MERCER COMPENSATION MANUAL

Theory and Practice

Roland Thériault, Ph.D.

MERCER COMPENSATION MANUAL

Theory and Practice

 morin

G. Morin Publisher Ltd

P.O. BOX 180, BOUCHERVILLE, QUÉBEC, CANADA
J4B 5E6   TEL. : (514) 449-2369   FAX : (514) 449-1096

ISBN 2-89105-414-8

Registered Copyright 1st quarter 1992
National Library of Canada

Guide Mercer sur la gestion de la rémunération :
théorie et pratique
© gaëtan morin éditeur, 1992
Tous droits réservés
Mercer Compensation Manual :
Theory and Practice
© G. Morin Publisher Ltd, 1992
All rights reserved

1 2 3 4 5 6 7 8 9 0   G M E 9 2   1 0 9 8 7 6 5 4 3 2

Révision linguistique : Dorothée Hobbs

PREFACE

The exchange process at the base of a compensation system is relatively simple and easy to understand. It involves offering pay and employee benefits in return for the services of willing, able, and motivated employees. This is accomplished by developing and implementing compensation policies and practices that are fair, adequate, and motivating.

Generally speaking, applying and managing this type of system proves highly complex, because of the constraints imposed by the limited resources of organizations, as well as of the various environments in which organizations operate, i.e. legislation, technology, individual expectations, competition, etc. The exercise must also be repeated regularly, because the most pressing constraints are constantly evolving, for example, the different expectations employees now have of their employers, as well as the change in economic conditions since the early 80s. Can employees still be offered pay increases as an incentive for improving job performance? How does one ensure that compensation is fair and adequate? Can one adopt equitable compensation policies and practices that satisfy, at the same time, the criteria of both individual and organizational efficiency?

Compensation has long been considered an essentially economic exchange. Recent findings in the behavioural sciences, however, broaden the perspective, so that compensation may no longer be viewed as simply an economic exchange, but rather as a psychological, sociological, political, and ethical transaction. Ignoring any one of these dimensions in no way diminishes its importance.

In recent years, organizations have been paying closer attention to operating costs, in which compensation is a key element. This has had a variety of effects:

- the introduction of pay structures less favourable for new than for existing employees;
- the implementation of benefit cost sharing programs;
- the proliferation of compensation surveys;
- greater interest in performance-based pay;

- the development of new compensation systems, e.g. based on competence and abilities rather than the job itself; and
- the return of old compensation systems such as profit-sharing and gain-sharing plans.

The coexistence of these different approaches within one organization may create an impression of inconsistency. As a result, an increasing effort is being made to streamline compensation methods. An organization's mission, objectives, strategies, and culture provide the guidelines needed for such a rationalization. From now on, the key word is strategy. It constitutes the basic orientation of this book, which examines compensation management in terms of four strategic decisions:

- degree of internal consistency desired;
- degree of competitiveness desired;
- the extent and forms of the rewards for individual contribution; and
- nature of the compensation administration.

Organizations are becoming increasingly aware that compensation is only one component of rewarding employees. A compensation system cannot be fully analyzed without also considering the other components the organization offers.

This book discusses the main factors to be considered in developing, implementing, and managing efficient and equitable compensation policies and practices. In reviewing the principal research findings, it provides readers with the information they need to proceed with this task. It also describes the practices and customs of numerous organizations.

While only one name appears as the author of this book, it is obviously the work of more than one person. First, my thanks go to management at William M. Mercer Limited, my employer, and particularly to our Chairman and Chief Executive Officer, Jean-Louis Bourbeau, for approving and supporting the project submitted to him. Nor may I overlook the contribution of André C. Magnan, also of Mercer, who initiated the project of updating an earlier version of this book entitled *Gestion de la rémunération: politiques et pratiques efficaces et équitables*, and transforming it into the *Mercer Compensation Manual: Theory and Practice*. Without his steadfast support and encouragement, this book would probably not have seen the light of day.

I also wish to express my gratitude to the many people whose comments and criticism have led me to revise countless pages of the manuscript. In particular, I would like to mention Georges Desgagnés of Alcan, and Yvan Paré of the Confédération des caisses populaires et d'économie Desjardins du Québec, as well as several of my colleagues at Mercer – Marc Chartrand, Jim Delaney, Roger Gurr, and Marilyn Sykes – whose comments and encouragement have been very helpful throughout the process of writing this book. Finally, I must single out the special contribution of Sylvie St-Onge, of the

École des hautes études commerciales de Montréal, who played a significant role in improving the structure of the entire book and its various chapters, as well as in clarifying the content. I extend to all these people my sincere thanks for their encouragement and criticism, while accepting full responsibility for my interpretation of their comments.

The content of a work may only be appreciated in the process of shaping it. This was done by Louise Cécyre, who coordinated the translation, and Nicole Barrette, who in addition to her ongoing duties serving other colleagues, shared the pressure with me by word processing the (too) numerous versions of this book in a sometimes unrealistic timeframe. Nor may I overlook the professional and scholarly work done by Dorothy Hobbs of Mercer in polishing the English text.

I am also grateful to the École des hautes études commerciales (University of Montréal) for providing me with workspace while I did the bibliographic research necessary for this book.

Finally, this new edition of my book could never have been published without the encouragement of my wife Michèle who, together with my children Marie-Élaine and Jean-François, created an environment conducive to this project by providing surroundings as pleasant to work in as they are to live in.

WARNING

In this book, the masculine is used to represent both genders not as a form of discrimination but simply in the interest of economy and readability.

TABLE OF CONTENTS

I
Introduction

1
Compensation and Its Management: Importance and Significance

2
Compensation: An Element of Strategic Management

II
Internal Equity and Job Evaluation

3
Job Analysis and Description

4
Job Evaluation: Definition and Methods

5
Managing Job Evaluation

III
External Equity and Compensation Surveys

6
Determining Pay Levels: The Labour Market and Compensation Policy

7
Compensation Surveys

IV
Pay Structure, Individual Pay and Pay Discrimination

8
Pay Structure and Individual Pay

9

Pay Discrimination

V
Rewarding Individual and Group Performance

10
Motivation and Merit Compensation

11
Individual Performance Evaluation
for Merit Compensation

12
Incentive Plans

VI
Managing Pay

13
Pay Management

VII
Employee Benefit Plans

14
Employee Benefit Plans: A Description

15
Managing Benefit Plans and Total Compensation

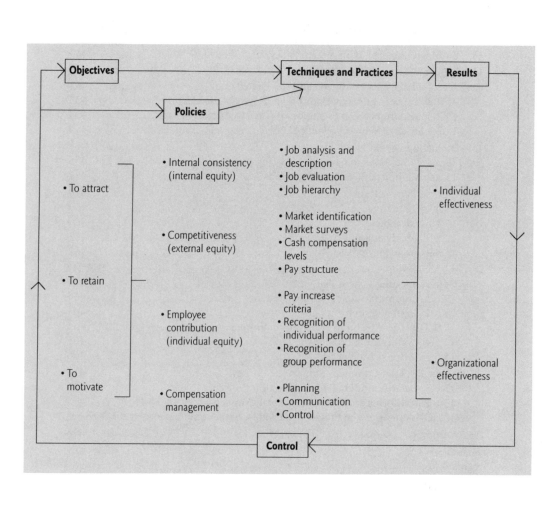

| Objectives | Techniques and Practices | Results |

Policies

• To attract	• Internal consistency (internal equity)	• Job analysis and description • Job evaluation • Job hierarchy	• Individual effectiveness
• To retain	• Competitiveness (external equity)	• Market identification • Market surveys • Cash compensation levels • Pay structure	
	• Employee contribution (individual equity)	• Pay increase criteria • Recognition of individual performance • Recognition of group performance	
• To motivate	• Compensation management	• Planning • Communication • Control	• Organizational effectiveness

Control

I

INTRODUCTION

The exchange process at the base of organizational compensation systems is relatively simple and easy to understand. The situation becomes complicated and problems arise once the system must be implemented and managed.

After discussing the importance of compensation for employers and employees, Chapter 1 focuses on the book's main theme: compensation as an exchange between employees and employers. This exchange may be analyzed from various angles (economic, psychological, sociological, political, and ethical), all of which are important and interrelated. Ignoring any one of these considerations does not make it less important. Chapter 1 concludes by presenting a model that integrates different factors involved in compensation management. This model serves as a background for developing the structure of the book and its chapters.

Chapter 2 discusses the underlying orientation of the book, namely, that compensation is a strategic management issue. It describes various concepts of compensation management, then focuses on strategic management, examining the impact of organizational strategy and culture on compensation management.

TABLE OF CONTENTS

1

COMPENSATION AND ITS MANAGEMENT: IMPORTANCE AND SIGNIFICANCE

The exchange process at the root of the organizational compensation system is relatively simple and easy to understand. In effect, organizations provide individuals with money and other benefits in return for their availability, capacity, and performance. However, complications and other problems arise as soon as such a system is established and managed. For organizations, the challenge becomes to plan, direct, organize, coordinate and control financial resources, to attract, retain and motivate the necessary workforce and to ensure the response that will allow the organization to meet its objectives.

After discussing the importance of compensation for organizations and individuals, this chapter examines various ways of analyzing compensation as a concrete element of the individual/organization exchange. Finally, the process of determining compensation is described by means of a model that will serve as a framework for subsequent chapters.

1.1 The Importance of Compensation

Compensation plays a complex and often misunderstood role in the functioning of an organization.

Compensation may well represent an organization's primary production cost: in some activity sectors, over 50% of total operating costs (Balkin and Gomez-Mejia, 1987). Yet, unlike other production factors, the organization cannot calculate the cost-effectiveness of this investment with the same degree of accuracy. Nor can the organization measure its contribution as readily as with its investments in equipment or other assets that make up its production infrastructure. Furthermore, decisions regarding compensation are dynamic. Today's increases affect not only the cost of employee benefits such as insurance and pension plans; they also have a cumulative effect on costs.

While compensation certainly represents the prime source of revenue for employees, it also has many other implications. Even though, as the Bible says, "One does not live by bread alone...", being mortal we all know how important bread is for life. The value employees assign to each element of compensation (salary and other benefits) depends essentially on how well each element meets their needs. Using Maslow's terminology (1954), for the individual, the importance of compensation is directly related to his or her needs – physiological, security, self-esteem, independence and self-actualization – as well as the relative importance of these needs.

In a critical analysis of 49 studies on the importance of the salary component of compensation compared to other possible rewards, Lawler (1971) found that salary ranked first, second, or third in 65% of the studies (32). As for the other elements of compensation (employee benefits), the critical analysis carried out by Heneman and Schwab (1975) reveals that their importance varies with the individual's age, marital status, sex, etc.

In brief, although compensation is not the only benefit an employee gets from the exchange with the organization, it remains one of the most important. Its importance, moreover, varies depending on individual characteristics. These characteristics will, therefore, occupy an important part of this book, as it explores the development and management of compensation policy and practice.

☐ 1.2 The Exchange Process

Compensation, which encompasses salary and employee benefits, is the concrete expression of an exchange between two parties: employee and organization. According to Belcher and Atchison (1987) as well as Mahoney (1987), this transaction has a number of facets, including economic, psychological, sociological, political, and ethical.

1.2.1 Economic Transaction

An employee's work is essential to an organization's operations, along with factors such as technology and raw materials. Compensation may therefore be viewed as a contract or economic transaction. It constitutes the price the organization pays to obtain the appropriate quality of labour in the amount it needs. Furthermore, the price of labour, i.e. the compensation employees receive, depends on supply and demand.

It is important to note certain characteristics of this approach. First of all, the demand for labour capacity is a function of the demand for goods and services. Any change in demand will affect the type and amount of labour required. Secondly, labour capacity that lies idle today cannot be used tomorrow; it is a perishable commodity. Finally, before doing a job, an employee asks for a fixed wage. The organization, however, can only calculate the actual price for the work after it has been done.

Viewing compensation from a strictly economic angle is, however, open to criticism. Since this perspective essentially focuses on the organization and economic conditions in general, it may be accused of ignoring or assigning the individual a passive role. It is also criticized for restricting the rewards of work solely to monetary compensation. Finally, this view neglects the psychological nature of the exchange.

Despite these criticisms, it is vital to emphasize that economic realities are relevant to compensation management. An organization's capacity to pay, its industrial sector, as well as geographic location, are all key factors that must be considered. Moreover, an organization's economic reality is not static. Today's decisions about compensation will have an impact on the organization's financial health for many years and, generally, this impact is difficult to reverse.

1.2.2 Psychological Transaction

The analysis of the psychological transaction, unlike that of the economic transaction, focuses on the individual and his or her relationship to the organization rather than on the organization and the economy.

Viewed in this way, a job represents a psychological contract between an individual and an organization. Under this contract, the individual agrees to adopt certain behaviour and display certain attitudes in exchange for compensation and other sources of job satisfaction that the organization promises to provide.

The psychological approach thus leads to an assessment of the compensation system through employees' eyes. Employees have varied needs and view them differently. The challenge for the organization therefore is to adopt compensation policies and programs that maximize employee motivation.

The concerns associated with this perspective include employees' satisfaction with their compensation and its various components, their needs, as well as the degree and nature of the motivation provided by the compensation system. The psychological perspective, then, explains organizational management's concern with instituting compensation systems that recognize each employee's personal contribution (i.e. performance and years of service).

1.2.3 Sociological Transaction

Compensation may also be viewed as a social contract. An organization is a group of individuals within a given cultural context. Compensation is also about status, both within the organization and in society.

This concept of status symbolized by rewards allows us to grasp the importance employees sometimes assign to even the slightest wage differences. It also explains why, in terms of status, the same significance does not attach to compensation by the job, by the hour, and on an annual basis. Furthermore, this view helps us understand why first line supervisors consider it important to be paid more than their subordinates, and on a different basis. The same applies to the various perquisites an organization provides to certain employees. Often, what counts with such benefits is not their monetary value but rather the prestige and status they confer.

From this perspective, compensation becomes a base against which individuals can measure their progress and success; it is the symbolic dimension of compensation that counts. The significance attached to compensation is all the greater since, in our North American society, most people see their jobs as a means of acquiring the material possessions they desire.

1.2.4 Political Transaction

Politically speaking, the level and forms of compensation result from the respective power of the parties who try to direct the transaction toward satisfying their own interests and preferences.

Organizations, unions, groups in the workplace, and individuals themselves all have some power, and therefore can, to a greater or lesser degree, influence the transaction in their favour. In this respect, for example, we need simply think of the power held by key people within a business, certain groups within an organization (such as doctors in a hospital), or certain divisions within an organization.

From a political perspective, the principles for determining levels and forms of compensation are fundamentally different from those underlying the economic approach. In the political perspective, organization and employee will tend to limit the communication of relevant information, in order to increase uncertainty and thereby maintain power. However, using an economic approach, the emphasis will be on gathering and disclosing information in order to determine and analyze the revenues and expenses of both parties more accurately.

1.2.5 Ethical Transaction

Finally, the entire question of compensation may be seen to contain an ethical element, issues of morality and justice. Any one of the following four justice issues – needs, egalitarian, legalistic or distributive – may form the basis for viewing and analyzing compensation.

One of these types of justice will prevail, depending on individual circumstances. In a situation where there is a heightened perception of each individual's "identity" (for example, within a family), justice based on needs will predominate. Everyone receives what they need, and the person who contributes the most is not necessarily the one who receives the most.

An egalitarian view may prevail when there is a perception of units distinct from one another, as in the case of the members of a team. In such a situation, the teammates share equally in the results. When the objectives of the individuals or parties involved come into conflict, behaviour is formally or informally motivated legalistically.

Finally, in situations where we recognize a difference or non-equivalence between the parties, as in a trade or market context, distributive justice should prevail. What each individual gets depends on what they contribute. The concept of contribution may have different meanings; what one person considers a contribution (e.g. years of service) may not be seen in that way by another. However, even though there may be agreement as to what constitutes a contribution, the transaction will not automatically be considered just. Hence, the process of setting pay should be analyzed in relation to how each party's contribution is perceived. This may represent a distinct advantage in reaching an agreement, since what is important for one party is not necessarily important for the other. The possibility of an exchange, therefore, exists.

Distributive justice predominates in North America, particularly in the area of wages. Yet not all individuals or groups see their salaries as a form of distributive justice; witness the egalitarian demands of certain unions.

Furthermore, even though distributive justice prevails when it comes to fixing monetary compensation, it is entirely possible to use other forms of justice in determining other elements of compensation. Hence egalitarian justice may prevail when it comes to vacations, whereas justice based on needs would apply to life or health insurance plans.

Consequently, in considering total compensation as an ethical transaction, it is important first to determine what type or types of justice apply in the overall analysis.

1.2.6 Conclusion

In conclusion, we have tried to show that compensation may be examined from various angles, i.e. as an economic, psychological, sociological, political, or ethical transaction. Of course, all of these dimensions are important and interrelated. Choosing to overlook any one of these factors in no way makes it less real or relevant.

Furthermore, regardless of what approach we take to compensation as a transaction between an individual and an organization, we must consider the objectives pursued by both parties as well as the content of the exchange.

Organizations and individuals pursue different objectives by means of compensation. For the organization, the exchange is designed to recruit and retain the necessary labour, and to elicit employee behaviour that will enable it to fulfil its mission. The relative importance of these goals, as well as the means of achieving them, varies from one organization to the next, from one class of employees to the next, and even from one job to the next.

For individuals, the objective may come down to satisfying needs. As mentioned earlier, these needs may differ considerably from one individual to another and may also change with time.

The content of the exchange process also varies with the parties involved. One party's contribution is the other party's reward. Compensation is a contribution for the organization, a reward for the individual. In addition, the value of each element relevant to the exchange varies, depending on the parties; this is where the possibility of an exchange exists. Otherwise, if each party considers the same elements essential to the exchange and assigns them the same value, the situation is no longer one of exchange but one of conflict.

☐ **1.3 The Elements of Compensation**

In a broad sense, compensation encompasses all the rewards received for a service or job. Often it is subdivided into two main components: direct or cash compensation and indirect compensation (employee benefits and perquisites). However, there is more. In fact, total compensation includes some items that involve a disbursement by the organization and others that involve none. In this book, we will be looking at all of these elements.

Diagram 1.1 depicts the key components of the compensation package.

Pay is the main element of the compensation package, the sum of money a person receives on an annual, monthly, weekly, or hourly basis for a service or job. In the case of an hourly salary, we speak of "wage rate" or "hourly wage"; production workers and tradespersons are generally paid by the hour. Personnel paid on a weekly, monthly, or annual basis are called "salaried employees".

The salary, or base pay, is the main element of the compensation package. There are two reasons for this. First of all, in general, salary represents at least 60% of an employee's compensation package, the other components making up the rest. Secondly, in most cases, the cash value of the other components is related to the base pay. For example, the cash value of a

DIAGRAM 1.1
Components of the compensation package

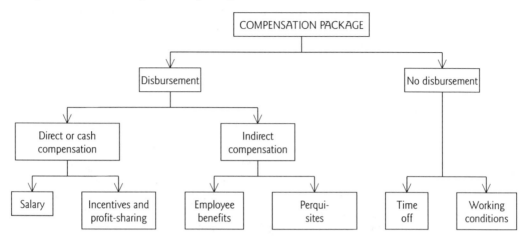

vacation plan depends partly on an employee's salary (and partly on the length of the vacation, which is usually tied to years of service). The cash value of an insurance plan also largely depends on a person's base pay. The same applies to most pension plans.

Organizations regularly adjust pay. This is done by taking into account many factors, such as changes in the economy, the amount of the changes made by other organizations in the community or similar labour market, the organization's ability to pay, as well as any increase in an employee's performance or years of service.

Sometimes a hardship premium is added to the base pay. This represents an amount paid to employees because of special circumstances surrounding their job. In practice, such premiums vary: overtime premium, shift premium, distance premium, weekend or holiday work premium, premiums for working with hazardous goods or under difficult conditions, call-back premium, minimum worktime bonus, standby premium, etc.

In addition to these various elements of direct or cash compensation, organizations offer some or all of their employees various incentive or profit-sharing plans. These may take the form of performance bonuses, organization shares or stock options, etc. Such plans represent the variable portion of direct or cash compensation.

Performance bonuses are lump sums paid to employees on the basis of their performance. Hence, each time they are obtained, these bonuses must be earned. Unlike salary increases, they are not included in an employee's base pay. They may depend entirely or only partially on individual perform-ance. In the latter case, the performance of a group or the whole organization is also a factor. Bonuses, moreover, may be based on short-term or long-term performance. Long-term plans are generally based on the entire organ-ization's performance, and are intended for senior management or certain professionals who have an impact on the organization's long-term (three- to five-year) performance.

Stock-purchase and stock-option plans have historically been reserved for senior management. They aim to link executive compensation to organ-izational performance.

As for indirect compensation, it is possible to distinguish between employee benefits and perquisites. Employee benefits include pension plans, as well as different insurance plans (life, disability, health) offered by most organizations. Then there are various forms of perquisites. Some organizations provide cars for certain employees, others pay for parking, meals, tuition fees, financial advice, employee assistance programs, etc.

In addition to these various components of direct and indirect com-pensation, a large part of the compensation package consists of elements that do not require an organizational disbursement. Nonetheless, they still represent a major cost. These include paid time off and working conditions.

Because of legal requirements – exceeded in most cases – organizations offer their employees vacations and various holidays (legal holidays, days off for personal business, sick leave, maternity leave, family leave for a funeral or marriage, etc.). The frequency of these days off has a direct impact on what the compensation package costs for the time worked. In addition to such time off, working conditions also influence compensation costs. Some conditions, such as hours of work, have a direct impact on compensation; others, such as unpaid leave and work schedules, have an indirect effect. For example, giving employees an unpaid leave may require training and devel-oping new employees to replace them.

☐ 1.4 Compensation Management Model

Compensation techniques and practices are not developed in the abstract. They are founded on a set of objectives and policies that stem as much from the nature of the individual as the organization, or the environment in which individual and organization evolve. This idea is depicted in Diagram 1.2, which stresses the importance of objectives and policies in the use of com-pensation techniques and the development of various practices.

Objectives are what the organization is trying to achieve through various compensation systems; policies are the foundation for managing such a

DIAGRAM 1.2
Compensation management model

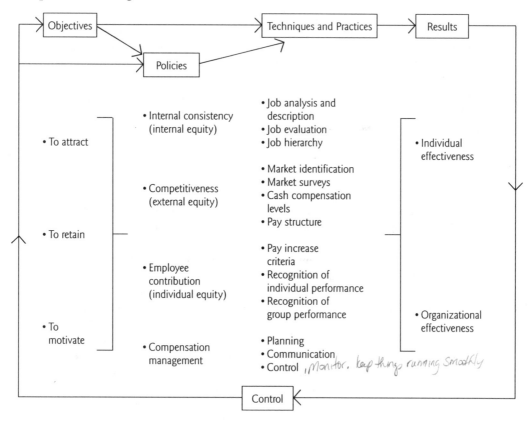

system. Techniques and practices represent the means available to the specialist for achieving the desired results in accordance with developed policy.

1.4.1 Objectives

Setting compensation management objectives is important for two reasons. First, the objectives are guides for developing necessary policies and practices. Thus, an organization wishing to motivate its workforce to improve productivity should consider using merit compensation techniques and practices and various performance bonus systems. To this end, it must ensure that it has flexibility in terms of total cash compensation. On the other hand, if the organization wishes to emphasize workforce stability, it will choose to attach more weight to the fixed portion of cash compensation, offering relatively high salaries in comparison to its reference market.

Secondly, compensation management objectives are ideal criteria for assessing the effectiveness of practice. For example, if an employer is trying to ensure a degree of labour stability among its computer personnel, it must measure that stability and this last one must translate into an improvement in certain indices of individual and organizational effectiveness. For example, it might have an impact on labour costs, productivity, and work atmosphere. The same applies if the employer changes its compensation practices to encourage its production workers to improve the quality of their work. One measure of organizational effectiveness in this case could be the number of goods returned by customers.

The various compensation systems found within organizations rest on a wide range of objectives (Belcher and Atchison, 1987; Gosselin and Thériault, 1985; Freedman, Montanari and Keller, 1982). Yet, they may be divided into three major groups: to attract an adequate number of highly qualified employees (recruiting), to maintain some degree of stability within the organization's workforce, and to offer employees compensation systems that will motivate them.

The relative importance assigned to each objective may vary from one employer to the next and from one job category to the next. In diversified organizations, objectives may even vary from one unit to the next (Salscheider, 1982; Kerr, 1985). Because of the multiplicity of these objectives, not all can be achieved; compensation management always involves a compromise. These compromises represent strategic choices (Chapter 2). In some cases, an organization will want to encourage innovation while recognizing the outstanding contribution of its employees. In other cases, it will be primarily concerned with keeping its compensation competitive with the market. Similarly, one organization will want to build team spirit among its employees, while another will encourage them to compete with each other.

1.4.2 Policies

Following Milkovich and Newman (1990), the compensation management model proposed here is based on four fundamental policies: internal consistency, competitiveness, employee contribution, and the nature of the compensation administration.

Internal Consistency

Internal consistency, or internal equity, implies a comparison of the various jobs within an organization to determine the value of each job's contribution in achieving the organization's objectives. For example, is the work of the analyst-programmer comparable to that of the purchasing manager or labour relations consultant? While the specific tasks involved in each of these jobs differ, are the skills required to handle them or the amount of responsibility they entail similar or different? Consistency or internal equity is therefore a relevant criterion for setting salaries within an organization. The degree of internal consistency has an impact on workforce stability, employee satisfaction, and productivity.

Competitiveness

A policy of competitiveness, or external equity, in compensation involves the level of pay offered by an organization in comparison to the market. What level of compensation does an employer wish to offer its supervisors compared to the market? While apparently simple, this question proves to be quite complex. For example, what market are we speaking of? Will the companies used as the reference market for supervisors' compensation be the same ones used as the reference market for the office staff's compensation? Do the organization's supervisors do basically the same work as those at the reference organizations? Does the organization want to (or should it) offer compensation above or below the reference market, and exactly what does this entail? Are we talking about the compensation package, total cash compensation, or simply salaries? Hence, the salaries paid to an organization's supervisors may be higher than those at the reference companies, whereas total cash compensation is lower because the organization has no performance bonus plan. A policy of competitiveness has an impact on the employer's ability to recruit, on labour stability, and on profitability.

Employee Contribution

A compensation policy based on employee contribution, or individual equity, gauges the importance an organization assigns to certain personal characteristics in determining compensation. For example, does the organization consider individual performance in setting salaries, or does it emphasize years of service? In addition to its potential effect on employee productivity, such a policy has a tremendous effect on personal job satisfaction and workforce stability.

Compensation Management

Compensation management policies are designed to ensure the effectiveness of the techniques and practices adopted to establish internal, external, and individual pay equity. How do an organization's practices compare to those of its competitors? Do these practices correspond to organizational objectives and strategies? What are its labour costs? To what extent will the organization disclose information about its compensation practices to its employees? Will it involve them in planning any changes to its policies and practices?

Compensation management policies constitute each organization's particular manner of coping with different situations and assuming its responsibilities in keeping with its culture, maturity, management style, objectives, and strategies. Hence, formulating such policies forces management to think about what it is doing and what it wants to do. It also gives employees a sense of security, because they know what to expect. However, care must be taken to ensure that the organization does not inadvertently discriminate.

1.4.3 Techniques and Practices

Compensation techniques and practices constitute another vital component of the compensation management model depicted in Diagram 1.2. They may be organized under the four main compensation policies the organization is trying to institute: internal consistency, competitiveness, employee contribution, and compensation administration.

Internal Consistency

An organization trying to ensure internal consistency in compensation must first analyze and describe its jobs. Then, using one of the existing techniques, it can evaluate the jobs and arrange them hierarchically. This process implies that internal consistency must be based on job content. Yet, as Atchison (1990) points out, this approach stems from a bureaucratic concept of work organization – a concept that is coming under increasing fire (cf. Chapter 3). Hence, some employers use techniques other than job evaluation to ensure internal consistency. These include the maturity curve or determining pay according to an employee's skills or competence. The maturity-curve technique is used, among other things, to set compensation for certain groups of professionals, such as engineers or scientists. The technique of basing pay on skills has been in use for some years now, mainly among production workers, while basing compensation on competence is occasionally used with office staff. Some organizations consider it worthwhile using a variety of techniques or practices to ensure that compensation is internally consistent.

Competitiveness

An organization interested in making its pay competitive must first define its labour market. It may have one or more reference markets, depending upon its employee categories. For office and sales personnel, the market may be local. For tradespersons or professionals, the market may be regional. For senior management, if we consider the markets opening up in the 90s, the reference market must be national, if not international.

Having selected the market or markets, the next step is to collect information about the various elements of compensation. This step raises other questions. How can we be sure that the content of the comparator jobs is similar when we know very well that job titles may be deceptive? For example, how do we ensure that another organization's job of buyer involves the same responsibilities and skills as does our own? Furthermore, just what information do we want to obtain? Is information about cash compensation enough, or should we also consider employee benefits and perquisites as well as working conditions? It is one thing to be paid $600 a week for 33 hours of work with 4 weeks of annual vacation and a pension plan to which the organization contributes the annual equivalent of 6% of an employee's salary a year; it is quite another to earn $650 a week for 38 hours of work with 2 weeks of annual vacation and no pension plan.

Once the survey or surveys have been done, the organization must determine the level of its compensation in relation to the market. Again, questions arise. Will we determine the degree of competitiveness based solely on salary, or will we consider total cash compensation or even the compensation package? Will the degree of competitiveness be the same for all job categories, or will we set different levels for each? The answers to these questions will lead to the establishment of one or more pay structures.

Employee Contribution

An organization that wishes to recognize the contribution of its employees may use techniques and practices that vary according to what contribution it wishes to emphasize (individual performance, group performance, years of service, training, etc.). An organization that wants to reward the individual performance of its employees may grant them salary increases or use a system of performance bonuses. In either case, the organization must develop an employee performance evaluation system, and determine criteria for measuring individual performance. On the other hand, an organization that wants to recognize the collective performance of its employees may do so through a group incentive plan (such as profit-sharing). An organization that wishes to retain its most experienced employees will favour years of service as a criterion for pay increases.

Compensation Administration

Organizations use a set of techniques and practices that reflect different types of compensation management. For example, employee surveys or focus groups might be used to allow the planning of any changes to the systems. Personalized compensation statements may be used as a means of communication, and salary increase grids as a control instrument.

1.4.4 Results

The institution of compensation techniques and practices within the framework of established policies will have a number of effects on organizational as well as individual effectiveness.

There are almost as many definitions of organizational effectiveness as there are organizations. For some, this effectiveness is measured by return on investment; for others, customer satisfaction; for yet others, profit, market share, return on equity, etc. Moreover, in diversified organizations, this effectiveness yardstick may vary from one division to the next.

Employee effectiveness is one of the most important elements in human resource management. Hence, the impact of various compensation techniques and practices on individual effectiveness is an important component of the proposed compensation management model. Once again, how one measures this effectiveness varies from one organization to the next. Normally, however, it includes measuring individual performance, quality of production or services, cost of labour, employee turnover, absenteeism, employee satisfaction, compliance with pay-equity legislation, etc.

Be that as it may, compensation techniques and practices sometimes prove to be so fascinating and complex that we lose sight of their objective. This is one of the greatest risks facing the compensation professional. The technique becomes an end in itself. What could be more enthralling than to develop a pay structure or a gain-sharing plan? For example, in the latter case, you would have to include employees' work organization, their specific contribution to overall productivity, the formulas for calculating and sharing gains, etc. The compensation specialist then runs the risk of forgetting the system's objective and, if this happens, the system may well be inefficient and not viable. For example, why should employees willingly agree to a gain-sharing plan if they believe the result will be fewer jobs?

In contrast to the past, today's compensation specialist should not only master the content of various techniques in the field, but should also be a management expert and have in-depth knowledge of the nature of the organization and the environment in which it operates. It is no longer solely a matter of developing practices. Such practices must correspond to very specific objectives and represent the most effective alternatives. For example, as Brown (1990) points out, more and more organizations are opting for merit pay practices that take into account the relationship between the chosen form of compensation and performance on the one hand and the cost of measuring performance on the other. Organizations must concern themselves with both the causes and effects of compensation policies.

☐ 1.5 Structure of the Book

The structure of this book is based on the compensation management model described in the preceding section. After providing a general outline of the book and the particular perspective of Part I, in the following sections we will discuss the various basic compensation policies one by one, as well as the techniques and practices associated with each.

Part II focuses on internal equity and job evaluation. After reviewing job analysis and description techniques (Chapter 3), the various methods for evaluating jobs are discussed (Chapter 4). Chapter 5 covers job evaluation management.

External equity and salary surveys are the subject of Part III. After briefly considering all the criteria for determining pay within an organization (Chapter 6), Chapter 7 describes the salary survey process, the tools available for it, as well as the questions it tries to address.

Part IV deals with individual equity and pay structures. Chapter 8 covers the considerations involved in developing pay structures. In brief, this means incorporating the conclusions reached from the study of internal, external, and individual equity into a coherent whole. Then, Chapter 9 reviews one of the major concerns in the field of compensation, that is, pay discrimination.

Recognition of performance is the topic of Part V. Whereas Chapter 10 covers compensation based on merit, Chapter 11 deals with measuring individual performance to determine merit compensation. This section concludes with a description of the most common incentive plans.

Part VI focuses on salary administration (Chapter 13). After discussing the importance of budgets to salary administration, it examines the salary increase process as well as the communication and control of salary policies and practices.

Finally, Part VII covers employee benefits, with a review and description of various employee benefit plans in Chapter 14, followed by a discussion of benefits management and total compensation in Chapter 15.

REFERENCES

ATCHISON, T.J., "What Should We Pay For?", in *Human Resource Strategies for Organizations in Transition*, edited by R.J. Niehaus and K.F. Price, New York, Plenum Press, 1990, pp. 63-81.

BALKIN, D.B. and L.R. GOMEZ-MEJIA, "Toward a Contingency Theory of Compensation Strategy", *Strategic Management Journal*, 1987, vol. 8, pp. 169-182.

BELCHER, D. and T.J. ACHTISON, *Compensation Administration*, Englewood Cliffs, New Jersey, Prentice-Hall Inc., 1987.

BROWN, C., "Firm's Choice of Method of Pay", *Industrial and Labor Relations Review*, 1990, vol. 43 N° 3, pp. 147-164.

FREEDMAN, S.M., J.R. MONTANARI and R.T. KELLER, "The Compensation Program: Balancing Organizational and Employee Needs", *Compensation Review*, 2nd quarter 1982, pp. 47-54.

GOSSELIN, A. and R. THÉRIAULT, "Designing Strategically Oriented Reward Systems", *Working Paper*, Montreal, École des hautes études commerciales, Université de Montréal, 1985.

HENEMAN, H.G. and D.P. SCHWAB, "Work and Rewards Theory", in *Motivation and Commitment*, edited by D. Yoder and H.G. Heneman, Washington D.C., Bureau of National Affairs, 1975.

KERR, J., "Diversification Strategies and Managerial Awards: An Empirical Study", *Academy of Management Journal*, 1985, vol. 28, pp. 155-179.

LAWLER, E.E., *Pay and Organizational Effectiveness: a Psychological View*, New York, McGraw-Hill, 1971.

MAHONEY, T., "Understanding Comparable Worth: A Societal and Political Perspective", in *Research in Organizational Behaviour*, vol. 9, edited by L.L. Cummings and B.M. Shaw, Greenwich, Connecticut, JAI Press, 1987.

MASLOW, A.H., *Motivation and Personality*, New York, Harper, 1954.

MILKOVICH, G.T. and J.M. NEWMAN, *Compensation*, Homewood, Illinois, Richard D. Irwin, 1990.

SALSCHEIDER, J., "Devising Pay Strategies for Diversified Companies", *Compensation Review*, 2nd quarter 1982, pp. 15-24.

THÉRIAULT, R., *Equity Theory: An Examination of the Inputs and Outcomes in an Organizational Setting*, doctoral thesis, Ithaca, New York, Cornell University, 1977.

TABLE OF CONTENTS

2

COMPENSATION: AN ELEMENT OF STRATEGIC MANAGEMENT

The compensation management model described in the preceding chapter emphasizes the importance of appropriate objectives and policies. These objectives and policies are not formulated in the abstract. They reflect individuals, their environment, and an era, and are based on value systems and theories about how individuals and organizations work. Moreover, the soundness and value of compensation techniques and practices are not ends in themselves. Objectives and policies are, on the one hand, guides for the development of techniques and practices and, on the other, criteria for assessing their effectiveness.

This chapter describes the fundamental perspective of this book. It will begin with the major trends that have shaped the design of corporate compensation management. Next, it will focus on the perspective espoused in this book, namely a strategic view. After determining the implications of this view for compensation management, it will take a closer look at the implications of various corporate strategies and cultures for compensation management.

☐ 2.1 The Concept of Compensation Management

Three main schools of thought on compensation management in North America have been identified since the turn of the century: the phase of the scientific organization of work, the social science phase, and the systemic and strategic management phase we are currently in. In practice, these phases do not supersede each other; rather, they are superimposed, and exist in varying degrees within each organization.

The phase of the scientific organization of work made its mark on compensation management primarily during the 30s and 40s. The vast majority of compensation management techniques and practices still in use today stem from that period, which is also known for its bureaucratic concept of work. From a scientific, bureaucratic viewpoint, compensation management is based first on the concept of "job", the job rather than the person should be the focus of special attention. It was during this period that analytic job evaluation techniques were developed, with an emphasis on measuring job requirements and the relative importance of jobs within the organization. This was the age of long, exhaustive, job descriptions. Jobs were arranged from the most junior to most senior, then compared with those on the market and, if a similarity was found, salary information was sought. This assured organizations of internal consistency as well as of some degree of salary competitiveness. With this model, the development of compensation systems became very important. Everyone was classified, and placed in a very precise niche. The human resources department, with its compensation experts and outside consultants, controlled the system.

The second period, the social science phase, brought major developments in the area of compensation during the 50s and 60s. Without denying the importance of jobs, attention began to focus on people. It was recognized that an organization is not a set of precisely hierarchically-arranged jobs, but a group of individuals with their own needs and values. While this period was marked primarily by a psychological emphasis, the other social sciences also entered the picture, particularly sociology. This phase was characterized by an attempt to understand human behaviour within an organization. The emphasis was on motivation and cooperation. Merit-based compensation and incentive plans were typical of this era, which raised the issue of measuring individual performance. Employers looked for the best way to evaluate performance; the attention shifted from developing to implementing various compensation systems. Decisions were no longer made solely in the human resources department. Line managers now participated in the decision-making process.

Since the early 80s, organizations have entered a new phase of compensation management. Now, the keyword is "strategy". We concentrate on the relationship between compensation management and the organization: its objectives, strategies, structure, and values. We have moved from a bureaucratic to an individual and finally to an organizational approach.

The North American business environment of the 80s was characterized by two basic phenomena. Competition became international rather than essentially domestic. Economic growth, meanwhile, was moderate at best, after the rapid growth of earlier decades. Both these phenomena focused more concern on production costs. Organizations with the same financial resources and production techniques could now be distinguished by their production costs.

This heightened concern with production costs, compensation being a key component, was reflected in various ways. Organizations introduced layoff and retirement incentive programs, and pay structures for new employees that were lower than the existing structures within the organization. This concern also led to programs designed to share the cost of benefits, the proliferation of salary surveys, more interest in compensation based on performance, the appearance of new compensation systems based on competence and skills rather than on the job itself, and the return of former compensation systems such as profit-sharing and gain-sharing plans. This variety, often within the same organization, could give the impression of inconsistency. Thus, in recent years, there has been a growing trend toward rationalizing these differing compensation techniques. An organization's mission, objectives, strategies, and culture are the guiding principles behind this rationalization.

The emphasis is now on planning, consistency, and synergy among the various management systems. The executive committee and board of directors now determine and articulate the organization's strategies and objectives. They also examine and approve the systems planned and developed by the human resource department, with help from in-house and outside specialists and line managers.

2.2 Strategic Compensation Management

Diagram 2.1 illustrates one way of viewing the relationships among an organization's strategic planning, the management of its human resources, its compensation management, and employee as well as organizational performance. The diagram requires some comment. The ultimate goal of compensation management is to influence employee behaviour to achieve a certain level of individual and organizational effectiveness. Moreover, like business strategy and financial strategy, formulation of the human resource strategy is an integral part of the organization's overall strategy. Human resource strategy has a direct impact on every component of human resource management, including compensation. Finally, the diagram illustrates that formulating these various strategies must also take into account the strategic context in which the organization is evolving.

Traditionally, human resource managers have not played a very important role in developing an organization's strategies and operations (Nininger, 1982; Misa and Stein, 1983). However, conditions change. More and more, an organization's competitive edge depends on how it manages its workforce. Increased competition has forced organizations to produce their products or services, and to enhance the quality of their customer service. Insofar as businesses use the same sources of capital, the same means of production, and the same marketing techniques, human resource management is increasingly becoming the differentiating factor. Thus, following Fombrun et al. (1984), it is not surprising to find that, with this new reality, human resource

DIAGRAM 2.1
Strategic Compensation Management

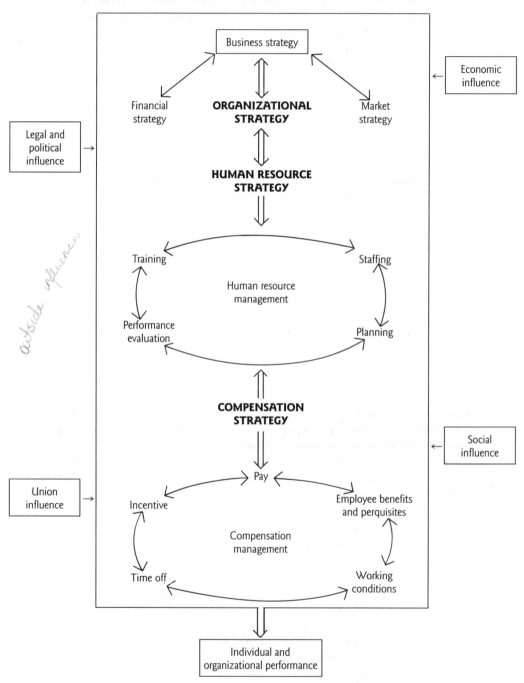

managers are playing an increasingly prominent role within organizations, getting involved in developing strategies and in organizational operations. On the other hand, more and more is expected from human resource managers. Introducing programs that simply match what is being done on the market will no longer be enough. The programs must integrate with the reality of the organization, its objectives, strategies, and culture. In other words, a strategic perspective is required.

Based on Chandler (1962), Miles and Snow (1978) and Mintzberg (1978), Dyer (1984, p. 159) defines human resource strategy as the image that emerges from a set of important human resource management decisions, especially those dealing with the organization's principal goals, and the means used to achieve them. Hence, a strategic approach to compensation management moves beyond the "recruit, retain, motivate" approach to address such questions as: Why have more structured compensation? What type of people do we want to attract? For what reasons? What compensation system will make it possible to attract them? Will it be consistent with other practices? What are our options? In brief, a compensation management strategy consists of an integrated set of practices with respect to salaries, bonuses, and other incentives, as well as employee benefits and perquisites, designed to achieve the organization's goals in keeping with its strategies and culture. Managing compensation strategically means seeing compensation systems as a means of communication, for they do convey a message. Are these messages the ones we want to communicate? Are the means used to convey them appropriate?

Regardless of how an organization manages its compensation, managers must always be able to answer certain questions. They must choose from among a set of alternatives. For example, human resource management has a number of options for dealing with a labour-cost problem: merit pay, individual or group performance bonuses or premiums, reducing planned pay increases, etc. Choosing a particular option, such as adopting a system of group performance bonuses, does not necessarily mean that an organization is strategically managing its compensation. What characterizes a strategic orientation is using a specific technique and determining the content of a system in response to objectives, taking into account internal limits as well as the strengths and weaknesses of the environment in which the business is evolving.

In summary, strategic compensation management involves establishing a link between, on the one hand, compensation policies and practices (the development process as well as content) and management of the organization. As Fay (1987) points out, strategic compensation management may even influence a company's compensation policies. The result may be less important attached to internal equity (through job evaluation) and more to individual equity (recognition of individual contribution). It might also mean a policy of differentiated treatment rather than consistency, guaranteeing fewer of the components of the compensation package – a greater shared risk – and assigning less importance to organizational level in determining an employee's status.

It is important to note that, as in other fields of endeavour, it may be easier to ask the questions than to find the answers, and even more difficult to apply them once found. It is relatively simple to copy current market practices; however, strategic compensation management requires a certain amount of innovation and, above all, a great deal of courage.

2.3 Factors to Consider

The numerous factors to consider in developing a compensation strategy may be divided into three categories: standard practice, organizational characteristics, and environmental influence.

2.3.1 Standard Practice

The purpose of monitoring standard practice is to determine the role of each component of the compensation package. What is working well? What is working less well? What objective is each component designed to meet? To what extent are these objectives being met?

Formulating objectives constitutes an important consideration in the orientation of compensation systems (Thériault, 1987). Obviously, you cannot do everything; this means making choices and setting priorities. In some cases, the organization wishes to encourage innovation. In others, it aims to emphasize performance or maintain its competitive position in the market. Similarly, one organization might want to stimulate team spirit, while another will try to spark competition among different units within the organization. These few examples make it clear that compensation objectives are not only diverse but may also conflict. Attaining one may keep you from achieving another.

A study by Gosselin and Thériault (1985) sheds some light on the problem of setting compensation objectives. A group of human resource vice-presidents from medium-sized and large Canadian corporations who were attending a seminar on compensation were asked what they thought about a set of hypothetical compensation objectives. Two questions were asked: "How much relative importance does your organization assign to each of these objectives?" and "What relative importance should they have?" Participants were then provided with a list of potential compensation problems and asked to indicate, in order of importance, how relevant each of

DIAGRAM 2.2
Actual and desirable importance attached to compensation objectives, and principal existing problems

	Rated by a sample of human resource vice-presidents	
Objectives that are being pursued	**Objectives that should be pursued**	**Principal shortcomings of existing methods of managing compensation**
1. Favour individual performance	1. Favour individual performance	1. Do not further the attainment of strategic objectives
2. Attract competent managers	2. Recognize outstanding contributions	2. Prevent development of an organizational culture
3. Remain competitive	3. Encourage innovation	3. Little connection between performance and compensation
4. Reinforce standards and values	4. Remain competitive	4. Compensation insufficient to promote better performance
5. Achieve short-term objectives	5. Ensure internal consistency	5. Do not take taxes into account
6. Ensure internal consistency	6. Promote implementation of strategies	6. Do not spark a productivity gain
7. Promote the implementation of strategies	7. Achieve long-term objectives	7. Emphasize quantity rather than quality
8. Recognize outstanding contributions	8. Attract competent managers	8. Do not promote the implementation of strategies
9. Achieve pay equity	9. Achieve short-term objectives	9. Do not encourage innovation
10. Encourage innovation	10. Engender job satisfaction	10. Do not recognize outstanding contributions

those problems was within their organization. Diagram 2.2 depicts the results of that study. Recognition of individual performance is the number one objective of these companies. Not only did participants rate it as the most important, they also felt it should be the most important. On the whole, the list of primary goals pursued corresponds closely to traditional compensation objectives. Yet, since the early 80s the situation has changed. Competition is no longer the same, and productivity is facing serious challenges. If we look at what objectives the organizations should pursue, it seems that these vice-presidents are aware of the new order. The list of desirable objectives is noticeably different from the list of those actually being pursued. When we note the discrepancy between these two lists, it is not surprising to find the kind of compensation problems that exist today within organizations.

These vice-presidents identified two main problems: their method of managing compensation does not promote the attainment of strategic objectives, and it prevents the development of an organizational culture. The sensitivity that compensation managers display toward employees' problems may lead them to assign more importance to the concerns of employees than to the concerns of the organization. A study conducted in the United States produced similar results (Freedman, Montanari and Keller, 1982).

2.3.2 Organizational Characteristics

A second set of determining factors in a compensation management strategy involves the characteristics of the organization.

Most current compensation systems were developed during the 70s in response to competition in the labour market. Competitiveness was the primary motivation. In the 90s, organizations must develop systems that comply with their characteristics and values. The key question is no longer, "Are we doing the right things?" but rather "Are we doing things right?" Less emphasis is placed on technique, more on strategy.

Each business has objectives, structure, culture, and environment that make it unique. In developing effective compensation systems and in determining their specific content, management must bear in mind the organization's specific nature.

Stage of Organizational Development

What is good for a fast-growing business may not be at all suitable to a fully mature business with a very low growth rate. A review of the literature enabled Balkin and Gomez-Meija (1987) to confirm that incentive pay should represent the largest portion of the compensation package in organizations experiencing rapid growth. The proportion of incentive pay should be even greater in growing high-tech firms. Moreover, the proportion of variable compensation should be greater in small organizations than in large ones.

On the subject of business growth rates, Stonich (1984) recommends that organizations assign greater or lesser importance, depending on their growth stage, to various organizational performance measurements. Thus, a fast-growing organization should assign less weight to return on investment in its overall assessment of business performance than one with an average growth rate (10% as compared to 25%). This criterion should be paramount in a slow-growing company (50% of the overall assessment of performance). On the other hand, an increase in market share should be significantly weighted (45%) in the overall assessment of the performance of a fast-growing business. This criterion should be weighted less (25%) in a business growing at a moderate rate.

Organizational Structure

An organization's performance measurement also depends on its structure. Thus, an organization with only one product line or product and a functional structure should use functional performance measurements for its various units.

On the other hand, an organization broken into decentralized divisions because of the diversity of its products or markets may use the criterion of divisional profitability as a performance gauge. However, problems are likely to occur unless there is a high degree of divisional autonomy. If, for instance, for the sake of vertical or horizontal integration, one wishes to stimulate cooperation among the various profit centres, it would be wise not to measure performance solely against divisional profitability. Some of the organization's measures of overall performance might better be used. On the other hand, for a holding company that controls a variety of businesses, the return on equity of each business might be a valuable gauge.

Presented in this way, the connections that must be drawn between performance measurements and the type of corporate structure seem relatively clear and simple. Yet, in practice, this matter may be quite complex. So what performance gauge should be used by a business with a functional structure that is converting into a holding company? Is it possible to keep compensation policies and practices centralized and to encourage employees to transfer from one company to the other within the holding company?

In a study of the relationship between the degree of business decentralization and compensation management, Kerr (1985) found that the more diversified the business, the more it tends to judge management performance solely on quantitative and financial criteria. Also, the more diversified the business, the more it tends to base itself exclusively on the performance of a unit or division to measure the performance of its managers. An analysis of all studies of the matter finally led the author to state that it is the process through which the company diversified, rather than the degree of diversification itself, that is crucial to compensation management. Was the diversification by acquisition or internal growth? Diversification by acquisition results in much greater divisional independence. The performance yardsticks for management may then be quantitative and focus on division. On the other hand, diversification by internal growth causes more dependency between the divisions and the parent company. In this case, it would be worth employing both quantitative and qualitative gauges, using both divisional and overall company performance to measure management performance.

Organizational Culture

In addition to the organization's unique characteristics and strategies, its culture is a fundamental factor in strategic compensation management. Culture reflects the values, beliefs, and attitudes of the organization's members. It is a set of beliefs and expectations shared by members, the effects of which appear as standards that modify the behaviour of individuals and groups within the organization (Schwartz and Davis, 1981). For Levy and Merry (1986, p. 277), culture includes not only beliefs, values, and standards, but also symbolic acts and things like myths, rituals, and ceremonies. The physical layout of the workplace, its appearance, as well as management style and prevailing interpersonal relationships are also part of an organization's culture.

Strategic compensation management emphasizes the consistency required between culture and compensation practices. This naturally raises certain problems. For example, management may deem it appropriate to replace the upper level of its salary scales with a performance bonus plan. Thus, from that point on, once employees reach a certain salary ceiling, their performance is rewarded by bonuses instead of salary increases. This way of doing things is theoretically justified. However, loyal employees whose salary is already above the new ceiling will receive no more salary increases. This illustrates the problem of the coexistence of concerns for performance and concerns for the individuals within the organization. What is the true nature of the organization's culture?

One of the important components of an organization's culture is its management philosophy. In this regard, Lawler (1984) makes several re-commendations about appropriate compensation practices. For instance, within an organization where a theory X management (autocratic) philosophy prevails, salaries should essentially be based on the job and should be high enough to attract the necessary resources. Decision-making regarding com-pensation should be at the senior management level, and only limited infor-mation should circulate. If, on the other hand, the prevailing management philosophy is of the Y-type (democratic), salaries should be based on com-petence, among other things, and be high enough to provide job security and attract the necessary personnel. Decisions, meanwhile, should be made hierarchically, as close as possible to the person whose compensation is being determined, and information should be readily available.

In practice, most traditional compensation systems in large organizations were developed to reinforce the culture of mature businesses (Bratkovich, Steele and Teesdale, 1990). These systems exercise prudence, avoid risk, control costs, and favour the short-term and functional aspect of the organ-ization. This situation is very different from the systems required by a new company or one wishing to stress innovation.

Not only does an organization's culture influence the compensation sys-tem and its management (Beck, 1987; Maidment, 1987), but the compen-sation system and its management influence the culture (Lawler, 1984; Kerr and Slocum, 1987). In fact, a large part of an organization's current culture may be attributed to earlier compensation policies (Stonich, 1984). In this context, the pertinent question is whether the compensation system should be adapted to the culture or whether the culture should support the compensation system (Lawler, 1981). In this respect, the message seems clear. If we want a major change in culture, we should not make compensation the driving force of the change, because the chances of failure are too high (Lawler, 1981). This view is shared by Kilman and Saxton (1985, pp. 14-15). The efforts to modify the culture may create more problems than they solve if the changes are not considered and controlled systemically.

Organizational Size

As Belcher and Atchison (1987) point out, the smaller an organization, the more limited the type of compensation plan it can offer. On the other hand, the more compensation decisions are made at lower organizational levels, the more salary increases may be linked to individual performance. The more employees perceive the connection between their performance and their pay, the more any discussions about pay are likely to be open.

In larger organizations, the trend is reversed. Since they have more capacity to pay, they can offer better compensation. On the other hand, compensation decisions are made through various organizational levels then confirmed at the top, and employees have a harder time seeing the connection between pay and performance. These size constraints help explain the problem large organizations face in sustaining employee motivation through their compensation practices. On the other hand, organizations might adopt decentralized compensation management to offset this constraint.

Characteristics of the Workforce

Compensation policies and practices may be formulated with an overall view, i.e. for all employees. Yet, for two reasons, it may be preferable to establish different policies and practices for different classes of personnel. First of all, financial restrictions may lead organizations to manage compensation differently for various employee categories. The form and the level of compensation offered to employees in certain categories may vary based on the organization's expectations: the importance of those employees' performance and their commitment to achieving the organization's goals.

Secondly, differences in what various employee groups need may also cause an organization to formulate separate compensation policies and practices. Some employees prefer to be paid for the time they work, whereas others, such as managers and professionals, want their compensation based not only on years of service but also on their contribution.

However, in establishing different policies and practices for different classes of personnel, the organization must take care not to inadvertently discriminate against one employee category or another.

Consistency with Other Facets of Human Resource Management

Compensation policies and practices must also be consistent with other human resource management activities. For example, the success of a compensation policy designed to recognize individual performance depends on the performance evaluation activity being properly managed and fully understood by employees. A policy of internal promotions – as opposed to outside recruiting – should be reinforced by a compensation policy that provides for sufficient salary differences between employees with different levels of responsibility. Offering high salaries to attract a high-quality workforce will not succeed unless the organization selects carefully from its pool of applicants.

2.3.3 Environmental Influences

Compensation cannot be managed strategically without taking into account the interaction between various environmental influences and the characteristics of the organization. Organizations do not operate in a vacuum. The main environmental variables they must cope with in regard to strategic compensation management include legal and political, union, social, and economic influences.

Legal and Political Influences

Through their laws, ordinances, and decrees, the various levels of government in a country set minimum and (occasionally) maximum limits on what an employer may pay workers. They also establish measures designed to protect individuals from loss of income and ensure certain minimum working conditions (e.g. vacations, holidays). One need only think of the acts on minimum work standards in various provinces across Canada, laws on salary discrimination, the Canadian Labour Code, the Fair Labor Standards Act in the United States, not to mention all the government legislation that defines the exchange relationship between employer and employee.

While government influence has increased in recent years, the parties concerned may still make most compensation decisions. For example, while the Labour Code establishes the rules of the game for labour relations, it leaves the parties concerned (organization and union) some decision-making leeway.

Legal and political influences also raise a number of questions. In terms of legislation, for instance, will organizations be proactive or reactive? In the case of an organization with employees in several provinces, will it apply the toughest legislation to all its employees, or will it manage compensation differently from one province to the next? This question arises, for example, with pension plans governed by federal and provincial laws that have not been fully harmonized.

Union Influences

In addition to legal and political influences, unions also advocate policies that have repercussions for an organization's compensation practices. This influence is somewhat more ambiguous. In fact, the policies put forward by various union headquarters do not always agree. For instance, while some unions insist on using their own job evaluation system in every organization where they operate, others use a more decentralized approach. Nonetheless, unions seem to have a common desire for job security and certain minimum wage levels for their members. Moreover, there seems to be an understanding about the importance of salary comparisons with the outside. As mentioned earlier, there is also an egalitarian emphasis in certain unions.

Social Influence

The values of the society in which the organization is evolving also define the limits of the exchange relationship between the organization and its employees. For example, these values lead to the standards used in determining salaries and employee benefits. While some countries, such as France, Germany and, to a lesser degre, Canada, force employers to protect their employees against insecurity in an industrial society, others, such as the United States, leave these problems for the most part to be solved by private initiative.

In the area of salary discrimination, it is interesting to note that what is considered inequitable toward women today presented no problem a few years ago. Social values change. New resources and constraints must now be considered in formulating compensation policies and practices. Such changes force companies interested in strategic compensation management to ask new questions. For example, will more women entering the labor market modify the pool from which we draw our workers? Will we continue determining the content of our compensation packages without taking into account the increasing number of women in the workforce and the rising number of families with both spouses working outside the home? Will the aging of the population projected for the next 20 years have an impact on one or more of the existing compensation systems?

Economic Influences

Economic conditions provide managers with strict limits within which compensation must fall so that the organization can obtain the labour it needs and ensure its own survival. These limits vary from one organization to the next as well as over time.

Analyzing economic influences brings certain other variables into play. For example, what is the relationship between economic conditions and our organization? Do interest rates, the value of the dollar, and the demand for goods and services put our organization in a favourable position? What can we expect in the coming months and even years? The less we are able to predict changes, the more flexibility we should build into the compensation program; otherwise, the organization will be forced to resort to layoffs.

In light of the Free Trade Agreement between Canada and the United States, and the increased pressure for productivity gains, it seems clear that organizations must opt for more flexible compensation systems. A closer relationship must exist between compensation and both employee and company performance. Establishing bonus plans is one way of achieving this. As Armstrong (1987) points out, the market will identify the participants in the bonus plan. When they survey the market about the criteria for participation in this type of plan, many companies ask: What kind of bonus system do you offer individuals with a salary of $75,000? $50,000? Should a distinction be made within any given salary grade between supervisory and staff jobs? If the goal is to manage employee behaviour, what the market reveals about participation in premium or bonus plans becomes incidental. Essentially, management must determine what behaviour they wish to promote within the organization, and to what end. Do they want to emphasize short-term profits? Ensure sustained growth? Increase market share? The answers to these questions will help not only to identify plan participants, i.e. those whose behaviour has a significant impact on objectives, but also to shape the content of the plans.

☐ 2.4 Summary

After explaining the three major schools of thought on compensation management, which are often superimposed within organizations, this chapter described the perspective adopted in this book, namely strategic compensation management.

Managing compensation strategically means emphasizing organizational traits and values. This does not, however, imply ignoring the market. The organization must always ensure that it remains competitive, whether or not it uses strategic management. Market surveys enable the company to formulate a compensation package that is as competitive as it wishes, rather than simply providing a model to copy.

While there are many ways to classify organizations according to their strategies, so far this exercise has contributed little to compensation management (Fay, 1987). Our knowledge of organizations is still too limited. It is difficult to understand clearly the reality of an organization described as being defensive or prospective; it is a start, but not enough. Moreover, whether you choose one classification or another, the recommendations for compensation management are still rather vague and very normative. But this is not surprising. Competent people interested in strategic compensation management are quite rare. It has only been recently that compensation has lost its essentially technical and forbidding nature. The way is clear for strategic compensation management. Yet, in practice, this creates some major challenges that must be faced in the future.

REFERENCES

ARMSTRONG, S.J., "Incentive Compensation: Incentive Design and Management Implications," in *Incentives, Cooperation, and Risk Sharing*, edited by H.R. Nalbantian, Totowa, New Jersey, Rowman and Littlefield, 1987, pp. 165-175.

BALKIN, D.B. and L.R. GOMEZ-MEJIA, "Toward a Contingency Theory of Compensation Strategy," *Strategic Management Journal*, 1987, vol. 8, pp. 169-182.

BECK, R.N., "Visions, Values and Strategies: Changing Attitudes and Culture," *Academy of Management Executive*, 1987, vol. 1, N° 1, pp. 33-41.

BELCHER, D.W. and T.J. ACHTISON, *Compensation Administration*, Englewood Cliffs, New Jersey, Prentice-Hall Inc., 1987.

BRATKOVICH, J.R., B. STEELE and G.N. TEESDALE, "The Reward System as a Tool for Reinforcing Innovation and Entrepreneurial Behaviour," in *Human Resource Strategies for Organizations in Transition*, edited by R.J. Niehaus and K.F. Price, New York, Plenum Press, 1990, pp. 63-81.

CHANDLER, A.D., *Strategy and Culture*, Cambridge, Massachusetts, MIT Press, 1962.

DYER, L., "Studying Human Resources Strategy: An Approach and an Agenda", *Industrial Relations*, 1984, vol. 23, N° 2, pp. 156-169.

FAY, C.H., "Using the Strategy Planning Process to Develop a Compensation Strategy," *Topics in Total Compensation*, 1987, vol 2, N° 2, pp. 117-128.

FOMBRUN, C., M.M. TICHEY and M.A. DEVANNA (Ed.), *Leaders and Managers*, New York, John Wiley and Sons, 1984.

FREEDMAN, S.M., J.R. MONTANARI and R.T. KELLER, "The Compensation Program: Balancing Organizational and Employee Needs," *Compensation Review*, 2nd quarter, 1982, pp. 47-54.

GOSSELIN, A. and R. THÉRIAULT, "Designing Strategically Oriented Reward Systems", *Working Paper*, Montreal, École des hautes études commerciales, Université de Montréal, 1985.

KERR, J.L., "Diversification Strategies and Managerial Rewards: An Empirical Study", *Academy of Management Journal*, 1985, vol. 28, N° 1, pp. 155-179.

KERR, J. and J.W. SLOCOM, "Managing Corporate Culture Through Reward Systems", *Academy of Management Executive*, 1987, vol. 1, N° 2, pp. 99-107.

KILMAN, R. and M. SAXTON, *Gaining Control of the Corporate Culture*, San Francisco, Jossey-Bass, 1985.

LAWLER, E.E., *Pay and Organization Development*, Reading, Massachusetts, Addison-Wesley, 1981.

LAWLER, E.E., "The Strategic Design of Reward Systems", in *Leaders and Managers*, edited by C. Fombrun, M.M. Tichy and M.A. Devanna, New York, John Wiley and Sons, 1984, pp. 127-147.

LEVY, A. and U. MERRY, *Organizational Transformation, Approaches, Strategies, Theories*, New York, Praeger Publication, 1986.

MAIDMENT, P., "No Small Change: A Survey of Japan," *The Economist*, December 5, 1987, pp. S1-S34.

MILES, P.E. and C.C. SNOW, *Organizational Strategy, Structure and Process*, New York, McGraw-Hill, 1978.

MINTZBERG, H., "Patterns in Strategy Formation," *Management Science*, 1978, vol. 24, pp. 934-948.

MISA, K.S. and T. STEIN, "Strategic HRM and the Bottom Line," *Personnel Administrator*, October 1983, 1, pp. 27-30.

NININGER, J.R., *Managing Human Resources: A Strategic Perspective*, Ottawa, The Conference Board of Canada, 1982.

SCHWARTZ, H. and S.M. DAVIS, "Matching Corporate Culture and Business Strategy," *Organizational Dynamics*, Summer 1981, pp. 30-48.

STONICH, P.J., "The Performance Management and Reward System: Critical to Strategic Management," *Organizational Dynamics*, Winter 1984, pp. 45-57.

THÉRIAULT, R., "Key Issues in Designing Compensation Systems," in *Canadian Readings in Personnel and Human Resource Management*, edited by S.L. Dolan and R.S. Schuler, New York, West Publishing Company, 1987.

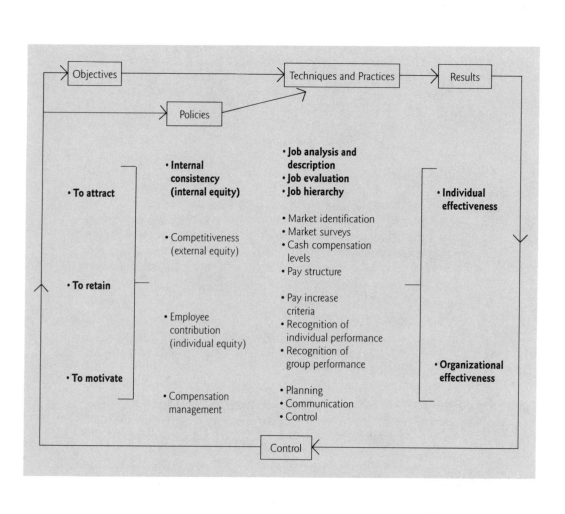

II

INTERNAL EQUITY AND JOB EVALUATION

Organizations rely on four fundamental compensation policies to determine pay: internal consistency, competitiveness, rewarding individual or group contributions, and the nature of the compensation administration. This section discusses the first of these policies, internal consistency, and how to ensure this consistency within an organization.

To make pay equitable, an organization must consider the content and scope of the duties and responsibilities attached to each job. Chapter 3 described the job analysis and description process.

Once jobs have been analyzed and clear descriptions written, job requirements may be determined. Various methods of doing this are presented in Chapter 4.

Establishing a job evaluation process is a sensitive task for an organization, because such a process generates considerable employee expectations. Also, regardless of what method is used, the evaluation remains essentially subjective. Therein lies the importance of critically analyzing evaluation results and any factors that might influence them. Chapter 5 discusses this, examining the management of job evaluation.

Finally, it should be noted that the purpose of establishing a job evaluation process is not to determine the pay for each job; rather, its purpose is to determine relative job requirements and thereby create a hierarchy of jobs. Individual pay cannot be determined without considering organizational policies on market competitiveness, as well as policies on rewarding individual or group contributions. These policies will be discussed in subsequent sections.

TABLE OF CONTENTS

3

JOB ANALYSIS AND DESCRIPTION

The value of an employee's contribution cannot be effectively determined without first knowing the requirements of the job. Therein lies the essential purpose of job analysis.

An individual's role within an organization is, in part, defined by his or her job description, which outlines the nature and scope of what the employer expects. Job analysis involves two dimensions. The first is the mandate, i.e. the accountability, duties, nature and level of decision-making, and the elements and tasks required of an individual. The second is the individual's contribution, in other words, the talents, skills, knowledge, experience, and performance, as well as effort put into work. The following chapters examine how to measure this contribution.

After defining the relevant terms and explaining the purpose of analyzing and describing jobs, this chapter focuses on the two principal methods of job analysis: the traditional or qualitative technique, and the so-called structural technique. The chapter concludes by discussing alternatives to written job descriptions.

☐ 3.1 Employment Terminology

Vocabulary is often misused in compensation management. Also, some definitions are confusing. This situation creates countless communication problems when orienting and training individuals in this discipline, as well as for practitioners in dealing with each other. Some organizations, for instance, refer to "job description", whereas others prefer "mandate" or "position description".

Sometimes, we speak about "position"; other times, about "job", "employment", "occupation", or "role". To understand the tools and techniques presented in this chapter, it is important to know exactly what the key concepts mean. Most of the definitions below are taken from a 1956 publication by

DIAGRAM 3.1
Employment Terminology

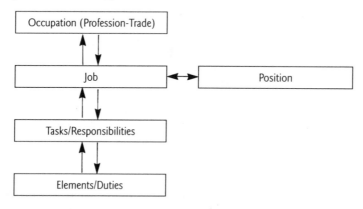

the European Productivity Agency of the Organization for European Economic Cooperation (OEEC). Although Canada and the United States are not members of the OEEC, they participate in all its activities. Many of the following definitions are taken from a document that emerged from a conference on job analysis organized jointly by the OEEC and the International Labour Organization (ILO). These definitions represent the results of a concerted effort on an international level to establish specific terms for job analysis and description. These definitions are in line with those later proposed by the American Compensation Association (Wallace, 1984).

Diagram 3.1 synopsizes the different components of employment terminology.

Before elaborating on these concepts, we must define some of the expressions used in job analysis and description.

Job analysis   A process by which jobs are broken down into their elements for the purpose of adopting a formal, systematic approach to compiling, analyzing, and synthesizing information about those elements. The components may be either tasks and elements or responsibilities and duties. There are different ways of conducting job analysis, among them interviews and questionnaires. Job analysis precedes job description.

Job description or mandate   A document containing the information gathered by job analysis in a practical and readily usable form. In addition to information about either tasks and elements or responsibilities and duties, a job description may include details about working conditions, as well as about the tools, materials, and instruments used. Another document containing **job specifications** is commonly attached to a job description. It lists the qualifications or personal qualities normally required of applicants for the position. Depending on the nature of a job, it may specify required level of education, type of training, experience, etc. However, as we will see below, job specifications are not an integral part of a job description.

Occupation   A group of jobs involving similar or closely related tasks, whose performance requires similar qualifications, knowledge, and skills.

Accounting, for instance, is an occupation. Within it, we find jobs such as internal auditor, controller, public auditor, cost accountant, bookkeeper, etc. All of these jobs involve similar or closely related tasks whose performance requires similar qualifications. These jobs may be related to a "profession" or to a "trade". Generally speaking, it is agreed that a trade involves the performance of manual tasks, whereas a profession primarily entails mental work.

Job   A group of positions that are identical in terms of the significant, major tasks they involve. For example, the job of teller is found in a credit union or bank branch. Yet the job may encompass several positions. There are as many teller positions as there are individuals working as tellers, plus teller vacancies. The same applies to the job of bookkeeper.

Position   A set of duties, tasks, and responsibilities requiring the services of an individual. An organization has as many positions as it has employees. Also, some positions may be vacant, meaning that no one holds them. In this case, those duties, tasks, and responsibilities are not being accomplished. A position may exist even if it is vacant.

Task   A set of activities required of an individual, demanding a mental or physical effort to achieve a stated objective. A task is a logical, necessary step in accomplishing an individual's work. A job may involve one or more tasks. An individual's position consists of the task or set of tasks that he or she performs.

Accountability/Responsibilities   A duty or set of duties used to determine and describe the main purpose or "raison d'être" of a job. For example, the job of personnel manager in an organization may include the responsibility of "defining and recommending policies, guidelines, systems, and methods to the executive committee, consistent with organizational objectives and needs in the area of human resource management".

Element   The smallest unit into which a task may be divided without analyzing the actual movements, actions, and mental processes it involves.

In general, a task consists of a number of elements. For example, "counter service" is one task assigned to the job of teller in a credit union or bank branch. The work is organized so that this task is comprised of a number of elements: accepting deposits from customers, closing accounts, paying interest on bond coupons brought to the counter, etc.

Duty   One or more of the elements required to carry out a responsibility associated with a job. Each responsibility attached to a job involves one or more duties.

Function   The nature of the tasks or responsibilities connected to a group of similar jobs. We may speak of a technical function or of a commercial function. In this context, the tasks or responsibilities of a job may be characterized by one or more functions. Similarly, but on a lower level of abstraction, the tasks or responsibilities of a job may stem from any of the various functions associated with management, i.e. planning, guidance, coordination, organization, and control.

These definitions apply throughout this chapter and the remainder of the book.

□ 3.2 The Value of Job Descriptions

Not everyone agrees that job descriptions should be set down in writing. Some executives see job descriptions as a yoke intended to keep employees from doing things. Some employees see job descriptions as useless pieces of paper, because they believe they know exactly what they have to do. Finally, some managers consider job descriptions utterly useless, because they are incomplete or obsolete when needed.

Yet all these criticisms focus on how job descriptions are used, rather than why they exist. Actually, job descriptions are simply management tools designed to achieve certain objectives, and are only valuable insofar as those objectives are being achieved. Here, a clear distinction must be drawn between how the means is used and the means itself. Ultimately, job descriptions are like money: useful, yet sometimes used in irrational and inefficient ways. This clearly indicates the importance of the objectives pursued in writing them.

Historically, the job analysis and description process has been used primarily for job evaluation (Asch, 1988; Primoff and Fine, 1988), because the content of a job must be known before its value can be determined. This makes it important to have descriptions complete and sufficiently well-organized to bring out the requirements of a job.

Job descriptions also prove valuable, if not essential, to numerous other human resource management activities, such as recruiting, selection, performance evaluation, training, management-labour relations, and human resource planning (Gael, 1988; Milkovich and Boudreau, 1988; Rock, 1990).

Thériault's survey (1986) of 200 Canadian organizations of every size and sector found that about 70% had job descriptions for some employee categories; this percentage reached almost 90% in corporations with over 250 employees. As for the objectives of job descriptions, 70% of the organizations stated that they used job descriptions for job evaluation and recruiting, 60% for establishing selection criteria, 50% for performance evaluation, and about 30% for training and human resource planning.

We may expect job analysis and description to be less focused on job evaluation in the future. In fact, new job evaluation techniques using structured questionnaires and involving incumbents in the evaluation process reduce the importance of job descriptions for job evaluation purposes (cf. Chapter 4). This does not mean that job descriptions will no longer be necessary, but rather that they will be utilized in other facets of human resource management, such as performance evaluation. Accordingly, their content will focus more on expected results and desired behaviour.

☐ 3.3 Managing the Job Analysis and Description Program

The process of establishing a job analysis and description program may be divided into the stages set out in Diagram 3.2.

3.3.1 Planning the Program

The effectiveness of a job analysis and description program depends primarily on the care taken in planning it. The resources and time required to implement such a program must not be minimized. It will take at least two to three months to plan a program properly for a medium-sized company (1,000 jobs).

Because of these requirements and, above all, the very nature of the program, support from senior management or the managers in charge of the unit in question is of primary importance. It is vital to ensure that senior management approves and supports the objectives of the program, the required information, the means of collecting it, and the personnel conducting the analysis. If management fails to convey the idea that job descriptions are useful, they will have no impact and will quickly fall into disuse, because managers will have no incentive for keeping them up to date.

DIAGRAM 3.2
Stages in a Job Analysis and Description Program

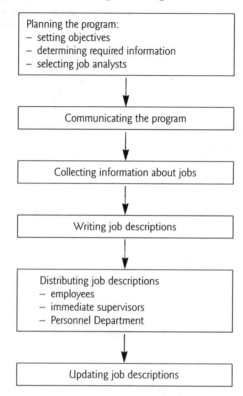

Setting Objectives

Job analysis and description are simply management tools. They have no inherent value; their value is measured by their impact on established objectives. The procedure used, as well as the content of descriptions, may vary, depending on the nature of these objectives.

The objectives most commonly pursued by a job analysis program relate to compensation (job evaluation and compensation surveys). How can one ensure internal and external compensation equity without first examining the specific content of each job? This type of job analysis and description program also proves valuable in areas of work organization, recruiting and selection, hiring and orientation, training and development, performance evaluation, and management-labour relations.

A summary of responsibilities and main duties is sufficient for a salary survey. It proves inadequate, however, if the organization wishes to use the job descriptions to evaluate employee performance. For the latter purpose, job descriptions must do more than define the various responsibilities attached to each job. They should indicate the behaviour required of employees and the performance expected of them.

Determining the Required Information

In addition to identifying objectives, the planning phase of a job analysis and description program requires that a number of decisions be made about the nature of the information to be collected, as well as about the methods and personnel used to collect it.

This information includes the tasks to be accomplished or the behaviour expected of the employee, the machines and tools used, the set objectives of the work, the context in which the job is performed, and the requisite qualifications. In practice, one or more of those items will be needed, depending on the objectives pursued and the nature of the jobs described (management, office staff, production personnel). For the purposes of compensation management (job evaluation and salary surveys), Table 3.1 sets out the minimum information required.

TABLE 3.1
Job Description Content: Minimum Information Required

1. Management, technical or professional jobs

Position of the job within the organization
- Official job title (alternatives in use)
- Department or division involved
- Place of work (if applicable)
- Immediate supervisor's job title
- Title(s) of employees reporting to this position

Purpose of the job

Specific regular and occasional responsibilities and duties

Relationship to other jobs within and outside the organization

2. Office staff or production personnel

Position of the job within the organization
- Official job title (alternatives in use)
- Department or division involved
- Place of work (if applicable)
- Immediate supervisor's job title

Purpose of the job

Specific regular and occasional tasks and elements

Machines, instruments, and tools used

This table calls for some elaboration. First, it indicates that a job may be described in two ways: in terms of responsibilities and duties and in terms of tasks and elements. Responsibilities and duties may be thought of as ends to attain; tasks and elements, as the means used to attain them. As this table illustrates, the nature of the job influences the terms used to describe it. Job description content for a management or professional position is generally expressed in terms of responsibilities and duties. Managers and professionals are usually free to do the tasks and activities they choose to accomplish their assigned responsibilities, insofar as they comply with certain ethical or organizational restrictions. On the other hand, the content of office and production job descriptions is usually formulated in terms of tasks and elements, since the means of fulfilling the responsibilities attached to the job are often specified in advance. This is not, obviously, ironclad. Office jobs may be described in terms of responsibilities and duties. Doing so would give office staff greater autonomy.

Secondly, the table draws a distinction between the *regular* and *occasional* duties and responsibilities of a job. "Occasional" does not refer to the frequency of tasks, but rather to tasks not normally performed by the incumbent, but which he or she is required to do under certain circumstances. For example, answering the telephone is not normally employee A's job, but employee B, whose job it is, sometimes cannot answer calls; in that case, the task is considered occasional in relation to employee A's job. In practice, an occasional task may be performed more frequently than a regular task. It is a matter of degree; if employee A in our example must answer the phone during employee B's mealtimes, the task is considered regular in relation to employee A's job. In practice, an occasional task may be performed more frequently than a regular task. It is a matter of degree; if employee A in our example must answer the phone during employee B's mealtimes, the task is considered regular in relation to employee A's job.

Thirdly, note that the table makes no reference to the basic *qualifications* for doing the job. Organizations, however, usually attach job specifications to job descriptions. These specifications must not be an integral part of the job description, because they depend essentially on the analyst's judgment, and information about job content must be as objective as possible.

Fourthly, it is important that job specifications be drawn up by those responsible for human resource management, and not simply by the job analyst. It is the human resource personnel, who will use the descriptions, that must determine job requirements, rather than the analyst. In fact, the content of job specifications may vary, depending on the objective pursued or the human resource management activity involved. For instance, depending on whether the objective is to evaluate or to fill a job, different conclusions could be drawn as to the nature of a specific requirement such as education. Those responsible for job evaluation must define what they mean by "requirement" before determining those requirements. Similarly, those who are responsible for recruiting and hiring must determine the personal characteristics required for these jobs. Having various human resource management personnel collaborate on job specifications helps ensure the consistency and validity of their respective judgments, since one person's view may be used to confirm another's.

Finally, job descriptions may be written in terms of tasks or of behaviour. In practice, task-oriented information is almost exclusively used, because of the great variety of behaviour the incumbent of a job can effectively use. In analyzing a job, however, it is often worth making a special effort to identify the characteristics in terms of both behaviour and task. In fact, to satisfy virtually all the potential objectives of job descriptions, the type of behaviour required must be specified. To determine relevant selection criteria and, following that, the means of measuring them, one must first set criteria of success or efficiency. This means identifying the behaviour that the incumbent must adopt. The same applies to both performance (Levinson, 1976) and job evaluation.

Choice of Job Analysts

There are three sources of information about a job: the persons doing it, their immediate supervisor, and job analysts. Which source is selected depends on the nature of the job, the kind of information required, the time and money available, the method of compiling information, and the objective or objectives being pursued. For example, management of a small or medium-sized business wishing to examine work organization may ask immediate supervisors to describe the tasks of their subordinates. Another organization, whose resources are limited, may ask employees to describe their own jobs, with the results subject to approval by their immediate supervisors. Finally, management of a large organization, interested in having complete job descriptions written in a standard form, may turn to analysts within or outside the organization. Depending on the method used to compile the information, and on the organization's management style, these analysts will allow incumbents and their immediate supervisors greater or lesser degrees of participation in the process.

Thériault's survey (1986) found that organizations most frequently ask a job analyst in their own human resource department to analyze jobs (45%); in 30% of cases, organizations use immediate supervisors and, in fewer than 10%, an outside consultant. For executive positions, however, the proportion of organizations using an outside consultant climbs to 20%.

3.3.2 Communicating the Program

The success of a job analysis and description program also depends on the quality of its communication. All too often, information about program implementation is conveyed by memorandum only, making it difficult for employees to obtain answers to their questions and concerns. Under such circumstances, negative rumors circulate and the program's chances of success are greatly reduced.

In one scenario, a small company, after successfully planning the implementation of a job analysis and description program, hired a consultant. The general manager of the company told close colleagues that the consultant would meet with employees in various positions to write job descriptions, to be used primarily to establish a new compensation program. The consultant, who already knew a little about the structure of the organization and nature of the jobs, arranged interviews. Those with office staff lasted over two hours each, and often stretched to almost three. This is because, each time, the consultant had first to introduce himself and explain the purpose of the interview, as well as what the information would be used for, before gaining enough employee confidence to obtain the required job information. Realizing that, the consultant asked the general manager of the company to convene a meeting of all employees. At the meeting, the general manager explained the program and its objectives, then introduced the consultant, who explained the implementation procedure. Employees were allowed to ask questions freely. After that meeting, the length of the interview decreased to about one hour, while at the same time the value of the information obtained increased.

This example emphasizes the type of information that must be conveyed before collecting data, and the importance of employees understanding the process. This improves a program's chances of success, because employees will be more inclined to cooperate, a prerequisite for obtaining high-quality information.

There is no magic formula for communicating a job analysis and description program. Many factors must be considered: the organization's style of internal communication, whether or not employees are unionized, the employee category for which the program is intended, the procedure adopted for collecting information, whether or not external analysts are used, the updating or development of job descriptions, etc. Every good communications program, however, has certain essential characteristics.

1. The information conveyed about the program must answer "Why?" (objectives), "What?" (type of information sought), and "How?" (steps to follow and manner of proceeding). If the job descriptions will be used to evaluate jobs, management must clearly indicate that the evaluation will focus on the jobs, not on incumbents.
2, Management must demonstrate total, unqualified support for the program.
3. If the jobs to be described are held by unionized employees, union representatives must, at a minimum, be informed about the program before information is disseminated more widely.

4. Line supervisors must be informed about the implementation of the program before their employees.
5. Employees whose jobs are to be described must be notified and given an opportunity to obtain answers to the questions this type of program raises.
6. If observation or interviews are being used to collect information, the job analysts – especially if they are outside consultants – must be introduced to line supervisors and to the employees directly affected by the program.

3.3.3 Collecting Information about Jobs

Information about the content of various jobs is normally collected using one of the so-called traditional or conventional job analysis techniques: observation, questionnaires, or interviews. In recent years, analysts have developed many other methods of analyzing jobs: so-called structural techniques, of which functional analysis and various structured questionnaires are the most familiar. The choice of technique is primarily determined by the program objectives, the work organization, the organization's culture, and available resources.

Traditional Techniques

Table 3.2 illustrates the most commonly used techniques.

TABLE 3.2
Methods of Collecting Information about Jobs

Methods	% of Companies
Observation	5
Questionnaires	
completed by incumbents	33
completed by immediate supervisors	37
Interviews	
of incumbents	34
of immediate supervisors	66

SOURCE: Thériault (1986, p. 100). Reproduced with the publisher's permission.

Observation

As the word suggests, this method involves observing the work being performed and noting what happens, either by way of a live observer (the analyst) or a video camera. Although employees must be notified of the fact as well as the purpose of the procedure, it is important that the observer exercise discretion.

Since this technique reveals only what can be seen, it is particularly useful for production jobs. In addition, analysts often use it to become familiar with a job before employing other methods (questionnaire or interview).

Questionnaires

Essentially, two types of questionnaires are used to analyze jobs: open and structured.

Open questionnaires, which are completed by incumbents or other individuals, are most commonly used to analyze traditional jobs. Diagram 3.3 provides a sample questionnaire for management positions.

Since this method requires incumbents to describe what they do in response to certain questions, this method is more valuable for jobs in which incumbents are accustomed to writing.

DIAGRAM 3.3
Job Analysis Questionnaire
Management Position

1. POSITION IDENTIFICATION

The basic purpose of this section is to determine your position within the organization.	
Family and first name	Immediate supervisor's title
Job title	Immediate supervisor's name
Region, area, or district (whichever applies)	Division

2. POSITION SUMMARY

State the purpose of your position. Summarize your basic responsibilities in your different spheres of activity. These responsibilities will be broken down into specific tasks in the next section.

3. YOUR RESPONSIBILITIES

Since this section constitutes the essence of your job description, we recommend that you take special care with it and use clear, complete sentences. Experience has shown that when managers are asked to describe what they do, a number of common words readily spring to mind: "administer", "plan", "control", "manage". While these words may express what the individual does, they may differ so much, depending on the position, that it becomes virtually impossible for the reader to determine exactly what they mean to the person using them. It is therefore important to be precise in describing your job.

EXAMPLE

Nearly all managers manage or supervise personnel. This responsibility, however, may involve different tasks, depending on the position in question. Hence, a manager may:

1. distribute and assign work to subordinates;
2. recommend candidates to the personnel department to fill vacancies under his/her supervision;
3. make the final choice of recommended candidates to fill vacancies under his/her supervision.

For some, "managing personnel" may mean doing one or more of these tasks; for others, it may mean doing all of them and more.

At times, you may have difficulty finding the exact words to describe what you do. Do the best you can, and you will have an opportunity to provide a fuller explanation during the subsequent interview.

Finally, we recommend that you describe what you do by beginning each statement with an active verb.

EXAMPLE

An individual's *tasks that directly involve his or her immediate supervisor* may be described by statements beginning with the following verbs:
- recommends...
- informs...
- submits...
- advises...

Describe, in as much detail as you consider necessary, the various tasks you must perform to accomplish the principal responsibilities you listed in the preceding section.

4. SPECIAL CHARACTERISTICS

4.1 Education

In your opinion, what academic background is normally required for assuming this position?

4.2 Experience

What experience would you consider adequate for assuming this position?

4.3 Supervision

Job titles under your direct supervision (first level)	Number of persons holding each job

Job titles under your indirect supervision (second level only)	Number of persons holding each job

4.4 Communication

Below, list the names of the work or organizational units with which communication is *regular* and *essential* for your job. Specify the purpose of the communication as well.

Internal communication *(within the organization)*

External communication *(outside the organization)*

4.5 Funds and budgets

Nature and amount of funds for which you are responsible:

Nature and amount of funds allocated to you:

DATE	y m d	Respondent's signature

As this example indicates, one of the main problems with open questionnaires lies in interpreting the compiled information. Respondents tend to express themselves in generalities, such as "does", "supervises", "controls", "manages". If the office manager, director of human resources, and vice-president of production all complete their questionnaires in rather vague terms, the ensuing job descriptions may be quite similar. Yet obviously, the behaviour expected of them and the latitude they enjoy in doing their jobs differ significantly. The more subtle distinctions can only be fully understood by using other methods (such as interviews) to define the meaning of those words.

Closed or *structured* questionnaires contain a list of phrases (sometimes followed by definitions) covering various aspects of the job. The person completing the questionnaire (the incumbent, immediate supervisor, or analyst) simply checks off the answers, which indicate whether or not a job has a specific characteristic, the amount of time required, or the degree of complexity of the expected behaviour.

Closed or structured questionnaires take much longer to develop than open questionnaires. One must ensure that the questions cover all the information essential for describing the job. The choice of words used is also of the utmost importance, because the resulting information must be *reliable* – consistent answers from different individuals holding the same job – and *valid* – the information obtained must accurately reflect reality.

One can readily see why this means of collecting information about jobs is rarely used to develop the kind of job descriptions normally found in organizations.

Interviews

A favorite tool of job analysts, interviewing, involves obtaining relevant information about a job directly from an employee or immediate supervisor. Such interviews are generally of the structured type.

A job analyst may interview the incumbents of a job one at a time or a number of them together, which saves time and may produce more information. On the other hand, interviewing several employees at the same time may have the disadvantage of inhibiting some from speaking freely about their work.

Some organizations interview immediate supervisors rather than incumbents, since supervisors are familiar with what their employees do, are responsible for their work and, possibly, are more objective about the job. This approach also reduces the number of employees whose work is disrupted, and may save time.

Nonetheless, this technique presents its own problems. First of all, the interview may bring out what "should be", rather than "what is", done, whereas the purpose of job analysis is to collect information about the work actually being done. Secondly, the fact that immediate supervisors are responsible for their employees' work does not necessarily mean that they have full and accurate knowledge of what those employees do. For example, one might cite the famous case of Maier (1961), who asked 58 pairs of supervisors/subordinates to enumerate subordinates' tasks. Each subordinate provided information about his or her work, which was then compared to the immediate supervisor's description of the subordinate's job. The results indicated that only 46% of the pairs agreed on more than 50% of the work done. The differences were even more pronounced concerning the principal hindrances to subordinates' performance, i.e. the more problematic jobs – only 8% of pairs agreed on more than 50% of the obstacles.

Finally, there is less chance of a job analysis program succeeding if incumbents are not interviewed, particularly when the results of the job analysis and description program directly concern them, e.g. job evaluation and determination of their pay level.

Generally speaking, collecting information through interviews avoids the disadvantages of a questionnaire. Face-to-face contact reduces semantic problems. In addition, different levels of writing skills or motivation do not affect the job descriptions, as is usually the case with open-ended questionnaires. Finally, since the information comes directly from the job incumbent, an interview has the advantage of allowing employees to express themselves directly about their work. Questionnaires also offer this advantage, but interviews are preferred. More accurate and relevant information can normally be gathered through face-to-face verbal communication than through written responses.

Yet, interviews are much more time-consuming than open-ended questionnaires, both for the analyst and the employees providing the information. They are also more expensive. And the cost rises when one considers the value of the time spent providing information about a job rather than doing it.

Structural Techniques

Traditional or conventional job analysis and description techniques typically involve writing sentences describing the tasks or responsibilities attached to various jobs. No matter how much care the analyst takes in writing, the results are always subject to interpretation. Structural job analysis and description methods were developed precisely to minimize this limitation and to produce what had been impossible using traditional methods – a quantitative analysis.

Structural techniques provide a set of instruments for collecting either task- or behaviour-oriented information about jobs, allowing similar tasks, behaviour, or jobs to be compared and analyzed using various logical or statistical techniques. McCormick (1979) and Gael (1988) describe almost twenty procedures or questionnaires based on structural job analysis techniques. We will limit ourselves here to three examples: functional analysis, critical incidents, and inventories with numerous structured questionnaires (standard or customized).

Functional analysis   The U.S. Department of Labor was among the first to use a structural technique to analyze work. During the 30s, it developed the *Dictionary of Occupational Titles* (DOT), which described all jobs on the market by so-called functional analysis. These descriptions have since been revised and updated.

Confronted with the problem of classifying the job market, the Canadian government made extensive use of the system developed in the United States and, in the early 70s, developed the *Canadian Classification and Dictionary of Occupations* (CCDO), based on a functional analysis of jobs.

The following assumptions underlie the functional analysis on which both classifications are based:

1. Everything a person may do as part of a job relates to three basic elements: people, information, and things.
2. An individual's functions in relation to each element are unique. Interpersonal resources are applied to people, mental resources to information, and physical resources to things.
3. Every job requires its holder to relate in varying degrees to each element.

Table 3.3 lists the functions identified for the three basic elements, as well as the hierarchical order of the CCDO.

Volume 1 of the CCDO contains a classification code for each of the 6,700 jobs identified in Canada, along with a three-digit code indicating each job's complexity in terms of information, people, and things.

Volume 2 provides the following information about each job:

– job specifications, i.e. required level of:
  • intelligence;
  • verbal skills;
  • mathematical skills;
  • spatial perception;
  • form perception;
  • reading perception;
  • eye/hand/finger coordination;
  • digital dexterity;
  • manual dexterity;
  • eye/hand/foot coordination;

TABLE 3.3
Hierarchy of Functions Used in the CCDO

Information	People	Things
0. Synthesizing	0. Mentoring	0. Setting-up
1. Co-ordinating	1. Negotiating	1. Precision working
2. Analyzing	2. Instructing	2. Operating-controlling
3. Compiling	3. Supervising	3. Driving-operating
4. Computing	4. Diverting	4. Manipulating-operating
5. Copying	5. Persuading	5. Tending
6. Comparing	6. Speaking-signaling	6. Feeding-offbearing
	7. Serving	7. Handling
7. No significant relationship	8. No significant relationship	8. No significant relationship

    • colour distinction.
    – degree of training generally required;
    – specific professional training required;
    – work environment;
    – physical effort required.

Volume 2 also lists:

    – chances for promotion and transfer;
    – various indicators of worker-job compatibility;
    – other required qualities and indicators.

Both volumes of the CCDO are of primary importance for employees in labour centres, professional guidance counsellors, and personnel managers in a human resource department. Volume 2 in particular gives them the benefit of valuable guidelines for job evaluation, personnel selection, career planning, etc.

Critical incidents   This method, developed by Flanigan (1954), involves collecting information about key job behaviours. This information may be compiled by line supervisors, incumbents, colleagues, or independent observers. This technique is especially useful in developing specifications used to establish criteria for personnel selection (Dunnette, 1966). It is also ideal for employee performance evaluation (Flanigan, 1954; Levinson, 1976).

Structured questionnaires   A number of structured questionnaires for collecting work information are also available on the market. Sometimes called "inventories", these questionnaires may focus on behaviour, tasks (or responsibilities), or skills. In practice, the organization's objectives determine the choice of instrument and of the kind of information sought. For instance, if the goal is to develop a training program, information about knowledge and skills, as well as behaviour, must be emphasized. For salary determination, information about all three is essential in order to comply with pay equity criteria, i.e. skills, responsibilities, effort, and working conditions.

Another important aspect of these questionnaires lies in whether their content is *standard* or *customized.*

Standard Questionnaires

Of all the various structured job analysis questionnaires available, the *Position Analysis Questionnaire* (PAQ), developed by McCormick and his team (McCormick et al., 1972), has undoubtedly attracted the most attention. In its present form, the PAQ contains 187 behaviour-centred characteristics divided into 6 main groups, including results of the work, interpersonal activities, and context of the job. The analyst, who may be the incumbent or a line supervisor, must rate the characteristics on various scales of importance, frequency, etc. Virtually every type of job at every organizational level may be analyzed and quantified with the PAQ. Although the PAQ was developed to determine job profiles and specifications for personnel selection, the information it yields is also useful for job evaluation.

Another example of a standard questionnaire is the *Executive Position Description Questionnaire* (EPDQ), developed and introduced by Hemphill (1954). It differs from the PAQ primarily in focusing on executive positions. It resembles the PAQ in that its characteristics are also behaviour-oriented and divided into 10 dimensions (work supervision, internal control over the organization, long-term planning, etc.).

Then there is the *Management Position Description Questionnaire* (MPDQ), created by Tornow and Pinto (1976). Unlike the PAQ and EPDQ, it focuses on task-centered characteristics. In its present form, the MPDQ contains some 200 questions to be answered by the incumbent. It is especially useful for evaluating management positions (Page, 1988).

Since the mid-80s, many compensation consulting firms use standard structured questionnaires to evaluate jobs (cf. Chapter 4). One example is the firm of TPF&C, with its *Weighted Job Questionnaire,* containing some 65 questions. More recently, Hay converted its traditional job evaluation grid into a standard structured questionnaire. These questionnaires generally focus on the three principal dimensions: tasks or responsibilities, required behaviour, and skills, so as to comply with pay equity legislation criteria, i.e. skills, responsibilities, effort and working conditions. In each case, questions are similar; the differences lie in how the questions are worded and the method of answering them.

Customized Questionnaires

Some consultants, rather than using a standard job analysis questionnaire, offer to customize structured questionnaires to evaluate the jobs in their client's organization. Such is the case with William M. Mercer Limited. This approach provides the client (the organization) with a questionnaire that more accurately reflects the particular nature of the jobs. Customized questionnaires are developed in five stages. First, after finding out about the jobs to be evaluated and the client's corporate values and culture, the consultant proposes a set of questions to a working committee, drawn from a question bank developed by the firm over time. The committee then revises the questions, adds or deletes questions and produces a first draft of the questionnaire. Some organizations prefer to become more involved in this questionnaire design stage. In this case, the consultant may begin by identifying potential target areas for questions through brainstorming sessions, instead of directly submitting possible questions to the committee. The consultant may also conduct a number of group interviews with incumbents of the positions concerned before drafting a questionnaire of 20 to 30 questions.

The second step in developing a customized structured questionnaire involves designing the response scale used to rate frequency, importance, required time, or degree of difficulty. Table 3.4 contains two examples of questions on a scale that rates degree of difficulty.

The third step in developing a structured questionnaire involves testing it with a sample group of employees. This ensures that the questionnaire makes the appropriate distinctions between jobs, that the questions are properly understood by respondents, and that all pertinent questions are asked.

At the fourth stage, the questionnaires are completed by incumbents. If a job has numerous incumbents, some organizations prefer to ask only a sample. In most cases, immediate supervisors are also asked to complete the questionnaire to validate their employees' responses.

The final stage entails analyzing the responses to the completed questionnaires. The quantitative nature of the information makes it possible to use a computer and statistical analysis to identify the different job profiles and compare them with each other. In practice, the results of these analyses are used primarily for job evaluation (cf. Chapter 4).

Timing the Information-Gathering

The value of the information gathered depends on the cooperation of the employees concerned, on the validity of the technique used to compile the

TABLE 3.4
Excerpt from a Structured Questionnaire

A. INTERNAL COMMUNICATION

For each of the groups listed below, enter the number corresponding to the *nature of your regular relations** with them.

* Nature of relations

1. Practically no contact.
2. Request or exchange information requiring courtesy and tact.
3. Explain or interpret information or ideas requiring courtesy and tact.
4. Advise or guide individuals in solving problems because of professional experience or expert knowledge.
5. Discuss problems to arrive at an agreement or cooperation requiring persuasiveness and empathy.
6. Reach agreements among individuals which necessitate a high level of persuasion and negotiating skills because of conflicting interests or objectives.

Groups	NATURE OF RELATIONS	
	Employee	Supervisor
– Employees in your department	_____	_____
– Employees in other departments	_____	_____
– Supervisors (other than your own)	_____	_____

B. REQUIRED WRITING SKILLS

Circle *the number of the statement that best describes* the type of writing *normally* required by your job.

1. No writing required.
2. Write form letters, messages or brief instructions consisting of *a few words* or symbols.
3. Write documents or notes several *paragraphs* long to communicate routine information.
4. Write or revise *documents* consisting of technical information, standard reports or the findings of studies (e.g. writing procedures).
5. Write or revise *detailed documents* discussing complex situations and containing recommendations.

---

information, and on the expertise of the analysts. It is also important to select the right time to collect the information. Organizations may know the peaks and slumps inherent in the nature of their business (i.e. industrial or production cycles). If such cycles can be identified, the appropriate time to collect job information is during a slower period. The labour relations climate must also be considered. For example, if the employees concerned are unionized, information should probably not be collected shortly before a collective agreement expires or during negotiations, when a spirit of cooperation is generally more difficult to achieve.

DIAGRAM 3.3
Job Description Process and Content

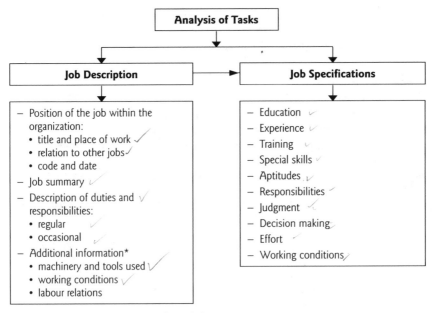

* This information is not always contained in a job description.

3.3.4 Writing Job Descriptions

Outline of a Job Description

Based on notes from observations, questionnaires completed by incumbents or supervisors, or notes from interviews, as well as any existing job descriptions, the job analyst can draft a job description. Diagram 3.3 outlines the content of job descriptions and specifications. It reflects what was mentioned previously, namely that job specifications are not an integral part of a job description. Despite the inherent disadvantages of the procedure, analysts are often asked to write specifications, which are then attached to each job description.

Some analysts go overboard, writing job descriptions eight to ten pages in length. On the other hand, many more sin by omission, and submit descriptions of less than one page. Generally speaking, job descriptions are one-and-a-half pages long for managerial and professional positions, one or two pages for office staff, and one page for production personnel.

First Section: General Information

As indicated in Diagram 3.3, the first part of a job description generally assembles information designed to situate the job within the organization.* For example, it might contain the following information.

Job title   This refers to the title of the job being described. Sometimes, alternative titles commonly used within the organization to refer to the position may also be listed. The title attached to a job must be accurate, because it confers a degree of status on incumbents, and may imply different responsibilities and salaries. For instance, the job of "executive secretary" generally involves making more independent decisions and therefore commands a higher salary than the job of "secretary". This makes it important to find out if the incumbent's job really involves the responsibilities listed. One must be on the lookout for titles designed solely to increase status and therefore command higher pay.

Department and division   This identifies the department or division, etc., in which the job is located, and gives some indication of the nature of the work. For example, a secretary in the accounting department undoubtedly does much the same work as one in personnel. Yet this does not automatically mean that their tasks or responsibilities are identical in nature. One must, therefore, write as many descriptions of secretarial jobs as there are different sets of tasks or responsibilities. In practice, this number often corresponds to the number of organizational divisions or departments.

Place of work   When an organization has more than one place of business, it is often useful to specify the geographical location of the job.

Immediate supervisor's job title   To trace the lines of authority surrounding a job, the title of the supervisor to whom the employee reports is generally included.

Titles of subordinates and number of positions   To indicate the level and scope of supervision involved in a job, it is important to list subordinates' job titles and the number of positions.

Job code   To simplify the management of job-related programs, some organizations develop their own job-coding system, while some use the standard codes of their business sector or industry. This code must appear in job descriptions.

---

* For an example of how an analyst can convert information obtained from the analysis of an executive position within an organization into a job description, see Wortman and Sperling (1975, pp. 89-101).

Date   Job content may change and require updating. Dating a job descrip-tion helps to ensure its accuracy, signal the necessity of revision, etc.

Second Section: Job Summary

Following the information indicating a job's position within the organization, job descriptions generally include a section entitled "Job Summary", "Job Synopsis", "Main Functions", or a similar title. This serves as a summary of the preceding (job's position within the organization) and following (descrip-tion of tasks or responsibilities) sections of the job description.

The summary should be worded as follows: "Reporting to..., the (job title) is responsible for (list of main tasks or responsibilities)." This section generally ends with a standard sentence: "The incumbent performs any other related tasks upon request." What is the purpose of this rider? Does it mean that the incumbent may be asked to do anything? Or is it intended to cover anything that the author of the description may have overlooked? Actually, there is a very basic reason for adding this sentence. It serves as a reminder to readers that the spirit and not the letter of the description is paramount. Its justification lies in the impossibility of anticipating every possible situation and always finding the right word when writing job descriptions. Obviously, the content implied by this sentence must not exceed what follows in the next section of the job description, i.e. the detailed description of tasks or responsibilities. One must also avoid interpreting the statement restrictively, as labour-relations arbitrators are wont to do.

Third Section: Description of Duties and Responsibilities

This section is the very essence of the job description. It is usually entitled "Tasks", "Duties and responsibilities", or something similar. This section of the job description must be written in such a way that anyone reading the list of tasks knows exactly what the employee does, and how and why. The decision as to whether this section should deal with "tasks" or "responsi-bilities" depends on the nature of the job in question, as well as other factors already discussed.

This section should be written in such a way that any reader unfamiliar with the job can understand its content, nature, and significance. This does not mean that the reader should then be able to do the job, but rather that he or she must know exactly what it entails. Therein lies the importance of making this section complete and accurate.

Depending on the nature of the job described, there are various ways of presenting the information: tasks and responsibilities in order of impor-tance, the order in which the work is done, the time spent on each task or responsibility, or the frequency of each activity. Use whatever most clearly describes the job. A job description for office or production personnel may include information about the machinery and tools used, working conditions, and labour relations. The description of a managerial or professional position might include information about the type of budget allocated to the position.

The European Productivity Agency included guidelines on how to write this section in its 1956 publication. Their advice is worth repeating:

1. Use a direct, concise, narrative style.
2. Begin sentences with functional verbs in the present active tense (e.g. "inspects", "sorts", "weighs"); the subject of each sentence, "this employee", is implicit.
3. Use precise terms. For example, do not say "makes wooden handles" or "produces wooden handles", when the employee actually "carves wooden handles". "Makes" and "produces" do not convey as precise a meaning as "carves". The same applies to words such as "plans", "manages", "coordinates", "controls", or "supervises", which are all-purpose words best kept out of job descriptions, because they fail to convey an accurate idea of an employee's responsibilities. One must also be precise in terms of quantities, weights, measures, and frequency. Do not write "carries boxes", but rather, for example, "carries 10-kg boxes". On the other hand, avoid excessive detail. For example, a job description need not elaborate on established, familiar procedures. "Posts the day's receipts and disbursements in the General Ledger according to established procedure" is sufficient.
4. Each sentence must make an explicit statement. Whatever is implicit must be obvious to the reader.
5. Do not describe the different elements that were observed separately. Rather, indicate the relationships among them, so as to bring out the significance of the job and convey a precise idea of it.

Finally, a job description must be complete. In this regard, Tables 3.5 and 3.6 contain descriptions of a technical and an office job.

Reviewing Job Descriptions

Once job descriptions have been drafted, they are first reviewed by the persons who gave the information to the analyst, i.e. immediate supervisors or incumbents. Having the originator of the information go over it first is important. Later, during the job description approval process, immediate supervisors and senior management will have no reason to think that incorrect information was provided when the analyst's misconception of the job is really to blame. The individuals who supplied the information are asked to confirm that the description is accurate, and reflects the reality of the job. The description need not use the incumbent's own words. What is important

TABLE 3.5
Technical Job Description

Date: March 11, 1988   **Code:** 7-02
Department: Boiler
Title: Draughtsperson/developer   **Grade:** 16
Source of supervision: Supervisor; receives instructions from group leader.
Supervisory duties: Assists. Informs other workers about details of the work.
Work:

1. Receives instructions, job orders, drawings, etc.
2. Reads and interprets drawings, and organizes the work based on the requisite materials and tools.
3. Obtains or makes arrangements to receive the specified materials.
4. Draws or develops templates, plates and structural or piping equipment for geometric construction and fabrication.
5. Develops proper materials such as combined transitions in circular, rectangular, conical, eccentric, etc. shapes by means of triangulation, radial lines, geometry, etc.
6. Produces drawings to ensure optimal use of materials.
7. Indicates holes, fold lines, shear lines, etc., by marking, drawing, painting, dotting centres, etc.
8. Logs and identifies materials by part, heat, or job number.
9. Informs management of defects in drawings and materials.
10. Moves materials manually or using lift mechanisms.
11. Keeps workplaces and equipment clean and tidy, and complies with safety regulations.

Tools and equipment:
Draughting table, tape, rulers, T-squares, levels, protractors, elliptical compass, dividers, compass, centring head, plumb line, straight-edge, drawings, sketches, mathematical table, soapstone, paint, centre-punches, hammers, lifting mechanisms, etc.

Materials:
Ferrous and nonferrous metals and alloys, plates, construction forms, welded and forged parts, etc.

---

is that the incumbent understands the words and that the description reflects reality. As a result of this process, the analyst may change a few words, add certain tasks or responsibilities, or even delete some.

Following this initial review, the analyst may submit the job descriptions to supervisors for approval. Any major changes they propose should be discussed with the subordinates concerned, to reach agreement and avoid the perception that the analyst changed the information originally provided.

Once consensus is reached with supervisors, the descriptions are submitted to management for final approval.

TABLE 3.6
Office Job Description

Job number: 121   Section: Reception
Job title: Receptionist   Date: December 1990
Department: General administration

JOB SUMMARY

Answers the phone at City Hall and transfers calls to the appropriate department, handles requests for information, opens the mail and forwards it to the appropriate department. Types letters and reports for the Public Relations Manager. Loads the photocopier and collects photocopy fees. Performs any other related task upon request.

TASKS

1. Telephone calls, information and mail
- Answers the phone at City Hall and transfers calls to the appropriate person.
- Takes messages when requested and gives them to the appropriate person.
- Greets visitors, gives them the information they request or directs them to the appropriate person.
- Answers any questions of a general nature.
- Provides information about public transit (routes, schedules, connections) and gives out the information brochure.
- Moves the phone console and connects the answering machine.
- Receives, opens and date-stamps mail, then forwards it to the appropriate department.
- Keeps the log of special delivery slips up to date and sends a report to Accounting.
- Receives tenders addressed to the Clerk, date-stamps them, and keeps them until the bids are opened.

2. Photocopier and Postage
- Cleans the photocopiers, ensures they function properly, and places service calls for repairs.
- Photocopies texts or documents for municipal departments, agencies or individuals based on priorities set by the City administration and, in some cases, with supervisor's approval.
- Remits the photocopy fees collected to the Tax Division.
- Puts postage on the mail of municipal departments and makes sure the postage metre is kept filled.
- Puts postage on the mail of agencies or individuals with supervisor's approval.

3. Assisting the Public Relations Manager
- Types certain documents, tables and correspondence on a PC (word-processor) for the Public Relations Department.

4. Miscellaneous
- Types certain documents on a PC (word-processor) for other departments with the supervisor's approval.
- Checks long-distance telephone charges and assigns them to the appropriate department.
- Collects the charges for personal long-distance calls from City employees.
- Prepares the City's press review by clipping relevant articles.
- Sells documents about the City to people who ask for them at the reception desk, balances cash and remits the proceeds to the cashiers.

5. Occasionally
- Types texts and reports from handwritten originals for the general administration, Clerk's office, and personnel department.

3.3.5 Distributing Job Descriptions

Job descriptions should be distributed to various parties. Obviously, incumbents need to have a copy of their own job description, since it gives them an indication of what the organization expects of them. Secondly, supervisors must have their employees' job descriptions on file, because they are directly responsible for managing their staff. Thirdly, job descriptions must be filed with the Human Resource Department, which should have a copy of every employee's job description so it can develop the various programs for which the descriptions were written. Finally, all job descriptions could also be made available to every employee, so as to provide firsthand information about career opportunities. In practice, however, office and production personnel rarely have access to executive and professional job descriptions. This secrecy surrounding job descriptions seems related to the fact that they are used primarily for salary administration, an activity considered confidential in most private sector organizations.

3.3.6 Updating Job Descriptions

As an organization evolves, its objectives and structures change. Similarly, no job description is fixed forever. Rather, it is an instrument that must change as the organization evolves. All too often, job descriptions are relegated to the archives or a bottom drawer once the original purpose for which they were drafted has been fulfilled. It is a high price to pay for a management tool that could remain useful for a modest additional investment.

Job descriptions should be updated whenever:

- all or part of the job content changes;
- there is a new incumbent; or
- the incumbent or immediate supervisor requests an update.

Berenson and Ruhnke (1976) recommend job audits every six months, but once a year seems more realistic. Thériault's survey (1986) found that the vast majority of organizations updated job descriptions when necessary (83%); only a few updated them regularly as a matter of policy (17%).

☐ 3.4 Alternatives to Job Descriptions

The practice of using job descriptions for determining compensation is based on the implicit assumption that job content is a basic element of compensation. It further implies that job content is relatively stable. In practice, these assumptions do not always suit the requirements of organizations striving for flexibility. The advent of new technologies and new forms of work organ-

TABLE 3.7
Levels of Competence – Scientist

Level I

Entry position. Has a B.Sc., no experience. Does laboratory work under the supervision of a higher-level scientist. Performs and records analytic tests and may do some analysis of experimental data.

Level II

Has a B.Sc. and 3 to 5 years of experience, or an M.Sc. with 0 to 2 years of experience. Does laboratory work requiring a high degree of scientific expertise. Develops methodologies for sections of large projects. May be asked to prepare and present experimental data.

Level III

Has an M.Sc. with 3 to 5 years of experience or a Ph.D. with 0 to 2 years of experience. Responsible for doing highly creative and independent work. Is also responsible for interpreting data and may develop and coordinate research programs and projects. May manage the work of lower-level scientists.

Level IV

Has a Ph.D. with 2 or more years of experience. Responsible for determining specific objectives and action plans. Coordinates the efficient implementation of research programs and projects. May supervise the daily work of lower-level scientists. Participates in decisions based on data interpretation, and makes scientific and technical recommendations. Has first-class knowledge and expertise of his/her discipline.

Level V

Has a Ph.D. and extensive experience. Also serves as group leader in charge of a large number of projects, and manages a research team consisting of 3 to 12 scientists and technicians. Assigns various projects, monitors their progress and evaluates the results. Must have advanced knowledge in a given field of specialization. May also participate directly in certain research projects.

ization affect not only job content, but also the qualifications required to do a job. Accordingly, some authors propose a strategic analysis of jobs (Schneider, Marcus and Konz, 1989) and descriptions of aptitudes or skills (Lawler and Ledford, 1985). Whereas strategic job analysis is still relatively new and impractical, the same is not true of aptitude or skill descriptions, that is, describing jobs in terms of what the person *is capable of* doing. This approach is especially suitable for professionals and technicians. The emphasis is on degree of competence at various levels (see Table 3.7). It is also suitable for academics, since an assistant, associate, and full professor have identical duties. What differentiates these three positions is level of competence.

This concept of work organization was first applied successfully to production workers in the early 70s by General Foods at its new plant in Topeka, Kansas (Walton, 1977). Rather than emphasizing degree of competence, as with professional and technical personnel, the focus was on the skills needed to master lateral and vertical tasks. Generally, levels of skill vary between four and seven (Gupta, Douglas Jenkins and Currington, 1986). An employee is normally hired at the lowest level. After a period of apprenticeship (which averages 26 weeks according to the same authors), the employee rises to Level 2, and so on. In some cases, the move from one level to the next is virtually automatic after a given time. In others, the employee must undergo an official evaluation. Procter & Gamble, Johnson & Johnson, General Motors, General Electric, Hyundai, and Alcan are among the companies that use skill, rather than job, descriptions. Many pulp and paper producers do the same.

According to Tosi and Tosi (1986), as well as Lawler and Ledford (1985), this approach to work organization has the following advantages:

- employees more motivated to acquire new knowledge and develop new skills;
- more flexible employees;
- more competent employees; and
- slightly less labour required.

On the other hand, the approach has its disadvantages as well (Tosi and Tosi, 1986; Luthans and Fox, 1989):

- higher training costs;
- creates false expectations among employees if they cannot apply what they learn for lack of opportunity;
- chance of higher employee turnover if the new skills are not used;
- higher labour costs; and
- work occasionally done by apprentices.

Furthermore, the fact that this approach does not lend itself directly to a review of the situation with regard to pay equity legislation may give rise to certain problems (cf. Chapter 9). Finally, like any other system, it too must be managed. In selecting employees, the importance of teamwork and participation rather than working alone must be stressed. Opportunities for training or upgrading must exist, and information about the system must be effectively communicated. If employees are unionized, union support is essential, because this system is the direct opposite of the conventional approach, which emphasizes the tasks to be performed. This undoubtedly explains why most of these systems are found in non-unionized surroundings, the pulp and paper industry being an interesting exception.

REFERENCES

AGENCE EUROPÉENNE DE PRODUCTIVITÉ, L'Analyse des tâches: instrument de productivité, Paris, Organisation européenne de coopération économique, 1956.

ASCH, R.A., "Job Analysis in the World of Work", *The Job Analysis Handbook for Business, Industry and Government*, edited by S. Gael, New York, John Wiley & Sons, vol. 1, 1988, pp. 3-13.

BERENSON, C. and H.O. RUHNKE, *Job Descriptions: How to Write and Use Them*, Costa Mesa, California, Personnel Journal, 1976.

CARLSON, S., *Executive Behavior: A Study of the Workload and the Working Methods of Managing Directors*, Stockholm, Stronberg, 1951.

DUNNETTE, M.D., *Personnel Selection and Placement*, Belmont, California, Wadsworth, 1966.

FINE, S.A., "Functional Job Analysis: An Approach to a Technology for Manpower Planning", *Personnel Journal*, November 1974, pp. 813-818.

FINE, S.A. and W.W. WILEY, *An Introduction to Functional Job Analysis*, Kalamazoo, Michigan, W.E. Upjohn Institute for Employment Research, 1971.

FLANIGAN, J.C., "The Critical Incident Technique", *Psychological Bulletin*, 1954, vol. 51, pp. 327-358.

GAEL, S. (editor), *Handbook for Business, Industry and Government*, vol. I and II, New York, John Wiley & Sons, 1988.

GOMEZ-MEJIA, L.R., R.C. PAGE and W.W. TORNOW, "Development and Implementation of a Computerized Job Evaluation System", *The Personnel Administrator*, 1979, vol. 24, N° 2, pp. 46-52.

GUPTA, N., G. DOUGLAS JENKINS and W. CURRINGTON, "Paying for Knowledge: Myths and Realities", *National Productivity Review*, 1986, pp. 107-123.

HEMPHILL, J.K., "Job Descriptions for the Executive", *Harvard Business Review*, 1954, vol. 37, pp. 55-69.

HORNE, J.H. and T. LUPTON, "The Work Activities of Middle Managers", *Journal of Management Studies*, 1965, vol. 1, pp. 14-33.

INFORMATION CANADA, *Canadian Classification and Dictionary of Occupations*, volumes 1 and 2, Ottawa, 1973.

JONES, J.J. and T.A. DeCOTTIS, "Job Analysis: National Survey Findings", *Personnel Journal*, 1969, vol. 48, pp. 805-809.

LAWLER, E.E. and C.E. LEDFORD, "Skill-Based Pay: A Concept That's Catching On", *Personnel*, September 1985, pp. 30-37.

LEVINSON, H., "Appraisal of What Performance", *Harvard Business Review*, July-August 1976, pp. 30 and ff.

LUTHANS, F. and M.L. FOX, "Update on Skill-Based Pay", *Personnel*, March 1989, pp. 26-32.

MAIER, N.R.S. et al., "Superior-Subordinate Communication in Management", New York, *AMA Research Study*, N° 52, 1961.

McCALL, M.W. Jr et al., "Studies of Managerial Work: Results and Methods", *Technical Report N° 9*, Greensboro, N.C., Center for Creative Leadership, not dated.

McCORMICK, E.J., "Job Information: Its Development and Applications", *Staffing Policies and Strategies*, edited by D. Yoder and H.G. Henemann Jr., Washington, D.C., Bureau of National Affairs, 1974, pp. 35-83.

McCORMICK, E.J., *Job Analysis: Methods and Applications*, New York, AMACON, 1979.

McCORMICK, E.J. et al., "A Study of Job Characteristics and Job Dimensions as Based on the Position Analysis Questionnaire (PAQ)", *Journal of Applied Psychology*, 1972, vol. 56, pp. 347-364.

MILKOVICH, G.T. and J. BOUDREAU, *Personnel/Human Resource Management: A Diagnostic Approach*, 5th edition, Homewood, Illinois, Richard D. Irwin, 1988.

MINTZBERG, H., "Le Travail du dirigeant: la légende et les faits", *Direction et Gestion*, 1976, N° 1, pp. 11-24.

MINTZBERG, H., *The Nature of Managerial Work*, New York, Harper and Row, 1973.

PAGE, R.C., "Management Position Description Questionnaire", *The Job Analysis Handbook for Business, Industry, and Government*, edited by S. Gael, New York, John Wiley & Sons, 1988, vol. II, pp. 860-879.

PRIMOFF, E.S. and S.A. FINE, "A History of Job Analysis", *The Job Analysis Handbook for Business, Industry, and Government*, edited by S. Gael, New York, John Wiley & Sons, 1988, vol. I, pp. 14-29.

PUBLIC SERVICE COMMISSION OF CANADA, BUREAU OF STAFF DEVELOPMENT AND TRAINING, *Charting Occupational Analysis through Semantics*, Ottawa, not dated.

ROCK, M. (editor), *Handbook of Wage and Salary Administration*, 3rd edition, New York, McGraw-Hill, 1990.

SCHNEIDER, B., A. MARCUS and A. KONZ, "Strategic Job Analysis", *Human Resource Management*, 1989, vol. 28, N° 1, pp. 51-63.

STEWART, R.M., *Managers and Their Jobs*, London, Macmillan, 1967.

STONE, C.H. and D. YODER, *Job Analysis: 1970*, Long Beach, California, California State College, 1970.

THÉRIAULT, R., *Politiques et Pratiques en rémunération globale dans les entreprises au Québec*, Montréal, Les Productions INFORT inc., 1986.

TORNOW, W.W. and P.R. PINTO, "The Development of a Managerial Job Taxonomy: A System for Describing, Classifying and Evaluating Executive Positions", *Journal of Applied Psychology*, 1976, vol. 61, pp. 410-418.

TOSI, H. and L. TOSI, "What Managers Need to Know About Knowledge-Based Pay", *Organizational Dynamics*, 1986, vol. 14, pp. 52-64.

U.S. DEPARTMENT OF LABOR, MANPOWER ADMINISTRATION, *Dictionary of Occupational Titles*, 3rd ed., Washington, D.C., U.S. Government Printing Office, 1965.

U.S. DEPARTMENT OF LABOR, EMPLOYMENT AND TRAINING ADMINISTRATION, *Dictionary of Occupational Titles*, 4th ed., Washington, D.C., U.S. Government Printing Office, 1977.

WALLACE, M.J., *Glossary of Compensation Terms*, Scottsdale, Arizona, American Compensation Association, 1984.

WALTON, R.E., "Work Innovations and Topeka: After Six Years", *Journal of Applied Behavioral Science*, 1977, vol. 13, pp. 422-433.

WORTMAN, M.S. and J. SPERLING, *Defining the Manager's Job*, 2nd ed., New York, AMACOM, 1975.

TABLE OF CONTENTS

4

JOB EVALUATION: DEFINITION AND METHODS

This chapter analyzes the importance of job content in determining pay. After describing several historical factors, we will focus on the significance and nature of job evaluation, and look at the main conventional methods as well as contemporary methods that are, at present, being increasingly used.

In addition to giving employees some indication of what an organization expects of them, job descriptions also provide the organization with a basis for assigning pay. From an economic standpoint, the compensation for various jobs within an organization must be based on the tasks and responsibilities they involve. Yet, as we saw in Chapter 1, compensation also represents a psychological, sociological, political, and ethical transaction. *All* these considerations come into play in determining pay, and job evaluation must be viewed within this perspective.

☐ 4.1 Defining Job Evaluation

4.1.1 Historical Factors

According to Patton, Littlefield and Self (1964), the first real job evaluation program appeared in 1871, when the U.S. Civil Service Commission, as an isolated experiment, organized a group of jobs into an official hierarchy. Then, in the early 1880s, Taylor proposed a formal and systematic analysis of assigning pay to jobs, to improve productivity at the Midvale Steel Co. This work eventually led to Lott publishing the first book on job evaluation in 1926. During the 20s and 30s, unions and certain employer groups, such as the National Metal Trades Association and the National Electrical Manufacturers Association in the United States, began evaluating production jobs. Their methods were quickly seen as an efficient means of establishing an equitable pay structure (Kress, 1939).

Job evaluation programs only really gained acceptance in the United States during World War II, with the creation of the National War Labor Board. Responsible for wage and price controls, the Board had to ensure that pay increases were only used to correct inequities in an organization's pay structure. It was during this period that the principal methods of job evaluation were developed, and from the early 50s to the late 70s, they remained essentially the same. The passage of new pay equity legislation and computerization of human resource management systems in the 80s gave rise to other methods or, to be more precise, different ways of using some of the conventional methods, not to mention extensive research into the assessment of each job evaluation method.

Treiman (1979) reported that job evaluation was commonly practised by virtually all American public-sector employers. In the private sector, Mahoney, Rynes and Rosen (1984) found that usage depended on organizational size; 89% of major corporations used one or more job evaluation methods, compared to 77% of smaller companies.

In Canada, Thériault's study (1986) indicated that slightly over 75% of employers used job evaluation to assign pay. This percentage varied with the job category in question and the size of the organization. He found that 81% of organizations used job evaluation systems to determine managerial and professional pay, while 67% applied them to production and maintenance employees. Almost 90% of large organizations used job evaluation, compared to less than 70% of small ones.

4.1.2 Job Evaluation and Internal Equity

Whenever different positions within an organization command different salaries, one may say that — implicitly or explicitly — jobs are being evaluated. There are various definitions of job evaluation. The ILO (1984, p. 2) defines job evaluation as a "technique for systematically determining the relative position of a job in relation to others in a pay hierarchy, based on the importance of the duties associated with that job." Treiman (1979) says that job evaluation involves the rational delineation of a hierarchy of jobs based on their worth, to establish an equitable pay scale. This book proposes the following definition: job evaluation is the process of arranging jobs within an organization into a hierarchy based on their relative requirements, so that employees are paid in proportion to the requirements of their job.

The Importance of Value Systems

Several key points emerge from these definitions. First of all, job evaluation means an assessment of the work, not the incumbent. It differentiates the job from its holder. Moreover, job evaluation involves *establishing a hierarchy of jobs based on their requirements.* While the ILO's definition (1984) refers to the concept of "importance" and Treiman's (1979) to "value", "requirements" is preferable. "Value" implies the idea of importance and, accordingly, job evaluation means establishing a hierarchy of jobs based on their importance. This approach clearly conveys the idea that some jobs within an organization are more important than others. Certain jobs might be considered very important, and others of little importance. In the real world, it is difficult to imagine an organization creating and maintaining jobs of little or no importance; that would be inefficient. It is also difficult to imagine individuals admitting that a large part of their lives (their work) is spent doing things of little or no importance. This makes it preferable to limit ourselves to saying that all jobs do not have the same requirements and do not make the same demands on an individual. Job evaluation means identifying what a job requires, and then organizing the evaluated jobs into a hierarchy based on those requirements and demands.

Furthermore, the definitions of job evaluation make it clear that its purpose is *to pay the incumbents of a position in proportion* to the requirements of their job, and not to determine pay levels or specific pay differentials. It involves identifying what jobs should have the same pay and what jobs should have different pay, i.e. ranking the jobs. Job evaluation must not be confused with pay determination. Although the varying demands of the positions within an organization are a worthwhile criterion for assigning pay, the importance of the market and individual characteristics cannot be ignored. Equity need not be based solely on job requirements. It may also depend on what the market pays or what the individual contributes.

The purpose of a job evaluation system is to create internal pay equity based on the various job requirements. Assigning pay on the basis of job requirements implies choosing a value system. Other value systems may be equally appropriate, leaving aside job requirements. Equity, in fact, is only one form of justice; others are based on needs, the law, or equality. Generally speaking, however, in North America, people tend to think that pay should at least reflect the relative requirements of a position. If all or some members of an organization fail to share that value system, job evaluation becomes a futile and even problematic exercise, because it may create pay differentials based on criteria considered irrelevant. And it may diminish rather than increase employees' satisfaction with their pay. The effectiveness of a job evaluation method, therefore, does not depend on its popularity with business or on its specific technical characteristics, but rather on whether or not its results correspond to the values of those concerned. Further, Mahoney (1979) affirms that, above all, a pay structure must reflect the value system of the individuals in question if they are to feel satisfied with their compensation.

In the final analysis, the concept of equity based on job characteristics is essentially subjective. What is fair for one person may not necessarily be fair for another. In this light, the technical characteristics of a job evaluation method are less important than the use made of them (Newman and Milkovich, 1989; Greenberg, 1990). The success of a job evaluation method is measured by the results it achieves. Acceptance of those results depends on the extent to which those concerned are engaged in the process and understand the method, and on the credibility of the evaluators and the evaluation procedure.

The Relative Importance of Internal Equity

As the ILO (1984) points out, job evaluation is only scientific to the extent that it addresses problems in a scientific spirit, i.e. a systematic, orderly fashion. One can readily understand why there is no objective job evaluation method. The process is essentially subjective. There are no universal or objective criteria for determining the value or requirements of a job (Hills, 1989), and all job evaluation methods involve some element of judgment, discretion, negotiation, and rationalization. The recent introduction of statistics does not make job evaluation more scientific; it simply leads to improved analysis and synthesis of the information obtained.

Because of the subjective nature of job evaluation and the importance of market supply and demand, the ILO (1984) notes that some people consider it a mistake to base pay differentials on internal equity. They think that the relative value of pay should depend exclusively on the relative supply and demand for each type of job, i.e. on economic factors. While this approach has its appeal, it creates new problems. It is far from true to say that *the market price of labour is an absolute gauge of its value.* There are also jobs for which the market has no measure. Furthermore, where pay equity legislation exists, as it does in Ontario, disregarding internal equity would simply be illegal.

Finally, on its own, job evaluation is an incomplete, limited tool. It only helps in weighing the most important differences between various job requirements. It attempts to isolate significant differences between jobs by comparing them, thereby leading to a more equitable distribution of pay within the organization. Job evaluation is simply one step in the process of establishing a pay equity program within an organization. In fact, how can a job evaluation reflect the elegance and poise of a fashion model, or the instant reflexes and skills of a racing car driver or a hockey player? In such cases, the characteristics of the individual and market supply and demand will carry much more weight in the compensation decision.

4.1.3 Objectives for Job Evaluation

Job evaluation may be used to reduce or eliminate certain pay inequities or to prevent their appearance. In any case, in a legislative environment, organizations may not have any choice. They have to comply with the law and prepare a pay equity plan (cf. chapter 9).

Correcting Pay Inequities

To correct pay inequities, it is essential to identify where they exist.

In practice, pay inequity has a negative impact on employee satisfaction with pay (Dyer and Thériault, 1976; Lawler, 1971; Weiner, 1979) which, in turn, causes increases in absenteeism, employee turnover, grievances, work stoppages, etc. Naturally, these do not result solely from low satisfaction with pay, just as low satisfaction is not caused exclusively by pay inequity. The appearance of these symptoms, however, may signal a perceived inequity in pay distribution.

Employees' comments about their pay may be a further sign that a job evaluation is necessary. This information may be systematically collected by means of questionnaires or interviews. Its usual source, however, is a formal or informal analysis by managers and executives of how they are managing their employees. The approach is definitely hazardous, since it may result in failure to conduct a systematic job evaluation at the opportune time. It may also trigger a job evaluation process when time, energy, and financial resources would better be invested in solving more pressing problems in other areas.

Take the example of a large organization whose managers were openly disgruntled about their pay. Discussions with a number of them made it clear that they were not dissatisfied with what they were being paid in comparison with each other, but rather compared to what the professionals and support staff within the organization were receiving. In these circumstances, a reevaluation of managerial jobs would have been an inadequate solution. One might also cite the case of the small business that hired an outside consultant to evaluate support staff positions. An exchange of views quickly revealed that it was members of management who felt that salaries paid to support staff were inequitable when compared one to another, and that this perception was caused by the embarrassment they felt in awarding pay increases to support staff. Here too, job evaluation was definitely not a useful exercise.

Preventing Pay Inequities

Introducing a job evaluation system may also help avoid the perception of pay inequity. In this context, various circumstances may justify implementation of a job evaluation program. These include, for example, a corporate merger, a significant increase in hiring, unionization of a group of employees, or institution of a more open compensation disclosure policy.

☐ 4.2 How Many Job Evaluation Programs?

The ultimate purpose of job evaluation, whether there is a specific pay equity law or not, is to ensure pay equity within an organization. What is required, then, is to compare all the jobs with each other and establish a hierarchy based on their requirements. This implies that there is only one cluster (family) of jobs within an organization, hence only one evaluation program to cover all the jobs and only one pay structure. As a matter of fact, this is the underlying assumption of most pay equity legislation.

However, the tremendous differences between jobs in many cases make such a comparison very difficult. To compare each job with all the others systematically, the criteria used for the comparison must be very broad to encompass every job. If the criteria are specific, some may not apply to certain jobs. In either case, it is difficult to evaluate the jobs accurately, making the results less reliable and less valid.

Moreover, even if we could identify the right factors for evaluating all the jobs within an organization, market comparison could still be a problem. In fact, just as certain jobs differ greatly, so too may the markets in which they are found. The market for some jobs is local, for others, regional, national, or international. In some cases, the market is restricted to one business sector; in others, it spans several industries. Limiting the comparison of all jobs to a single geographic or industrial market skews the results. The question of compensation surveys is further discussed in Chapter 7.

In addition to variations in content and market, unionization may also be a factor. Employees may be affiliated with different bargaining units, so that their jobs may (or must) be handled differently. The Ontario government recognized this in its pay equity legislation (cf. Chapter 9). Each bargaining unit may have its own job evaluation program, unless the various unions within an organization agree on a common program.

For these various reasons (nature of the job, the labour market, union characteristics, etc.), the usual procedure is to create job clusters and evaluate the jobs within each cluster. Since an organization has numerous job clusters, it may also have more than one pay structure.

4.2.1 The Concept of Job Cluster

Dunlop (1957) defined a job cluster (family) as a stable group of jobs (wage-determining unit) within an establishment, interconnected through technology, administrative organization, production operations, or social habits, which provides common characteristics for assigning pay. In contrast, the ILO (1984) offers a much simpler definition of job cluster: any group of jobs that are closely related when pay rate is compared to job requirements. In this book, a job cluster is defined as a group of jobs similar enough to be compared with each other on the basis of a common set of specific characteristics and located in similar markets. However, where pay equity law exists, as it does in Ontario, it may be necessary to apply the job evaluation system across job clusters (cf. chapter 9).

4.2.2 Number of Job Clusters

It is important to determine the number of job clusters within an organization, because there will be as many job evaluation methods as there are job clusters. This is, however, no easy task. The fewer job clusters there are, the fewer evaluation methods there are to develop and administer, and the closer one gets to the ultimate goal of systematically comparing the requirements of every job within the organization. However, jobs will be more dissimilar and thus more difficult to compare, the resulting comparison less accurate.

The answer to *how many job clusters should there be* lies somewhere between one and the number of jobs within an organization. In practice, large organizations have the following job clusters: management, professional and technical, office staff, production and maintenance and, in some cases, sales personnel. In other organizations, executives may be distinguished from management, and professional from technical staff, and the list goes on. Such distinctions are impractical in a smaller organization, however, where all jobs are generally classified into only one cluster. Take, for example, a radio station with some 15 jobs and 30 employees. The job of technical director and production technician may very well fit into a different job cluster from those of program host and news editor, which in turn will be in a different job cluster from accountant and bookkeeper, etc. These jobs are so different in nature that a systematic comparison of their various requirements is pointless. Does this mean station management has to develop and administer at least three job evaluation methods and pay structures? In practice, the answer is no. Yet grouping all these jobs into one cluster makes comparison more difficult.

The presence of one or more unions within an organization also has a significant effect on the number of job clusters. In practice, each bargaining unit is a job cluster, which may imply the need to develop a separate job evaluation program.

It is important to remember that, while defining job clusters more strictly may facilitate job comparison, translating the job evaluation methods into pay structures is likely to produce inequities. Because job requirements in the different clusters are not systematically compared, there is a high risk of inequity between clusters. Chapter 9 describes some ways of reducing the chances of such inequities.

4.2.3 Illegal Discriminatory Effects

Job clusters are determined subjectively, using judgment. It may very well be that certain job clusters are overwhelmingly dominated by women and others by men, and this may or may not be the product of chance. Moreover, the job evaluation results may be logical, consistent, and fair within a job cluster, but this does not automatically guarantee that the same is true of compared clusters. In this respect, while the proliferation of clusters within an organization makes it easier to compare the jobs within each, it increases the likelihood of inequity within the organization as a whole.

Actually, organizations were traditionally relatively less concerned about inequities between job clusters than between the jobs within a cluster. Yet, in theory and increasingly in law, pay equity must exist, not only between the jobs in a cluster, but also between jobs in different clusters. This is a major recommendation of the leaders in the fight against sex-based pay discrimination. Inasmuch as women form a majority in some job clusters and men in others, there is a risk of illegal discrimination. The answer to the question of potential discrimination lies in a comparison of jobs in different clusters. Paradoxically, it is interesting to note that some American legal experts recommend using multiple job evaluation programs to avoid comparing clusters (Schlei and Grossman, 1983). To date, the United States has no proactive pay equity legislation (cf. Chapter 9).

Yet how do you create equity within an organization as a whole when there are good reasons for creating different job clusters and where it is not contrary to the law? One might first of all examine the overall pay implications of the job evaluation results for each cluster. There is also a relatively simple analytic technique for comparing the pay implications of job evaluations in two clusters (Henderson, 1989), which involves identifying two clusters that resemble each other in terms of what some employees in each are paid (e.g. the technical and the professional job cluster). The lowest-paying jobs in the cluster with the higher average pay (e.g. the professional jobs) are evaluated by the method used for the jobs in the other cluster. The highest-paying jobs in the latter (e.g. the technical jobs) are then evaluated by the method used for the cluster with the higher-paying jobs. The next step is to work out the pay implications for these jobs within the pay structure of the opposite job cluster, to see whether the ensuing conclusions are justified. In reality, very few organizations go through this process. But

TABLE 4.1
Classification of Job Evaluation Methods

Comprehensive methods

Ranking	• General ranking
	• Alternative ranking
	• Paired comparison
Market-pricing	• Ranking by pay
	• Smyth-Murphy

Analytic methods

Qualitative
  • Classification
  • Decision-making responsibility (Woods-Gordon)

Quantitative
  • Factor method
  • Point method
    – Conventional
      – Customized
      – Standard
        – CWS
        – NEMA-NMTA (or MIMA)
        – Hay
        – Aiken (Peat, Marwick, Stevenson and Kellogg)
    – Contemporary
      – Customized
        – Structured questionnaire (Mercer)
        – Multicomp (Wyatt)
      – Standard
        – WJQ (TPF&C)

this relatively subtle form of discrimination, i.e. between job clusters, may be found in many organizations.

☐ 4.3 Selecting a Job Evaluation Method

The wide variety of job evaluation methods is usually divided into qualitative and quantitative techniques. The ranking and classification methods are examples of qualitative techniques. Factor and point methods are quantitative techniques.

Recent developments in job evaluation methods have rendered this division inadequate. This book proposes a slightly different distinction (cf. Table 4.1). It divides job evaluation methods into whole-job and compensable-factor techniques. Whole-job techniques include ranking and those based on the labour market. Compensation-factor techniques may be either qualitative or quantitative, with the latter subdivided into conventional and contemporary, both of which may be further subdivided into customized and standard.

4.3.1 Whole Job Evaluation Methods

Whole job evaluation methods include ranking and market pricing. These relatively unsophisticated techniques are useful for quickly checking the reasonableness of compensable-factor evaluations.

Ranking

This method involves using job descriptions, which in some cases are relatively brief, to grade the jobs within a cluster on the basis of a single factor or overall criterion, namely, requirements. The evaluation committee may do this with any of the following techniques.

General Ranking

Committee members are asked, first individually and then in committee, or in committee only, to rank all the jobs of a particular cluster in relation to each other on the basis of their requirements. The ranking is no more precise than that. In practice, this procedure may become rather complicated and result in considerable inaccuracy and frustration, the greater the number of jobs, i.e. 15 or more.

Alternative Ranking

This technique makes it slightly easier for committee members to rank jobs. After reviewing the job descriptions, the committee first identifies the most demanding job and then the least demanding one. This process is repeated with the remaining jobs until all have been ranked. Here too, the danger exists of not systematically comparing all the jobs.

Paired Comparison

Paired comparison is the most systematic ranking technique. It involves comparing all the jobs with each other to determine the more demanding job in every possible pair.

To date, this has meant comparing jobs with each other on the basis of a single criterion (or factor), namely, requirements. This method may be slightly modified to use more than one criterion; in this case, the job hierarchy is determined by the resulting average grade. If one decides to assign different weights to criteria, this technique becomes very similar to the point method.

Whatever technique is adopted, application of the ranking method is relatively time-consuming when the evaluation involves a large number of jobs. Moreover, it is not particularly conducive to reaching consensus among committee members, and often leads to an impasse. The whole-job perspective of this technique limits constructive exchange of information.

In addition, this method provides no information about the differences between jobs. The differential between two jobs in successive grades may be totally inconsistent with the differential between the next two. This method is therefore not very useful for constructing a pay scale. It also lacks flexibility, because the entire process of comparison must be repeated for each new job or change to an existing job. Because of its whole-job perspective, the jobs may be graded on the basis of incomplete information, and the evaluation results may have a significant impact on existing pay rates as well as on employees.

Despite the disadvantages of this method, one must not underestimate its main advantage – simplicity. It is very suitable for a small organization, where use of a more complex technique would make the job evaluation process only marginally more effective. It may also be used initially by an evaluation committee as a means of learning about the process and its problems, and highlighting the advantages of whatever method is ultimately chosen. Lastly, as mentioned earlier, it is useful for testing the reasonableness of the results of other job evaluation methods.

Market Pricing

This method uses the labour market to determine the value of jobs. Based on job descriptions (which may be more or less detailed), the organization undertakes a market survey to determine the monetary value of its jobs.

In addition to being readily comprehensible and swiftly applicable (especially with a limited number of jobs), this method has the advantage of simplicity. And, as Livy (1975, p. 74) points out, simplicity is very important in the business world, where arriving quickly at a satisfactory decision is sometimes preferable to waiting for the perfect solution. According to Thériault's study (1986), 25% of Canadian organizations used the market-pricing method. This percentage depended on job categories and organizational size. For example, it appeared to be most commonly used for top-management personnel (31%), and in small organizations, i.e. with less than 100 employees (45%).

On the other hand, this method overlooks the question of internal pay equity and considers only external equity. The resulting job hierarchy is based solely on market price. In this context, it is implicitly, if not explicitly, prohibited where pay equity laws exist, as in Ontario (cf. Chapter 9). Furthermore, this method also virtually ignores the fact that pay is only one component of compensation.

The problems and mistakes a compensation survey may cause by using incomplete and inaccurate job descriptions present yet another disadvantage of this method. Moreover, the method does not consider the specific characteristics of organizations. It is one thing to find an identical job at another organization (albeit no easy task), and quite another to find a similar job at an organization with the same working conditions and operating methods. There are always some jobs whose content is unique to an organization, and they call for the use of another method. Finally, the market-pricing method simply perpetuates existing pay inequities in the market and those related to individual characteristics. If an organization had to justify the equity of the results obtained by this method, it would find itself in a very precarious, if not indefensible, position.

4.3.2 Compensable-Factor Job Evaluation Methods

Compensable-factor job evaluation methods encompass both qualitative and quantitative techniques, with the latter subdivided into conventional and contemporary.

Qualitative Methods

Qualitative methods of analysis include classification and decision-making responsibility (the so-called broadbanding method, based on the decision band theory developed by Paterson and Husband (1970) and used by the firm of Ernst & Young). Both are described below.

Classification

The classification method is essentially a product of the work done by the Carnegie Institute of Technology Personnel Research Bureau in 1922 (Livy, 1975). Although every job evaluation method may be used to create classes, this phase usually follows the actual job evaluation. In the classification method, the establishment of job classes comes at the outset.

Once the job descriptions have been written and the evaluation committee formed, the classification phase involves identifying and defining a number of classes into which all jobs in the particular cluster in question can fit. This is a delicate and complex procedure.

Identifying the classes means determining the various job categories that appear to emerge from the job cluster under study. Next, the committee decides on criteria for defining the various classes. These definitions may be obtained by enhancing the adopted criteria through the addition of permutations, degrees, or levels. In practice, however, the same criteria are not used to define every class. The accepted considerations (various degrees of different criteria) must result in each class having different levels of requirements. For example, one class might be defined as "jobs of a relatively repetitive nature with little independence and requiring a minimum of education and experience". Another might consist of "jobs with average independence, requiring previous experience in related jobs, and involving the supervision and coordination of a limited number of persons".

The committee normally spells out exactly what it means by each definition by following it with an example of a job in that class. Once the classes have been identified and defined, all that remains for committee members is the actual job classification, i.e. assigning each job to a class based on the definitions.

● Advantages and Disadvantages

In general, this method may be used for a centralized evaluation of a large number of jobs. In other words, it allows for fewer job clusters within an organization; more jobs may be systematically compared.

This method has the further advantage of being simple and inexpensive. In fact, the classification roughly corresponds to the general idea that people within an organization have of the job classes or hierarchy. The relatively vague nature of the class definitions means more flexibility and latitude, particularly when creating new jobs or modifying existing ones, which avoids a repetition of the entire evaluation process.

On the other hand, this method has certain disadvantages. First among them is class identification and definition, an exercise that calls for extensive knowledge of the nature of the jobs under evaluation and a remarkable capacity for synthesis. Moreover, the class definitions might seem to be the outcome of an arbitrary process designed to differentiate certain jobs.

● Frequency of Use

Perhaps the most visible application of this type of method (at least because of the number of jobs involved) is the General Schedule (GS), used to evaluate federal government office jobs in the United States. Established by the 1949 Job Classification Act, which replaced the Act of 1923, the GS is used to evaluate about half of all federal government jobs. The GS consists of

18 classes, which in turn may contain subclasses. GS-1 to GS-4 are used to classify jobs requiring less than a college education, GS-5 to GS-11 for intermediate technical and administrative jobs and, finally, GS-12 to GS-18 for higher-level jobs. For instance, GS-1 is defined as follows:

> Includes those classes of positions the duties of which are to be performed, under immediate supervision, with little or no latitude for the exercise of independent judgment:
> 1. the simplest routine work in office, business or fiscal operations; or
> 2. elementary work of a subordinate technical character in a professional, scientific or technical field.

The jobs of typist and messenger fit into this category.

On the other hand, GS-5 covers jobs that are "difficult" and involve "responsible work". These jobs require "broad working knowledge of a special subject matter or of office, laboratory, engineering, scientific, or other procedure and practice, and the exercise of independent judgment in a limited field". This class also includes jobs that involve "performing, under immediate supervision, and with little opportunity for the exercise of independent judgment, simple and elementary work requiring professional, scientific or technical training." The jobs of chemist and accountant fit into this class.

Similar classification methods are used to evaluate public-sector jobs in Canada. Yet, properly speaking, these methods may not be ranked under the same heading as the General Schedule of the U.S. federal public service. For example, unlike other Canadian provinces, and except for management jobs in the social affairs sector, Quebec uses the classification method. Yet its classification depends more on the nature of the jobs than on their requirements, so that it looks like the ranking method. In the education sector, for instance, one finds the classes of technical and administrative support staff. The latter class, defined simply as all "jobs characterized by doing different standard routine administrative work", encompasses the following job groups: buyer, office worker, office assistant, secretary, and telephone operator. The job groups are organized in relation to each other and, in some cases, subdivided. Thus, there are three classes in the secretarial job group: secretary, senior school secretary, and executive secretary. The same applies to the office worker job groups. This is not really an example of the use of the classification method, even though the jobs have been classified. Rather, it illustrates the problem of semantics raised earlier. Using classes does not necessarily imply use of the classification method.

Decision-Making Responsibility

In a 1970 article, Paterson and Husband indicated that one of the main problems of conventional job evaluation methods (ranking, classification, factors, and points) is that they cannot be applied to every job within an

TABLE 4.2
Levels of Responsibility According to the Paterson Method

Band	Decisions	Title	Level	Decisions	Title
E	General policy	Senior executive	10 9	Coordinating Policy	Director general Director
D	Programming	Upper manager	8 7	Coordinating Programming	General manager Manager
C	Interpreting	Middle manager	6 5	Coordinating Interpreting	Department manager Division manager
B	Routine	Skilled operator	4 3	Coordinating About process	Shop manager Tradesperson
A	Automatic	Semi-skilled operator	2 1	Coordinating About operation	Unit manager Machinist
O	Defined	Unskilled worker	0	About the job	

SOURCE: Paterson and Husband (1970, p. 23). Reprinted by permission of the publisher.

organization (requiring job clusters). So, they proposed the Paterson method, based on a universal (*sic*) job evaluation factor – decision-making responsibility. This method certainly recalls others based on a single factor, such as time-span of discretion (Jaques, 1961, 1969) and problem-solving (Charles 1971). Developed by Paterson and Husband, the broadbanding method is used by the firm of Ernst & Young (Kelly, 1988).

Paterson and Husband (1970) claim that there are six decision bands within an organization (cf. Table 4.2). The higher the decision band, the more demanding the job and the higher the salary it should command. Furthermore, to refine the analysis as the authors do, each decision band except O has two levels.

For example, band C (middle manager) has two separate levels – coordinating and interpreting – those in the latter level under the supervision of those in the former.

With the decision-band chart and an interview guide, it is suggested that a properly trained job analyst can evaluate all the jobs with no need for an evaluation committee. In practice, however, a job evaluation committee is normally used.

This method has the advantage of not entailing the creation of different job clusters for the various groups of jobs, with all the human resource problems involved in administering numerous pay structures. In addition to reducing the human resource requirement to a minimum, this method is also relatively simple (at least *a priori*), based on an important organizational criterion (decision-making) and employs a familiar concept, namely, the job hierarchy.

Yet this method does have its problems. First of all, the use of a single criterion makes the judgment of evaluation committee members crucial. Secondly, the types of decision bands used do not fully apply to every size and type of organization. Here, one need only think of an organization with a relatively flat hierarchy, or one with a matrix-type structure. Thirdly, basing pay structure essentially on job hierarchy may seem somewhat simplistic to someone who knows that hierarchy involves not only decision-making level, but also other specific considerations like status. Fourthly, this method is based solely on an allegedly universal criterion. This apparent simplicity engenders scepticism. Finally, as Kelly notes (1988, p. 151), Ernst & Young has developed an argument aimed at proving that this method, while based on a single criterion, covers the four main dimensions required by Canadian pay equity legislation, namely skill, effort, responsibility, and working conditions. While plausible, the truth of this assertion remains to be seen.

Quantitative Methods

Generally speaking, the quantitative methods combine efficiency with administrative simplicity. These characteristics, however, cannot guarantee the success of a job evaluation method, which above all depends on how the method is developed and on the participation of those concerned.

Quantitative methods are especially conducive to that participation. It should also be noted that legal institutions (i.e. the Canadian and the Quebec Human Rights Commission, the Pay Equity Commission in Ontario, and its equivalent in other provinces) favour the use of so-called quantitative analysis methods for job evaluation.

There are two principal means of evaluating jobs quantitatively: the factor method and the point method.

Factor Method

Eugene Benge and his colleagues developed what is considered to be the first application of the factor method for the Philadelphia Rapid Transit Co. in 1926. This method involves the following steps:

1. determining job clusters;
2. identifying and defining evaluation factors;
3. identifying benchmark jobs;
4. ranking the benchmark jobs for each factor;
5. assigning the pay in the benchmark jobs by factor;

6. comparing the results and eliminating discrepancies;
7. ranking the remaining jobs for each factor; and
8. adding up the results.

1. Determining job clusters

   The factor method does not easily lend itself to general application within an organization, because it uses specific evaluation factors (or criteria). The considerations raised about the number of job evaluation programs an organization should have are particularly applicable to the factor method.

2. Identifying and defining evaluation factors

   Unlike whole-job evaluation techniques, the factor method requires that evaluation factors be identified and defined.

   The evaluation committee's first task, then, is to identify these evaluation factors. Based on their knowledge of the jobs being evaluated and the job descriptions (which for this purpose must be complete and accurate), committee members begin identifying factors that make some jobs more demanding, and more highly paid, than others. For example, if the committee thinks that some jobs require more manual dexterity than others, and that the employees doing these jobs should be paid more than those whose jobs require less dexterity (all else being equal), then manual dexterity becomes an evaluation factor. The situation would be different if every job in question required the same (or almost the same) degree of manual dexterity, or if the committee was divided on the idea that pay should be based on the level of manual dexterity. In either case, this factor would not be worth retaining, because it would not help distinguish jobs in terms of requirements.

   In practice, a limited number of factors are used. The five employed by Benge when he originally applied this method are frequently adopted. They are: (1) mental requirements, (2) skill requirements, (3) physical requirements, (4) responsibility, and (5) working conditions.

   The most common are; [handwritten margin note]

   There is, however, no inherent reason for using these five factors rather than any others that might be considered relevant to the jobs under evaluation.

3. Identifying benchmark jobs

   The next step is to identify a number of benchmark jobs within the cluster. About 20% of all the jobs being evaluated should be selected. A benchmark job is one whose incumbent the committee feels is being properly paid. "Properly paid" may mean the jobholder's current salary, the one planned following the compensation survey, or the pay resulting from negotiations. These benchmark jobs must be repre-

TABLE 4.3
Benchmark Jobs Ranked for Each Factor

Job	Experience Required	Mental Requirements	Sociability	Responsibilities	Working Conditions
			Ranking		
Programmer	5	5	10	5	8
Clerk-cashier	7	7	4	7	10
Print shop manager	4	4	2	4	1
Computer clerk-operator	11	9	11	9	4
Programmer-analyst	2	1	6	3	7
Receptionist	9	10	7	10	9
Lab manager	1	2	5	2	3
Personnel secretary	8	8	9	8	5
Building inspector	3	3	1	1	2
Public service clerk (library)	10	11	8	11	11
Accounts payable clerk	6	6	3	6	6

sentative of the other jobs under evaluation and of the compensation levels within the job cluster. The holders of these jobs are therefore representative of everyone in the job cluster concerned in terms of seniority and performance, inasmuch as pay is based on these two factors. Finding jobs that satisfy all these criteria is no easy task! The views of committee members should be obtained at this stage, and the next two stages used to validate their perceptions, i.e. to ensure that the benchmark jobs identified at this stage really are benchmark jobs.

4. Ranking the benchmark jobs for each factor *Vertical comparison*
   The evaluation committee must now rank all benchmark jobs for each factor, beginning with the most demanding job in terms of a particular factor and ending with the least demanding. This step must be carried out first individually, then in committee, until a consensus is reached.

Table 4.3 shows how this step applies to 11 municipal office jobs ranked for each factor. Note that no two jobs have the same rank for a given factor. In reality, nothing in this method precludes the possibility that a number of jobs may be assigned the same rank for a given factor.

5. Assigning pay in the benchmark jobs by factor

    While the previous step required that the evaluation committee compare jobs vertically, this step calls for a horizontal comparison. For each benchmark job identified, committee members must allocate the pay received among the various factors selected. If a job has more than one incumbent, average pay may be used.

    Underlying this comparison is the assumption that the evaluation factors selected represent all the things employees are paid for. Thus, the portion of total pay explained or justified by each factor must be identified (by making a judgment) for each job.

    Table 4.4 illustrates this procedure using the same jobs as in Table 4.3. According to the committee, the programmer's $532 weekly salary breaks down into $110 for the experience required to do the job, $145 for mental requirements, $110 for sociability, $125 for responsibility, and $42 for working conditions. The same method is applied to each benchmark job selected.

    Once the pay received has been allocated among the various factors for each job, each one may be ranked for each factor based on the amount of pay assigned to that factor. Thus, for "required experience", the job of lab manager ranks first, building inspector second, programmer-analyst third, and so on, for the remaining factors.

6. Comparing the results and eliminating discrepancies

    The next step involves comparing the results of the vertical and horizontal analyses performed in the two previous stages. This work is done by committee.

    Table 4.5 combines the results of the two previous stages. It indicates to what extent the results of two independent comparisons of each job concur. It is essential that the results agree for each factor, since the benchmark jobs are used in the next stage as reference points for evaluating the remaining jobs. A maximum discrepancy of 20% between the two evaluations is considered acceptable. The above tables contain 11 jobs, which means the maximum discrepancy for selecting genuine benchmark jobs is 2 grades. This step hones the choice of benchmark jobs. Of the 11 jobs selected by the evaluation committee in our example, only 3 fail to qualify as genuine benchmark jobs.

7. Ranking the other jobs for each factor

    After the committee has made its final selection of benchmark jobs,

TABLE 4.4
Breakdown of pay for benchmark jobs by factor

Job	Weekly salary $	Salary Distribution				
		Experience Required	Mental Requirements	Sociability	Responsibilities	Working Conditions
Programmer	532	110 (4)*	145 (5)	110 (11)	125 (5)	42 (8)
Clerk-cashier	505	90 (7)	135 (8)	130 (6)	118 (7)	32 (11)
Print shop manager	595	100 (5)	138 (7)	125 (7)	127 (4)	105 (1)
Computer clerk-operator	475	50 (11)	135 (9)	112 (10)	115 (8)	63 (4)
Programmer-analyst	669	120 (3)	252 (1)	123 (8)	130 (3)	44 (7)
Receptionist	419	54 (10)	93 (11)	135 (5)	97 (9)	40 (9)
Lab manager	712	142 (1)	226 (2)	144 (4)	135 (2)	65 (3)
Personnel secretary	505	80 (8)	140 (6)	145 (3)	90 (10)	50 (5)
Building inspector	632	125 (2)	150 (4)	150 (1)	140 (1)	67 (2)
Public service clerk (library)	419	75 (9)	94 (10)	121 (9)	90 (11)	39 (10)
Accounts payable clerk	595	94 (6)	188 (3)	148 (2)	120 (6)	45 (6)

* The numbers in parentheses indicate the job's rank for each factor.

members, first individually and then as a group, classify the remaining jobs in reference to the benchmark jobs. Table 4.6, which contains the job comparison scale, completes our illustration of the preceding steps.

The committee should identify another set of jobs (about 20%) that are not strictly benchmark jobs, but rather ones whose pay is not excessively inequitable, and then evaluate them. They should continue in this way until every job has been ranked in the job comparison scale.

It goes without saying that the pay for the latter jobs is ignored at this stage. In other words, in the case of print shop manager, not considered to be a benchmark job, this means determining how much

TABLE 4.5
Comparison of the Results of Tables 4.3 and 4.4

Job	Evaluation Factors									
	Experience Required		Mental Requirements		Sociability		Responsibilities		Working Conditions	
	4.3	4.4	4.3	4.4	4.3	4.4	4.3	4.4	4.3	4.4
Programmer*	5	4	5	5	10	11	5	5	8	8
Clerk-cashier*	7	7	7	8***	4	6	7	7	10	11
Print shop manager**	4	5	4	7	2	7	4	4	1	1
Computer clerk-operator*	11	11	9	9***	11	10	9	8	4	4
Programmer-analyst*	2	3	1	1	6	8	3	3	7	7
Receptionist*	9	10	10	11	7	5	10	9	9	9
Lab manager*	1	1	2	2	5	4	2	2	3	3
Personnel secretary**	8	8	8	6	9	3	8	10***	5	5
Building inspector*	3	2	3	4	1	1	1	1	2	2
Public service clerk (library)*	10	9	11	10	8	9	11	11***	11	10
Accounts payable clerk**	6	6	6	3	3	2	6	6	6	6

* These may be used as benchmark jobs.
** These are not genuine benchmark jobs.
*** When pay is equal, the ranking of the requirement determines precedence.

the jobholder should be paid for each factor based on what the incumbents of benchmark jobs earn for that factor.

8. Adding up the results.
The final step involves adding up the amount of pay assigned to each factor for each job. Once the totals have been obtained, all the jobs may be ranked in relation to others within the job cluster in question. In this way, the factor method takes into account each factor's relative importance in each job.

● Advantages and Disadvantages

With its crosscheck of benchmark jobs, this method may produce the most reliable results (Nash and Carroll, 1975). It has the further advantage of

TABLE 4.6
Job Comparison Scale

Monetary value	Experience required	Mental requirements	Sociability	Responsi-bilities	Working conditions
			Factors		
300					
295					
290					
285					
280					
275					
270					
265					
260					
255					
250		Programmer-analyst			
245					
240					
235					
230					
225		Lab manager			
220					
215					
210					
205					
200					
195					
190					
185					
180					
175					
170					
165					
160					
155					
150		Building inspector	Building inspector		
145		Programmer	Lab manager		
140	Lab manager			Building inspector	

Monetary value	Factors				
	Experience required	Mental requirements	Sociability	Responsibilities	Working conditions
135		Clerk-cashier	Receptionist	Lab manager	
130		Computer clerk-operator	Clerk-cashier	Programmer-analyst	
125	Building inspector		Programmer-analyst	Programmer	
120	Programmer-analyst		Public service clerk (library)	Clerk-cashier	
115			Computer clerk-operator	Computer clerk-operator	
110	Programmer		Programmer		
105					
100				Receptionist	
95		Receptionist			
90	Cashier-clerk	Public service clerk (library)		Public service clerk (library)	
85					
80					
75	Public service clerk (library)				
70					Building inspector
65					Building inspector
60					Computer clerk-operator
55	Receptionist				
50	Computer clerk-operator				
45					Programmer-analyst
40					Receptionist Programmer
35					Public service clerk (library)
30					Clerk-cashier
25					

determining pay directly, without any intervening step. Finally, it allows all jobs to be compared systematically, not only as a whole, but also on the basis of compensable factors.

Like all job evaluation techniques, the factor method has its disadvantages. As mentioned, it supports the assumption that only evaluation factors or criteria are important in determining pay. The effects of seniority and employee performance, for example, are ignored. In addition, the pay of key employees is considered accurate and definitive *a priori*. Furthermore, the use of pay in job evaluation increases the chances of biasing it. In practice, however, pay may always be replaced by points, so that the job with the highest ranking for a factor earns a particular number of points while the one with the lowest rank scores zero, and so on for the jobs in between. This procedure minimizes the risk of bias in the final stage of the evaluation. Then, however, the only way of breaking down the pay for benchmark jobs by factor is to use a number of points in proportion to the pay; this calls for considerable ingenuity. Finally, the fact that this method is difficult to explain to everyone concerned is a major disadvantage.

● Frequency of Use

Many companies claim to use the factor method in evaluating jobs. However, considerable confusion surrounds the definition of this technique. As we have seen, the process involved is complex and precise. However, using evaluation factors does not mean that an organization is using the factor method. The point method described below also uses evaluation factors. Cognizant of this problem of terminology, Thériault (1986) found that in fact, only about 5% of organizations, in most cases small companies, use the factor method.

Point Method

The point method is definitely the oldest and most widely used job evaluation method. Thériault's survey (1986) found it the most widespread technique in Canada. On average, 46% of organizations use it for certain employee groups. The same study found that the point method is used primarily by medium-sized or large organizations (82%), very little by small ones (11%). In breaking jobs down into their various facets, this method represents a compensable-factor technique. Since it uses numeric values, it constitutes a quantitative technique. It is sometimes called the point-factor method instead of simply the point method.

This job evaluation method has changed considerably over the years, engendering numerous variations on a theme. In practice, these may all be classified on the basis of two criteria: content (standard or customized) and process (conventional or contemporary).

Table 4.7 shows how the principal point methods used by organizations today are classified.

TABLE 4.7
Classification of the Principal Point Methods on the Market Today

Content	Process	
	Conventional	Contemporary
Customized	Mercer	Mercer
	Wyatt	Wyatt
Standard	Hay	TPF&C
	Aiken	Hay
	CWS	
	NEMA	

● Standard and Customized Methods

In the job evaluation field, one commonly hears of standard methods, whose content is usually specific and definitive, and customized methods, whose content is determined by the organization using them. The best-known standard techniques are the Hay method, used by Hay Management Consultants, the CWS (Cooperative Wage Study) method, primarily used in the steel industry, and the NEMA (National Electrical Manufacturers Association) method. In addition, many consulting firms have developed their own job evaluation method. The firm of TPF&C has its WJQ method, while Peat, Marwick, Stevenson & Kellogg has the Aiken method. Others prefer to offer their clients customized methods, as is the case with William M. Mercer Limited and Wyatt.

The main advantage of a standard over a customized method is that it avoids the delicate task of determining and defining the evaluation factors and degrees the organization will use. In addition, the use of one job evaluation method by numerous organizations may make it easier to conduct compensation surveys, since jobs may be matched more closely. Finally, its standard nature in itself is reassuring. The client sees the product from the start, and knows that the product has been used many times in the past. These advantages, however, are offset by some disadvantages.

First of all, standard methods use evaluation factors and degrees that are not necessarily entirely relevant to the specific jobs within an organization and, in particular, more or less valid in the eyes of those concerned (employees and management). Since most standard methods on the market today were developed during the 30s and 40s, they accurately reflect the values of that era, with its preferred methods of work organization. The question therefore becomes one of knowing to what extent these historical values still apply today.

In fact, job evaluation consists of organizing jobs based on their requirements, with the aim of paying employees fairly. Like equity, job requirement is essentially a subjective concept. What is fair to one person is not necessarily fair to another. In this light, just because a standard method has produced satisfactory (though not necessarily proven) results for one job cluster within an organization does not mean it will produce equally satisfactory results when applied to another job cluster. The same is true of an equivalent job cluster within another organization in the same business sector, and much more so if another business sector is involved. Objectives and procedures vary from one organization to the next and, since people differ, it is naive to expect that what one group has perceived as equitable will also be considered fair by others. In fact, many organizations have learned this lesson at their cost.

Secondly, the advantage that standard methods provide in compensation surveys must be examined more closely. While job evaluation aims to ensure internal equity in terms of pay, a compensation survey strives for external equity. People do not necessarily attach equal importance to these aims, and each involves a different process. Just as job evaluation must be distinct from wage negotiations, so too a compensation survey must be kept separate from a job evaluation. Without such distinctions, one no longer knows what considerations determine pay.

Thirdly, the argument that standard methods save time by eliminating the necessity of identifying and defining factors is misleading. The time saved is partly spent training committee members in the standard method. Also, since the factors with their specific wording may not necessarily suit the evaluation committee, there may be much more discussion of the job ratings (because of differences in interpretation) than if members had developed their own. All in all, in practice, a standard method may consume as much time, if not more, than a customized method.

Fourthly, even if we assume that the deliberations of a job evaluation committee using a customized method produce the same results (identical factors, degrees, and weighting) as a standard method, there is still an important difference between them. In one case, the results are the work of the committee, in the other they are not. This distinction has a significant impact on the degree to which job evaluation results are accepted.

Finally, standard methods are based on a set of "universal" factors, so-called because they are used everywhere. Yet there are no suitable criteria for determining the value or requirements of every job in every organization (Treiman and Hartman, 1981; Hills, 1989).

Other arguments for using a customized method have been developed by Gray (1950), Brett and Cumming (1984), and Milkovich and Newman (1990).

- Conventional Methods

As Table 4.7 indicates, conventional point methods may be divided into customized and standard.

Customized Conventional Methods

Based on job descriptions, customized conventional methods involve six basic steps:

1. determining job clusters;
2. identifying and defining evaluation factors and degrees;
3. rating the jobs;
4. weighting the evaluation factors;
5. assigning points to evaluation factor degrees; and
6. adding up the points for each job.

1. Determining job clusters

   Because this method uses weighted evaluation factors, it is difficult to apply to every job within an organization. Given the differences between jobs, this method lends itself more readily to a specific cluster. Inasmuch as the jobs within a cluster differ, some of the factors used by the point method may be more or less relevant and, in practice, distort the weight assigned to the various factors. Therefore, the first step in the point method involves grouping jobs similar enough to be comparable with each other based on a set of specific common characteristics and located in similar markets. In reality, the point method has as many applications as an organization has job clusters.

2. Identifying and defining evaluation factors and degrees

   Evaluation factors represent what makes certain jobs more demanding, thereby justifying higher pay for their incumbents. A job evaluation factor has three dimensions. First, it is a characteristic constituting the jobholder's required contribution on the basis of the nature of the job. Secondly, the degree of that contribution may vary from job to job. For example, if all the jobs in a cluster call for the same level of education, education should be omitted as an evaluation factor, since it cannot be used to distinguish the jobs with a view to creating a hierarchy — one of the goals of job evaluation. Finally, it must be accepted that the characteristic will be compensated, which is the second goal of job evaluation. For example, if the physical working conditions of the jobs in a cluster vary, this characteristic may be an appropriate factor. However, if the parties agree that employees should not be compensated on the basis of physical working conditions, this characteristic then becomes inappropriate. As we can once again see, while job requirements may be determined objectively (though this too is open to question), the concept of what should be compensated is essentially a matter of perception.

a) The importance of using specific evaluation factors

As standards defining the hierarchy, job evaluation factors represent the individual contribution associated with jobs, which the organization officially recognizes and compensates. This makes the concepts of exchange (contribution-reward), motivation, and satisfaction particularly important. According to the exchange model, the individual recognizes that the nature and degree of contribution required vary from job to job, and that a certain contribution must be made in exchange for a certain reward from the organization. The extent to which an employee perceives a balance between contribution and reward obviously affects his or her sense of fair play, satisfaction, and motivation.

The exchange model makes it clear that evaluation factors stem from the very nature of jobs, and must be suited to each situation. These factors result from the perception of those concerned by the question of what a job requires (the expected contribution officially recognized by the organization) and what it demands. In this context, it is difficult to develop a universal job evaluation scheme applicable to every job in an organization and even more so to different organizations. Therein lies the importance of creating job clusters.

The exchange model also implies that decisions about evaluation factors are made jointly by management and the jobholders in question or their representatives. This increases the likelihood that what the jobholder perceives as the required contribution will actually correspond to what is expected (the evaluation factors and their relative importance, as well as the evaluation results – the ratings).

b) Selecting evaluation factors

While most job evaluation experts agree that the factors must be suited to each situation, they provide very few specific guidelines for identifying factors. Aside from the lists of factors used by other organizations to classify employees (cf. Table 4.8; also, Otis and Leukart (1954) suggest over a hundred factors for office and production jobs), the parties concerned are on their own. There are numerous sources of information about potential job evaluation factors. However, factors taken from the methods in use, or even from books on the subject (including this one), may be inappropriate for any given situation.

The following has proved to be a relatively efficient and satisfactory method of selecting evaluation factors. After agreeing on the nature of an evaluation factor, committee members then hold a brain-storming session to identify evaluation factors based on a sample of job descriptions representative of the jobs being evaluated. This means first identifying factors without criticizing them; the chair simply notes each factor suggested. Next, members are asked to elaborate on each factor. This provides them with information for defining the factors and ensuring that the jobs differ in terms of those factors. Next, the chair gives committee members lists of the factors used by other organizations to evaluate similar jobs. This brings the committee to the step of identifying potentially appropriate factors. With this information in hand, the chair draws up a set of factors, which is submitted to the committee. At a subsequent meeting, the committee fine-tunes the factors one last time, making sure they are independent (each factor measures a unique component of the jobs) and complete (the factors take into account all facets of the job requirements).

TABLE 4.8
List of Job Evaluation Factors and Weighting Used for Different Classes of Employees

I. **NATIONAL ELECTRICAL MANUFACTURERS ASSOCIATION (NEMA) SYSTEM ADOPTED BY THE NATIONAL METAL TRADES ASSOCIATION (NMTA) AND OTHER RELATED ORGANIZATIONS, COORDINATED BY THE MIDWEST INDUSTRIAL MANAGEMENT ASSOCIATION (MIMA)**

1) PRODUCTION AND MAINTENANCE JOBS (FACTORY)

Factors and subfactors*	Number of degrees	Weighting
Skill		250
1. Education	5	70
2. Experience	5	110
3. Initiative and ingenuity	5	70
Effort		75
4. Physical	5	50
5. Mental or visual demands	5	25
Responsibility		100
6. Equipment or process	5	25
7. Material or product	5	25
8. Safety of others	5	25
9. Work of others	5	25
Conditions		100
10. Working conditions	5	50

11. Unavoidable hazards	5	25
Total points		<u>500</u>

* Some job evaluation systems distinguish between factors (criteria) and subfactors (subcriteria). The term "factor" applied to systems that do not make this distinction corresponds to the "subfactors" of those that do.

2) OFFICE JOBS

Factors	Number of degrees	Weighting
1. Education	6	100
2. Experience	7	150
3. Complexity of work	6	100
4. Required supervision	5	60
5. Consequence of errors	6	80
6. Relations with others	6	80
7. Confidential information	5	25
8. Mental or visual demands	5	25
9. Working conditions	5	25
Total points		<u>645</u>

3) MANAGEMENT JOBS

The same factors, with the same weighting as office jobs, to which we add:

Factors	Number of degrees	Weighting
10. Type of management	6	80
11. Scope of management	7	100
Total points		<u>825</u>

Source: NMTA Associates, *The National Position Evaluation Plan*, Westchester, Illinois, Midwest Industrial Management Association, undated. Reproduced by permission of the NMTA.

2. COOPERATIVE WAGE STUDY – C.W.S.

PRODUCTION AND MAINTENANCE JOBS (FACTORY)*

Factors	Number of degrees	Weighting
1. Preliminary training	3	1,0
2. Professional training and experience	9	4.0
3. Mental dexterity	6	3.5
4. Manual dexterity	5	2.0
5. Responsibility: materials	32	10.0
6. Responsibility: tools and equipment	16	4.0
7. Responsibility: operations	8	6.5
8. Responsibility: safety of others . .	5	2.0
9. Mental effort	5	2.5
10. Physical effort	5	2.5

11. Work environment.	5	3.0
12. Hazards	5	2.0
Total points		43.0

* For office and technical jobs in the industrial sector, the list and weighting of the factors is the same as for maintenance jobs. However, the definition of factors 1,3,5,7, and 9 differs. The number of factors always remains the same.

Source: United Steelworkers of America, *Co-operative Wage Study (C.W.S.) Manual for Job Description, Classification and Wage Discrimination*. Montreal, United Steelworkers of America, 1976 reprinted by permission of the publisher.

3. QUEBEC HUMAN RIGHTS COMMISSION
(illustration of a form; job classes are not indicated)

Factors and subfactors	Number of degrees	Weighting
Skill		225
1. Required education or knowledge	5	65
2. Training and experience acquired on the job	10	100
3. Mental aptitude	5	60
Effort		100
4. Mental or visual demands	3	25
5. Physical requirements	5	50
6. Manual dexterity	5	25
Responsibility		100
7. Materials	5	25
8. Tools and equipment	5	25
9. Safety of others	5	25
10. Taking charge.	5	25
Conditions		75
11. Working environment	5	50
12. Occupational hazards	5	25
Total points		500

Source: Commission des droits de la personne du Québec, *À travail équivalent, salaire égal, sans discrimination*, cahier n° 3, Quebec Human Rights Commission, 1980, p. 145, reprinted by permission of the publisher.

4. RADIO STATION JOBS

Factors	Number of degrees	Weighting
1. Sociability	5	180
2. Supervision	5	140
3. Learning and experience.	4	260
4. Autonomy and initiative	4	240
5. Responsibility	4	280
6. Manual skills	3	120
7. Education	4	160
8. Physical work conditions	3	80

9. Flexibility and cooperation	4	140
10. Work stress	4	200
11. Memory of transactions or events	4	200
Total points		2000

Source: *Convention collective de travail*, Valleyfield, Quebec, Radio-Valleyfield et Syndicat des employés de Radio-Valleyfield, 1981.

5. TRADE JOBS

Factors	Number of degrees	Weighting
1. Professional training and experience	8	5.00
2. Manual skill	5	2.50
3. Mental effort	5	2.50
4. Physical effort	5	1.25
5. Responsibility: materials	5	4.00
6. Responsibility: work	4	2.00
7. Responsibility: safety of others . .	5	1.50
8. Working conditions	5	2.00
9. Risk of accidents	5	1.75
Total points		22.50

Source: Commission hydro-électrique du Québec et Syndicat des employés de métier d'Hydro-Québec, section locale 1500 S.C.F.P., *Système d'évaluation des emplois de métiers*, Montréal, 1969. Reprinted by permission of the publisher.

6. OFFICE JOBS (municipal sector)

Factors	Number of degrees	Weighting
1. Educational factor	7	250
2. Experience and learning	9	150
3. Analytical and judgement abilities	13	300
4. Initiative and ingenuity	16	150
5. Internal and external contacts . . .	44	200
6. Supervisory responsibility	22	350
7. Physical requirements	15	100
8. Visual requirements	6	50
9. Working conditions	6	50
Total points		1600

Source: Syndicat canadien de la Fonction publique, *Système de classification utilisé par le S.C.F.P. Secteur municipal, Bureau*, Montreal, undated. Reprinted by permission of the publisher.

7. MANAGERS IN THE SOCIAL AFFAIRS SECTOR (Quebec)

Factors and subfactors	Number of degrees	Weighting
1. Nature of position		
– complexity of decisionmaking .	7*	270
– freedom of action	6	135
– impact of decisions	5	45

2. Knowledge required for the position
   - formal education   7   115
   - practical experience   6   115

3. Supervision involved in the position
   - nature of supervision   5   135
   - number of employees supervised   11   90

   Total points   905

* Each of these degrees is subdivided into 3 sub degrees.

Source: Department of Health and Social Affairs, Province of Quebec. Reprinted by permission of the Department.

c) Optimal number of evaluation factors

There is no precise way to determine the optimal number of factors to use. On the one hand, too small a number reduces the method's capacity to draw distinctions and risks giving those concerned (especially employees) the impression that certain aspects of the job have been ignored. On the other hand, too great a number risks creating the problem of duplication. In practice, conventional point methods have 7 to 15 factors, with the average being around 10. It is important when identifying appropriate factors to consider the perceptions of those concerned, which will, equally, affect the acceptability of the job evaluation results.

The classic studies by Lawshe et al. (1944, 1945, and 1946) attempted to determine the optimal number of evaluation factors. They tested the single factor, the two factors, the three factors, etc. whose results had the highest correlation with the outcome of using all factors. The most important factor was experience (actually, learning time), and the next two were risk and initiative. These studies proved that a very limited number of factors may be enough to produce the same results as a much longer list. Of course, there remains the problem of identifying this limited number of evaluation factors. As Otis and Leukart (1954) point out, identifying a number of specific factors is only possible after a statistical analysis of a larger number of factors has been carried out. In addition, the factors adopted will be suitable for the situation; applying them to other circumstances may be a hazardous undertaking. Before a set of factors may be considered universal, it must be proved to be such.

d) Number of degrees of intensity in evaluation factors

After identifying and defining the evaluation factors, their different levels or degrees of intensity must be determined for each job under evaluation. In brief, this means classifying all the jobs within a given cluster on the basis of each factor, making sure that each degree of the factors is found in at least one job.

There is a simple rule for identifying the degrees of intensity for each factor. In practice, each factor may have from two or three to six or eight degrees or levels. The factors chosen may all have the same number of degrees (as, for example, in the NEMA-NMTA method). This situation, however, is something of an exception, given the objective of presenting the range of degrees for various factors in the different jobs.

Some studies offer guidelines for identifying the degrees of intensity in evaluation factors. The psychophysical research of E. Weber (1795-1878)* demonstrated the existence of some regularity in the perception process. The result, known as the Weber-Fechner law, indicates that, for an increase in the amount (intensity) of a stimulus to be perceptible (distinguishable from the preceding level), the increase must be a constant of the preceding level of stimulation. The greater the intensity of a stimulus, the greater any increase must be for humans to perceive a difference in intensity.

The Weber-Fechner law gave rise to a number of applications, particularly in the field of job evaluation. For example, Hay (1950) found that an intensity differential of about 15% is needed between two situations for the difference to be perceptible. Based on that rule, the maximum possible number of degrees is 7, (100% divided by 15%). More than that would only create imperceptible differentials, and needlessly complicate the job evaluation method in use. Also, if the unnecessary degrees exceed those defining the range of evaluated jobs, employees will think that committee members evaluated the jobs too harshly and will think that they have to contest the results to attain higher degrees.

It is not mandatory for each factor to have six to eight degrees; these are maximums. The objective is to establish degrees that match the real differences between the jobs being evaluated. If committee members only see three levels for the manual dexterity factor, namely low, average, and high, that factor should only have three degrees.

The delicate process of identifying and defining degrees of intensity is not irreversible. If, in rating the jobs (the next step), members identify a degree midway between two others, which would result in a more accurate evaluation, there is nothing to stop them from using it. Obviously, this would mean reviewing the ratings of jobs already evaluated for that factor in light of the addition.

---

*   *Micropædia*, vol. X, 15th edition, Chicago, Illinois, *Encyclopædia Britannica*, 1974, p. 595.

TABLE 4.9
Description of the "Manual Dexterity" Factor in Terms of
Intensity and Frequency

Intensity	Frequency			
	Rarely 10%	Occasionally 10-25%	Often 25-60%	Very Often 60-100%
Low	A1	B1	C1	D1
Average	A2	B2	C2	D2
Very high	A3	B3	C3	D3

e) Defining degrees of intensity in evaluation factors

The job evaluation committee must define the degrees of its evaluation factors as precisely as possible. This simplifies the next step of rating the jobs. While precision may be rather easy to achieve with a factor like "required education", the same is not true of others such as "initiative" or "complexity of tasks". For such factors, a quick solution is to define the degrees in general, subjective terms such as "very little", "average", "above average" and "a lot". Yet this merely defers the problem to the rating stage, which calls for judgments based on those expressions. The use of such vague language may also give those concerned the impression that the results are more random than they actually are. The evaluation committee would be wise to define the various degrees as specifically and concretely as possible. The ease with which the next step of rating the jobs is carried out and the credibility of the evaluation system depend on it.

One way of defining degrees of intensity in evaluation factors is the critical incident technique (Flanagan, 1949). Bergeron (1979) has since used it to advantage in developing a job evaluation system for school administrators.

Degrees may be defined not only in terms of intensity, but also the duration or relative frequency of each factor. Table 4.9 illustrates this approach. Based on it, a job would be classified D1-B3 if it requires very little manual dexterity most of the time, with an occasional high degree. This job would be slightly less demanding than another classified D1-C3. While these evaluations may reflect reality, this method of evaluating jobs may also be challenged, and acceptance of the results might pose a problem. Most opponents of this approach would hold that it is the most demanding element that may be required of the employee that should be considered. As the ILO points out (1960, p. 45), would an employee agree to lower compensation while driving to a meeting than while attending it? The argument certainly warrants consideration!

3. Job rating

Rating a job involves specifying the appropriate degree of each factor for each job. Preferably, job evaluation committee members should first rate jobs individually, then in committee. The committee's ratings, moreover, should be determined by consensus rather than by averaging.

Most of the literature on job evaluation suggests rating the jobs after weighting the factors. We recommend the opposite. The sole purpose of rating the jobs is to identify the appropriate degree of each factor, and this may be done without weighting them. Moreover, the definitions of degree are subjective and therefore open to interpretation. Having points alongside degrees risks making the evaluators' judgments more biased, in direct proportion to the subjectivity of the degree definitions and the magnitude of the point differential between two degrees under consideration. The ratings are likely to be less biased when evaluators have no information about the number of points assigned to each degree. Of course, they know that one degree is higher than another. But not knowing to what extent, they cannot see the effect of their rating on pay. Obviously, this recommendation to rate degrees before weighting factors only applies to an initial job evaluation.

4. Weighting the evaluation factors

The quantitative nature of the point method stems from the fact that the evaluation factors are weighted on their relative importance. There are four principal approaches to weighting. The first involves determining the relative importance of each factor based on market pricing. Using the statistical technique of a multiple regression analysis, one arrives at the relative weight attributable to each factor, so that the sum of the points derived from the rating corresponds as closely as possible to the pay assigned to the jobs concerned. The factor weights used by the CWS job evaluation system (cf. Table 4.8) were obtained in this way. The main weakness of this approach is that it confuses the concepts of internal and external equity. As a result, compensation survey results become entangled in the job evaluation process, with all the inequities found in the market. By way of example, one need only mention market discrimination in terms of the pay for jobs filled predominantly by women.

The second approach involves determining the importance of each factor based on what the organization pays. A regression analysis is used here as well. This approach has the advantage of making the weighting consistent with the complete hierarchy of salaries paid by the organization. Yet it also reproduces existing pay inequities. One way of solving the problem of sex-based inequity is to make the percentage of women in each job an independent variable in the multiple regression, or to do separate regression analyses for predominantly male and female jobs.

The third approach involves determining the relative importance of the various factors by collecting committee members' views until a consensus is reached. This may be an arduous and somewhat painstaking task, but it can be done. Moreover, it corresponds more closely to the very nature of the job evaluation process, which combines the judgments of all the individuals concerned to organize jobs into a hierarchy based on requirements. The following procedure has proved effective for weighting factors by committee. First, each member ranks all the evaluation factors in order of importance, ideally by paired comparison. Next, members assign a weight of 100 to the factor they have identified as the most important. The second factor's weight is a percentage of the first, the third, a percentage of the second, etc. The fourth approach to determining the relative weight of the evaluation factors combines the other approaches. First, a multiple regression analysis, based either on current pay within the organization or market pricing, is done (monitoring the effects of the sex of job-holders). Then the job evaluation committee can adjust the results to align them with the value system of the corporate culture. This is the best approach, minimizing the disadvantages of the other three.

5. Assigning points to evaluation factor degrees

   Each factor's degree of presence may be assigned points by means of an arithmetic, geometric, or random progression. Conceptually, an evaluation factor's weight equals the difference between the number of points assigned to its highest degree and the number assigned to its lowest, divided by the result of adding up the total differentials for each factor. For example, in Table 4.10, "previous experience" is weighted 10%, or 125 (the sum of the differentials between the highest and the lowest degree) divided by 1250 (the result of adding up of the total differentials for each factor). Mathematically, a factor's weight corresponds to the slope of a vector in a graph; where it begins and ends is not important, the distance between the two points is. For example, the points for the "previous experience" factor could very well have ranged from 75 to 200, with a differential of 25, instead of from 25 to 150; the differentials would still add up to 125 and the weight would remain 10% (125 divided by 1250). The absolute

nothing important.

TABLE 4.10
Weight Grid for Job Evaluation Factors

Factors	Degrees						Total differentials
	1	2	3	4	5	6	
Previous experience	25	50	75	100	125	150	125
Training	30	60	90	120	150		120
Supervision	0	15	30	45			45
Financial responsibility	30	60	90	120	150		120
Working conditions	10	20	30	40			30
...	...	...	...	...			...
TOTAL							1250

number of points is not important for determining relative job requirements. Whether the points range from 25 to 150 or from 75 to 200,
with a differential of 25, the difference between the total number of
points obtained by two jobs rated as having a degree of difference in
"previous experience" will always be 25 points.

a) Arithmetic progression

An arithmetic progression implies a constant differential between
an evaluation factor's degrees of presence. For example, if, as in
Table 4.10, the differentials total 1250 and a weight of 10% is
assigned to a factor, 125 points must be distributed among that
factor's degrees. The differential between its degrees equals the
points assigned to that factor divided by the number of degrees
minus 1:

$$\frac{\text{Points assigned to a factor}}{\text{Number of degrees} - 1}$$

Therefore the differential between degrees of "previous experience"
in Table 4.10 is:

$$\frac{125}{6 - 1} = 25$$

As mentioned earlier, the number of points assigned to the first
degree of a factor is arbitrary and unimportant. But if the lowest
degree is defined as "nil" or "none", as it might be in the case of
the "supervision" factor in Table 4.10, it seems preferable to assign
0 points to that first degree. This is only a question of appearance;

in practice it changes nothing. Furthermore, if the lowest degree is defined positively, it may be assigned the same number of points as that factor's differential (see the other factors in Table 4.10).

b) Geometric progression

A geometric progression is a sequence of numbers, each of which is the product of its predecessor multiplied by a constant. Thus, if the first number in the progression is a_1 and the constant is k:

the second term, $a_2 = a_1 \times k$;

the third term, $a_3 = a_1 \times k^2$; etc.

For example, a factor with a first degree of 10 and a constant of 2 would have a progression of 10, 20, 40, 80, 160, etc. Change the constant to 1.5 and the progression becomes 10, 15, 22.5, 33.8, 50.7, etc. A geometric progression creates a constantly increasing differential between degrees. If the point spreads are ultimately translated into pay differentials, a geometric progression will create more differences between the salaries assigned to jobs than an arithmetic progression.

c) Random progression

Whereas the two preceding types of distribution involve a regular progression from one degree to the next, the differentials in a random progression are irregular. An example of a random progression in the differentials of 6 consecutive degrees is: 10, 20, 25, 40, 60.

In practice, an arithmetic progression may be used for some factors, a geometric progression for others, and a random progression for still others. Organizations, however, tend to use the same kind of progression for different factors, usually arithmetic.

Why select one type of progression over another? We have already pointed out that an arithmetic progression results in smaller differentials between jobs and hence a more horizontal pay structure than does a geometric progression. The type of progression chosen is also important in terms of the message it implicitly conveys about the value of job requirements.

Take, for example, the progression for the "education" factor defined by the following degrees:

	Points
1st degree: Grade 10 completed	30
2nd degree: High School graduate	60
3rd degree: High School graduate plus 2 years of specialization	90
4th degree: Bachelor's degree	120
5th degree: Master's degree	150

This progression indicates that the 2nd degree is twice as demanding as the 1st, and the 4th four times as demanding, etc. The same arithmetic progression might also be used for all the other evaluation factors. Since the hierarchy established by job evaluation is mirrored in the pay structure, a jobholder with a 2nd-degree rating for every evaluation factor should be paid twice as much as one with a 1st-degree rating for each factor.

This is obviously an entirely hypothetical situation, since no job is evaluated at the same degree for every factor, and a pay structure is not a mirror image of the hierarchy established by job evaluation. However, this example shows that weighting sends messages that must correspond to what the organization wants to convey. Returning to our example, does the perception that completing high school is twice as demanding as finishing Grade 10 correspond to the perception of evaluation committee members and the jobholders concerned? If not, a progression other than arithmetic must be used.

This process often leads to the adoption of a random progression with irregular differentials between degrees. In the final analysis, a random progression has the important advantage of more accurately reflecting how individuals perceive differences in job requirements from one degree to the next. Yet this benefit comes at a high cost. It makes the job evaluation system more complex and more difficult to understand and explain. So, before opting for a random progression, one must consider the way in which the system was developed and the capacity of those for whom it is intended to understand it. A random progression is likely to create more doubts about the value of a system than a constant regular one (such as arithmetic or geo-metric).

6. Adding up the points for each job
   The results obtained in the preceding steps may be translated two ways: first, into an evaluation grid containing the various factors with the number of points assigned to each degree, secondly, into a doc-ument indicating each factor's degree of presence in each job. Table 4.11 is a sample of the former.
   Once the value assigned to each degree of the evaluation factors has been determined, it is simply a matter of adding them up.

Advantages and Disadvantages

The point method has a number of advantages. First, once the evaluation grid has been developed, it is relatively stable. When new jobs are added or existing ones modified, they may be evaluated without the need to reconstruct the entire system from scratch and compare every job.

In addition, this method allows the various elements of a job to be rated separately and analyzed in depth. Because of its quantitative nature, this method also simplifies and accelerates the classification process, while numer-

TABLE 4.11
Job Rating Grid

Job	Relevant degree selected for the various evaluation factors					
Factors	1	2	3	4	...	10
A	2	4	3	1	...	2
B	1	2	1	4	...	3
C	2	2	1	1	...	3
D	4	1	3	2	...	1
E	1	1	2	5	...	2
F	3	1	2	3	...	1

ically rating relative job requirements. Finally, the results of this method are less likely to be biased, since it uses points rather than monetary values to classify jobs.

On the other hand, the point method also has its disadvantages. To begin with, it is relatively difficult to develop, apply, and explain. It eliminates certain typical job requirements from consideration since only factors common to all jobs in a cluster may be used. With this method, there is also a risk of error in weighting the factors, in determining what value to assign to each degree, and in rating the jobs. Moreover, one of the biggest problems with this method is *its false scientific character*. It may be considered scientific because it uses a precise procedure, but certainly not on the basis of its results. The results are neither scientific nor objective simply because they are quantitative. The sum of the points assigned to each job is definitely the result of a precise procedure, but the content of each step is essentially subjective. Subjectivity is not necessarily wrong. The accuracy of the results depends on the specific procedure followed, as well as on the competence of the evaluation committee members. Finally, as Lawler (1986) points out, this and other job evaluation methods were developed to support a conventional type of organization of a bureaucratic nature. He also notes that a compensation system based on capacity or competence would be more in line with the requirements of contemporary organizations (cf. Chapters 3 and 8).

Standard Conventional Methods

Conventional, quantitative, compensable-factor job evaluation methods include those in which the content is prefabricated (standard) and those with no predetermined content (customized).

The number of standard methods is relatively large. In fact, to qualify as standard, a method need simply be developed for an organization and its content – "as is" – applied elsewhere. Many management consulting firms use such methods and, in some cases, modify the content slightly to adapt it to their clients' needs. In addition, the champions of these methods tend to describe their content as universal, i.e. applicable to all kinds of jobs in any type of organization. In practice, however, "universal" describes how the method is applied more than the results of studies on the validity and value of the method's content under different conditions.

Another characteristic of standard methods involves exclusive rights to their use by their owners (copyright). In most cases, an organization interested in using one of these methods must hire the firm or organization that holds the copyright.

The best-known standard methods – CWS, NEMA-NMTA (or MIMA), Hay and Aiken – are discussed below.

The CWS Method

The CWS method was developed in 1944 by a taskforce known as the Cooperative Wage Study. Formed by 12 American steel companies, its objective was to address the chaotic situation prevailing at the time in steel industry pay. The 12 founders were later joined by 39 other companies, with the result that, combined, they accounted for almost 90% of the unionized jobs represented by the United Steelworkers of America (CIO).

The taskforce, in conjunction with the union, wanted to develop a job evaluation system that would be applicable to the entire industry and would reflect the existing pay structure as much as possible. This system was covered by an initial agreement, signed in October 1945 during negotiations between Carnegie Illinois Steel Corp. and the United Steelworkers. The evaluation method was subsequently modified in April 1946, May 1946, and January 1947. Since then, it has been accepted by other companies and undergone virtually no change, aside from the introduction of a similar system for technical and office jobs in 1971.

Applied to line jobs, this method uses 12 factors, each of which has 3 to 9 degrees. Both factor weighting and point distribution are based on a multiple regression analysis. Therefore, the pay structure almost perfectly matches the one used in those days by the American steel industry. Table 4.8 lists the factors with number of degrees and point distribution. For technical and office jobs, there are 7 factors, weighted by the same system as the line jobs.

In addition to these instruments, the CWS system includes an extensive collection of about 662 benchmark jobs with descriptions and evaluations. With all this, a committee with equal union and management representation has solid documentation for evaluating the jobs at a steel plant. The problem lies in applying this system outside the steel industry for which it was designed.

In brief, the CWS method is an application of the point method to a specific industrial sector. The system was developed jointly by the companies and the union. It is also worth noting that this method creates problems for companies that adopted it some years ago, particularly in evaluating new jobs created by emerging technologies or reflecting new forms of work organization. Management at many organizations is questioning the relevance, in the 90s, of the values conveyed by an evaluation system developed in the mid-40s.

NEMA-NMTA (or MIMA) Method

Amid all the attempts by Benge and Lott in the United States in the 20s to identify evaluation factors, three leading electrical equipment manufacturers of the day – Western Electric, General Electric, and Westinghouse – joined forces to develop a job evaluation system. The system was intended for their own use and for members of their industry association, the National Electrical Manufacturers Association (NEMA). In 1937, the method was applied to manual jobs in their plants. Later, in 1947, the Association introduced a method for evaluating technical, office, and management jobs.

Since there is no copyright for this method, it is widely used in the manufacturing sector in the United States and, to a lesser extent, in Canada. In particular, the National Metal Trades Association (NMTA), now known as the NMTA Association, adopted it in the late 30s. Since then, other organizations associated with the NMTA combined to form the Midwest Industrial Management Association (MIMA), and they also use this method to evaluate jobs.

The NEMA-NMTA (or MIMA) method has 11 factors with 5 degrees each. In contrast to the CWS system, its factor weights do not derive from a multiple regression analysis to reflect the industry's existing pay structure. Instead, they are based on the judgment of the method's creators as to the relative importance of each factor. Once again, see Table 4.8 for the factors and weights used in this system.

In brief, this method is another application of the points method. Yet unlike the CWS system, it was not developed by a joint union-management committee, but rather by a few leading members of a management association.

The Hay System

Throughout the 30s, E. Hay, under the guidance of E. Benge and S. Burk, worked at putting into practice the factor method originally developed in 1926 by Benge and his colleagues for the Philadelphia Rapid Transit Co.

Then, in the 40s, Hay and his colleague D. Purves created the so-called guide-chart profile method of job evaluation. Stemming from Hay's work at a leading American bank, and enhanced by a standard point system, it is now marketed around the world by Hay Management Consultants as the Hay method. In certain countries, such as France, it is sometimes referred to as the Hay-Métra method, and in England, as the Hay-MSL system. But the method is one and the same.

The Hay method is a combination of the point and factor methods. It essentially involves three operations: evaluating the jobs using grids with standard content, determining the profiles and, finally, comparing the two evaluations as a quality control check.

The standard evaluation grid has three factors, in turn divided into subfactors. The first factor, know-how, includes scientific and technical, human relations, and managerial skills as subfactors. The second, problem-solving, has two dimensions: the thinking environment in which the problems are solved and the thinking challenge presented by the problems. Finally, the accountability factor has three dimensions or subfactors: freedom to act, magnitude (the budget that the job clearly affects), and impact (of the job and end results).

The know-how and accountability factors each have a number of standard points. The problem-solving factor, however, is evaluated by percentages, which are subsequently converted into points. The point score is obtained by the application of these percentages to the points assigned for the know-how factor. As for the magnitude dimension of the accountability factor, its various degrees are annually updated by the Hay firm, using what is known as the Accountability Magnitude Index (AMI) to ensure that accountability of jobs does not increase owing to inflation.

In the early 80s, a fourth factor, working conditions, was added, primarily to satisfy legislative requirements. It has four subfactors: physical effort, environment, hazards, and sensory attention.

Once jobs have been evaluated on the know-how, problem-solving, and accountability grid, the three factors are used to establish a profile for each job. Thus, the job of regional manager might have a profile of 41-23-36, whereas a scientist's might be 49-32-19. The difference of emphasis is immediately apparent; the scientist's job would imply a greater requirement for problem-solving than accountability, whereas the regional manager's job emphasizes accountability above problem-solving.

Once the profiles have been established, they are then compared to the number of points assigned to each factor on the evaluation grid, to test for reasonableness and as a quality-control check.

Readers interested in this method should refer to Hay (1946, 1948, 1950 and 1958), Hay and Purves (1951 and 1954), and Henderson (1989).

In practice, like all other methods, the Hay method has its drawbacks. Besides the disadvantages stemming from its standard and universal nature, which have already been mentioned more than once in this chapter, the Hay method allows for much more differentiation at the top of the hierarchy and less at the bottom than most other point methods (whether standard or customized). In this regard, it is worth remembering, as Treiman (1979) points out, that the Hay method is suited primarily to management jobs. This becomes apparent simply by looking at how the factors are defined. Treiman (1979, p. 23) adds that the language used to define the factors emphasizes judgment much more than other evaluation methods. He also finds that virtually no importance is attached to the working conditions factor when it is used. Another not insignificant disadvantage of this method is its complexity.

In addition, like other conventional job evaluation methods, the Hay method requires the initial preparation of job descriptions. Since the content of the evaluation method used is predetermined and focused on a set of specific factors, the firm has its own job description technique. The content of its descriptions is basically oriented toward the evaluation factors. Anything unrelated to those factors is ignored. In practice, Hay job descriptions no longer represent a document describing what an organization expects of an employee, but rather describe organizational expectations likely to influence job evaluation. Thus, at least one U.S. court has ruled, in the 1986 case of *Equal Employment Opportunity Commission vs. Sears, Roebuck & Co.* (Barrett and Sansonetti, 1988), that the factors used by the Hay method are not equivalent to those specified in the Equal Pay Act, and are therefore inadequate for proving the similarity of work. According to the Equal Pay Act, a job analysis must be based on real rather than assumed content.

Finally, as Arvey (1986) points out, the Hay method, which consolidates subfactors within a subtotal for each factor, does not explicitly indicate the relative weight of evaluation subfactors. This lack of transparency in terms of weighting gives rise to many general objections, especially from unions.

On the other hand, this method is reassuring because it is tried and true. In addition, the complementary service of compensation surveys offered by Hay allows the organization using the method to compare its pay rates with those of other companies using the same evaluation method. However, the question of whether facilitating compensation surveys is really the purpose of a job evaluation method remains open to debate.

Aiken Method

The Aiken method, developed in the late 40s by J. Aiken, an employee of Stevenson-Kellogg, uses 9 evaluation factors, including initiative, consequences of errors, education, and working conditions. These factors were weighted at that time, and the weighting has remained the same. One might suspect that it was based on the author's judgment rather than on the hierarchy of pay in the market.

Unlike the Hay method, this one is relatively simple. While the factors and weights are different, and the method is not the result of management-union collaboration, it very closely resembles the CWS method. It has been used by the Treasury Board in Canada to verify pay equity in evaluating public-sector jobs. Today, the copyright for the method is held by Peat, Marwick, Stevenson & Kellogg.

● Contemporary Methods

In the mid-60s, job evaluation benefited from the convergence of two fields: data processing and quantitative methods.

A typical example of job evaluation methods using these disciplines is the original work done by McCormick and his team. Based on the *Position Analysis Questionnaire* (PAQ) (cf. Chapter 3), they used a multiple regression analysis to statistically identify weights for various PAQ factors and organize the jobs on the basis of requirements (McCormick, Jeanneret and Mecham, 1972; Gomez-Mejia, Page, and Tornow, 1982). Their work foreshadowed con-temporary job evaluation methods. Yet, the PAQ and similar instruments (Tornow and Pinto, 1976) have been used primarily for research purposes.

Since the early 80s, many consulting firms have developed their own job evaluation methods that could be described as contemporary. Kenneth Foster, the then compensation research director at TPF&C, a member of the Towers-Perrin group, was a pioneer in this field. In fact, he was one of the first consultants to propose the virtually exclusive use of objective variables to determine the relative value of jobs within an organization. Thus, for managers and professionals, compensation factors such as hierarchal level of the job, number of employees supervised, the organization's total sales, rate of return on investment, etc., are used in the form of statistical regression models.

While interesting, this essentially statistical job evaluation method based on a set of variables viewed as objective has its limitations. In fact, it fails to consider job content, and therefore ignores one of the four main dimensions required by the federal and provincial legislation.

All this has led to a new way of using the point method, namely the structured questionnaire. Like conventional point methods, the contem-porary point, or structured questionnaire, method may be either customized or standard. Below, we describe the procedure for using a customized struc-tured questionnaire, followed by a few examples of standard methods.

Customized Structured Questionnaire Method

What is a structured questionnaire? How does it differ from the conventional point method? The structured questionnaire method is essentially a point method that entails designing a questionnaire to be completed by the employee or immediate supervisor, or both. The resulting information is then statistically processed by computer before ultimately being verified by those responsible for the job evaluation. In practice, the customized structured questionnaire method involves the following steps:

1. determining job clusters;
2. developing a structured questionnaire;
3. administering the questionnaire;
4. verifying responses to the questionnaire;
5. weighting the evaluation criteria; and
6. adding up the points assigned to each job.

1. Determining job clusters

There are no special considerations involved in determining job clusters for a structured questionnaire. The procedure is essentially the same as for the conventional point method described earlier. Furthermore, a single questionnaire may be developed to evaluate different job families.

2. Developing a structured questionnaire

Developing a structured questionnaire is a crucial phase of this evaluation method. The questionnaire is the instrument used to identify the various elements (criteria or factors) on which the job evaluation is based. In reality, its content corresponds to the evaluation factor grid of the conventional method. In contrast to the grid, however, the questionnaire must have more specific content. Each requirement of the jobs under evaluation must be specified. These dimensions are then expressed in measurable and often quantifiable questions. Hence, unlike the conventional approach, with its single evaluation factor covering the supervision of other employees, a structured questionnaire might contain at least three questions covering this aspect:

- nature of supervision (assignment of tasks, training, control of work, performance evaluation, etc.);
- number of employees under direct or indirect supervision;
- nature of jobs supervised, etc.

As mentioned in Chapter 3 regarding job analysis and description, this type of questionnaire is developed in four stages. The first involves preparing a set of potential questions. The only legal requirement here stems from provincial and federal legislation, which stipulates that a job evaluation must cover at least four main dimensions: knowledge and skills, effort, responsibility, and working conditions. Therefore the questionnaire must contain at least one question on each of these aspects.

There are at least two ways of identifying questions. First, after learning about the jobs to be evaluated, as well as about the organization's values and culture, the consultant may suggest a series of potential questions to a task force within the organization. These questions are taken from a question bank compiled by the firm over the years. The committee then makes whatever adjustments are necessary to those questions in preparing a first draft of the questionnaire. Alternatively, to satisfy the desire of some organizations for greater involvement in developing the questionnaire, the committee may identify potential topics for questions through brainstorming sessions. In addition, there may be a number of group interviews with the incumbents of the jobs concerned, with the gathered information then used by the consultant in drafting the questionnaire.

Regardless of how the questions are determined, in practice, the questionnaire contains 20 to 30 questions and sometimes more. One relevant factor in this regard is the nature of the jobs under evaluation. In fact, the more the nature of the jobs varies and the more job families the evaluation program encompasses, the more questions the questionnaire is likely to contain.

The second step in the process of developing a structured questionnaire is determining a scale of possible responses to each question. The responses may be formulated in such a way as to indicate frequency, importance, or duration time. Other scales may simply refer to degree of difficulty (see page 61 in Chapter 3 for sample questions). After the questions and measurement scales have been determined, the third step involves testing the questionnaire on a group of employees. This ensures that appropriate distinctions between jobs have been made, that the questions are readily understandable by those concerned, and that all relevant topics are covered.

3. Administering the questionnaire

After any necessary adjustments are made, the next step is to determine who will complete the questionnaire. Normally, jobholders are asked to complete a questionnaire about their own job. When a job has numerous incumbents, some organizations prefer to question only a sample. Immediate supervisors are also asked to verify their employees' responses. On occasion, immediate supervisors are asked to complete a questionnaire independently for each job under their supervision so as to avoid internal tension.

Even though the trend in management is toward direct employee participation in the job evaluation process, an organization's culture may not lend itself to this approach. In some cases, only immediate supervisors are asked to complete a questionnaire for each job they oversee.

There are many ways of having quationnaires completed. The human resource department might distribute them by internal mail to all respondents, with instructions to contact the department if necessary. Alternatively, group sessions might be organized. There are advantages to the latter; it guarantees that the questionnaires are completed and returned on time, and increases the likelihood of all respondents receiving the same instructions and explanations.

4. Verifying responses to the questionnaires

There are normally three stages in verifying responses to the questionnaire. First, human resource management or the task force must identify one set of responses for each job. If a number of incumbents in the same job have completed the questionnaire, their responses should be examined to determine which one will be used for each question. This exercise also highlights differences between jobs that were assumed to be identical.

The second step in the validation process involves determining the predicted values for various questions, notably by means of a multiple regression analysis. This process is called "auto-check" at Mercer, and "devil's advocate" at Wyatt. The responses to many questions are interrelated. Thus, if an incumbent indicates that a job requires a high-school education, it should come as no surprise that the mathematical skills required by the job involve analyzing ratios and percentages. It is doubtful that the jobholder would be required to use advanced statistical methods. The response to a question may therefore be predicted on the basis of responses to other related questions. Using statistical methods makes it easier to establish a profile of the expected responses for each job.

The use of these expected responses helps make the process more objective. Subjectivity creates problems with the conventional point method. Yet, it must be emphasized that predicted values may only be determined with a minimum number of jobs (about 100 to 120), because of the statistical techniques involved. A structured questionnaire may still be used with a smaller number of jobs, but this step of verifying the responses will be omitted.

The final step in the validation process is handled by the task force. The information obtained from the questionnaires and the predicted values are given to the task force (or job evaluation committee). The committee need not do evaluations on the basis of a wide range of job descriptions; instead, it can focus on correcting inconsistencies and monitoring results. In this way, the committee is able to ensure more harmony among jobs and among the organization's various departments and administrative units.

5. Weighting the evaluation criteria

Like the traditional point method, the relative value of each evaluation factor in the structured questionnaire may be determined using statistics, judgment, or a combination of both. Depending on whether organizational or market salaries are used, a multiple regression analysis identifies the weight that, on the whole, produces the job hierarchy most representative of the organization's or the market's pay structure. In the former case, the weight corresponds to the values inherent in the organization's pay structure; in the latter, it reflects the market's values. Given the possibility of the organization's current salaries being discriminatory and of systemic discrimination in the market, the use of only one weighting method will only perpetuate existing problems. Verifying the impact of the sex of jobholders on the weighting is also recommended before making a decision.

The second approach involves using judgment to do the weighting. In practice, the judgment of evaluation committee members will be either indicative or final, depending on its mandate. If the committee is playing an advisory role, management must then decide the job content for which the organization will compensate employees. To ensure that the weighting is non-discriminatory, special attention must be paid to how the responses to the questions are distributed by sex of jobholder.

Finally, statistical methods provide some indication of an organization's present situation, with the results subsequently modified in line with corporate values.

Regardless of which procedure is used, the relative weight of evaluation criteria is not determined in a vacuum. The weighting will only be acceptable to the extent that it results in a satisfactory job hierarchy.

6. Adding up the points assigned to each job

This step is identical to its counterpart in the traditional point method described above.

As attractive as the method may be, structured questionnaires are no miracle solution to job evaluation. In fact, validating the information may prove to be a major undertaking. Because of this, some consulting firms reduce the validation committee's workload by attaching considerable importance to predicted values. In our view, doing so is risky. A statistical relationship will always be no more than just that. Statistics cannot replace human judgment, although they may provide guidance.

Nonetheless, significant progress has been made in the area of job evaluation methods through structured questionnaires. Members of the job evaluation committee can now use their time more wisely, because they are given information and appropriate statistical tools on which to base their judgments. The process allows for direct employee participation, and eliminates the need to write detailed job descriptions.

Standard Structured Questionnaire Method

As with the traditional point method, some consulting firms have developed standard versions of structured questionnaires. In practice, what distinguishes the standard from the customized method is the questionnaire itself. The questionnaire for a standard method is prefabricated. Although the methods of processing the information vary, their differences relate not to the type of method used but rather to the type of intervention favoured by the consultants. Some emphasize technique to the point of creating a "black box". Others, while relying on technique, prefer more transparency.

The firm of TPF&C, a member of the Towers-Perrin Group, uses a standard questionnaire consisting of 65 questions covering the four main dimensions stipulated by law, i.e. skill, effort, responsibility, and working conditions. Coding the responses, however, is rather complex. This has led some (Kelly, 1988) to say that this method is particularly suitable for computer fanatics or people working in high-tech.

More recently, Hay Management Consultants has also offered its clients a standard structured questionnaire, which is actually a conversion of the firm's well-known standard evaluation grid into a set of questions.

☐ 4.4 Summary

This chapter has examined various job evaluation methods. A burst of activity in the 30s and 40s furnished organizations with most of the job evaluation methods still in use today. There are two versions of the point method: customized and standard. The main advantage of the customized approach is its ability to reflect organizational values and the nature of the jobs under evaluation. The standard method, on the other hand, appears, *a priori*, more reassuring.

With McCormick's PAQ, the early 80s saw the development of a new evaluation technique based on the point method – the structured questionnaire – which uses statistics and computers to process the resulting information.

REFERENCES

ARVEY, R., "Sex Bias in Job Evaluation Procedures", *Personnel Psychology*, 1986, pp. 315-335.

BARRET, G.V. and D.M. SANSONETTI, "Issues Concerning the Use of Regression Analysis in Salary Discrimination Cases", *Personnel Psychology*, 1988, vol. 41, N° 3, pp. 503-516.

BERGERON, J.L., "Designing a Job Evaluation Plan for School Administrators", *Working Paper 79-1*, Sherbrooke, Université de Sherbrooke, 1979.

BRETT, E. and C. CUMMING, "Job Evaluation and Your Organization: An Ideal Relationship", *Personnel Administrator*, 1984, vol. 29, N° 4, pp. 115-128.

CHARLES, A.W., "Installing Single-Factor Job Evaluation", *Compensation Review*, Spring 1971, pp. 9-20.

Commission des droits de la personne du Québec, À *travail équivalent, salaire égal, sans discrimination*, cahier N° 3, Quebec City, Quebec Human Rights Commission, 1980.

Commission hydro-électrique du Québec et Syndicat des employés de métiers d'Hydro-Québec, Local Section 1500, Canadian Public Service Union, *Système d'évaluation des emplois de métiers*, Montreal, 1969.

DUNLOP, J.T., "The Task of Contemporary Wage Theory", in *New Concepts in Wage Determination*, edited by G. Taylor and F.C. Pierson, New York, McGraw-Hill, 1957, pp. 127-139.

DYER, L. and R. THÉRIAULT, "The Determinants of Pay Satisfaction", *Journal of Applied Psychology*, 1976, vol. 29, pp. 233-242.

FLANAGAN, J.C., "A New Approach for Evaluating Personnel", *Personnel*, 1949, vol. 26, pp. 35-42.

GOMEZ-MEJIA, L.R., R.C. PAGE and W.W. TORNOW, "A Combination of the Practical Utility of Traditional, Statistical and Hybrid Job Evaluation Approaches", *Academy of Management Journal*, 1982, vol. 25, N° 4, pp. 790-809.

GRAY, J.S., "Custom Made System of Evaluation", *Journal of Applied Psychology*, December 1950, vol. 31, pp. 378-380.

GREENBERG, J. "Looking Fair vs. Being Fair: Managing Impressions of Organizational Justice", *Research in Organizational Behavior*, vol. 12, edited by B.M. Staw and L.L. Cummings, Greenwich, Connecticut, JAI Press, 1990.

HAY, E., "Characteristics of Factor Comparison Job Evaluation", *Personnel*, 1946, vol. 22, N° 6, pp. 370-375.

HAY, E., "Creating Factor Comparison Key Scales by the Percent Method", *Journal of Applied Psychology*, 1948, vol. 32, pp. 456-464.

HAY, E., "Setting Salary Standards for Executive Jobs", *Personnel*, January-February 1958, pp. 63-72.

HAY, E., "The Application of Weber's Law to Job Evaluation Estimates", *Journal of Applied Psychology*, 1950, vol. 34, pp. 102-104.

HAY, E. and D. PURVES, "A New Method of Job Evaluation: The Guide Chart-Profile Method", *Personnel*, September 1954, pp. 72-80.

HAY, E. and D. PURVES, "The Profile Method of High Level Job Evaluation", *Personnel*, September 1951, pp. 162-170.

HENDERSON, R., *Compensation Management*, Englewood Cliffs, New Jersey, Prentice-Hall, 1989.

HILLS, F.S., "Internal Pay Relationships", in *Compensation and Benefits*, edited by L.R. Gomez-Mejia, Washington, D.C., The Bureau of National Affairs Inc., 1989, pp. 29-69.

International Labor Office, *La Qualification du travail*, Geneva, International Labor Office, 1960.

International Labor Office, *L'évaluation des emplois*, Geneva, International Labor Office, 1984.

JAQUES, E., *Equitable Payment*, New York, John Wiley, 1961.

JAQUES, E., "Fair Pay: How to Achieve It", *New Society*, November 1969.

KELLY, J.G., *Pay Equity Management*, Don Mills, Ontario, CCH Canadian Limited, 1988.

KRESS, A.L., "How to Rate Jobs and Men", *Factory Management and Maintenance*, 1939, vol. IIIc, N° 10.

LAWLER, E.E., *Pay and Organizational Effectiveness: A Psychological View*, New York, McGraw-Hill, 1971.

LAWLER, E.E., "What's Wrong with Point-Factor Job Evaluation", *Compensation and Benefits Review*, March-April 1986, pp. 20-28.

LAWSHE, C.H., "Studies in Job Evaluation II: The Adequacy of Abbreviated Point Ratings for Hourly Paid Jobs in Three Industrial Plants", *Journal of Applied Psychology*, 1945, vol. 29, pp. 177-184.

LAWSHE, C.H. and A.A. MALESKI, "Studies in Job Evaluation III: An Analysis of Point Ratings for Salary Paid Jobs in an Industrial Plant", *Journal of Applied Psychology*, 1946, vol. 30, pp. 117-128.

LAWSHE, C.H. and G.A. SATTER, "Studies in Job Evaluation I: Factor Analysis of Point Ratings for Hourly Paid Jobs in Three Industrial Plants", *Journal of Applied Psychology*, 1944, vol. 28, pp. 189-198.

LIVY, B., *Job Evaluation: A Critical Review*, London, George Allen and Unwin Ltd., 1975.

LOTT, M.R., *Wage Scales and Job Evaluation*, New York, Ronald Press, 1926.

MAHONEY, T.A., *Compensation and Review Perspectives*, Georgetown, Ontario, Irwin-Dorsey Ltd., 1979.

MAHONEY, T.A., S. RYNES and B. ROSEN, "Where do Compensation Specialists Stand on Comparable Worth", *Compensation Review*, 1984, vol. 16, N° 4, pp. 27-40.

McCORMICK, E.J., P.R. JEANNERET and R.C. MECHAM, "A Study of Job Characteristics and Job Dimensions as Based on the Position Analysis Questionnaire (P.A.Q.)", *Journal of Applied Psychology*, 1972, vol. 56, pp. 347-364.

Métallurgistes unis d'Amérique, *Manuel - Description et classification des occupations et administration des salaires. Occupations techniques et de bureau. Étude conjointe des salaires (C.W.S.)*, Montreal, Syndicat des métallos, 1976.

Métallurgistes unis d'Amérique, *Manuel - Description et classification des occupations et administration des salaires. Occupations techniques et de bureau. Étude conjointe des salaires (C.W.S.)*, Montreal, Syndicat des métallos, not dated.

Midwest Industrial Management Association, *Job Evaluation Plan for Production and Related Jobs*, N° 100, Westchester, Illinois, Midwest Industrial Management Association, not dated.

Midwest Industrial Management Association, *MIMA'S Job Evaluation Plan (Office) for Clerical, Technical & Supervisory Positions*, N° 200, Westchester, Illinois, Midwest Industrial Management Association, not dated.

MILKOVICH, G.T. and J.M. NEWMAN, *Compensation*, Homewood, Illinois, Richard D. Irwin Inc., 1990.

NASH, A.N. and S.J. CARROLL, *The Management of Compensation*, Belmont, California, Wadsworth Publishing Co., 1975.

NEWMAN, J. and G. MILKOVICH, "Procedural Justice: Applications and Hypotheses in Compensation Management", *Working Paper Series No. 734*, Buffalo, State University of New York at Buffalo, 1989.

OTIS, J.L. and R.H. LEUKART, *Job Evaluation*, 2nd Ed., Englewood Cliffs, New Jersey, Prentice-Hall, 1954.

PATERSON, T.T. and T.M. HUSBAND, "Decision-Making Responsibility: Yardstick for Job Evaluation", *Compensation Review*, Summer 1970, pp. 21-31.

PATTON, J.A., C.L. LITTLEFIELD and S.A. SELF, *Job Evaluation: Text and Cases*, 3rd Edition, Homewood, Illinois, Richard D. Irwin, 1964.

Radio-Valleyfield et Syndicat des employés de Radio-Valleyfield, *Convention collective de travail*, Valleyfield, Québec, 1981.

SCHLEI, B.L. and P. GROSSMAN, *Employment Discrimination Law*, 2nd Edition, Washington, D.C., The Bureau of National Affairs, Inc., 1983.

Syndicat canadien de la Fonction publique, *Système de la classification utilisé par le S.C.F.P. Secteur municipal. Bureau*, Montreal, not dated.

THÉRIAULT, R., *Politiques et pratiques en matière de rémunération globale dans les entreprises au Québec*, Montreal, Les productions INFORT inc., 1986.

TORNOW, W.W. and P.R. PINTO, "The Development of a Managerial Job Taxonomy: A System for Describing, Classifying and Evaluating Job Positions", *Journal of Applied Psychology*, 1976, vol. 61, pp. 410-418.

TREIMAN, D.J., *Job Evaluation: An Analytical Review*, Washington, D.C., National Academy of Sciences, 1979.

TREIMAN, D.J. and H.I. HARTMAN (editors), *Women, Work and Wages: Equal Pay for Jobs of Equal Value*, Washington, D.C., National Academy Press, 1981.

WEINER, N., "A Comparison of Two Models of Pay Satisfaction", *Academy of Management Proceedings*, Atlanta, Georgia, Academy of Management, 1979, pp. 221-225.

TABLE OF CONTENTS

5

MANAGING JOB EVALUATION

This chapter focuses on managing job evaluation. It opens with a discussion of the proper time to evaluate jobs, then moves to the importance and potential content of the program for communicating the job evaluation system. Next, it looks at the parties involved in developing the system. Following sections deal with communicating the results, appeal mechanisms, and updating the evaluations. Finally, the chapter closes by discussing the assessment of evaluation results, as well as the costs of developing, administering, and implementing a job evaluation system.

First and foremost, job evaluation is a subjective process, whose purpose is to ensure internal equity among jobs within organizations. Its outcome — the job hierarchy — is crucial. Acceptance of the results is equally important. Given the subjective nature of the process, this acceptance depends not only on the results themselves, but also, largely, on how the organization obtained them. How a decision is made is as important as its outcome. This raises the concept of "procedural justice" (Thibault and Walker, 1975; Greenberg, 1987, 1990): the degree of equity in the process used to determine and manage the pay assigned to various jobs. Distributive justice, on the other hand, relates to the equity of the pay itself.

The concept of procedural justice applies to various facets of compensation management (Newman and Milkovich, 1989), and plays a key role in the management of job evaluation. Job evaluation must satisfy certain criteria of procedural justice (Leventhal, Karuza and Fry, 1980) if it is to be perceived as properly managed.

It must be:

- consistent: procedures must be applied uniformly to different jobs at different times;
- bias-free: personal interests must not enter into the application of procedures;
- flexible: there must be mechanisms for appealing or modifying job evaluation decisions;
- accurate: application of the procedures, as well as the ensuing decisions, must be based on factual information;

- ethical: accepted moral principles must guide application of the procedures; and
- representative: all affected employees must have an opportunity to express their concerns, which must then be considered.

In addition, development and management of the job evaluation system must be in keeping with organizational objectives, strategy, and culture. This will determine the effectiveness of the system and its acceptance by those concerned.

☐ 5.1 Timing Job Evaluation

Whether implementation of a job evaluation system is intended to correct existing inequities or to prevent potential inequities from occurring, its success depends on timing. During contract negotiations is obviously not an opportune time to determine job requirements judiciously, for suspicions related to the bargaining will likely interfere with the exchange of information and the sound judgment required for job evaluation. Periods of peak business, when those directly affected by the job evaluation are very busy, should also be avoided.

It may be worthwhile to make conversion of job evaluation results into pay coincide with a general pay increase (assuming there is one). This gives management more latitude in dealing with the incumbents of different jobs, and may make it easier for those identified as overpaid to accept the consequences. Rather than applying to some jobs and not others, a pay increase might extend to all employees, but in different amounts.

☐ 5.2 Communicating the Job Evaluation Program

The ultimate purpose of evaluation is to ensure that jobholders are paid fairly. As we have already indicated on more than one occasion, the perception of equity is a subjective phenomenon with practical consequences to which employees react. While management must believe that it is paying fair salaries, even more important is that employees judge their compensation to be equitable. This perception of equity depends not only on the actual compensation, but also on employees' confidence in the procedure for determining their pay.

The evaluation program must be communicated properly if employees are to consider that the resulting job hierarchy is fair. The program's success depends on the extent to which employees accept its results. This makes communication a key factor in a job evaluation program, all the more so because, in most cases, employees do not understand the process. Many people expect job evaluation to eliminate pay differentials between men and women. Others consider job evaluation a waste of time. Still others see it as a means of obtaining higher pay increases or abolishing certain positions.

A good communication program begins by defining the scope and limits of the job evaluation program. It is also important to reassure the employees concerned, by clearly specifying that the program will not result in the elimination of positions, reductions in pay, or pay increases for all women, even less for all employees.

The content of the communication program will vary, depending on the job cluster in question and the management style on which the evaluation is based. When jobholders are unionized, union officials should be informed in advance of the program, and the plan of action discussed with them. The union might then be invited to play a leading role, by appointing representatives to sit on the evaluation committee along with management representatives. This increases the likelihood of both parties reaching an agreement. Such an agreement, incidentally, is mandatory in Ontario under the province's pay equity legislation. The same applies to public sector employees in the Canadian provinces and one territory that have proactive pay equity legislation, namely, Manitoba, Nova Scotia, New Brunswick, Prince Edward Island, and the Yukon. Elsewhere, management alone may perform the job evaluation, with the union reserving the right to review the results. Alternatively, management may decide not to consult the union, or else the union may decide not to participate and to respond only when a member's pay is involved – but this approach is rare.

Efficient vertical lines of communication must be established: from management to the immediate supervisors of the employees concerned, and to the employees themselves. Those affected by the program must be able to obtain answers to any questions they have.

Organizational traits and culture determine what medium of communication is chosen. In some instances, written media will prevail. Organizations that favour oral communication will organize meetings with small groups of employees, or with immediate supervisors; still others will use audiovisual presentations. Whatever the medium, the key is to incorporate a mechanism for responding to the questions of those concerned. To this end, organizing focus groups has proved highly effective.

The content of the communication program must convey certain basic points: What is job evaluation? How will jobs be evaluated? How will the results affect pay? What can employees do if they consider the results unfair?

Some elements of content may also vary, to comply with provincial pay equity legislation. Regardless of the circumstances, however, certain basic points must be conveyed, as listed in Table 5.1.

TABLE 5.1
Principal Components of a Job Evaluation Communication Program

- What is pay equity?
  - How is it defined by law?
  - What is the intent of the legislation?
  - What are the principal characteristics of the legislation?
- How is pay equity achieved?
  - What is the purpose of job evaluation?
  - What procedure will be used? How will the information be obtained? How will it be analyzed?
  - What is the composition and role of the evaluation committee?
  - What jobs will be compared with each other?
  - How will the necessary pay adjustments be determined?
- What role will employees play in the program?
- What role will immediate supervisors play?
- What is the timetable for the program?
  - What are the principal stages?
  - When will pay adjustments occur?
  - What happens if the program falls behind schedule?
- Are results open to appeal?
- Credentials and role of the external consultant (if applicable).

In addition to the information specified in Table 5.1, the program should provide employees with access to one or two representatives of the human resource department who can answer their questions. Unionized employees may also be referred to a union representative.

Because the program may span several months, management must monitor progress periodically, by means of follow-up meetings or information provided in the organization's newsletter.

In sum, an effective communication program must make three things clear. First, job evaluation is only one of the factors used to determine pay. Secondly, job evaluation is not used to determine pay directly, but rather to establish a job hierarchy based on job requirements. Finally, job evaluation focuses on the job, not on its holder, on the nature of the work, not of the worker.

☐ 5.3 The Job Evaluation Committee

The success of a job evaluation program further depends on whether its development follows authoritarian or democratic lines. Authoritarianism will most likely breed suspicion and antagonism, if not outright hostility.

A democratic procedure is more likely to provide a basis for constructive dialogue and discussion on pay determination.

5.3.1 Committee Composition

Generally speaking, the committee's mandate is to evaluate jobs by whatever method management chooses. However, under some pay equity legislation, the committee chooses the method. If a customized method is selected, the committee usually determines its content. This task may be assigned to an individual, or to a team of compensation or human resource management specialists, immediate supervisors, representatives of the employees directly concerned, or any combination of two or more of these groups. All too often, job evaluation committees consist exclusively of management, with no employee representation. The contemporary trend, however, is toward greater employee participation in evaluation committees.

Thériault's survey (1986) of a sample of Canadian companies found that job evaluation was primarily assigned to committees composed of human resource specialists and the immediate supervisors of the jobs under evaluation (23% of cases on average, depending on the employee categories). Job evaluation was handled exclusively by the human resource manager in 18% of the cases, and by a team of specialists in 14%. A survey by the American Compensation Association (1989, p. 9) reveals a similar situation in the United States.

The number of men and women on the committee should be proportionate to the gender distribution in the jobs concerned. Employees from various departments or divisions, as well as from various organizational levels, must also be represented. Ideally, the committee should consist of open-minded individuals of high credibility. These individuals should possess enough experience with the organization to be thoroughly familiar with its culture and procedures, and should also have a sound knowledge of the content of many of the jobs they will evaluate.

Finally, committee members' positions within the organization should, ideally, be balanced, since experienced evaluators may influence the judgment of other members (Elliot, quoted by Livy, 1975, p. 21). Achieving this balance seems difficult to reconcile, however, with the desire to form a committee representative of all parties concerned.

5.3.2 Joint Committees

A joint evaluation committee consists of representatives of both management and the jobholders concerned. It is surprising to find that very few organizations adopt this approach, despite its advantages. In fact, many studies have proved the positive effects of involvement in decision-making (Viteles, 1953; Vroom, 1964; Vroom and Yetton, 1973). Others have confirmed that employee participation in decisions about pay and job evaluation affect satisfaction with pay, confidence in management, and the quality of communication (Lawler and Hackman, 1969; London, 1976; Jenkins and Lawler, 1977). The importance and visibility of decisions regarding pay make employee participation vital. As early as 1955, Lanham noted that it was no accident that job evaluation systems based on employee participation and full disclosure were more effective. The concept of procedural justice further supports these contentions (Folger and Greenberg, 1985; Greenberg, 1987, 1990). If jobholders are not represented on the evaluation committee, results will probably be relevant only to management. Employees are likely to perceive them as the outcome of an irrational management decision. With a joint committee, while some employees may still view the results as irrelevant and irrational, the onus for defending them rests with the employee representatives, rather than with management.

On the other hand, two reasons are often cited for excluding employees from job evaluation committees: their lack of information about the jobs and their tendency to overestimate jobs requirements. In our opinion, the "lack of information" argument applies equally to human resource specialists and immediate supervisors, and the problem is easily solved by using job descriptions or employee questionnaires (the contemporary approach). The "overestimate" argument is just as weak. If the overestimate is consistent from one job to the next, the problem vanishes, since what matters is not the absolute level of the evaluation results, but rather the differences between jobs. If the overestimate argument focuses instead on the fact that the pay assigned to jobs tends to be higher with joint committees, then the committee's role has been misunderstood. The committee does not determine pay. Pay is determined by the human resource department in organizations without a union, and, where there is one, by management-union negotiations.

Finally, in some cases, employee representation on the evaluation committee may be undesirable for reasons such as corporate culture. This does not mean that the jobholders concerned will automatically reject the results of the committee's work. Acceptance depends primarily on the credibility of the process. Employee representation on the committee is only one of many factors that affect credibility. Confidence in management and the perception that management has sound information are equally, if not more, important.

5.3.3 Committee Size

Research indicates that the most efficient committees have six to eight members, representative of the parties concerned. Often, the committee is chaired by someone from the human resource department or by an outside consultant. Human resource staff generally play a supportive, rather than decision-making, role on these committees. This reduces the likelihood that the evaluation will be perceived as simply another of the department's many activities. The department, then, becomes merely a tool for implementing the job evaluation program.

5.3.4 Committee Procedure

Since the evaluation committee consists of non-specialists, the organization's human resource department (or consultant, if the committee has one) must train members in their roles. In addition to receiving information about the different stages of the process and their role in each stage, committee members might be asked to take part in simulation exercises, to acquire a better understanding of the nature and implications of their work.

There are many ways for the committee to function. One is to carry out all the work (identifying and determining the content of the chosen evaluation method and job ratings) in committee. In theory, this procedure gives everyone a chance to be heard. In practice, however, it proves to be a long and painstaking process. Moreover, the hierarchical position of some members may give their opinions more weight, and prevent certain ideas from being put forward. One solution to this drawback is to have committee members first do the required work individually. Their respective conclusions are then presented to the committee and discussed. At least this way, all members have an opportunity to state their views on each item. If the committee is chaired by an outsider, the value of members' opinions and judgments may be more readily appreciated, regardless of their position in the organization.

In some cases, an approach similar to the Delphi method suggested by Henderson (1989) may be used. Developed in the 60s by the Rand Corporation in the United States, this system translates as follows when applied to job evaluation. Each committee member delivers individual evaluation results to a central committee, which then compiles them in terms of averages, variances, etc., and submits the results to all members. After reviewing the compilation, members may modify or maintain their evaluations. The central committee then analyzes them, draws certain conclusions, and convenes members for the final evaluations. This approach allows committee members to carry out the initial stages of job evaluation without holding meetings. It also limits the influence of members' hierarchical positions or of any pseudo-experts on the committee, since individuals are not identified.

Finally, is it better to evaluate all jobs against one factor at a time, or to evaluate one job at a time against all factors? The first approach is preferable, because it ensures a better understanding of the factor, a sounder relative judgment, and a more consistent application of the factor from one job to the next.

5.3.5 Committee Decision-making: Consensus or Average

A comment is in order on how the final evaluation results are determined. Averaging the evaluations of individual committee members may speed up the process, but the result corresponds to no one's judgment in particular. This is similar to telling someone with one hand in boiling water and the other in ice water that, on average, the water is lukewarm! Despite the tediousness involved, job evaluations should be determined by a consensus of committee members built around the most frequent response. The conflicting views of committee members on the precise meaning of a particular evaluation factor and their variable knowledge of job content may sometimes make a consensus difficult to achieve. On the other hand, their variable knowledge of job content may also result in members sharing such information and thereby enhancing the quality of the results (Stasser and Titus, 1985).

What little research has been done on this point, however, fails to show that the results of a consensus are superior to those obtained by averaging individual evaluations. Schwab and Heneman's study (1986) found no systematic difference between the results achieved by these two methods. On the other hand, contrary to all expectations, Caron's study (1988) revealed that averaging individual evaluations produces better results than a consensus. The convergence indices of the various job evaluation methods were higher with averaging than with a consensus.

Before any final conclusion may be reached, more empirical findings are definitely needed. It would be worthwhile if future research in this area also included, as a criterion of success, the degree to which the employees concerned accept the results. Considering the concept of procedural justice, consensus should result in a higher degree of acceptance than averaging individual evaluations. With the consensus formula, more facets of employees' work should be considered during committee discussions. However, this remains to be seen.

☐ 5.4 Communicating Job Evaluation Results

As with the composition of the evaluation committee, an organization's management style will determine how the results of the job evaluation are communicated. Therefore, the same comments apply.

If the primary objective is to achieve an internal pay structure that management considers relevant and rational, management alone will conduct the job evaluation and generally not announce the results. Employees may learn about the evaluation of their own job, but no more. Any other approach in such a closed context would require management to provide numerous explanations, which might be perceived as mere justification of its decisions.

When job evaluation is perceived as a means of establishing a pay structure considered fair by all concerned (employees, management, and the union, if any), the evaluation committee will consist of representatives of those parties, and the results will generally be made public (at least within the job cluster concerned). Such disclosure increases the likelihood of some results being challenged, but the onus for justifying them rests not solely with management, but rather with the entire committee. Explanations should clear up any misunderstandings and, ideally, there should be an appeal mechanism for handling justified complaints.

Ontario's pay equity legislation obliges employers to post what the law calls the "Pay Equity Plan" for each target group. The regulation applies to all employers with 100 or more employees, as well as to any with 10 to 100 employees who choose to post the plan voluntarily. The employer must disclose the following information about the pay equity program:

— the name of the establishment;
— the identity of the bargaining unit or group of employees concerned;
— the list of female-predominant and male-predominant jobs (note that these are the only jobs covered by the law; this excludes evenly distributed jobs as well as male-predominant jobs not used as the equivalents of jobs held predominantly by women - cf. Chapter 9);
— a description of the job evaluation method used;
— the classification (cf. Chapter 9) of the jobs concerned and the results of the comparisons;
— the jobs for which pay differentials are justified, and the reasons;
— the amount equal to 1% of the employer's total payroll in Ontario and the percentage of that amount that must be allocated among the employer's various Pay Equity Plans;
— a description of the planned adjustments; and
— the earliest adjustment date.

□ 5.5 Appeal Mechanisms

Job evaluation will always be an essentially subjective process. While the results are obtained through a precise, rational procedure, errors may always creep in. And even if there are no mistakes, some people may still believe that one has been made in the case of their job.

When employees are unionized, job evaluation disputes are referred to the general arbitration mechanism specified in the collective agreement. In some cases, a special mechanism is established to contest job evaluations. This, for instance, may be to ensure that the arbitrators who hear such cases are familiar with job evaluation.

In non-unionized organizations, formal appeal mechanisms are rare, despite the advantages of instituting them. For example, disputes may initially be submitted to the evaluation committee for review. Assuming that the committee has done an honest job in the first place, a distinction must then be drawn between a dispute over the job evaluation results and one over the assigned pay. In the latter case, modifying the job evaluation results will only alter the balance among jobs and trigger further disputes. If the committee upholds its decision after justifying it, an employee might refer the case to one or two individuals in the organization for a final decision. These individuals must not be associated with the evaluation committee, and should hold high-ranking positions within the organization. These days, more and more organizations have someone specifically in charge of employment equity or equal opportunity programs, as is the case with Hydro-Québec and Canadian National. Such individuals are in a good position to serve as final arbitrator in job evaluation disputes.

Finally, in every Canadian province, individuals may file a complaint about pay discrimination with the body responsible for applying that province's legislation (or with the federal government, in the case of organizations under its jurisdiction).

☐ 5.6 Updating Job Evaluations

Job evaluation, which occurs at a given point in time, is simply one way of ensuring that an organization has an equitable salary structure. As the organization changes, creating and modifying jobs, a process for updating job evaluations must be established to maintain an equitable pay structure. This means that the committee must rate new jobs, as well as any that have been modified.

The committee responsible for the initial job evaluations should also handle any job updates and revisions, to give the process continuity. It is equally important that the composition of the committee remain reasonably constant over time. To ensure some stability, committee members are generally replaced one at a time rather than all at once.

In evaluating new jobs, the committee follows its initial procedure. Updating evaluations because a job has changed, however, is a more delicate process, requiring the committee to examine only the effects of the modifications on the evaluation. Hence, any changes to the ratings must be justified by those made to the content of the job description. Any other approach would risk upsetting the original balance of the job evaluations.

About 25% of the organizations surveyed by Thériault (1986) had a formal, regular process for updating job evaluations; the others did so only when necessary.

☐ 5.7 Assessing Job Evaluation Results

So far, we have focused on the results of job evaluation and the procedure used to obtain those results. Now, we will examine the question of the value or usefulness of such a program. No research appears to have been done on the impact of the job evaluation follow-up process and results on the behaviour of the incumbents covered by the program. There is abundant research, however, on the reliability and validity of evaluation methods, as well as on the effects of the system used on the results.

5.7.1 Reliability

Reliability means the degree of constancy or stability of the results obtained by different evaluators or at different times, and is normally expressed by a correlation index. The reliability indices for job evaluations may range from 1 (perfect positive correlation between two sets of results) to 0 (absolutely no correlation between two sets of results). The reliability indices referred to in job evaluation literature generally represent estimates of the degree of similarity between job evaluation results arrived at by different evaluators, i.e. the extent of agreement between them (Madigan, 1985; Treiman, 1979).

Most studies on the reliability of job evaluation methods predate the early 80s. Treiman (1979) summarized those findings as follows. In general, the extent of agreement between evaluators is high in terms of the overall results of the evaluation, but not so high for the results of each evaluation factor. His study reported reliability indices of 0.94 (Ash, 1950), 0.88 to 0.95 (Jones, 1948), 0.77 for the NEMA-NMTA system, and 0.84 for an abridged four-factor system (Lawshe and Wilson, 1947; Lawshe et al., 1948), regarding overall results. For particular factors, the reliability indices were lower: from 0.39 to 0.93 (Ash, 1948), from 0.80 to 0.86 (Ash, 1950), from 0.34 to 0.84 for the NEMA-NMTA system, and from 0.51 to 0.89 for the abridged system (Lawshe and Wilson, 1947; Lawshe et al., 1948).

While a reliability index of 0.90 is considered high for purposes of research, this standard may be inappropriate when employees' pay is at stake. Any reliability index other than 1 indicates discrepancies between the points assigned to each job by an evaluation committee at two different times or

TABLE 5.2
Example of Job Distribution among Salary Grades

Grade	Number of Jobs	%
1	534	4.2
2	419	3.2
3	294	2.3
4	268	2.1
5	979	7.7
6	429	3.4
7	747	5.9
8	1,887	14.9
9	819	6.5
10	624	4.9
11	751	5.9
12	1,620	12.8
13	1,203	9.5
14	556	4.4
15	30	0.2
16	377	3.0
...	...	...
Total	**12,706**	**100%**

SOURCE: International Labour Office (1960, p. 112). Reproduced by permission of the publisher.

by two committees evaluating the same job. In practice, the problem is to detect potential discrepancies in the points assigned to each job in the two evaluations to determine the implications.

Based on Nunnally's original work (1967, p. 120), Treiman (1979) proposes that a standard error of measurement be calculated to estimate the impact of discrepancies in the points assigned each job in two separate evaluations. This measurement is expressed by the following formula:

$$\sigma_{\text{measurement}} = \sigma_x (1 - r_{kk})^{\frac{1}{2}}$$

in which σ_x is the typical variance in the results of the value scale and r_{kk} is the reliability index for the entire scale. To illustrate the effects of the job evaluation reliability index on potential errors in determining the total number of points assigned to each job, consider the figures in Table 5.2. For the purposes of the example, we assume that the point differential between job grades is constant, and that the reliability index for the overall results is 0.90. The typical variance for this job distribution among grades is 4.44 grades. Completing the formula results in the following equation:

$$\sigma_{\text{measurement}} = 4.44 (1 - 0.90)^{\frac{1}{2}} = 1.40$$

Based on the 95% confidence index used in this type of study, or a confidence interval of $\pm 1.96\ \sigma$, one may conclude that the potential error in the correspondence of jobs to each grade is 2.74 grades (1.40 $\times$ 1.96). Hence, the precise statement about the classification of each job is the specified grade ± 2.74 grades. In other words, a job whose evaluation indicates it belongs in Grade 6 could be assigned to another grade if evaluated by others. More precisely, if 100 people evaluate that job using the same method, 95 of them will conclude it belongs in Grade 6 ± 2.74 grades. The job therefore fits between Grades 3 and 9, which may mean large pay differences.

This example indicates that it is risky to estimate the reliability of job evaluation results with only one correlation index. In fact, despite a high correlation index, the measurement error may result in large differences in classification (Madigan, 1985). However, we should not exaggerate this problem. Job evaluation is only one stage in determining pay. It is the result of evaluations by a number of people, and is often reviewed by an evaluation committee, which may improve the reliability of results. The Spearman-Brown formula (Stanley, 1971, p. 394-398) may be used to estimate the exact improvement in the reliability index.

$$R_n = \frac{nr_{kk}}{1 + (n - 1)\ r_{kk}}$$

In this formula, R_n is the predicted correlation index for the average results assigned by groups of n persons, and r_{kk} is the index of reliability of the evaluators' results by themselves (this index is normally obtained by calculating the average correlation of each result of the evaluators, paired). The correlation index for the average results assigned by groups of n evaluators may be calculated using the above formula. This reveals that the reliability of job evaluations may be significantly improved using a committee.

For a 2-person committee:
$R_2 = (2)\ (0.8) / [1 + (2 - 1)\ (0.8)] = 0.89.$

For a 3-person committee:
$R_3 = (3)\ (0.8) / [1 + (3 - 1)\ (0.8)] = 0.92.$

For a 6-person committee:
$R_6 = (6)\ (0.8) / [1 + (6 - 1)\ (0.8)] = 0.96.$

This discussion of the reliability of job evaluation indicates the value of using relatively standard psychometric techniques (standard error of measurement, Spearman-Brown formula, etc.). At present, very few organizations bother to analyze their job evaluation results with such statistical tools.

5.7.2 Validity

The validity of job evaluation consists in assessing the degree of accuracy of the evaluation system established to measure the relative requirements or relative worth of jobs. This raises a fundamental problem because, unlike a person's height or weight, the worth of a job is difficult to measure objectively. Determining the validity of job evaluation methods depends on the purpose of the evaluation. How can you know that an instrument is useful without first knowing what it is supposed to do? Job evaluation may pursue many possible objectives:

1. to assess the relative worth of jobs;
2. to achieve a socially fair pay distribution;
3. to determine fair pay for jobs; and
4. to measure job requirements.

In practice, the salary distribution in effect on the labour market may be used to determine the validity of the job evaluation (Schwab, 1980; McCormick, 1981). However, using external pay structures to rationalize what an organization pays as the result of a job evaluation simply confuses matters.

Another way to highlight the biases of a job evaluation method is to apply another method to the same set of jobs, and compare the results. The degree of similarity is measured by the statistical index of correlation, r; if r is high, the technique produces valid results. However, caution is necessary, because the second technique may simply replicate the problems of the first so that, instead of confirming the validity of the first, it is merely redundant.

As we have seen in Chapter 4, there is a wide range of job evaluation methods, many of which have been in use for almost 40 years. It is surprising, then, to find that few such comparisons have been made. However, following are some comparative studies that have been carried out.

The most commonly cited study is probably Chesler's (1948), which obtained a 0.94 average correlation index for the hierarchy of a number of jobs established by means of the point, factor, and ranking methods. There is also Satter's study (1949), in which the author compared the paired comparison technique (ranking method) with the point method. The evaluation results obtained by both methods were similar. The study by Sales and Davies (1957), cited by Livy (1975), compared job evaluation results obtained by the National Coal Board of England, using the ranking method, to those obtained by Sales and Davies with the point method. Again, the results were virtually identical. Finally, Treiman (1979) cites the study by Pappas et al. (1976), in which the results of evaluating a set of U.S. federal public service jobs (classification method - General Schedule) were compared with those obtained for the same jobs by the Hay method. As in Chesler's study, the correlation index was 0.94. Treiman subsequently points out that this result may be readily understood, given that the General Schedule assigns a lot of importance to the skill- requirements criterion, as the Hay method does with the know-how factor. However, Treiman adds that, for certain jobs, such as those involving human resource management, there were significant differences in the results using the two methods.

These studies, along with others predating the early 80s, give the impression of a broad convergence of the various job evaluation methods. The degrees of correlation obtained are very high. However, as Madigan notes (1988), such high degrees of correlation should not be surprising, because of the limited samples used: jobs from the same cluster, jobs with well-defined relative standards of worth. Moreover, often the comparison only covers benchmark jobs rather than all jobs. Finally, the degree of convergence used, i.e. the degree of correlation, raises serious problems. It is one thing to say that the ranking of a set of jobs is statistically similar to the results of another method. It is another to say that the various methods have the effect of arranging the jobs within the same grade. Since pay is generally based on grade, the grade to which a job is assigned, and not simply its rank, is important. It makes little difference if the job rankings within a grade are inverted, for the pay for all jobs in a given grade is the same. The situation is different, however, if inverting ranks places a job in another grade. The more the various methods place jobs in the same grade, the more we say they converge. This convergence has been dubbed the "hit rate". To illustrate this, compare the results of evaluating 30 jobs by two methods:

2 (7%)	9 (30%)	14 (47%)	4 (13%)	1 (3%)
2 grades lower	1 grade lower	same grade	1 grade higher	2 grades higher

In fact, a high correlation index does not necessarily mean a high hit rate (Gomez-Mejia, Page and Tornow, 1982). A correlation of 0.82 may be associated with a lower hit rate than a correlation of 0.63, because the standard error of measurement is higher in the second case. A high correlation does not indicate the degree of measurement error in a calculation.

Caron (1988) found four studies whose authors had used a hit rate (or similar measurement of classification) as an indicator that the methods agree. Three of them noted discrepancies, depending on the method used (Gomez-Mejia, Page and Tornow, 1982; Madigan, 1985; Madigan and Hoover, 1985). Caron's own study shows that, depending on the method used, 30% to 60% of jobs fall into different grades. Moreover, as Caron states, what criterion do we consider acceptable? If we use ± 1 grade of difference, is a 90% hit rate acceptable when only 47% of the jobs have been assigned to the same grade? (cf. the example above). There is no final answer to this question. The pay differential between grades is definitely one of the factors to consider in determining the acceptability of a hit rate. Obviously, a variance of ± 1 grade is more acceptable for a pay scale with small differences between grades than one with large differences.

5.7.3 Acceptability

On the whole, the results of the studies cited in the previous sections challenge the validity of evaluation results. Yet – and this is the important point – do some job evaluation methods produce more reliable and valid results than others? This raises another question: How do we determine that some job evaluation results are better than others? In practice, these questions cannot be answered. It is worth repeating: job evaluation is essentially a subjective process.

In this context, perhaps the question of the validity of job evaluations should be viewed from a broader perspective. As the ILO (1960, p. 30) and Livy (1975, p. 130) suggest, this means determining whether the results improve individual performance and increase satisfaction with pay. A method that produces these results is considered valid. However, once again, it is not that simple. Internal equity and how the compensation system is administered (Dyer and Thériault, 1976) are not the only variables affecting individual job performance and satisfaction with pay.

A second way of dealing with the question of the validity of evaluations is to adopt a utilitarian approach (such as in personnel selection). This involves analyzing the costs and benefits associated with each evaluation system. A system's validity is one element of its utility (and obviously a benefit). Its capacity to increase satisfaction with pay, productivity, motivation, etc., represents further benefits. Its costs are related to implementation, review, etc. The utilitarian approach has the value of being associated more with management than with psychometry. It is therefore more likely to spark management's enthusiasm.*

In brief, regardless of how we see the question of the validity of job evaluation, it remains highly complex and is far from being resolved, if it ever will be. We might even be tempted to conclude, as Livy does (1975, p. 29), that job evaluation may only be a myth created to justify inequities. Yet this conclusion would simply shift the problem to the political arena, without any assurance that it would be more adequately resolved there.

As things stand, it is impossible to say that one job evaluation method produces better results than another. All we can say is that the more the results of one job evaluation method are accepted and understood by everyone concerned (management and employees), the better it works. In fact, the ultimate test of a pay structure is not whether the evaluation process used is objective, but rather whether it is accepted and considered credible by management and all the employees concerned.

☐ 5.8 Job Evaluation Costs

There are two major elements of cost associated with job evaluation: the development and the implementation of the program.

---

*   This approach to examining the question of validity was suggested to the author by Jean-Yves Lelouarn, a professor at the École des hautes études commerciales in Montreal.

When an organization develops its own evaluation program, its development costs involve, first, the cost of the time spent on the project by members of the organization (internal). Some refer to the cost of replacing those individuals; had they not been assigned to this project, what would they be doing?

Secondly, program development costs include fees paid to outside consultants, depending on the extent of their involvement and the degree of expertise required. The role of outside consultants may be limited. For example, they may simply inform the organization of the available options and monitor progress. On the other hand, the consultants may become deeply involved and propose a turnkey project. In this case, with support from members of the organization, the consultant develops the program from the start and takes it as far as determining individual pay. While the fees for this kind of assignment vary, depending on the circumstances, they may run from $40,000 to $50,000 for a program covering about 100 jobs and 300 to 400 employees. For a smaller assignment (e.g. a program covering about 30 jobs), the fees might range from $20,000 to $25,000. For a program evaluating hundreds of jobs, the fees may reach $100,000 or more. These figures warrant comment. First, they do not include the potential costs of compensation surveys. Secondly, the relationship between the number of jobs being evaluated and the fee is not direct. Certain steps require the same amount of time, regardless of the number of jobs involved, for example developing the evaluation instrument for a customized method. On the other hand, the fees for a customized and a standard job evaluation are, for all practical purposes, identical. In the case of a customized method, the firm is selling its expertise. With a standard method, it is selling its product.

Implementation costs normally range between 1% and 3% of total payroll, sometimes higher in the context of pay equity. Generally, provinces and states with proactive pay equity legislation, however, limit employers' required adjustments to an annual rate of not more than 1% of total payroll. The adjustment cost depends on a number of factors (Madigan and Hills, 1988), such as the number of employees in underpaid jobs, the difference between the present and appropriate wage, or the speed with which the results are implemented. The job evaluation method used influences the first two factors and therefore the adjustment cost. Hence, the Madigan and Hills study found that the number of incumbents for whom adjustments were required varied by 25%, depending on which evaluation method was used. The average monthly pay differential between the results of pairing the various methods ranged from $76 to $206. The question of the validity of evaluation results discussed above does not simply create theoretical problems; it eventually comes down to dollars and cents.

☐ 5.9 **Summary**

At the beginning of this chapter on managing job evaluation, we emphasized the fundamental importance of communication in developing and implementing a job evaluation program. Next, following a description of the composition and role of the job evaluation committee, we discussed the mechanisms for appealing evaluation results and updating the evaluations. Then, we described a number of studies on the reliability and validity of evaluation results, and the impact of various aspects of a job evaluation program on the results. This emphasized the concept of procedural justice in developing and managing a job evaluation program, to ensure acceptance of the results by the employees concerned. Above all, such acceptance depends on the credibility of the procedure adopted to develop the program, and on how it is managed. Finally, we closed with a look at job evaluation costs.

This chapter concludes Part II of this book, which deals with internal pay equity. The following section examines a second aspect of compensation policy, namely, the degree of competitiveness desired.

REFERENCES

American Compensation Association, *ACA News*, September 1989, p. 9.

ASH, P., "A Statistical Analysis of the Navy's Method of Position Evaluation", *Public Personnel Review*, 1950, vol. 11, pp. 130-138.

ASH, P., "The Reliability of Job Evaluation Rankings", *Journal of Applied Psychology*, 1948, vol. 32, pp. 313-320.

BERGERON, J., *Effets du sexe de l'évaluateur, du sexe du titulaire et du niveau de salaire sur les résultats d'évaluation d'emplois*, directed study for a Master's degree, Montreal, École des hautes études commerciales, Université de Montréal, 1990.

CCH Canadian Limited, *Canadian Pay Equity Compliance Guide*, Don Mills, Ontario: CCH Canadian Limited.

CARON, I., *Étude sur la convergence des résultats d'évaluation de deux méthodes de points d'évaluation des emplois*, Master's thesis, Montreal, École des hautes études commerciales, Université de Montréal, Montreal, 1988.

CHESLER, D.J., "Reliability and Comparability of Different Job Evaluation Systems", *Journal of Applied Psychology*, 1948, vol. 32, pp. 622-628.

DYER, L. and R. THÉRIAULT, "The Determinants of Pay Satisfaction", *Journal of Applied Psychology*, 1976, vol. 29, pp. 233-242.

FOLGER, R. and J. GREENBERG, "Procedural Justice: An Interpretative Analysis of Personnel Systems", in *Research in Personnel and Human Resource Management*, edited by K.M. Rowland and G.R. Ferris, 1985, vol. 3, pp. 141-184.

FOSTER, K.E., and S. GIMPLIN-PORIS, "Job Evaluation: It's Time to Face the Facts", *Personnel Administrator*, 1984, vol. 29, N° 10, pp. 120-125.

GOMEZ-MEJIA, L.R., R.C. PAGE and W.C. TORNOW, "A Comparison of the Practical Utility of Traditional, Statistical and Hybrid Job Evaluation Approaches", *Academy of Management Journal*, 1982, vol. 25, N° 4, pp. 790-809.

GREENBERG, J., "A Taxonomy of Organizational Justice Theories", *Academy of Management Review*, 1987, vol. 12, pp. 9-22.

GREENBERG, J., "Looking Fair Vs Being Fair: Managing Impressions of Organizational Justice", in *Research in Organizational Behavior*, vol. 12, edited by B.M. Staw and L.L. Cummings, Greenwich, Connecticut, JAI Press, 1990.

HENDERSON, R.I., *Compensation Management: Rewarding Performance*, Reston, Virginia, Prentice-Hall, 1979.

HILLS, F.S., "Internal Pay Relationship", in *Compensation and Benefits*, edited by L.R. Gomez-Mejia, Washington, D.C., The Bureau of National Affairs, Inc., 1989, pp. 29-69.

International Labour Office, *La Qualification du travail*, Geneva, International Labour Office, 1960.

International Labour Office, *L'Évaluation des emplois*, Geneva, International Labour Office, 1984.

JENKINS, G.D. and E.E. LAWLER, *Impact of Employee Participation in Development of a Pay Plan*, Ann Arbor, Michigan, Institute for Social Research, 1977.

JONES, A.M., "Job Evaluation of Non-Academic Work at the University of Illinois", *Journal of Applied Psychology*, 1948, vol. 32, pp. 15-19.

KOZIARA, K.S., "Comparable Worth: Organizational Dilemmas", *Monthly Labor Review*, 1985, pp. 185 and ff.

LANHAM, E., *Job Evaluation*, New York, McGraw-Hill, 1955.

LAWLER, E.E., *Pay and Organizational Effectiveness: A Psychological View*, New York, McGraw-Hill, 1971.

LAWLER, E.E., "Reward Systems", in *Improving Life at Work: Behavioral Science Approach to Organization Change*, edited by J.R. Hackman and J.L. Suttle, Santa Monica, California, Goodyear Publishing Co., 1976.

LAWLER, E.E. and J.R. HACKMAN, "The Impact of Employee Participation in the Development of Pay Incentive Plans: A Field Experiment", *Journal of Applied Psychology*, 1948, vol. 32, pp. 118-129.

LAWSCHE, C.H., E.E. DUDEK and R.F. WILSON, "Studies in Job Evaluation. VII: A Factor Analysis of Two-Point Rating Methods of Job Evaluation", *Journal of Applied Psychology*, 1969, vol. 53, pp. 467-471.

LAWSCHE, C.H. and R.F. WILSON, "Studies in Job Evaluation. VI: A Factor Analysis of Two-Point Rating Systems", *Journal of Applied Psychology*, 1947, vol. 31, pp. 355-365.

LEVENTHAL, G.S., J. KARUZA and W.R. FRY, "Beyond Fairness: A Theory of Allocation Preferences", in *Justice and Social Interaction*, edited by G. Mikula, New York, Springer Verlag, 1980, pp. 167-218.

LIVY, B., *Job Evaluation: A Critical Review*, London, George Allen & Unwin Ltd., 1975.

LONDON, M., "Employee Perceptions of the Job Reclassification Process", *Personnel Psychology*, 1976, vol. 29, pp. 67-77.

MADIGAN, R.M., "Comparable Worth Judgements: A Measurement Properties Analysis", *Journal of Applied Psychology*, 1985, vol. 70, pp. 137-147.

MADIGAN, R.M. and D.J. HOOVER, "The Impact of Alternative Job Evaluation Methods on Pay Equity Decision", *Academy of Management Annual Meeting*, San Diego, 1985.

MADIGAN, R.M. and E.S. HILLS, "Job Evaluation and Pay Equity", *Public Personnel Management*, 1988, vol. 17, N° 3, pp. 323-330.

McCORMICK, E.J., "Minority Report", in *Women, Work and Wages: Equal Pay for Jobs of Equal Value*, edited by D. Trieman and H. Hartman, Washington, D.C., National Academy Press, 1981, pp. 115-130.

MILKOVICH, G.T. and J.M. NEWMAN, *Compensation*, Homewood, Illinois, Richard D. Irwin Inc., 1990.

NEWMAN, J.M. and G.T. MILKOVICH, "Procedural Justice: Applications and Hypotheses in Compensation Management", *Working Paper Series No. 734*, State University of New York at Buffalo, School of Management, August 1989.

NUNNALLY, J.C., *Psychometric Theory*, New York, McGraw-Hill, 1967.

PAPPAS, L.D. *et al.*, *A Comparison of the Civil Service Classification and the Hay Method of Job Evaluation*, Washington, D.C., Hay Associates, August 1976.

SALES, W.H. and J.L. DAVIES, "Introducing a New Wage Structure into Coal Mining", *Bulletin of the Oxford University Institute of Statistics*, August, 1957, pp. 201-204.

SATTER, G.A., "Method of Paired Comparisons and a Specification Scoring Key in the Evaluation of Jobs", *Journal of Applied Psychology*, 1949, vol. 33, pp. 212-226.

SCHWAB, D.P. and H.G. HENEMAN, "Job Evaluation and Pay Setting: Concepts and Practices", in *Comparable Worth: Issues and Alternatives*, edited by R. Livernash, Washington, D.C., Equal Employment Advisory Council, 1980.

SCHWAB, D.P. and H.G. HENEMAN, "Assessment of a Concensus-Based Multiple Information Source Job Evaluation System", *Journal of Applied Psychology*, 1986, vol. 71, N° 2, pp. 354-356.

STANLEY, J.C., "Reliability", in *Educational Measurement*, edited by R.L. Thorndike, 2nd ed., Washington, D.C., American Council of Education, 1971, pp. 356-442.

STASSER, G. and W. TITUS, "Pooling of Unshared Information in Group Decision Making: Biased Information Sampling During Discussion", *Journal of Personality and Social Psychology*, 1985, vol. 48, pp. 1467-1478.

THÉRIAULT, R., *Politiques et pratiques en matière de rémunération globale dans les entreprises au Québec*, Montréal, INFORT Productions, inc., 1986.

THIBAULT, J. and L. WALKER, *Procedural Justice: A Psychological Analysis*, Hillsdale, New Jersey, Lawrence Erlbaum Associates, 1975.

TRIEMAN, D.J., *Job Evaluation: An Analytical Review*, Washington, D.C., National Academy of Sciences, 1979.

TRIEMAN, D. and H. HARTMAN (editors), *Women, Work and Wages: Equal Pay for Jobs of Equal Value*, Washington, D.C., National Academy Press, 1981.

VITELES, M.S., *Motivation and Morale in Industry*, New York, Norton, 1953.

VROOM, V.H., *Motivation and Morale in Industry*, New York, Norton, 1953.

VROOM, V.H. and P.W. YETTON, *Leadership and Decision-Making*, Pittsburgh, University of Pittsburgh Press, 1973.

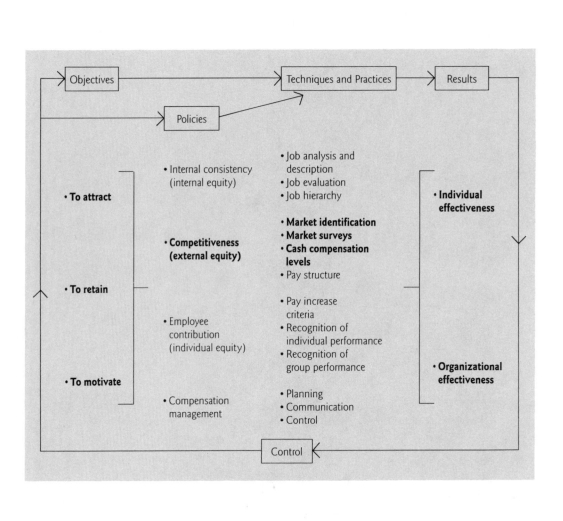

III

EXTERNAL EQUITY AND COMPENSATION SURVEYS

In addition to ensuring that pay is internally consistent, an organization must determine its pay structure's degree of competitiveness. This section examines the second fundamental compensation policy, namely, determining the desired degree of competitiveness in pay, referred to as external equity.

To establish external pay equity, the organization must first identify the labour market with which it wishes to compare itself. The variables to be considered include the organization's market, business sector, location, and size.

Once an organization has identified its comparator market, it must adopt a policy on competitiveness: Does it wish to pay more, less, or the same as most organizations in its market? and Why should it adopt one of these policies over another? Chapter 6 provides some answers to these questions.

After the labour market has been identified, appropriate information must be gathered. Compensation surveys, based on suitable job descriptions, as well as on the sensitive yet fundamental exercise of job matching, provide valuable indications about how much jobholders should be paid. Chapter 7 discusses survey methods, sources of information, and the limitations of such surveys.

TABLE OF CONTENTS

6

DETERMINING PAY LEVELS:
THE LABOUR MARKET
AND COMPENSATION POLICY

This chapter describes the factors an organization must consider in comparing its compensation with the market to ensure external equity. Pay may be determined on the basis of feelings or impressions. However, the entire process of pay determination may then have to be repeated, with more or less reversible consequences. One need only think of the impact on the organization of a high level of dissatisfaction with pay among employees, or of a total payroll too large and difficult to reduce.

Pay determination results in a payroll whose size has a direct impact on organizational operating costs and competitiveness. This effect is all the more pronounced when labour accounts for a high percentage of operating costs. In service corporations, where labour may represent over 50% of total operating costs, pay levels have a significant direct impact on competitiveness.

After discussing the principal factors affecting pay levels, this chapter focuses on the nature of an organization's policies relative to the market, then concludes with a discussion of the most important factors in the development of an organization's compensation policy.

☐ 6.1 Importance of the Market

As stated in earlier chapters, job evaluation aims to determine the relative requirements of various positions, making it possible to establish a hierarchy of job requirements and, depending on the method used, highlighting differences in job requirements. While the purpose of this type of job classification is to ensure internal pay equity, it cannot be used directly to determine individual pay; there it reaches the limit of its usefulness. However, an organization is already paying salaries when it undertakes a job evaluation, so it can now undertake to determine the relative external equity of its present compensation. Unfortunately, doing so fails to answer a number of questions, including: What market should an organization use for comparison? Are its salaries competitive? Is the organization overpaying or underpaying all or part of its workforce?

While far from being a complete mechanism for determining pay level and structure, the market remains an important criterion. In Chapter 1, we pointed out that compensation represents an economic transaction through which an organization obtains the services of individuals. The wages and salaries it pays must be partly related to market supply and demand for the type of services and workers required. A compensation survey is one way to obtain this information (cf. Chapter 7).

Chapter 1 also described compensation as an ethical transaction. While job evaluation makes it possible to create some equity within an organization, a compensation survey ensures equity in relation to the labour market. This external equity, as it is called, makes it easier for an organization to recruit and retain competent personnel, while giving employees more reason to be satisfied with their compensation. Yet, as Rynes, Schwab and Heneman (1983) point out, pay level has neither a direct nor a linear effect on recruitment. In fact, its impact is significant only insofar as the pay offered on the market varies. It would appear that when the pay offered by an organization represents an acceptable minimum, it has no influence on recruitment, because other variables may have a compensatory effect. These variables include, for example, the organization's prestige, job security, career opportunities, or even such basics as transportation options or the time required to travel to work.

☐ 6.2 Factors Influencing Pay Levels in the Organization's Market

Table 6.1 provides an overview of the principal factors affecting pay levels in an organization's market: the business sector in which the organization operates, pay legislation in its labour market, labour supply and demand, the organization's location and size, and the productivity of organizations in the base reference market.

6.2.1 Business Sector

Contrary to what many people think, there is no specific economic market for each type of job, just as it is impossible to determine a single wage for each job.

The concept of "market" is complex and subjective. There may be large differences in the pay offered on the market for "identical" jobs. Table 6.2

TABLE 6.1
Principal factors influencing pay levels in the organization's market

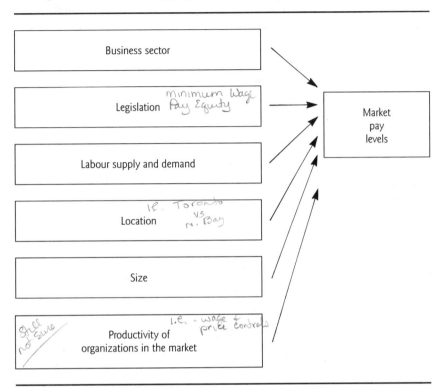

presents a sample of the range of salaries paid by different-sized companies in various business sectors for a chief financial officer. There are significant differences from one business sector to another. Whereas some companies pay less than $77,800 for the job, others pay over $160,500.

One also finds variations within the same business sector. For instance, in the insurance industry, pay at the 11 companies that provided information for the position of chief financial officer at the parent company ranges from $79,100 to over $110,000.

Dunlop (1957) was among the first to describe the impact of business sector on pay levels within a local market. He found that, in Boston in 1953, firms in the scrap metal business paid truck drivers $1.27 an hour, whereas those distributing merchandise to stores paid $2.49 an hour.

Pay differentials between industries are strongly influenced by the pro-portion of labour to total production costs. The more labour-intensive the business, the less it is likely to pay, because the company's survival is at stake.

TABLE 6.2
Chief financial officer's salaries by business sector for companies with annual sales or operating expenses in the $100 to $500 million range

Business sector	Base salary ($000)			
	25th Percentile	50th Percentile	Average	75th Percentile
Manufacturing – nondurables	85.5	97.5	101.2	120.0
Manufacturing – durables	93.6	100.0	107.5	123.0
Transportation, communication and public service	98.8	104.0	129.7	160.5
Wholesale and retail	91.3	107.0	114.5	141.5
Insurance	79.1	95.9	95.8	110.0
Public service	77.8	86.3	89.2	95.2

SOURCE: William M. Mercer Ltd. (1990), adapted

For example, hotel industry wages are much lower than those in mining. The same applies to the furniture and textile industries compared to the chemical and petroleum industries.

The public sector is an exception to this rule. While labour accounts for a relatively high percentage of total costs, it is not always true that the pay for public servants is lower than in less labour-intensive industries. Public service salaries follow a slightly different logic. Many people see governments' pay policies as designed to increase the population's income level and standard of living. However, in the public sector, such an objective may become dangerous. Even if it is not a question of profit and survival, as it is with a private firm, the government's capacity to pay is limited by its capacity to raise taxes. Moreover, every government must be concerned, not only with the income level of its people, but also with employment levels and the quality of the social programs available to its citizens. In the 70s, in a number of Canadian provinces, especially Quebec and British Columbia, governments offered a relatively high level of compensation in comparison to the market. This was believed to influence companies to increase salaries and thus increase the standard of living for the entire population. Since the end of the 80s, government policy in virtually every Canadian province has been to align public service pay with that offered by private industry.

6.2.2 Legislation

Government legislation also affects pay levels, for example the tax and social legislation of different provinces or countries as well as the minimum wage

TABLE 6.3
Minimum wage decreed by Canadian provinces and territories and selected American States (December 1990)

Canada	$4.00	United States	$3.80
Alberta	$4.50	California	$4.25
British Columbia	$5.00	Connecticut	$4.25
Manitoba	$4.70	Maryland	$3.80
New Brunswick	$4.50	Massachusetts	$3.75
Newfoundland	$4.50	New Jersey	$3.80
Northwest Territories	$5.00	New York	$3.80
Nova Scotia	$4.50	Pennsylvania	$3.70
Ontario	$5.40	Texas	$3.35
Prince Edward Island	$4.50	Vermont	$3.85
Quebec	$5.30		
Saskatchewan	$5.00		
Yukon	$5.97		

laws. The latter have various names, e.g. the federal Minimum Hourly Wage Order, or the Quebec Act respecting labour standards.

Table 6.3 lists the minimum wages decreed by Canadian and American legislation. In Canada, each province or territory sets the minimum wage for employees of organizations under its jurisdiction, while the federal government sets one for employees under its jurisdiction (banks, interprovincial transport, telecommunications, etc.). Most American states have their own minimum wage legislation, many of which are based on the federal government's minimum wage. Some have the same minimum wage as the federal government (as does Maryland), while others adopt the federal minimum wage plus a fixed percentage or amount (e.g. in Connecticut, the minimum wage equals the federal, plus 0.5%).

While seemingly simple, minimum wage legislation does have its peculiarities. For instance, the minimum wage in Quebec is $5.30, but $4.58 for employees who earn tips. Ontario's minimum wage is $5.40, but $4.55 for students under 18. In Alberta, salespersons are exceptions; in Newfoundland, domestic servants are exceptions.

Generally speaking, organizations cannot predict minimum wage increases in advance. Governments are rarely helpful in this area, with the exception of the United States federal government; it was known that the minimum wage of $3.80 applicable in December 1990 would rise to $4.25 in April 1991. In Canada, the Ontario government has also warned business of an upcoming large increase in the minimum wage, but no timetable has been established.

It should be noted that minimum wage legislation does not apply solely to the lowest paid workers. Indeed, given existing pay structures, a pay increase at the lowest level of jobs eventually leads to pay increases at every level.

Finally, the impact of the minimum wage on an organization's labour costs depends on its sector. Increasing the minimum wage is likely to have no effect on labour costs in the petrochemical or pharmaceutical industries, since they pay well over the minimum. On the other hand, the opposite is true of the retail trade, where a large percentage of employees work for minimum wage. and wether or not they pay more than the minimum wage

6.2.3 Labour Supply and Demand

As Reynolds (1970) pointed out, supply and demand in the labour market also defines the parameters within which organizations determine pay for a job. The pay rate and unemployment level in an organization's market, as well as labour supply and demand related to the activities of its competitors, dictate the minimum that the organization must pay to obtain the labour it needs. Moreover, the maximum an organization can afford to pay its workers is influenced by conditions in the market for its goods or services, namely:

1. the elasticity of the demand for the products it makes or services it renders;
2. the trend in demand for its products;
3. labour as a percentage of total production costs;
4. whether or not the prices of its goods or services are tied to the market or controlled through legislation or regulation;
5. the organization's relative efficiency; and
6. the demands of the owners for a return on investment.

Organizations use compensation surveys to collect information about labour market conditions. Depending on its accuracy, this information is used to determine actual, as well as minimum and maximum, pay. However, the limitations inherent in such surveys — including a degree of inaccuracy as well as a lack of detail and information about certain jobs — mean that managers have to use other criteria for determining organizational pay levels and structure.

Therefore, no matter how we look at the labour market, whether economically or in terms of comparative salaries (with their apparent equity and measurability), it is only one criterion among others in determining pay, and an imprecise one still.

TABLE 6.4
Salary of a human resource manager in organizations with 100 to 499 employees in various regions of Canada

Region	Base salary ($000)			
	25th Percentile	50th Percentile	Average	75th Percentile
Maritimes	59.4	65.4	70.2	86.0
Greater Montreal	66.6	85.0	80.9	95.0
Elsewhere in Quebec	49.5	54.6	62.4	72.6
Eastern Ontario	55.8	67.3	72.7	92.3
Metro Toronto	65.7	73.5	78.8	91.5
Elsewhere in Ontario	63.5	67.4	70.4	80.4
Manitoba and Saskatchewan	*	72.4	74.8	*
British Columbia	*	*	69.4	*

* Insufficient data.
SOURCE: William M. Mercer Ltd. (1990), adapted.

6.2.4 Location

The general level of pay in an organization also depends on its location. Multinational organizations must consider this fact when planning the careers of their employees. For example, because salaries in Germany are much higher than in England, promoting a German executive to a position in England may create compensation problems.

Closer to home, despite the Free Trade Agreement, Canada's tax system significantly limits the transfer of human resources from the United States. The total compensation of someone from New York who wishes to maintain the same standard of living in the Toronto, Montreal, or Calgary area must be increased by 44%, 18%, and 21% respectively. For someone from Chicago, the increases would have to be 59%, 34%, and 35%. These estimates assume a married employee with two children, earning $100,000 in the United States, (Brown and Gimbert, 1991). The highest U.S. tax rates are clearly below the top rates in Canada.

There are also pay discrepancies within Canada. In this regard, Table 6.4 illustrates the pay range for the job of human resource manager at organizations with 100 to 499 employees in various parts of Canada. We find a difference of over 25% between the lowest average salary ($62,400 in Quebec outside of Montreal) and the highest ($78,800 in Metro Toronto). The table further reveals pay discrepancies within provinces. In Quebec, for instance, the average salary for a human resource manager in Greater Montreal is

TABLE 6.5
Salary of a marketing and sales manager in the manufacturing sector, by size of company

Size (total annual sales)	Base salary ($000)			
	25th Percentile	50th Percentile	Average	75th Percentile
Less than $50M	54.3	64.6	69.8	81.0
$50 < $100M	82.1	100.0	98.0	116.3
$100 M < $500M	78.1	96.7	104.6	131.0
$500M < $1B*	89.3	130.0	123.3	153.9
$1B and over	**	**	142.2	**

* B = Billion
** = Insufficient data.
SOURCE: William M. Mercer Ltd. (1990), adapted.

$80,900; elsewhere it is $62,400, almost 30% less. In Ontario, the difference between the average salary paid in Metro Toronto and elsewhere in the province is about 10%.

An organization interested in adopting a national compensation policy must consider such regional differences when transferring employees. Many major corporations provide relocation assistance to employees they wish to transfer to Toronto, in view of the higher cost of living in general, and housing in particular.

6.2.5 Size

As Table 6.5 and numerous previous surveys indicate, the size of an organization influences the level of pay it offers. Large organizations, obviously, tend to pay more (Lester, 1967; Ingham, 1970). According to Mellow (1982), this positive correlation between organizational size and level of pay was also found in organizations operating in the same business sector or competing in the same product market.

The nature of the relationship between organizational size and pay level is far from clear. To some extent, it is the question of which came first – the chicken or the egg! Does offering higher pay and thereby recruiting potentially more qualified personnel help an organization grow? Or is a larger organization in a better position to pay higher salaries (Nash and Carroll, 1975)? According to Evans and Leighton (1989), salaries are higher at large companies than at small ones partly because the former tend to have better educated, more stable employees who accumulate more years of service, and these elements have a positive impact on pay.

6.2.6 Productivity Rate

not sure

within GNP.

industries that produce ie. agric. mining export

The productivity rate of a province or country has always been the most commonly used criterion for determining pay, especially in recent years. Governments cannot allow periods in which wages rise faster than the productivity index to continue indefinitely (a major inflationary situation). The arguments developed to control salaries under these circumstances hold primarily that inflation is partly caused by wages, and that higher wages are not compatible with the public interest. Governments may take such action as a simple wage freeze, or else may institute controls that allow increases more in line with economic conditions. In this regard, one might recall the legislation passed by the Canadian government in the mid-70s. Bill C-73, which represented an extreme case of wage and price controls, made the maximum increase in compensation for a three-year period the function of two coefficients. First, depending on the expected increase in the Consumer Price Index during those three years, a basic protection coefficient was set at 8%, 6%, and 4% respectively. Secondly, based on national productivity, which represents the long-term trend in productivity increases, a productivity coefficient of 2% per annum was set. Thus, pay was determined specifically on the basis of productivity.

The productivity rate may be relevant to the entire economy but, because of the difficulties with measurement, organizations rarely use it as a criterion. Moreover, taking the productivity rate into account may cause distortion. Organizations and economic activity sectors have a wide range of productivity rates, which fluctuate with major business cycles, as well as seasonally. Even if a method of measuring organizational productivity is agreed on, applying this criterion alone would result in unskilled workers in industries subject to swift technological change being better paid than most skilled labour in other industries.

6.3 Nature of Compensation Policies Relative to the Market

An organization's compensation policy may lead, trail, or fall in line with the market. This is a matter of strategy, determined by weighing four sets of factors.

First, the relative position of a pay curve depends on whether or not the organization is unionized, the bargaining power of those unions, corporate prestige and tradition, as well as the degree of difficulty in recruiting, the calibre of the required labour, and the involuntary turnover rate.

Secondly, its position depends on whether or not certain compensatory factors are present. For example, a prestigious organization may allow its pay curve to fall below that of one with less prestige. Similarly, an organization with abundant opportunities for promotion may position its pay curve below that of other organizations with fewer promotional opportunities.

Thirdly, the conclusions drawn from examining these factors may be modified by the organization's capacity to pay (its productivity rate, as well as both the current and the projected profit positions).

Finally, given the growing number of incentive and profit-sharing plans within organizations (cf. Chapter 12), this factor cannot be overlooked in positioning the pay curve. In practice, this means having a pay policy in relation to the base reference market, as well as a total cash compensation policy. An organization might fix its pay policy at 5% below the average for a group of 25 major Canadian organizations. Its total cash compensation policy might place it at the median within its market if performance objectives are achieved; if they are surpassed, it might want its total cash compensation to exceed the market in proportion to its surplus earnings.

An organization's pay position relative to the market always depends on the base reference market used. It is one thing for an organization's pay policy to be in line with the market average for a certain number of organizations. It is another if those organizations rank in the upper quartile of all Canadian organizations.

Among other objectives, a policy of leading the market aims to attract and retain the most highly skilled individuals. Yet, this type of compensation policy cannot guarantee the presence of that workforce, unless recruiting and selection policies pursue the same objective. This also applies to the subsequent performance of those employees. A policy of market leadership is, in itself, no assurance of higher productivity.

Such a policy may also be adopted to offset certain organizational disadvantages compared to the market, such as location or limited promotion opportunities.

A lag policy relative to the market may be necessitated by a difficult financial position, and may limit the organization's appeal when recruiting. Yet this policy has not been established as having an impact on employee turnover (Lee and Mowday, 1987; Noe, Steffy and Barber, 1988). It might be offset, for example, by a policy of leadership in total cash compensation (salary and bonuses), if justified by the organization's performance.

It is interesting to note that few, if any, organizations dare admit to a lag policy relative to the market. The reality is entirely different. Any distribution of pay levels invariably has an upper quartile, a median, and a lower quartile. The differential between the upper and lower quartile may, in fact, be small, and so justify the statement that the compensation policies of the vast majority of organizations are consistent with each other. However, the situation is often otherwise, and differences in compensation levels are often large enough to indicate that some organizations are clearly leading the market, while others are lagging.

A policy of falling in line with the market is very often adopted by organizations in a specific market. It has no particular advantages or disadvantages. To attract and retain a top-quality workforce, employers who opt for this compensation policy must apply more dynamic policies in other areas of human resource management.

Finally, as we will see in Chapter 8, which deals with pay structures, an organization's pay policy and what it actually pays may be two different things. The former is the objective, the latter the reality.

6.4 Factors Influencing an Organization's Compensation Policy in Comparison to the Market

After collecting information about market pay, the organization must determine the position of its compensation (pay, total cash compensation and overall compensation) relative to the market. This decision is affected by numerous variables, such as the organization's business strategy, union influence, corporate prestige or tradition, company policy and practices related to other aspects of human resource management, the organization's capacity to pay, and other compensatory factors (cf. Table 6.6).

In practice, few organizations adopt a single pay policy. Since the effect of the variables listed above may differ from one job or job cluster to the next, organizations often adopt a variant of their general policy for particular jobs or job clusters. For example, after examining all of these factors, an organization may decide to position itself in the upper quartile of the market for certain jobs, at the median for others, and in the lower quartile for yet others.

The use of different pay policies for different job groups or grades is, however, seriously limited by pay discrimination legislation, which is based on the principle of "equal pay for jobs of equal value". In fact, if the value of two jobs can be shown to be equal, the organization must pay their incumbents equally (cf. Chapter 9 on pay discrimination).

6.4.1 Business Strategy

Business strategy is among the key factors determining an organization's compensation policy relative to its market. As noted in Chapter 2, this

TABLE 6.6
**Principal factors influencing an organization's compensation policy
in relation to the market**

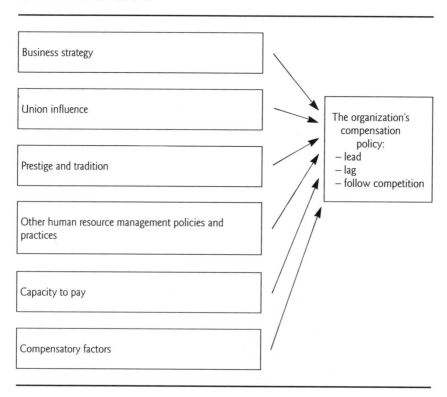

relationship between an organization's business strategy and compensation policy may be deliberate and explicit, or may flow from its actions.

An organization's compensation policy answers the question of why it wishes to pay its employees. The message is intended for them. A business strategy indicates what direction an organization wishes to take, and serves as an action guide. The more integral an organization's various human resource policies, including compensation policy, are with its business strategy, the more efficient the organization will be.

6.4.2 Union Influence

Studies by economists (Raimon and Stoikov, 1969; Livernash, 1970) have confirmed that the presence of one or more powerful unions within a company operating in an industrial sector that generates healthy revenues has a major positive impact on pay levels. They also found that the pay level of employees who were not unionized, but where the possibility of unionization existed, was affected by what unionized employees were paid. This applies to different companies in the same industrial sector and even to different plants belonging to the same company. For example, employees at Alcan's non-unionized plants are paid the same as, if not more than, those at unionized plants. This effect is clearly less evident when the jobs differ in nature (Nash and Carroll, 1975). The pay of unionized production personnel has a much less noticeable effect on the pay of non-unionized office staff.

In their study of the 1967-75 period in Canada, Cousineau and Lacroix concluded that unionization does not eliminate the impact of market forces, but modifies the channels and mechanisms through which the economic players in question learn about them (1977, p.121). Their empirical results, however, failed to confirm that a strike atmosphere had a positive effect on pay trends. There may be many reasons explaining this lack of correlation. Actually, unions' influence on pay depends on a number of variables. According to Lewis (1983), the effect of unions, whose presence may lead to a pay increase of 5% to 15%, depends on the period under study. During the Great Depression in the early 30s, unionized workers were paid approximately 25% more than non-unionized. By the mid-80s, the gap had shrunk to 10%. The effect of unions on pay also depends on the degree of industry concentration (i.e. the number and size of the companies within that industry) and the possibility of passing pay increases on to consumers by charging more for goods or services. Readers will recall, for example, the behaviour of the big three American automobile manufacturers before and after the Japanese penetrated their market. The extent of unionization in an industry and the size of the unionized companies are also significant variables in determining unions' influence on pay. According to Mellow (1982), the positive effect of unionization on pay was more pronounced in small than in large companies.

Finally, it must be pointed out that the presence or absence of a union affects not only pay, but also the criteria used to determine pay increases. Unlike non-unionized organizations, unionized organizations are inclined to grant pay increases based on length of service rather than on performance. Unionization also has a major effect on how total compensation is divided between pay and employee benefits (Fossum, 1985). History reveals that unions have had an important positive impact on the presence and level of various employee benefits, including pension and insurance plans, vacations, and statutory holidays.

6.4.3 Prestige or Tradition

The general level of an organization's pay may reflect the corporate image the organization wishes to project. For example, a bank may use its pay policy to reinforce its image as a "good corporate citizen".

DIAGRAM 6.7
The relationship of an organization's compensation policy to other human resource management policies and practices

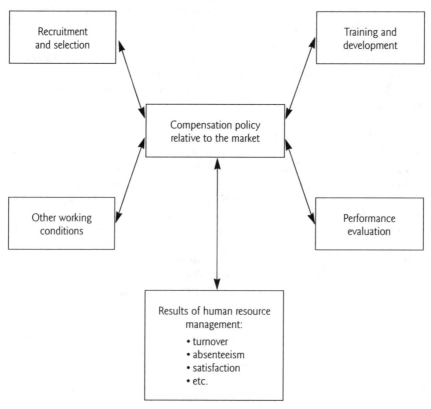

Until the late 70s, the general level of pay of many organizations was a matter of tradition, built up over time. Few employers can afford that luxury any longer. The globalization of product markets is forcing organizations to improve productivity and tighten cost controls. Generally speaking, therefore, corporate tradition now has much less effect on compensation policies than in the past. Yet it remains an important factor. In fact, what else but tradition could account for a compensation policy unconnected with an organization's business strategy?

6.4.4 Other Human Resource Management Policies and Practices

Diagram 6.7 illustrates the fact that other human resource management policies and practices (recruitment, selection, training, performance evaluation, etc.) must also be considered by an organization in determining its compensation policy in relation to the market. An organization with high hiring standards must offer candidates real opportunities for a meaningful reward. Furthermore, an effective recruiting process, which attracts an adequate number and calibre of applicants, is affected by an organization's compensation level. In establishing pay policy, an employer must be concerned with the extent of satisfaction with pay, because this affects the employee turnover rate. As we will see in Chapter 10, an organization's compensation policy must be closely tied to its performance evaluation policies and practices. A policy of leading the market will only prove effective if based on sound performance evaluation practices. Otherwise, the organization's survival is in jeopardy. Moreover, as mentioned earlier, rewarding performance means that more and more organizations can adopt a pay policy in line with the market or trailing it, because of the bonuses that result from individual performance in many cases.

6.4.5 Capacity to Pay

An organization's capacity to pay determines the maximum compensation it can afford. Its profits and survival are at stake. The importance of this factor depends on the organization's ability to recover pay increases through the prices of its products or services. This, in turn, depends on competitive conditions (regional, national, and even international) in its business sector. The more intense the competition and the lower the demand for its products or services, the less an organization is able to pass on pay increases by raising prices. On the other hand, the more favourable an organization's market position and the greater the demand for its products or services, the more it can afford to lead the market in compensation. There are a number of laws governing competition and, hence, the ability of an organization to recover pay increases through the prices of its products or services. The GATT (General Agreement on Tariffs and Trade) agreements signed by various countries, including Canada and, more recently, the Free Trade Agreement between Canada and the United States illustrate that.

A criterion such as capacity to pay obviously becomes particularly important during an economic recession. In the early 80s, many unionized as well as non-unionized organizations limited or postponed pay increases, while others resorted to temporary pay reductions to overcome their financial problems. This occurred in the automotive industry, where employees had to agree to certain pay sacrifices to ensure the survival of their employer. This situation is recurring in the early 90s. While capacity to pay and profits are justified and understandable arguments, employees must accept the validity of these arguments and consider the information they receive credible. This attitude is influenced by their perception of management's ethics and morality in decision-making. Many executives respond to these circumstances by paying at least the market price and making arrangements to stay in business.

6.4.6 Compensatory Factors — *can't be measured*

A pay policy may be determined on the basis of compensatory factors, such as the chances of promotion, the atmosphere at work, and the opportunities for training and development. An organization whose pay policy lags the market can still continue attracting and retaining high-quality personnel by emphasizing employee growth. On the other hand, an organization with little opportunity for promotion and development might offset this disadvantage through more generous compensation policies and practices. Organizations located far from major urban centres may have to pay distance bonuses in addition to salary (as is the case with companies operating in the northern areas of British Columbia, Ontario, and Quebec) or as a component of salary (as with organizations whose principal activities are situated in remote regions, such as mining companies).

☐ 6.5 Conclusion

Generally speaking, there are minimum and maximum limits determining what an organization can pay. These limits may be estimated, but are never exact. They also change over time in response to economic conditions, union activities, or organizational management. This applies to both the private and public sectors, except that, in the latter case, maximum pay may be determined by law (which is also true for some non-profit organizations and such organizations like the Quebec construction industry, which is regulated by decree).

This chapter grouped the various factors influencing an organization's compensation level into two categories: those with an effect on what the market pays and those the organization considers in positioning its compensation policy relative to the market. Having discussed these various factors, the next step is to collect relevant information about the market, so that the organization can position its policy as it wishes relative to that market. This will be the focus of the next chapter.

REFERENCES

BROWN, R.D. and R. GIMBERT, "The Tax Scoreboard", *The Globe and Mail*, January 12, 1991, pp. D-1 and ff.

COUSINEAU, J.M. and R. LACROIX, *La détermination des salaires dans le monde des grandes conventions collectives: une analyse des secteurs privé et public*, Ottawa, Conseil économique du Canada, 1977.

DUNLOP, J.T., "The Task of Contemporary Wage Theory", in *New Concept in Wage Determination*, edited by G.W. Taylor and F.C. Pierson, New York, McGraw-Hill, 1957.

EVANS, D.S. and L.S. LEIGHTON, "Why Do Smaller Firms Pay Less?", *Journal of Human Resources*, 1989, vol. 24, N° 2, pp. 299-318.

FOSSUM, J.A., *Labor Relations*, Plano, Texas, Business Publications, 1985.

HAREL, G., "Job Evaluation and Wage Setting in the Public Sector of Israel", *Relations Industrielles*, 1976, vol. 31, N° 2, pp. 284-302.

INGHAM, G.K., *Size of Industrial Organization and Worker Behavior*, London, Cambridge University Press, 1970.

LEE, T.W. and R. MOWDAY, "Voluntary Leaving an Organization: An Empirical Investigation of Steers and Mowday's Model of Turnover", *Academy of Management Journal*, December 1987, pp. 721-743.

LESTER, R.A., "Pay Differentials by Size of Establishment", *Industrial Relations*, 1967, vol. 7, pp. 57-67.

LEWIS, H.G., "Union Relative Wage Effects: A Survey of Macro Estimates", *Journal of Labor Economics*, January 1983, pp. 1-27.

LIVERNASH, E.R., "Wages and Benefits", *A Review of Industrial Relations Research*, 1970, vol. 1, pp. 79-144.

MELLOW, W., "Employer Sizes and Wages", *Review of Economics and Statistics*, 1982, pp. 495-501.

MERCER, WILLIAM M., *1990 Executive Benchmark Compensation Report*, Toronto, 1990.

NASH, A.N. and S.J. CARROLL, *The Management of Compensation*, Monterey, California, Brooks/Cole Publishing Co., 1975.

NOE, R.A., B.D. STEFFY and A.E. BARBER, "An Investigation of the Factors Influencing Employees' Willingness to Accept Mobility Opportunities", *Personnel Psychology*, 1988, vol. 41, N° 3, pp. 559-580.

RAIMON, R.L. and V. STOIKOV, "The Effect of Blue-Collar Unionism on White-Collar Earnings", *Industrial and Labor Relations Review*, April 1969, pp. 358-374.

REYNOLDS, L.G., *Labor Economics and Labor Relations*, Englewood Cliffs, New Jersey, Prentice-Hall, 5th Edition, 1970.

RYNES, S.L., D.P. SCHWAB and H.G. HENEMAN, "The Role of Pay and Market Pay Variability in Job Application Decisions", *Organizational Behaviour and Human Performance*, 1983, vol. 31, pp. 353-364.

RYNES, S.L. and G.T. MILKOVICH, "Salary Surveys: Dispelling the Myths About the "Market Usage"", *Personnel Psychology*, 1986, vol. 39, pp. 71-89.

TABLE OF CONTENTS

7

COMPENSATION SURVEYS

Organizations cannot offer competitive compensation unless they know their labour market. This chapter focuses on compensation surveys, i.e. collecting market data about compensation. After examining the value of compensation surveys and corporate participation in them, we describe the five critical stages in conducting a survey: determining requirements and objectives, defining scope, selecting a method, deciding on the source, and interpreting the results. Then we discuss employee participation in compensation surveys, and the limitations of surveys, before concluding with a look at the implications of unfair competition legislation.

☐ 7.1 Compensation Surveys: Value and Participation

The first American salary survey was probably the one conducted in 1891 by the Bureau of Labor Statistics. Organizations only began using them regularly after the National War Labor Board was founded during World War II. A survey by Mahoney, Rynes and Rosen (1984) found that over 80% of American companies used both commercial surveys from outside sources, and in-house ones done by their own human resource department.

In Canada, a recent survey by Thériault (1986) found that most organizations used salary survey results. About 50% of the organizations used the data from salary surveys of specific employers, and over 80%, the results of more general market surveys. Thériault also found that the larger the organization, the more it tended to consider the findings of general salary surveys. Only 25% of organizations with less than 100 employees used general surveys, compared to over 65% of those with more than 1,000 employees.

Organizations generally use the results of more than one compensation survey. Some take three, or even four, into account. It appears that they consider a larger number of surveys when they relate to the general market as opposed to specific employers. Organizations also make extensive use of compensation surveys (Belcher, Ferris, and O'Neill, 1985). They are consulted in making decisions about pay scale adjustments, merit compensation budgets, pay rate adjustments, hiring rates, pay scale control points, in prep-aration for collective negotiations, and in the analysis of the causes of employee turnover.

At the same time, most organizations participate in numerous compen-sation surveys. Belcher (1974) mentions about 100 surveys for a large organ-ization. While that figure is undoubtedly the exception, it is not rare to find a medium-sized organization responding to at least 10 annually. It is worth noting, in this regard, that an organization's participation in numerous surveys has an impact on what employees earn in the market. The more surveys the organization responds to, the more the results resemble the organization. Consequently, the more the organization influences the market, the more the market resembles it, with the result that external equity more closely resembles what the organization offers.

7.2 The Critical Stages of a Compensation Survey

There are five stages to conducting a compensation survey (cf. Figure 7.1).

The first step involves determining the requirements and objectives of the survey, as well as the type of information desired. Is it information about salaries, bonuses, and employee benefits, or about only one of these elements?

The second step is to define the scope of the survey. Should it extend to all jobs, or only to some? If the latter, which ones? And where will the desired information be obtained — from what population or what sample of organizations? In brief, in what market will the survey be conducted, and will it cover one market for all jobs or different markets for various jobs.

The third step is to select a method. How will the content of jobs covered by the survey be compared with that at participating organizations? Will there be an approximate or intuitive comparison, job by job, by job class? Or is it better to match jobs by means of the evaluation system used by the organization that is conducting or needs the survey?

The fourth step is to decide what source of information to use. Will the organization conduct its own survey? If so, will it be informal, approximate, or formal? Will the organization also consult the results of surveys conducted by government agencies or management consultants? And if so, which ones?

The final step is to interpret the survey results. In other words, what messages does this information convey with respect to establishing or updat-ing a pay structure?

7.2.1 Determining Requirements and Objectives

Compensation surveys are used to collect information about what the market pays. They allow an organization to ensure that its compensation is com-

FIGURE 7.1
Stages of a Compensation Survey

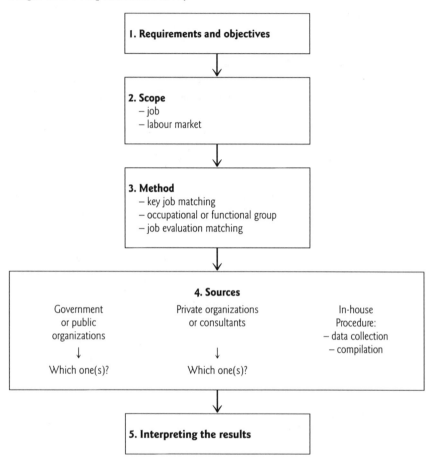

petitive. Such external equity has a twofold importance. First, jobs have no intrinsic value, only whatever value the market assigns to them. Secondly, competitive compensation is an important factor in attracting the required human resources to the organization (Rynes, Schwab, and Heneman, 1983), and in retaining them. In brief, salary surveys (or to be more precise, compensation surveys) are an essential element of compensation planning, and therefore, of overall organizational planning.

The concept of external equity may be less relevant to organizations with an internal recruiting policy (Fay, 1989), i.e., those that fill their entry-level jobs through outside hiring and the rest through internal mobility (employee promotions, transfers, etc.). This does not mean that compensation for employees beyond the entry level need no longer be competitive, but rather that it need not be as competitive as for entry-level jobs, because of the opportunity for other forms of rewards.

"Salary" surveys were common a few years ago; they tended to be limited to collecting information solely about pay levels and increases in the competitive job market. "Compensation" surveys tend to be the norm today. They gather information not only about pay, but also about bonus plans, employee benefits, perquisites, and other supplemental benefits (cf. Chapter 14).

In practice, there are two types of surveys. The first consists of the wage increase forecasts for the coming year, which are published annually in the business pages. These figures come primarily from membership or general surveys conducted by private organizations, such as the Conference Board of Canada, or consulting firms. Some consultants, however, do not publish their forecasts for fear of fuelling inflation. We do not feel that this is generally true – it seems like blaming a hot day on the thermometer. However, general averages may easily be misinterpreted, and the results cited out of context. Reliance on statistics is actually dangerous without complete knowledge of the surrounding circumstances. Hence, some firms prefer to restrict circulation of their forecasts to survey participants – not to avoid fuelling inflation, but rather as a precaution against the risks of misinterpretation (Mercer, 1985).

The second type of survey gathers information about pay, bonuses, working conditions, and employee benefits on the market. This is the type primarily discussed in this chapter.

7.2.2 Defining Scope

Two factors define the scope or extent of a compensation survey: the jobs or job clusters about which information is gathered and the specific market surveyed.

Target Jobs and Job Clusters

The scope of a salary survey may be specific or general. The former covers specific jobs, whereas the latter extends to one or more job classes. When an organization needs data to update its pay structure, differentiate pay levels, ascertain the mix of total compensation components assigned to jobs, or plan a market-based pay increase, the scope of the survey tends to be general. It extends to the entire scope of jobs within the relevant job clusters. However, in the case of newly created jobs, or a highly active market (e.g. computer programmer and other related jobs in the 80s and still to some extent in the early 90s), the survey may be limited to specific positions.

Target Market

Defining the target market involves two dimensions: determining the geographic range of the survey and selecting the organizations to be surveyed within a territory.

Geographic Range of the Survey

The geographic range of a survey depends essentially on the job market. A good idea of the geographic market for a survey may be obtained by simply finding out what media are used to recruit candidates for the jobs in question – local, regional, national, or other media? The market for certain executive or senior management positions may span an entire province or country, and sometimes may even be global. The market for clerical or unskilled production workers is local. It may be defined by outlining the areas in which these employees live on a map.

Importance of a Survey's Geographical Boundaries

A compensation survey's geographical boundaries depend on two principal considerations: labour mobility and compensation differentials based on location. The compensation assigned to a job is not identical across a country (in Canada, for example, salaries are currently higher in Ontario than in Alberta), or within a province (salaries in the province of Quebec, for instance, are higher in Montreal than in Quebec City, where they are, in turn, higher than in Sherbrooke). Poor demarcation of survey boundaries may therefore lead to (1) an *overestimate* of salaries, resulting in an undue increase in an organization's labour costs or (2) an *underestimate* of salaries, leading to problems with employee recruitment and turnover. For example, a regional compensation survey of a job with a national market may result in an overestimate, or in an underestimate, of the salaries paid. It is equally important to consider the effective mobility of the present jobholders, which may be limited to a region, despite a national job market. In such a case, a national survey would be pointless, since it would risk producing an overestimate of salaries if pay is lower in the region in question, or an underestimate if compensation in the region is higher than elsewhere.

Selecting Organizations to Survey

After determining the geographic range of a survey, the next step is to select organizations within those boundaries to participate in the survey. It is common practice to survey organizations of the same size and in the same business sector. These restrictions, though, are not always adequate. The market for some jobs (such as office work) is not limited to any one industrial sector, and even less to organizations similar in size. Yet while a secretary may work in different business sectors for organizations of any size, the same is not true of a telecommunications engineer, an x-ray technician, or a university professor.

Furthermore, restricting a survey to organizations of the same size has its limitations. Since compensation levels in a business sector are proportional to the size of the organization, large corporations often serve as an important reference point. One must obviously consider that, even though large organizations generally pay higher salaries than medium-sized or small ones, the latter may compensate with other advantages such as opportunities for promotion, the work environment, etc.

Finally, the characteristics of the organization that needs the survey will influence its choice of targets. Take the example of a job with a local market. Half the people filling that job in the region work at 4 companies, while the other half are spread out among 20 other firms. A large organization might decide to survey the three other large companies and a limited sample of smaller firms, whereas a small business might be interested in surveying a wider selection.

In brief, a compensation survey is not intended to collect information solely about organizations known to pay their employees well or poorly. Rather, it means *gathering information about the potential labour market for the jobs concerned,* so that the survey accurately reflects what is offered by all organizations in that market. The statistical technique of sampling may then prove useful.

Use of the Sampling Technique

A very large population may call for random or stratified random sampling. Stratified random sampling is more commonly used in salary surveys, because it is generally more practical. Organizations are first sorted on the basis of specified characteristics (such as size, business sector, or location), and then a larger or smaller sample of organizations is taken from each group, with the size of each sample dependent on the importance (weight) assigned to the class of organizations concerned. It is important to note that the survey results will reflect the weighting system used. If in our example of 4 large and 20 small companies, we assign more weight to small ones, it is highly probable that the survey results will be lower, because salaries are usually lower in smaller organizations than in larger ones.

Use of a Potential or Specific Job Market

Some surveys are designed to obtain information about specific organizations, rather than about the general labour market. An example might be a municipality interested in basing its salaries on specific municipalities as opposed to the potential labour market for numerous jobs. Another would be a large industrial firm that wishes to compare its salaries with those paid by a dozen other industrial giants located in the same metropolitan area, but involved in a variety of business sectors.

Nonetheless, compensation surveys generally target the entire potential labour market, if not more. While such surveys certainly provide some indications about salary, they reflect the compensation conditions at participating organizations, rather than those of the entire potential population. A list of participants must therefore be attached to the results of these surveys. Otherwise, the figures will have no practical significance, and it will be virtually impossible to determine their value (validity). Meanwhile, surveys covering the entire potential population also create problems when comparing results from one year to the next. *Inasmuch as participating organizations change from one survey to the next, it is practically impossible to draw valid conclusions about salary changes.* In fact, one can then only determine what part of the changes from year to year is attributable to a real salary change, and what to other conditions prevailing within the participating organizations.

7.2.3 Selecting a Method

There are essentially three methods of conducting a compensation survey: key job matching, the occupational or functional survey method, and matching by job evaluation.

Key Job Matching

Key job matching is undoubtedly the most commonly used method of conducting a compensation survey. It consists of comparing and estimating the degree of similarity in the content of the key (or benchmark) jobs used, and those in the organizations surveyed. The degree of accuracy of the job matches is of fundamental importance, and will depend on how the information is gathered.

For example, when survey data is collected by questionnaire, the key job descriptions cannot be printed in full. Sometimes only the job title is listed, with a brief indication of content. Summary job descriptions, such as those in Table 7.1, are more commonly used. In this case, survey respondents must identify the jobs within their organization that most closely correspond to those listed in the questionnaire, and provide the desired information. The value, or validity, of the data provided by participants is, therefore, subject to the quality of the key job descriptions in the survey questionnaire.

TABLE 7.1
Illustration of Job Summaries Used for Salary Surveys

Job code: **340**   Job title: **Sales representative**

Responsible for selling products and services to a vast clientele consisting of medium-sized companies. Must have, as a minimum requirement, complete sales skills, and must meet specific sales targets.

Job code: **412**   Job title: **Buyer**

Following detailed instructions, negotiates with authorized suppliers, selects suitable ones and places orders based on needs (quantities and dates) as determined by the inventory planning department. Generally has two to four years of experience. Reports to the senior buyer or purchasing manager.

Job code: **530**   Job title: **Recruiting manager**

Determines recruitment policies. Supervises recruiting, interviewing, selection, and assignment of management, salaried, and hourly-wage employees, or handles it personally. Supervises the writing and publication of job offers, or handles it personally. Is responsible for relations with outside personnel recruiting agencies. Manages tests and training programs. Sees that affirmative action and pay equity objectives are met. Occasionally supervises orientation programs for new employees and their integration into staff. Provides counselling for dismissed employees.

The description of the *sales representative* in Table 7.1, for example, might cover several jobs. As a result, it comes as no surprise to find large differentials (over 50%) in the pay assigned to the job by various organizations. In addition to reflecting salary differences from one organization to the next, this pay differential is explained by the different types of sales representative jobs covered. To narrow down the scope and level of jobs for which information is being sought, some compensation surveys follow each summary job description with the incumbent's characteristics (experience, education, etc.). Some authors suggest using statistical techniques to ensure the quality of the job matches. Weinberger (1984), for instance, recommends the multiple regression technique to clarify the issue of the validity of "forced" matches. Moreover, some survey questionnaires (such as those used by William M. Mercer Limited) are designed to obtain details about the quality of the match made by respondents. They indicate whether the job described involves equivalent, lesser, or greater responsibilities than those attached to the job for which they are providing information.

Key Jobs

A survey focused on a job cluster does not, in practice, cover *every* job in that cluster. Such a survey would be a long, arduous task for both the surveying organization and respondents. In addition, it would raise complex problems with comparison. Actually, it is rare to find two organizations with the same work organization, even if operating in the same business sector and identical in size. Different job contents underlie identical or similar titles. The content of a *certain number* of jobs, however, is virtually identical from one organization to the next. A salary survey only covers these so-called key or benchmark jobs. More specifically, *a key job is one whose content is relatively stable, clearly defined, and rather typical in the labour market.* In identifying key jobs, organizations must ensure that they satisfy various levels of requirements within the job cluster, and that they include jobs encompassing a large number of positions.

The Limitations of Key Jobs

Limiting the compensation survey to key jobs facilitates comparison and reduces the time required to collect the data, but also creates a potentially serious problem. To the extent that the key-job data is accurate and valid – achieving which is, in itself, no small task – it will be relevant for those jobs. In practice, organizations assume the key-job data applies to other jobs in the cluster with similar requirements. But that remains an assumption! The market compensation for a key job depends not only on its requirements, but also on a host of other factors: the relative scarcity of candidates to fill the job, industrial sector, location, capacity to pay. In all likelihood, these factors do not have the same effect on a key job as they do on other jobs in the cluster with similar requirements.

Occupational or Functional Group Survey

Another compensation survey technique gets around the problems involved in matching key jobs by collecting information about all the jobs in an occupational or functional group, such as office or administrative jobs. Survey respondents must provide information about the hierarchical level of the jobs in their organization, as well as about the number of employees filling those jobs. The technique used by government agencies (e.g. Statistics Canada) for salary surveys provides a good illustration of this approach. It produces relatively accurate salary data, broken down by economic sector and organizational size. Moreover, considering the functional nature of the jobs in an economic sector and organizational size, the most important factor in this technique is not the specific content of jobs, but rather their hierarchical level.

Surveys of the salary conditions of members of a profession use a variation of this technique; they also consider how long members have worked in their profession since receiving their diploma or degree. An example might be the engineer salary surveys conducted in various provinces across Canada.

They match not only responsibilities, but also criteria unrelated to job content, such as length of time worked since earning the most recent university degree, type of degree (specialization), level (undergraduate, Master's, doctorate).

Matching by Job Evaluation

Another compensation survey technique involves matching jobs by means of a job evaluation system. It may be used in two situations.

The first is when the organizations participating in the survey use the same job evaluation system and provide the evaluation information about their jobs. This results in superior matching, to the extent that the job evaluations used by the responding organizations are standardized to take into account the degree of rigour with which the job evaluation system was applied. This matching is therefore based on job content in relation to the job evaluation results. This can only be done if all participating organizations use the same job evaluation system, with standardized results. The Hay Management Consultants' salary surveys of their clients provide a good example of this approach, which has its problems (Foster, 1983). First, the conversion of each participating organization's evaluation results into standard points is a subjective process, whose effectiveness is difficult to assess. Secondly, participants in this type of survey do not know (unless they ask for special analyses) the market compensation for a specific job, because its content depends on its evaluation result, rather than on its nature. For example, respondents do not know how much a plant controller is paid on the market. What they do know is what the market pays for jobs whose "standardized" evaluation results equal the result for their plant controller. Thirdly, a technique such as this only has relevance if the job evaluations of all participants are up-to-date, which is not always the case. Finally, this technique limits the reference market to organizations that use the job evaluation system in question. In practice, this may rule out many others that are pertinent.

This compensation survey technique may also be used when the participating organizations have different job evaluation systems. The organization conducting the survey tries to obtain relatively complete information (job descriptions) about the jobs in question, then applies its own job evaluation system to them. The value of the matching in this case depends on the quality of the job descriptions provided by respondents and on the objectivity of the job evaluators. This technique is more time-consuming, but yields more valid salary data. In fact, the matching is superior because it considers both the nature of job content and the requirements of jobs evaluated by a common system.

7.2.4 Deciding on a Source

There are essentially five sources of compensation surveys: (1) government agencies; (2) consulting firms and private organizations; (3) employer and professional associations; (4) informal employer groups; and (5) in-house surveys. Table 7.2 lists the salary survey sources in each of the first three categories.

TABLE 7.2
Compensation Survey Sources

GOVERNMENT AGENCIES

Pay Research Bureau (Ottawa):
— Compensation for different employee categories except executives.
— Real starting salaries offered to university, CEGEP, and community college graduates.
— Frequency, characteristics, and relative expenditures on employee benefits and working conditions.

Treasury Board, Government of Quebec:
— Executive compensation in the public and private sectors in Quebec.

Quebec Department of Labour:
— Total compensation for a set of clerical, technical and professional jobs in Quebec.

Health and Welfare Canada:
— Compensation for different employee categories in Canadian hospitals.

Statistics Canada:
— A variety of surveys on unionized employee compensation and, more general, on clerical, production and maintenance workers in Canada, by province.
— Survey of Canadian pension plans.

Labour Canada:
— Wage rate trends for all major collective agreements in force in Canada.

PUBLIC ORGANIZATIONS

Association of Professional Engineers, Geologists and Geophysicists of Alberta:
— Engineer salaries in Alberta with comparative data on the engineering profession in Quebec, Ontario, and British Columbia, as well as various professional and nonprofessional employee categories in Alberta.

Association of Professional Engineers of British Columbia:
— Engineer salaries in the Province.

Metro Toronto Board of Trade:
— Clerical job compensation.
— Data-processing job compensation.

Montreal Board of Trade:
— Compensation of hourly-wage employees, clerical staff, executives and sales personnel.

Central Ontario Industrial Relations Institute:
— Compensation for about 100 professions in three groups: production, nonproduction, and foundries.
— Clerical worker compensation.

Conference Board of Canada:
— Compensation of members of boards of directors in Canada.
— Comparison of the compensation for certain clerical, executive, professional, and production jobs in Canada, and the United States.

Quebec Industrial Relations Institute:
— Executive compensation in Quebec and Ontario.
— Clerical job salaries in Greater Montreal.
— Production, maintenance and service job salaries.

Ordre des ingénieurs du Québec:
— Engineer salaries in Quebec.

Vancouver Board of Trade:
— Clerical worker compensation.

PRIVATE ORGANIZATIONS

Sobeco Group Inc.:
— Executive compensation in Canada.
— Chief executive officer compensation in Canada.
— Sales representative compensation in Canada.

Hay Management Consultants:
— Executive compensation in organizations that use the Hay job evaluation method.
— Management employee compensation.
— Compensation in health, education and government units, as well as in associations that use the Hay job evaluation method.

MLH + A Inc.:
— Executive compensation.

Peat, Marwick, Stevenson & Kellogg:
— Data-processing job compensation.
— Senior executive compensation.
— Sales and marketing personnel compensation.
— Frequency and cost of employee benefits in Canada.

Towers, Perrin, Forster & Crosby:
— Executive compensation.
— Employee benefit surveys.

Mercer
(William M. Mercer Limited)
— Senior executive compensation in Canada.
— Management and supervisory personnel compensation in Canada.
— Data-processing personnel compensation.
— Survey of salary increase forecasts for non-unionized employees.

Wyatt Company:
— Senior executive compensation in Canada.
— Clerical worker compensation.

SOURCE: Some of the above is taken from *Collective Bargaining Information Sources*, published by Labour Canada, Ottawa, 1988.

Relative Frequency of Survey Sources Used

Thériault (1986) notes that third-party surveys were the most commonly used source of information about market compensation. Over 80% of organizations made formal use of third-party surveys. These surveys came primarily from government agencies such as the Pay Research Bureau (33%), management consultants (25%), and public organizations such as the Canadian Manufacturers' Association (21%). Government agencies were used more as a source of information about administrative support, production, and maintenance personnel, whereas management consultants were used more for management employees, executives, and professionals. His study also found that almost 70% of organizations had their human resource department conduct compensation surveys. Organizational size appeared to have no effect on conducting in-house surveys. More than 20% of the organizations hired consulting firms to do their in-house surveys. This figure varied, however, with employee category. About 10% of organizations commissioned in-house surveys from consultants for administrative support staff. This figure rose to 30% for management and professionals, and to almost 40% for executives.

This data indicates that organizations often use more than one source of information for a compensation survey, and participate in many surveys. In some cases, it even appears that quantity is favoured at the expense of quality! Nonetheless, organizations seem to be increasingly concerned about the quality of the compensation surveys they use, and in which they agree to participate. In this regard, they now take a closer look at information about survey methodology and procedure.

Third-party Surveys

Third-party surveys have both advantages and disadvantages.

Their advantages include:

– they cost relatively little, virtually nothing in the case of government agencies;
– users have the assurance of a survey conducted with some degree of professionalism and impartiality;
– the data is analyzed and summarized for users; and
– the surveys cover a relatively vast population, which makes them likely to represent a better statistical sample.

Among the disadvantages of third-party surveys are:

– users have no control over the selection of jobs covered, and respondents are generally anonymous;
– apart from requesting special studies, users cannot weigh survey results based on the magnitude of the economic sector to which they belong;
– users have no control over the information that is collected; some may be irrelevant, and information considered important may be missing;

– the geographic scope of the survey may not be entirely relevant;
– the results may not be released at an opportune time; and
– the results are difficult to compare, because the respondents change from one survey to the next.

The last disadvantage applies especially to salary surveys conducted by non-government firms. In most instances, they do not use a sampling of all organizations, but instead rely on organizations' willingness to cooperate. In that case, since one has no control over the degree of representativeness of the data, the list of respondents must be annexed to the report so that users can ascertain the relevance of the results.

In-house Surveys

Organizations also conduct their own in-house surveys, or commission a consulting firm to conduct a survey on its behalf.

The advantages of in-house surveys include:

– the organization selects the key jobs;
– it does its own job matching;
– it has the option of selecting and determining survey participants; and
– it gains the assurance of a professionally and impartially conducted survey.

But they also have certain disadvantages:

– organizations do not necessarily have qualified researchers;
– the organization may run up against a lack of cooperation from certain participants because of the large number of surveys they face, or the confidential nature of some of the requested information;
– surveys are time-consuming; for instance, an experienced researcher could require a minimum of 30 days to survey 15 key jobs at 20 organizations in the same geographic sector; and
– the employees concerned may challenge the credibility of the survey results, because the organization is both referee and player.

Many of these disadvantages are eliminated, however, when the organization turns to a consulting firm.

7.2.5 Survey Procedure

The survey procedure is based on four major decisions: (1) What information will be collected? (2) What method will be used to collect the information?

(3) What statistics will be used to analyze the data? (4) What form will the results take?

What Information Will Be Collected?

The purpose of a compensation survey is to collect information about the compensation offered in the labour market, in order to establish salaries that represent fair market value. In practice, it is often a matter of the "going rate", which might lead one to believe there is only one rate of pay. But a salary survey produces a set of pay rates, for which one can determine "main trend" indices (such as average, mode, and median).

Moreover, pay is only one part of compensation. It is equally important to obtain information about the other components of compensation, such as employee benefits, perquisites, and working conditions. There is a big difference between earning $700 for 32 hours of work, with 13 paid holidays, a month of vacation, and a pension plan 75% paid by the employer, and earning $700 for 40 hours of work, with 9 paid holidays, 2 weeks of vacation, and no pension plan. The various components of compensation must be interpreted in a relative manner, since each has its own importance.

A case could also be made for the importance of information such as working environment, opportunities for promotion and training, living conditions in the community where the organization is located, etc. These factors come into play when someone compares their work situation with that of people holding similar jobs in the labour market. It is often difficult, in practice, to weigh these variables objectively. The chance to live within 25 kilometres of downhill skiing facilities may mean a great deal to one person, and be irrelevant to another. And how does one compare the value or importance of that, with the opportunity to go to a different movie theatre every week? This problem certainly does not make the question any less relevant. As we shall see in the following section, certain methods of collecting information produce a more complete and accurate picture of working conditions. In addition, Chapter 15, on the management of employee benefits, provides a glimpse of existing methods of determining total compensation.

Table 7.3 lists the usual information a compensation survey must gather. It indicates that data must be collected not only about specific pay conditions, but also about the participating organization, so that it can be situated in relation to other respondents. As well, one must find out about employee benefits and general working conditions for the job class covered by the survey.

Thériault's study (1986) found that the following percentages of in-house surveys, whether conducted by the organization or by outside consultants, collected information on the subjects listed: 66% on the average wage paid to holders of the jobs under study, 58% on minimum and maximum wages paid for the job, 67% on employee benefits, 34% on the criteria for pay adjustments within pay grades, 58% on pay grade minimums and maximums, 52% on organizational size, 63% on business sector, and 25% on profit-sharing plans. The nature of the information requested also appears to vary with the characteristics of the organization for which the study is being conducted. The larger the organization, the more it tends to collect information about pay grades and average wage paid. Furthermore, public and parapublic sector organizations have a stronger tendency than those in the private sector to seek information about pay grades.

Methods of Collecting Information

The required information may be collected formally or informally. The *informal approach* involves gathering approximate or partial data randomly, as

TABLE 7.3
Usual Information for a Compensation Survey

I.   General information on the organization

  1. Business sector
  2. Location
  3. Number of permanent and full-time employees
  4. Annual sales
  5. Percentage of unionized employees in each job class

II.   Information on pay

For each job, find out:

  1. Base pay: 1) hourly
               2) weekly
               3) annual

  2. Number of employees

  3. Pay scale: 1) minimum pay
              2) midpoint, control point, or normal maximum
              3) merit maximum pay

  4. Real wage: 1) minimum wage paid
              2) maximum wage paid
              3) weighted average of real pay

  5. Basis of pay increases: 1) merit or individual performance
                       2) seniority
                       3) cost of living
     If seniority is used as a basis for pay increases, how long does it take to go from scale minimum to maximum?

  6. Bonuses (% of pay): 1) target
                  2) maximum possible
                  3) paid.

III. Information on working conditions and employee benefits

1. Number of hours of work per week

2. Number of paid holidays

3. Special leave (length of time):   1) birth or adoption
    (Beyond legislated requirements)   2) death: i. immediate family
                                                        ii. other
                                             3) marriage: i. employee
                                                          ii. family member
                                             4) personal reasons
                                             5) other

4. Annual vacations: number of days and time required to qualify

5. Insurance and retirement:

	In force		Contribution	
Plan	Yes	No	Employer	Employee
1) pension				
2) group life insurance				
3) long-term disability				
4) short-term disability				
5) accident and health				
6) medication				
7) dental care				
8) other				

6. Overtime pay: 1) after a normal day
                   2) after a normal week
                   3) weekends
                   4) holidays

---

people are encountered, or as job offers appear in newspapers and periodicals. The resulting information may provide some indications about wages and salaries, but there is a strong possibility that will be inaccurate, because it is often incomplete. Consequently, a hasty implementation of the conclusions of such a survey may create more problems than it solves. It may give rise to a sense of unfairness and dissatisfaction, excessive labour costs, too-high employee turnover rate, etc. The *formal approach* entails collecting information by means of instruments such as a questionnaire, telephone, or personal interviews. The relevance of the conclusions drawn from these surveys depends on the quality of both the instrument and the analysis of the results. Regardless of which method is used to collect the required information, a minimum of 8 to 10 respondents are needed to obtain data that may be considered valid while respecting the confidential nature of the information collected by the survey.

Questionnaire

Questionnaires are without a doubt the most widely used method of collecting information (Henderson, 1989; Thériault, 1986). Most surveys conducted by public and private organizations, as well as consulting firms, use questionnaires. Compared to other methods of information-gathering, questionnaires make it possible to obtain compensation information from more organizations at a clearly lower cost. Obviously, this cost advantage depends very much on the overall approach: Is a letter or telephone call used to solicit respondents? Is a covering letter used to request relevant background information? Are closed rather than open-ended questions used? Are participants provided with the possibility of receiving a summary of the results?

A few precautions are necessary. First, it may be complicated to complete a compensation survey questionnaire, hence the importance of asking a reasonable number of precise, closed-ended questions. Secondly, a questionnaire readily lends itself to collecting information on compensation policies and practices, and planned pay increases, but less so to information on hiring rates, minimum-maximum differentials, and total compensation, because these items are liable to be interpreted differently. Also, questionnaires leave the problem of job matching up to the discretion of respondents, who have, to a greater or lesser degree, the skills, competence and motivation to do it properly, and who have varying amounts of time to spend on the survey. Finally, after receiving the questionnaires, it is worthwhile telephoning participants to confirm one's interpretation of the results.

Telephone Survey

The second method of collecting information, the telephone survey, is used primarily for production, maintenance, and administrative support personnel (Thériault, 1986). It is particularly effective when those conducting the survey and the respondents already know each other, and when the survey involves a small number of readily identifiable jobs. Otherwise, this method may prove very tedious.

Personal Interview

The third method of collecting information is the personal interview. Thériault's study (1986) found it used for 36% of in-house surveys conducted by organizations or consulting firms. According to the U.S. Bureau of Labor Statistics — one of the organizations with the most experience conducting compensation surveys — "There is no real substitute for trained interviewers possessing good job descriptions if accurate, complete, comparable information is to be obtained." (Douty and Kanninen, 1949; quoted by Nash and Carroll, 1975, p. 85). This method allows the interviewer to control the degree of job comparability in a relatively uniform manner, to obtain clarification of information, and to control the information received from respondents by eliminating semantic problems. It also provides a better indication of total compensation and working conditions. Finally, when this method is used on an ongoing or annual basis, its costs may be reduced by alternating it with telephone calls or questionnaires. Furthermore, if participants are given an opportunity to prepare for the interview properly, this considerably reduces the time involved, because the information obtained need simply be confirmed.

Analyzing the Information

Once the information has been collected, indices for summarizing it must be identified and established, so that the data may be properly interpreted, and valid conclusions drawn. The two types of indices commonly used are "main trend" (such as average, median, and mode), and distribution (such as quartile and decile).

Average

Survey results may be *averaged* simply by adding the figures provided by each respondent and dividing them by the number of participating organizations. Other indices, such as *weighted averages*, may also be calculated (cf. Table 7.4). Weighted averages are determined by taking into account the number of times each pay rate is found. They are therefore much more indicative of the status of market supply and demand than simple averages. One may also calculate *adjusted weighted averages* by eliminating the extremes of a distribution, given their questionable nature (cf. Table 7.4). Extreme figures may, in fact, indicate suspect job matching rather than real pay differentials. The decision to include or exclude the extremes of a distribution must nonetheless be based on the nature of the job in question. A *difference of over 50% between the pay rates collected for the same production and maintenance job may be the result of dubious job matching.* A difference of that magnitude is not uncommon for a management job, however, and while it may point to a problem with the job matching, it may also indicate real pay differences. Finally, one may calculate an adjusted weighted average and diminish the effect of a particular organization by subtracting its employee count from the total number of employees of all participating organizations. This adjustment may be worthwhile when one of the respondents pays a slightly higher, or slightly lower, salary for a particular job, and has a larger number of employees. Such is the case with Company F in Table 7.4; it has many more employees than the others, and pays more.

As the Table 7.4 illustrates, these various calculations do not yield the same results. Whereas the average salary is $586.67, the weighted average is $623.76. When Company F is excluded, based on the assumption that the job is not similar, the adjusted weighted average becomes $576.24. Finally, the average may be further adjusted to $606.60, by reducing the number

TABLE 7.4
Compensation Survey Statistics: Main Trend Indices for Job Y

Company	Real average salary	No. of employees	Total salaries
A	450	15	6,750
B	500	7	3,500
C	520	3	1,560
D	625	6	3,750
E	700	20	14,000
F	750	32	24,000
G	565	16	9,040
H	660	8	5,280
I	510	10	5,100
TOTAL	5,280	117	72,980

Average: $\dfrac{\$5,280}{9} = \$586.67$

Weighted average: $\dfrac{\$72,980}{117} = \$623.76$

Adjusted weighted average (excluding Company F data):
1. Total real salaries   : $\$72,980 - \$24,000 = \$48,980$
2. Number of employees   : $117 -$ $32 =$ 85
3. Adjusted weighted average: $\dfrac{\$48,980}{85} = \$576.24$

Adjusted weighted average (reducing the effect of Company F)
1. Number of employees per company: $\dfrac{117}{9} = 13$
2. Relative surplus of employees in Company F: $32 - 13 = 19$
3. Reduction of the effect of the number of employees in Company F (arbitrary reduction factor of 75% of the relative employee surplus):
   $75\% \times 19 = 14$
4. New number of employees used for Company F:
   $32 - 14 = 18$
5. Calculation of the new adjusted weighted average:
   New total salaries: $62,480
   New total number of employees: 103
   New adjusted weighted average: $\dfrac{\$62,480}{103} = \$606.60 \ \$$

of employees in Company F by a part of the amount by which its employee count exceeds the average for all participants.

Other Statistics

Two other main trend indices may be measured: the median and the mode. In a distribution of salaries, the median represents the midpoint above and

TABLE 7.5
Compensation Survey Statistics Distribution Indices for Job XYZ

Company	Number of incumbents	Individual salary	Decreasing order of salaries
A	2	22,000	5
		24,100	2
B	3	20,000	9
		19,000	12
		18,800	13
C	1	25,500	1
D	2	19,800	10
		20,200	8
E	1	18,000	15
F	1	18,500	14
G	2	21,000	6
		20,400	7
H	1	23,900	3
I	1	23,800	4
J	1	19,100	11
Total	15	314,100	

Presentation of results
Job XYZ

	Number of participants	Number of incumbents	Q1	Median	Q3
Salary	10	15	19,000	20,200	23,800

below which 50% of the salaries are located. The mode represents the figure appearing most frequently in a distribution.

Other statistics related to salary distribution are also used: deciles and quartiles. In a set of data arranged in decreasing order, the first decile is the point above which 90%, and below which 10%, of the figures are located. The ninth decile is the opposite; 10% of the salaries lie above it and 90% below it. The concept of quartile is similar. The first quartile (Q1 or P25), in a distribution arranged in decreasing order, is the point above which 75%, and below which 25%, of the figures lie, while the third quartile (Q3 or P75) is the opposite (cf. Table 7.5). The salary distribution obtained from the survey may also be analyzed by calculating the averages of both minimum and maximum salaries. The same applies to minimum and maximum salary ratios. The former is the highest minimum salary divided by the lowest, and the latter the highest maximum divided by the lowest. These ratios may indicate a problem with the job matching in the survey. For example, a ratio higher than 2 for production and maintenance jobs indicates questionable matching, meaning that some of the data may refer to different jobs.

In concluding, we might note that organizations have many other methods of analyzing market data. One study of 24 organizations found them using over 100 methods of analyzing compensation survey results (Belcher, Ferris and O'Neill, 1985). For instance, it is relatively common for organizations to adjust the market data for time. Data collected on April 1st and analyzed on November 1st is often adjusted to reflect increases in the Consumer Price Index during that period. Some organizations whose figures are included in the market data will want them excluded. Others may adjust the calculations by removing extreme figures, or any that diverge sharply from the resulting profile. Finally, some might wish to compare themselves to companies whose employees are unionized, or in other cases, non-unionized.

Presenting the Results

Presentation of the survey results is limited above all by the specificity and quantity of the information gathered. For example, if the survey only collects scale minimums and maximums, adjusted weighted average pay cannot be calculated, and the status of market supply and demand for the job cannot be determined accurately. This makes it necessary to collect precise and complete information during the survey. Data presentation also depends on the scope of the survey. The more respondents there are, the more important summarizing the results becomes – and the more arduous, owing to the greater quantity of information.

In practice, compensation survey results may be presented in any of the following forms: (a) reproduction of the information collected from each respondent; (b) statistics representative of the complete data; or, (c) distribution of the statistics by means of linear or multiple regression analyses.

Table 7.6 illustrates reproduction of the data collected from each respondent. To protect the confidential nature of the information, each participant is assigned a code, which may change from one job to the next. The main advantage of this approach is that it provides precise information about each participant. It is especially used for surveys with a limited number of respondents (e.g. less than 30). In the case of a regional survey, however, it may be relatively easy to identify an employer based on the number of employees; an example is employer No. 234 in Table 7.6.

Table 7.7 illustrates survey results presented by means of a statistical description of all the data collected. This format is useful for summarizing data from a large number of respondents.

TABLE 7.6
Salary data: presentation of information for each participant

Job No. 422: Senior bookkeeper
Number of organizations: 18
Number of employees: 209
Unionized: 20%   Non-unionized: 80%

Org. code	No. of employees	Salary scales			Salaries		
		Mid-Minima	Points	Maxima	Minima	Avgs.	Maxima
249	25	25,641	32,427	42,950	25,641	26,267	30,944
212	4	25,244	28,564	33,157	25,244	26,204	26,538
250	23				18,186	25,662	31,216
220	12	21,486	28,856	34,640	24,367	25,369	26,434
206	3	22,279	27,833	33,408	22,279	25,160	28,439
234	44	23,072	27,687	32,322	22,279	25,077	30,547
226	26	21,381	25,662	29,942	21,381	25,077	29,086
204	3	23,323	27,499	31,675	23,135	24,889	26,100
236	7	22,175	30,318	38,461	22,028	24,638	28,188
251	6				19,001	23,553	27,290
214	1	21,673	24,910	28,146	23,469	23,469	23,469
216	12	21,089	26,392	31,633	21,360	22,759	24,972
231	15	19,335	25,390	31,445	19,335	22,717	28,710
225	5	19,210	23,699	28,188	19,210	22,216	25,160
254	3	22,049	26,455	30,882	22,049	22,049	22,049
252	20	19,377	22,383	25,390	18,813	21,151	23,344
230	0	23,239	27,875	32,510			
221	0	21,402	25,745	30,109			
Average		21,998	26,981	32,179	21,736	24,141	27,030
Weighted average		22,097	27,238	32,822	21,539	24,464	28,481

Finally, Figure 7.2 illustrates the presentation of compensation data based on the results of a linear regression analysis. Unlike the preceding approach, which gives no indication of the salaries paid in organization with gross revenues of about $200 million (data was obtained for the $100-499 million group), a linear regression can estimate salaries on the basis of the organization's precise revenue.

7.2.6 Interpreting the Results

The value of a compensation survey essentially depends on three factors: the person requesting the information, the person providing it, and how the

TABLE 7.7
Salary data: presentation of information by means of descriptive statistics

POSITION CODE: 501	POSITION TITLE: HUMAN RESOURCE MANAGER

SUMMARY ANALYSIS BY ACTIVITY SECTOR

Type of Industry	Number of organizations	Number of incumbents	Base salary				Average bonus	Average total compensation	Average bonus target percent	Percent eligible for bonus	Average bonus as percent of salary	Number of firms reporting range	Average: mid point/job rate
			25th Percentile	50th Percentile	Average	75th Percentile							
Manufacturing non-durable goods	33	33	60.0	75.0	78.8	92.0	14.0	88.1	20.7	87.9	16.7	26	79.0
Manufacturing durable goods	29	29	62.1	76.0	81.2	93.5	17.9	92.9	21.6	82.8	20.3	21	83.5
Transport, communic. and utilities	12	12	90.4	106.4	105.3	117.5	13.7	114.5	20.6	75.0	12.7	9	111.9
Natural resources	4	5	72.4	72.4	81.6	95.0	4.5	82.5	7.0	20.0	7.1	3	98.5
Wholesale/retail	9	9	85.0	100.0	93.3	103.5	27.9	115.0	34.8	88.9	27.8	4	91.0
Finance, bank and trust	11	13	61.5	70.5	79.1	78.2	15.4	88.6	14.7	69.2	18.7	8	94.9
Insurance	16	16	73.0	81.5	82.6	93.3	13.8	86.9	30.5	50.0	14.8	12	77.7
Public service	24	24	59.6	76.6	76.2	92.0	10.5	77.1	15.0	29.2	9.7	19	75.9
Services	16	16	51.5	63.4	68.4	82.5	10.3	72.9	5.0	50.0	14.5	7	55.0

SUMMARY ANALYSIS ACCORDING BY GROSS SALES/GROSS REVENUE

Range	Scope ($million)	Firm count	Incumbent count	Base salary				Average bonus	Average total compensation	Average bonus target percent	Percent eligible for bonus	Average bonus as percent of salary	Number of firms reporting range	Average: mid point/job rate
				25th Percentile	50th Percentile	Average	75th Percentile							
Under $50 million	18.6	10	10	50.0	61.9	63.8	66.0	10.2	70.9	15.0	80.0	14.5	6	68.5
$50 to $99 million	71.4	29	29	58.5	65.1	67.2	74.1	11.8	73.7	19.3	86.2	16.6	20	67.4
$100 to $499 million	245.9	40	40	74.9	90.0	88.9	104.3	15.2	99.9	22.1	80.0	16.7	26	89.3
$500 ro $999 million	582.3	7	7	102.0	105.6	114.3	135.0	31.5	132.2	24.0	57.1	25.7	5	115.3
$1 billion and over	2 677.7	11	12	85.2	106.0	109.0	130.0	27.7	127.4	31.7	75.0	23.6	8	119.5

			Base salary				Average bonus	Average total compen- sation	Average bonus target percent	Percent eligible for bonus	Average bonus as percent of salary	Number of firms reporting range	Average: mid point/job rate
SUMMARY ANALYSIS ACCORDING TO REGION													
Region	Firm count	Incum- bent count	25th Per- centile	50th Per- centile	Average	75th Per- centile							
Atlantic Region	5	5	62.1	68.7	77.3	91.7	12.5	82.3	25	60.0	20.7	4	77.8
Montreal Region	49	51	61.2	76.8	80.5	92.21	6.3	98.81	16	72.5	18.3	34	80.9
Elsewhere – Quebec	23	23	50.0	62.7	66.4	80.0	10.7	69.2	16	47.8	14.9	13	67.9
Ontario	11	11	61.5	91.2	85.1	105.9	3.9	86.5	15	63.6	4.8	9	87.1
Toronto Region	43	43	72.1	83.0	88.9	110.0	18.7	100.2	28	76.7	19.8	30	89.2
Elsewhere – Ontario	7	7	63.0	69.7	81.3	105.3	16.1	88.2	20	42.9	18.2	7	76.0
Manitoba – Saskatchewan	5	6	72.4	76.0	79.1	92.8	0.9	79.3		33.3	1.6	5	86.7
Alberta	6	6	66.0	79.3	82.3	88.6	16.8	90.7	22	66.7	18.9	3	84.5
British Columbia	5	5	68.2	77.0	84.7	107.2	15.5	90.9	20	60.0	14.3	4	92.2

SOURCE: Mercer (1990).

results are analyzed. In the case of analysis, this means knowing if pay, employee benefits, and bonuses are included, or if these three components of compensation are analyzed separately. If the latter, it would be misleading to draw conclusions based on only one component. An organization may, in fact, pay less than the market, but offer superior employee benefits, or vice versa.

To take into account differing lengths of work week from one organization to the next, some compensation surveys standardize the base pay period by converting it into hours. Generally speaking, this practice is incorrect. Employees paid on a weekly or annual basis think of their salary in those terms; they do not convert it into an hourly wage. In other words, when asked how much they earn, they respond with the normal frame of reference, and do not reply with an hourly wage if they are paid on a monthly or annual basis. During collective agreement negotiations, it is plain that a union representing employees who work 37.5 hours per week stands to gain from converting weekly or annual salaries into an hourly wage, if the normal work week in the market for comparable jobs is 35 hours. From a cost perspective, it would be more appropriate to collect information about "pay for time worked". Besides taking into account the number of hours worked per week, this concept also encompasses all the factors that affect the hourly cost of labour, such as vacations, statutory holidays, etc.

FIGURE 7.2
TOTAL COMPENSATION: PRESENTATION OF INFORMATION THROUGH THE RESULTS OF A
STATISTICAL LINEAR REGRESSION ANALYSIS

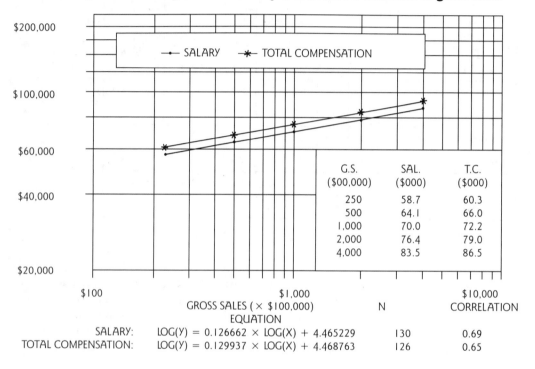

HUMAN RESOURCES MANAGER
Linear regression: salary and total compensation as a function of gross sales

G.S. ($00,000)	SAL. ($000)	T.C. ($000)
250	58.7	60.3
500	64.1	66.0
1,000	70.0	72.2
2,000	76.4	79.0
4,000	83.5	86.5

	EQUATION	N	CORRELATION
SALARY:	$LOG(Y) = 0.126662 \times LOG(X) + 4.465229$	130	0.69
TOTAL COMPENSATION:	$LOG(Y) = 0.129937 \times LOG(X) + 4.468763$	126	0.65

Furthermore, in interpreting survey results, some people stress the value of the average, while others emphasize the median. As Greene (1981) states, both have their advantages. The average may be used to calculate changes from one year to the next. It is statistically superior to the median with a small sample to which a regression analysis will be applied. On the other hand, the median truly represents the typical case around the middle of a distribution, and is much less influenced by extreme values. As Greene also points out, the average, median, and mode rarely correspond to a single value, because the distribution pattern for salaries in a labour market is not normal, but rather non-parametric. Hence, the average is often slightly higher (3% to 5%) than the median. So, if an organization wishing to pay salaries equal to what "typical employees" on the market earn for the same job uses the average, it risks paying more than it really intends.

As already stated, the interpretation of compensation survey data must also consider the participating organizations. The changes within an organization or in the number of positions they have from one survey to the next modifies the results and conclusions from year to year.

Finally, in view of these limitations, Greene (1978) asks how one might react to a market survey for a product that concludes, "Assuming that $635,000 is spent on newspaper advertising, that consumer confidence remains stable, that economic forecasts calling for a 3% to 4% increase in consumer purchasing power are accurate, and that the winter is not too harsh, we predict an 11.381% increase in market share." Precision may be the hallmark of a good technician, but in this case, its value is for the professional to judge!

☐ 7.3 Employee Participation

As mentioned at the beginning of this chapter, the purpose of a compensation survey is to ensure external equity, in order to achieve employee satisfaction, obtain good performance, minimize involuntary employee turnover, recruit competent personnel – and all at the lowest cost possible. In practice, compensation surveys are conducted at the request of the management of an organization, and on the basis of their own points of reference (i.e. organizations relevant from their point of view). The employees' external points of reference may very well differ, however, from those of management. In such a case, the results may not be accepted by employees, and the data may be considered useless. People react on the basis of what they perceive! In this context, there are two alternatives: replace the employees' points of reference with those of the organization, or have the employees concerned participate in the compensation survey.

Convincing employees of the relevance of the organization's points of reference may be a relatively long, complex process. On the other hand, the reasons for involving the employees concerned in developing a compensation survey and analyzing its results are essentially the same as those for including them on job evaluation committees. In theory, all those concerned (or their representatives) should be involved: greater employee participation in determining the organizations used as reference, and in analyzing the data, can help improve their understanding of survey results. To our knowledge, however, no research has ever established the validity of this statement.

☐ 7.4 The Limitations of Compensation Surveys

Compensation surveys are essential tools for compensation planning within the organization. They are used, accordingly, in making compensation decisions that shape the future. The surveys, however, essentially produce retrospective data, i.e. about the past. In a rapidly changing world, organizations must ensure the validity of the results. Some organizations even conduct more than one survey a year for certain jobs. The retrospective nature of survey data may help perpetuate some forms of discrimination in the market, because the surveys indicate what is paid, but not why. This explains why the various agencies responsible for enforcing pay equity legislation have reservations about market surveys (cf. Chapter 9).

Given these limitations of compensation surveys, Alexander's comments (1978) on how to view such surveys are well worth repeating:

1. **Do not have blind faith in compensation surveys.** After analyzing the salary data from a compensation survey and doing a few calculations, a technician will say, "We are 4.23% below the market. Not 4%, nor 5%, but 4.23%." Technicians rarely know what they are analyzing, ask few questions about the survey, and tend to give an exaggerated degree of precision. On the other hand, a compensation survey professional must ask questions: Of what value is the survey? Which organizations participated? To what extent have the various components of compensation been taken into consideration? What statistical techniques were used? How valid are the results? And so on.

2. **Do not attach too much importance to compensation surveys.** Compensation surveys are all too often perceived as the keystone of compensation management. They contain numbers, which we have come to trust. A 7 is a 7, and not a 6 or an 8. Compensation surveys, however, simply provide a frame of reference and nothing more. They must not be peered at so closely that the trees prevent us from seeing the forest! In fact, compensation surveys are merely a summary of certain factors, including pay levels, trends, and practices. They provide no indication of how organizations respond to specific internal needs, objectives, or policies. Nor do they reveal how compensation is related to financial and operational planning and to business development efforts. In practice, a multitude of factors involved in determining pay are not covered by survey results: for example, seniority with the organization and in the job, time since the last pay increase, trends compared to the external market, changes in the Consumer Price Index, the relative level of salaries, salary levels within minimum and maximum scales, individual and organizational performance, etc.

3. **Avoid bias in analyzing compensation surveys.** If numerous surveys yield different results, should one only use those that confirm the position one wants to uphold? The purpose of compensation surveys is not to collect information solely from a particular group of employers (e.g. those with a reputation for paying more, or less,

than the market, or of paying at a certain level, etc.). Rather, they try to provide indications of the *general* status of compensation for specific jobs in competing organizations.

☐ 7.5 Unfair Trade Practices Legislation

In the early 80s, a number of organizations in the United States expressed fears about compensation surveys, because of unfair trade practices legislation. Fisher's review (1985) of U.S. Supreme Court rulings in unfair trade practice cases reveals the following. First, surveys and exchanges of information about compensation do not in themselves violate American unfair practice legislation (Sherman Act, Clayton Act). Secondly, the Court has ruled that the law was broken every time participants used information taken from compensation surveys to push prices (upward or downward) artificially. Thirdly, when the entire exchange of information resulted in a price change, participants were found guilty of price-fixing, even in the absence of an explicit agreement.

In the United States, there have only been two cases of prosecution for unfair trade practices in compensation surveys: *Goodspeed vs. Federated Employers of The Bay Area* in 1976, and *Boston Survey Group* in 1982. In the former, Women Organized for Employment (WOE) charged that the employer association in question was using a salary survey of its 350 members to keep clerical workers' pay low. Fisher (1985) notes that this case was settled out of court. The 1982 case also involved a charge that some 40 employers belonging to the Boston Survey Group were using the results of their survey to keep women's salaries low. The survey report used by the Boston association presented individual salaries for each participant, as well as results by industry. In this case, there was no friendly settlement, but the Boston Survey Group complied with the Attorney General's order to the effect that henceforth there would be (1) no identification of results by participant; (2) no individual information, but only aggregate results; (3) no information published for less than 10 observations; (4) no information published by industry; and (5) no information on salary forecasts. As Carmell (1987) points out, the content of this order is interesting, but still not a real court decision. We have yet to learn what the courts think of it.

Canadian unfair trade practices legislation (the Competition Act, which replaced the Combines Investigation Act) allows an exchange of compensation statistics, unless its purpose is to influence prices and reduce competition. To date, no charge involving compensation surveys has been filed in court. Actually, compensation surveys are not very likely to give rise to charges of unfair trade practices. Collusion based on compensation surveys is rather improbable, given the diversity of markets, the numerous uses made of the surveys, and the various methods of analyzing the results.

☐ 7.6 Summary

Compensation surveys provide indications to help the organization ensure that its compensation is competitive relative to the market. Many people think that obtaining useful, precise information about the market is not difficult. This chapter has shown that the opposite is true. As with job evaluation, there are no objective answers to the question of what the market pays. Important decisions about the scope of the survey, the method and sources used, as well as the general nature or thrust of the survey, will all influence the results. This chapter emphasized the fact that the quality and the nature of the information obtained is always a major limitation on analysis and interpretation. In summary, compensation surveys simply present a frame of reference that provides data about the market. The figures they contain have value only to the extent that the market surveyed is relevant, the jobs are carefully matched, the methodology is correct, and the results are properly analyzed and interpreted.

REFERENCES

ALEXANDER, C.E., "Problems of Information Exchange and How to Use Salary Results", *National Conference Proceedings 1978*, Scottsdale, Arizona, American Compensation Association, 1978.

BELCHER, D., *Compensation Administration*, Englewood Cliffs, New Jersey, Prentice-Hall, 1974.

BELCHER, D.W., M.B. FERRIS and J. O'NEILL, "How Wage Surveys are being used", *Compensation and Benefits Review*, 1985, pp. 34-51.

CARMELL, W.A., "Compensation Strategies for Avoiding Liability Under Fair Employment Laws", *Topics in Total Compensation*, 1987, vol. 2, N° 2, pp. 197-206.

DOUTY, H.M. and T.P. KANNINEN, "Community Approach to Wage Studies", *Monthly Labor Review*, 1949, vol. 71, pp. 365-370.

FAY, C.H., "External Pay Relationships", in *Compensation and Benefits*, edited by L.R. Gomez-Mejia, Washington, D.C., The Bureau on National Affairs, 1989, pp. 70-100.

FISHER, G.D., "Salary Surveys - An Antitrust Perspective", *Personnel Administrator*, 1985, vol. 30, N° 4, pp. 87 and ff.

FOSTER, K.E., "Measuring Overlooked Factors in Relative Job Worth", *Compensation Review*, 1983, vol. 15, N° 1, pp. 44-55.

GREENE, R.J., "Problems of Information Exchange and How to Use Salary Results", *National Conference of Proceedings 1978*, Scottsdale, Arizona, American Compensation Association, 1978.

GREENE, R.J., "What Does Median Mean?", *Personnel Administrator*, 1981, vol. 26, N° 5, pp. 40-44.

HENDERSON, R.I., *Compensation Management: Rewarding Performance*, Reston, Virginia, Reston Publishing Co., 1989.

MAHONEY, T., S. RYNES and B. ROSEN, Where do Compensation Specialists Stand on Comparable Worth?", *Compensation Review*, 1984, vol. 16, N° 4, pp. 27-40.

MERCER (William M. Mercer Limited), "Mercer Survey Shows Emphasis on Compensation Linked to Results, *The Mercer Bulletin*, 1985, vol. 35, N° 10.

MERCER (William M. Mercer Limited), *1990 Executive Benchmark Compensation Report*, Toronto, 1990.

NASH, A. and S.J. CARROLL, *The Management of Compensation*, Monterey, California, Brooks/Cole Publishing Co., 1975.

RYNES, S.L., D.P. SCHWAB and H.G. HENEMAN, "The Role of Pay and Market Pay Variability in Job Application Decisions", *Organizational Behavior and Human Performance*, 1983, vol. 31, pp. 353-364.

THÉRIAULT, R., *Politiques et pratiques en matière de rémunération globale dans les entreprises au Québec*, Montreal, Les Productions INFORT inc., 1986.

Labour Canada, *Collective Bargaining Information Sources*, Ottawa, Labour Canada, 1979, and updates.

WEINBERGER, T.E., "A Way to Audit the Job Matches of Salary Survey Participants", *Compensation Review*, 1984, vol. 16, N° 3, pp. 47-58.

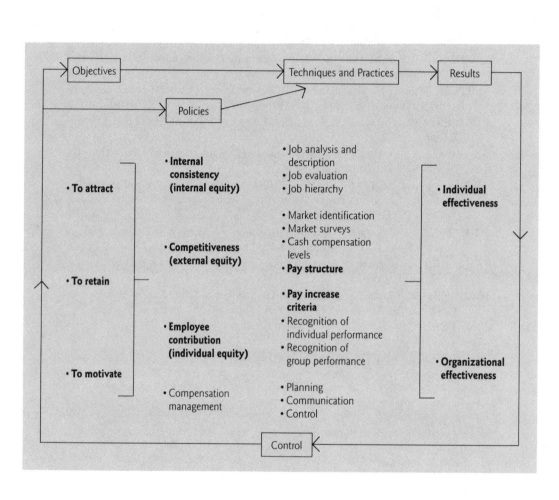

IV

PAY STRUCTURE, INDIVIDUAL PAY AND PAY DISCRIMINATION

After constructing a job hierarchy based on requirements (internal equity), identifying an appropriate labour market, collecting the necessary information from organizations in this market, and determining the desired degree of competitiveness (external equity), an organization is ready to establish its pay structure. Chapter 8 looks at this phase. After providing pertinent information about relative job requirements and market salary data, this chapter discusses how many pay structures an organization should establish, then describes ways of developing these structures and how pay functions within the different types of pay structures. Finally, Chapter 8 addresses the question of how to integrate individual pay into pay structures.

Chapter 9 focuses on pay discrimination within organizations. Its existence is an established fact, but what is its impact on the pay differentials between men and women in the labour market? The first part of Chapter 9 examines this point, the second details Canadian legislation on pay discrimination and the consequences of this legislation for employers.

TABLE OF CONTENTS

8

PAY STRUCTURE AND INDIVIDUAL PAY

Determining an organization's pay structure requires integration of three principal compensation policies: (1) internal equity, considering relative job requirements; (2) external equity, determining the degree of competitiveness desired, and (3) individual equity, considering individual factors, such as performance and length of service.

Establishing such a structure and determining individual pay may be depicted as a decision-making process, the various stages of which are listed in Figure 8.1.

☐ 8.1 Integrating Internal and External Equity

8.1.1 Graphic Representation of Job Evaluation Results

A logical way to establish a (new) pay structure is to begin by making a graphic representation of job evaluation results and the pay currently attached to those jobs. Exhibit 8.1 provides an example of such a representation. The y-axis depicts the various pay levels, the x-axis, job requirements – in this instance, expressed by the number of evaluation points allotted to each job.

8.1.2 Plotting an Organization's Pay Line

The preceding step resulted in a graph of the pay distribution for various jobs within an organization, on the basis of their requirements. A pay line is frequently used to better visualize this relationship. It shows how pay and job evaluation result coordinates are distributed. It may be either a straight line or a curve.

FIGURE 8.1
Steps in Establishing a Pay Structure

I.   Integrating internal and external equity
                 (pay lines of the organization and its market)
                                    ↓
2.   Selecting one or more pay structures
                                    ↓
3.   Determining job grades
                                    ↓
4.   Pay policy relative to the market
                                    ↓
5.   Selecting criteria for determining individual pay
                 (individual equity)
                                    ↓
6.   Determining pay ranges and intergrade differentials
                                    ↓
7.   Determining procedure within pay ranges
                                    ↓
8.   Determining individual pay and adjusting pay rates
                                    ↓
9.   Relationships between various pay structures

Plotted as a Straight Line

There are three ways to plot a pay line as a straight line. Exhibit 8.2 shows two ways for the data in Exhibit 8.1. The first involves linking the lowest to the highest pay with a straight line. This assumes that the lowest and highest pay levels are correct (or more correct than the others). Since this is not necessarily the case, this technique is rarely used. The second way of plotting a pay line is to draw, freehand, the straight line that best represents the distribution of pay and job evaluation result coordinates. The third involves using the statistical method of "least squares" to plot the straight line that best represents the distribution of the graph's coordinates. This method is the most accurate, since the points on the pay line are determined by means of the statistical equation $y = a + bx$, in which:

y = present pay,
x = number of job evaluation points allotted,
a = point where the straight line crosses the y-axis, and
b = slope of the line.

EXHIBIT 8.1
Graphic Representation of Job Evaluation Results

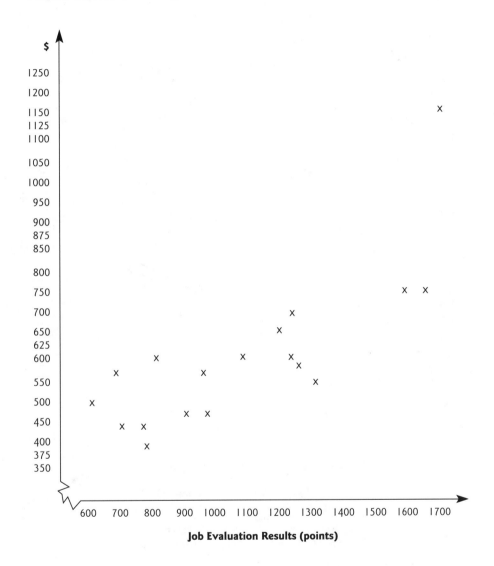

Job Evaluation Results (points)

The decision as to whether to use the least-square or freehand method depends on the degree of precision required and on the target population. While the former method is more precise, in most cases, in the past, a freehand line sufficed. However, in this age of personal computers and software, statistics are more commonly used. Furthermore, the degree of precision one obtains from using such statistics is highly desirable.

EXHIBIT 8.2
Pay Lines

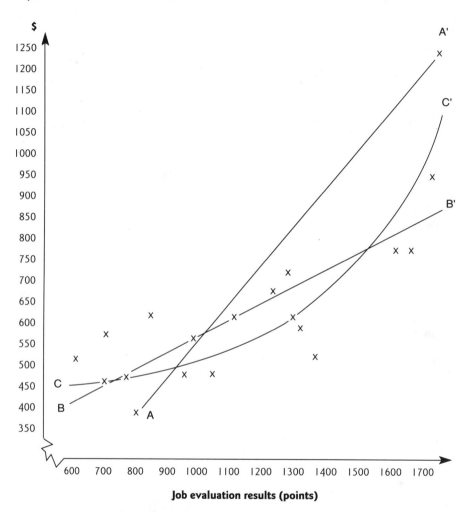

A-A': Straight line connecting the lowest with the highest pay.
B-B': Freehand straight line representing the distribution of coordinates.
C-C': Freehand curve representing the distribution of coordinates.

Drawn as a Curve

Although the term "pay line" has been used since the beginning of this section, it has, to this point, referred to a straight line, which in some cases may be the most accurate representation of pay distribution. Most of the time, however, the distribution is more accurately represented by a curve with an increasing rather than a constant slope. This indicates that pay differentials between jobs increase, because fewer individuals are ready to assume, or are capable of holding, the more and more demanding jobs within the organization. As with a straight line, a pay curve may be drawn freehand or statistically. The statistical equation for the least-square method is then $y = a + bx + cx^2$, in which c represents the degree of deviation from a straight line. A positive value indicates an ascending curve (the usual case), whereas a negative value indicates a descending curve. Plotting pay distribution by curve or straight line may be compared in Exhibit 8.2, which reveals that a curve provides a more accurate picture.

8.1.3 Comparison with the Market Pay Line

This step involves drawing a graph to depict the results of the salary portion of the compensation survey, so that the organization's pay distribution may be compared with that of the market. The market pay line may be plotted using the weighted averages of the actual pay on the market. Other indications may be obtained from market data, for example, pay lines to represent the band within which the various market salaries for equivalent jobs are located. For example, the minimum line might consist of the salaries in the 25th percentile for the various jobs, and the maximum, those in the 75th.

Exhibit 8.3 is an illustration of such a pay distribution comparison. The points marked "x" represent what the organization actually pays, and those marked "o" what the market pays.

The market pay line in this exhibit does not have the same slope as that of the organization; it is less steep. Note too that the market pays more for the jobs with lower requirements and less for those with higher requirements.

☐ 8.2 Choice of Pay Structures

The concept of "job cluster" (a group of jobs, similar and comparable) has already been discussed in Chapters 4 and 5 on job evaluation, as well as in Chapter 7 on compensation surveys. Drawing a graph of pay and job evaluation results makes it possible to determine whether one or more pay structures are needed, based on the number of job clusters identified. The point distribution in the graph provides an indication of the number of job clusters. If there is only one job cluster, the points may be connected by a straight line; if the jobs do not belong to the same cluster, a curve is more appropriate. Exhibit 8.3, for example, reveals that the jobs scoring over 1,400 evaluation points belong to a second cluster. The distribution of both

EXHIBIT 8.3
Comparison of Organizational and Market Pay Lines

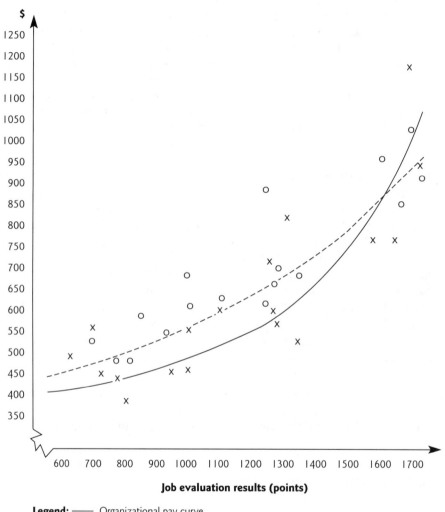

Job evaluation results (points)

Legend: —— Organizational pay curve
------ Market pay curve

organizational and market pay for those jobs lies along a different line than the pay for the others. This explains why a curve, rather than a straight line, was needed to better represent overall pay distribution. In fact, two straight lines with different slopes might have been used instead. The first would have covered the jobs in the 600 to 1,400 point range, and the second, those that scored over 1,400 points in evaluation.

Whether to adopt a simple or a multiple pay structure is an important question, given the varying nature of the jobs and economic factors (cf. Chapter 6), which may differ from one job cluster to the next. It has been common practice to establish as many pay structures as there are job clusters. Nowadays, however, there is a clear tendency to limit the number of different pay structures so as to reduce potential systemic discrimination. Furthermore, in a pay equity context, all female-dominated jobs and their comparable male-dominated ones ought to be within the same pay structure (cf. Chapter 9).

8.3 Determining Job Grades

At this point in establishing a pay structure, the organization must decide whether pay differentials will be based on individual jobs or on job grades. The usual practice is to create job grades (also called "pay grades"), i.e. groups of jobs with similar or equivalent requirements that are paid the same.

8.3.1 Why Group Jobs by Grade?

There are three principal reasons for organizing jobs into grades. First, job evaluation, however logical, remains essentially subjective. One weakness of quantitative job evaluation methods (such as the point system) is their "false" scientific character. The point distribution resulting from job evaluation is the product of a set of subjective decisions and, therefore, more or less accurate. Since job evaluation is neither an exact science nor a completely random process, the quality of its results lies somewhere between these two extremes. Thus, the limited accuracy of job evaluation must be considered in establishing the pay structure. This means determining which jobs have similar or equivalent requirements, despite different point scores. In other words, the various job grades within the overall pay structure must be identified.

A second reason for establishing job grades is to facilitate the administration of the pay structure. Classifying jobs limits the number of decisions that must be made to the number of grades, rather than separate decisions having to be made for each individual job.

Finally, the use of job grades makes it easier to communicate and justify a pay structure. It would otherwise be difficult to justify pay differentials between jobs with similar, but not equal, evaluation scores; such jobs would likely be perceived as having equal requirements and consequently meriting equal pay.

8.3.2 How Many Job Grades?

While there is no set rule for determining the number of job grades, various criteria may be established. First, the number of grades depends on the number of jobs concerned. The more jobs there are, the more grades there may be. Secondly, the number of grades depends on variations in job requirements. The more requirements vary, the more grades there tend to be. Hence, the fewer pay structures an organization establishes, the more they tend to encompass different job clusters and the more grades are likely to result. Thirdly, the number of grades depends on the difference between the highest and lowest pay. The greater the difference, the more grades there may be. Finally, the number of grades depends on organizational policies on pay increases and promotions. A large number of grades is needed when an organization chooses to pay all holders of equivalent jobs at the same rate; then only a promotion will lead to a pay increase. On the other hand, if an organization chooses to vary the pay for equivalent jobs, a smaller number of grades may be used, because pay increases may be obtained without changing jobs. Pay, in this case, is primarily a function of seniority or performance.

Belcher and Atchison (1987) reported that a pay structure may contain anywhere from 4 to 60 job grades. Most have 8 to 15. Henderson (1989, pp. 282-5) provides a mathematical table for determining the required number of grades, based on the ratio of the highest to the lowest pay, as well as on the percentage pay differential between each grade. In practice, however, few organizations use such a table to determine the number of job grades within a pay structure.

The fewer the job grades, the larger pay differentials will be between them; conversely, the greater the number of grades, the smaller the pay differentials. Finally, it should be noted that the trend in recent years has been to reduce the number of grades within pay structures, thereby enabling organizations to deal with the problem of pay compressions resulting from a narrowing gap between lowest and highest pay. It also ensures that employees perceive financial gain in being promoted from one job grade to another.

8.3.3 Determining Job Grade Boundaries

There are at least five ways of determining the boundaries or limits of job grades, by examining: (1) the distribution of job evaluation results, (2) the point distribution between the different degrees of job evaluation factors, (3) the threshold of perception (i.e. just noticeable differences), (4) the standard error of measurement, and (5) a combination of the above.

TABLE 8.1
Example of Job Evaluation Results

Job	Points	Job	Points
A	600	H	957
B	620	I	1,055
C	645	J	1,069
D	675	K	1,070
E	688	L	1,092
F	846	M	1,102
G	918		

Examining the Distribution of Job Evaluation Results

Examining the distribution of job evaluation results allows one to identify breaks in the spectrum of points. For example, Table 8.1 lists the evaluation scores for 13 jobs.

A brief look at this distribution indicates three possible job grades: A to E, F to H, and I to M. The difference between the top and bottom scores in each grade is less than that between the top score in one and the bottom score in the next; the difference between 688 and 600, for instance, is less than that between 846 and 688. These differences may be used to draw the boundaries between job grades.

Grade boundaries must not, however, be so broad as to encompass jobs perceived as having requirements that differ enough to warrant pay differences. Neither should they be so fine as to create pay differentials between jobs that are perceived as having insignificant differences in requirements.

Examining the Point Distribution between the Different Degrees of Job Evaluation Factors

Another way of determining grade boundaries is to examine the point distribution between the different degrees of the job evaluation factors (cf. Table 8.2).

Based on this data, a constant evaluation error of plus or minus one degree on each factor will result in a 225-point overvaluation or undervaluation of the jobs (the sum of the point differentials between degrees for

TABLE 8.2
Grid of Points Between Evaluation Factor Degrees

Evaluation factors	Point value of degrees						Point differential between degrees
1	10	20	30	40			10
2	15	30	45	60	75		15
3	50	100	150	200	250		50
4	30	60	90	120	150	180	30
5	60	120	180	240	300		60
6	20	40	60				20
7	15	30	45	60	75	90	15
8	25	50	75	100			25
Total							225

all factors). In practice, such an error is not likely to occur with a job. One factor may be overvalued and another undervalued so that some errors will cancel each other out. But since the risk of error remains, a rule of thumb must be adopted. One possibility is to divide the constant error by 3 and have the grade boundaries mark differentials of 75 points, or 225 divided by 3. The division by 3 is based on the assumption that two thirds of the errors will cancel each other out. Another assumption might well be equally valid. Finally, based on this logic, the differential between grade boundaries would be constant. In Table 8.2, the differential between boundaries is always 75 points, regardless of grade. This is justified in this case because the differential between degrees is constant for each factor (an arithmetic progression was used), regardless of which degrees are considered. In fact, the differential between grade boundaries may be constant, increasing, or decreasing. Therefore, one must ensure that the classification (all job grades with the differentials between them) reflects the point grid used. If, unlike Table 8.2 with its constant differentials between degrees, the differentials of some factors increase, then the differentials between grade boundaries must also increase, since the higher degrees one assigns to a job, the greater the impact of an error with this point grid.

Threshold of Perception

As mentioned in Chapter 4 on job evaluation methods, the Weber-Fechner law, applied to job evaluation by Hay (1950), showed that a difference between the requirements of two jobs becomes perceptible only when evaluation

TABLE 8.3
Job Classification

Grade	Grade boundaries	Job	Score
I	100-115	A	100
		B	104
II	116-133	C	116
		D	117
		E	127
III	134-154	F	138
		G	150
IV	155-178	H	163
		I	170
		J	172
		K	173

results differ by at least 15%. Since the purpose of classification is to group jobs considered equivalent, one may therefore consider two jobs equivalent if their evaluation results differ by 15% or less. This criterion may be used, accordingly, to determine the differential between boundaries. While this procedure provides an indication of possible differentials between group boundaries, in practice, certain jobs whose scores differ by less than 15% will fall into two different grades. In Table 8.3, for example, the differential between boundaries is 15%; yet the difference between Job B in Grade I and Job C in Grade II is less than 15%. There is no perfect method of determining grade boundaries. Each method suggests a possible classification.

Standard Error of Measurement

The fourth way of determining boundaries is suggested by the mathematical formula for the standard error of measurement (cf. Chapter 5) developed by Nunnally (1976). By way of reminder, the formula is as follows:

$$\sigma_{\text{measure}} = \sigma_x (1 - r_{kk})^{\frac{1}{2}}$$

in which σ_x is the standard deviation of the distribution of job evaluation results and r_{kk} is the reliability index of the results. While both indices may be calculated, it was pointed out in Chapter 5 that the reliability index for job evaluation results is generally around 0.90. Therefore, if we calculate the standard deviation of the distribution of results with the 0.90 reliability index (assuming that the exact index for the system in use cannot be ascertained), the standard error of measurement may be determined by substituting those values for the mathematical symbols in the formula. Grade boundaries are then based on that index, and the differential between them should be constant.

Combination of Methods

Finally, the fifth way of determining the boundaries between job grades is to use all of the above-mentioned methods to establish a satisfactory job classification.

Before concluding this discussion of determining grade boundaries, it is important to note that a system with small differentials may well be unstable, since the slightest change in evaluation results could result in a change of grade. This could cause employees to demand a re-evaluation of their jobs and, consequently, complicate pay administration. On the other hand, if differentials are very large, job requirements within each grade may not be equivalent at all.

8.3.4 Vacant Job Grades   *"Harvey"   allow room for growth*

Regardless of what method is used to determine job grade boundaries, certain job grades may be vacant, i.e. contain no job. These empty grades make the pay structure more flexible, which is important for growing organizations. It leaves room for potential changes in job content and, consequently, evaluation results. In other words, the vacant grades may eventually be filled. It is important, however, not to have too many vacant grades. Otherwise, employees whose jobs are situated immediately below a vacant grade may think the evaluation committee was especially harsh on them, making sure their jobs fit into a lower grade and paid less. Finally, it should be noted that the number of vacant grades may be increased or reduced by changing the grade boundaries.

8.3.5 Jobs Near Grade Boundaries

Certain jobs may be located very close to a grade boundary. In a grade ranging from 650 to 750 points, one job may score 745, another 740, and a third 725. How does one handle that?

The first possibility is to do nothing. If the job evaluation results and grade boundaries are common knowledge, however, this may provoke dissatisfaction among employees whose jobs scored 740 or 745 points. This is even more likely to occur, given that the employees know very well that job

TABLE 8.4
Job Evaluation Results by Committee Member

Evaluation factor	Committee member	Results (degrees assigned) by committee members						Final result
		1	2	3	4	5	6	
A		2	3	2	3	2	3	3
B		3	3	3	3	3	4	3
C		1	1	2	1	1	2	1
D		4	4	5	5	4	5	5
E		3	2	3	2	3	3	3

evaluation results always involve some degree of subjectivity and error. They will therefore be tempted to request a review of their job evaluation, which in many cases will produce higher results. This also sends the message, "Next, please!", because employees holding the job that scored 725 points will in turn request a re-evaluation, and so on. A few years of playing around with the same system will make the job evaluation results so inconsistent as to lack any apparent logic.

A more appropriate solution for jobs near the boundaries is to review the evaluation committee's initial results for any discrepancies in its members' individual results, and to see how they were handled. For example, if a six-member evaluation committee arrived at the results illustrated in Table 8.4, certain conclusions may be drawn.

Three committee members assigned Degree 3 to Factor A, and the other three members assigned Degree 2. The same applies to Factor D: three members chose Degree 4 and the other three, Degree 5. With the remaining factors, one degree is always in the majority. The final scores (Degree 3 for Factor A and 5 for Factor D) were reached by discussion. Once these results were converted into points, the job in question scored 745, putting it very close to the boundary of 750. In this case, the job evaluation results for Factor A or D could be lowered without violating the spirit of the evaluation committee's work. This would reduce the total evaluation score and move the job an acceptable distance from the boundary. Had Degrees 2 and 4 ultimately been selected for Factors A and D, they could be raised without contravening the committee's decision; this would then move the job into a higher grade.

In some cases, job evaluation results cannot be changed without violating the spirit of the committee's work. The committee should then be given an opportunity to review its evaluation. The purpose of this exercise is not to change the results as much as to look for a possible error. This situation resembles that of a student who earns 58%, when 60% is required to pass. Before the grade is finalized, it must be reviewed for possible error, since the consequences of a two-point grading error are much greater for this student than for one who earned 40% or 82%. Similarly, in the case of job evaluation results, the committee must re-analyse the job, and decide whether the results should be modified or remain as is. If the committee decides on a modification, it must make sure that the new results are consistent with the evaluations of the other jobs. Once the review is complete, the results become final; they may then be announced and, if necessary, justified. Sometimes, job evaluation results are not modified, because they contain no apparent errors or because changing them would create more problems than it would solve. In this case, it is important to be resolute with employees who will eventually express their dissatisfaction. The consistency of the evaluation system, as well as the sense of equity felt by all employees concerned, depends on it. Adopting a firm attitude definitely does not mean having a closed mind. Modifications to job content, for instance, may justify a re-evaluation. In brief, the important thing is to ensure that solving one problem does not create other, bigger ones.

☐ 8.4 Pay Policy Relative to the Market

Once job grades have been determined, the jobs within each grade are considered equivalent, and differences in job evaluation results within a grade are no longer relevant. Those in charge of compensation may then determine the general level of pay they wish to assign to the various grades. Essentially, this means applying the organization's pay policy (cf. Chapter 6) by positioning the organization's pay line at the desired level relative to the market.

An organization's pay position relative to the market is always a function of the reference market used. There is a clear difference between knowing that a pay policy reflects the market average for a specific number of organizations and knowing that it lies in the upper quartile for all Canadian organizations. In addition, a position relative to the market is taken at a given point in time, e.g. at the annual adjustment of the pay structure. Thereafter, the market continues evolving, whereas the organization's pay structure remains in force until the end of the year. As a result, an organization that adopts a policy of leading the market at the beginning of the year may, by the end of the year, be offering average or below-market pay. Figure 8.4 illustrates such a shift in position over time.

FIGURE 8.4
Evolution of an Organization's Relative Position over the Course of a Year (Assuming a 6% Market Increase)

(a)   Market average at the beginning of the year:

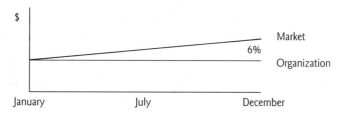

(b)   Market average at mid-year:

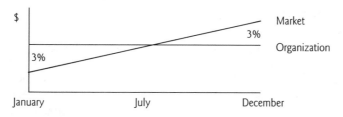

(c)   Market average at year's end:

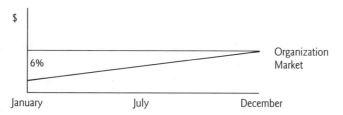

Let us assume that the organizations in the market modify their pay structures throughout the year – some in January, others in February, still others in March, etc. In Figure 8.4 a) above, the organization revises its structure in January to be in line with the market average, then during the course of the year, falls behind the market. In practice, this organization's pay structure only reflects its market policy at one point in the year; for the remainder, it lags behind the market. The organization in b) revises its structure in July, for the first half of the year, paying less than the market, for the second half, more. For the year as a whole, it is in line with the market average. Finally, in c), the organization's pay structure is in line with the market average at year end, after paying more than the market throughout the year.

☐ 8.5 Selecting Criteria for Determining Individual Pay

An organization's pay line represents what it pays for various jobs. It constitutes an integration of its internal equity policy with its external one, which is aimed at competitiveness. After determining the pay rates for various jobs, an organization must decide whether it will pay all holders of a job the same (single rate), or whether pay will vary within a range from one holder to the next based on various individual characteristics, such as experience, length of service, and performance. Considering these characteristics enables the organization to ensure the *individual equity* of its pay.

8.5.1 Experience

Experience is one possible criterion for determining individual pay. The argument, in this case, is that it is equitable and accepted that two employees who hold the same job but have different work experience will be paid differently. On the other hand, it has been pointed out that this criterion is valid to the extent that the experience influences the performance of the jobholder or of colleagues (the jobholder as either "voice of experience" or role model).

Applying this criterion, however, raises certain problems. The first stems from the fact that experience is a function of time. The longer an employee holds a job, the more experienced that person is considered to be. However, this is certainly not a general rule. Some jobs are so simple that, after a week or a month, the work becomes merely a repetition of what has already been learned. Other jobs may take two or more years to master. Hence, it is not possible to apply monetary rewards for work experience uniformly from one job grade to the next.

A second problem may arise if one uses experience as a criterion to determine pay. If experience (the time required to do the work adequately and satisfactorily) has already been considered in the job evaluation, it would then receive double recognition – in job evaluation and in determining individual pay. In practice, this problem can only be avoided by distinguishing the nature (definition) of the experience considered in job evaluation from that used in determining individual pay. On the one hand, experience, for job evaluation, refers to the prior experience required to hold the job, which may be measured in terms of time (number of years, months, etc.), but above all on the basis of content (prior work experience). For determining individual pay, on the other hand, the criterion of experience emphasizes the experience acquired in the job in question. It too may be measured in terms of time (seniority in the position), but how the employee does the work is even more important.

8.5.2 Seniority – Length of Service

The most commonly cited reason for using seniority to determine individual pay is to reward an employee's years of service.

In North America, this criterion is primarily used for clerical, technical, and professional jobs (e.g. lawyers and engineers). In the latter case, the expression "maturity curve" or "learning curve" is sometimes used. Seniority is also used, though considerably less often, to determine individual pay levels for production workers. It is never used officially, outside of the public sector, for management and executive positions. In Europe, however, it is common practice to officially recognize an employee's years of service (seniority) in determining individual pay levels, regardless of employee category. In some cases, an individual's seniority is recognized out of gratitude for years of service. Although the basic idea is to recognize an employee's past performance, in practice, the criterion is applied uniformly to all employees, regardless of performance. In other cases, rewarding seniority is a recognition of an employee's greater experience, which can only result in their doing a better job and having a positive influence on the performance of colleagues with less seniority. In this case, "seniority" is being confused with "experience" – an idea that would seem naive even if there may be some relationship between the two. It also assumes that experience has a positive effect on job performance, although this relationship is far from clearly proved. Evidently, certain notions are hard to break.

8.5.3 Performance

Behaviour (what people do, their actions) and performance (the results or consequences of those actions) may also serve as criteria for determining individual pay. Recognition of employee performance is, in fact, one of the most universally accepted concepts in pay administration. Failure to reward the relative merit of employees monetarily will certainly lead to serious problems of inequity. Yet, while the idea of rewarding performance is largely taken for granted, it is not treated the same everywhere, nor does it carry the same weight in all pay policies. This question will be discussed further in Chapter 10.

☐ 8.6 Determining Pay Ranges and Intergrade Differentials

If an organization decides to ignore individual characteristics in determining pay, it then has a single pay rate for each job grade and no need to establish

EXHIBIT 8.5
Degree of Intergrade Overlap

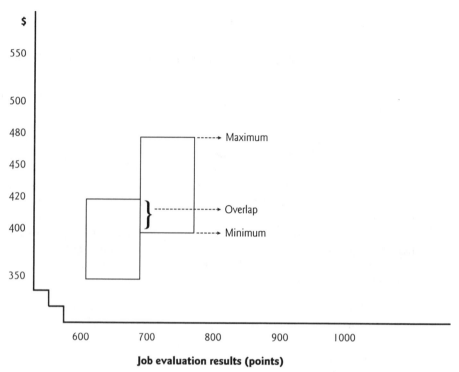

Job evaluation results (points)

pay ranges. It need only determine or set the pay differential between adjacent job grades. On the other hand, if it decides to consider individual characteristics and therefore use pay ranges, it must determine both the minimum and maximum for each job grade, as well as the degree of overlap (or intergrade differential) between adjacent pay ranges. The minimum corresponds to the pay received by someone with no experience in the job. The maximum represents the highest amount paid by the organization, when warranted by experience, length of service, or performance. The degree of overlap represents the extent of duplication between two adjacent pay ranges. Exhibit 8.5 is an illustration of this situation. All the pay ranges together comprise the pay structure.

8.6.1 Types of Pay Range

Exhibit 8.6 indicates that there are two types of pay range: the simple minimum-maximum range, and the range with two maximums: the normal

EXHIBIT 8.6
Two Types of Pay Range

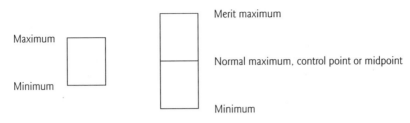

maximum, or control point and the merit maximum. The normal maximum in the latter case corresponds to the pay received by jobholders whose performance is entirely satisfactory, and therefore at a normal level of merit. This often corresponds to the midpoint of a minimum-maximum range.

A new incumbent's pay normally lies between the minimum and normal maximum, depending on experience, and gradually increases to the normal maximum on the basis of performance. An employee whose performance is consistently above average should be paid between the normal and the merit maximum. The normal maximum therefore serves as a control point, which gives rise to the expression, "pay at the control point". In practice, however, the situation is rarely this clearcut (cf. Chapter 10).

8.6.2 Determining Pay Ranges

After having plotted its salary survey results, an organization can determine its desired pay line. It represents the maximum when a minimum-maximum range is used or the normal maximum where a merit range exists. This leaves the minimum, or the minimum and merit maximum to be determined.

Salary survey results provide one indication for determining minimums and maximums. If the organization wishes to position itself at the market median, it might plot the curves representing the first and third quartiles of the market pay distribution. These pay lines then serve as a guideline for determining the minimums and maximums for each job grade in the pay structure. Range minimums represent the pay offered when recruiting employees with no experience at the job in question. Accordingly, they must be set so as to induce individuals on the market to apply, particularly in the case of lower job grades, where more applicants without experience are hired.

8.6.3 Nature of Pay Ranges

Pay ranges may either be constant, or may increase from one grade to the next in the structure. Narrower ranges are more common at the bottom of the pay structure, because the jobs at that level are generally transitory and take less time to learn, and their incumbents have relatively less impact on the organization's overall results than those at the top of the pay structure.

On the other hand, the pay ranges at the top of the structure must be wider than those at the bottom because, with jobs at this level, more time is often required to reach satisfactory performance, incumbents generally have more impact on the organization's overall results, and the progressive tax rates must be taken into consideration.

8.6.4 Spread of Pay Ranges

The spread of a pay range corresponds to the differential between the minimum and maximum pay rate, and is influenced by various factors.

First, the characteristics of the jobs concerned influence this spread. The more differences that may be established in how a job is being carried out, the greater its pay range should be, to allow for variations in individual performance.

Secondly, organizational policies also have an impact on pay range spread. The more an organization wishes to monetarily reward differences between employees (based on seniority or performance), the broader its pay ranges should be.

Promotion policies and opportunities constitute the third factor influencing pay range spread. In fact, to control its employee turnover rate, a mature organization with few opportunities for promotion must have wide pay ranges, to provide an incentive for employees to stay. On the other hand, a fast-growing organization with numerous opportunities for promotion may use smaller pay ranges, its employees anticipating pay increases through promotion.

In practice, ranges of 10% to 25% are common for production and maintenance workers, 25% to 35% for office staff, 30% to 50% for professionals and managers, and 50% to 100% for senior executives of major corporations. In other words, the norm of $\pm 10\%$ to $\pm 30\%$ around the control point (normal maximum) is regularly cited. Exhibit 8.7 illustrates a pay structure for management positions. For executives, in particular, one may use a split structure, with a smaller range below the control point than above. For example, there may be a 15% spread between the minimum and control point, and a 25% spread between the control point and the merit maximum. Obviously, in this case, different rules apply to pay increases below and above the control point.

Pay range spread may be determined using more or less established standards. For example, there is a traditional mathematical formula for deter-

EXHIBIT 8.7
Pay Structure

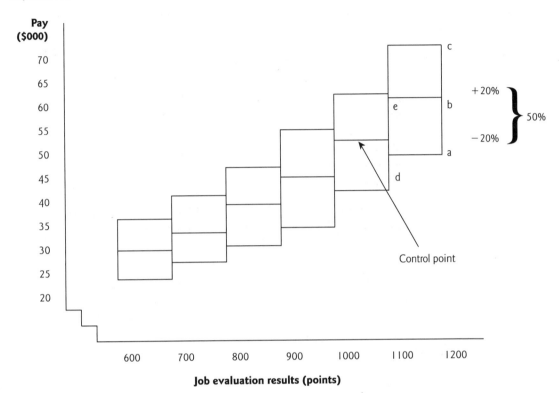

a : Pay range minimum
b : Control point or normal maximum
c : Pay range merit maximum
d-e: Degree of pay range overlap

Pay data for the exhibit

Grade	Minimum	Control point	Merit maximum
I	24,000	30,000	36,000
II	27,600	34,500	41,400
III	31,740	39,675	47,610
IV	36,501	34,626	54,751
V	41,976	52,470	62,964
VI	48,272	60,340	72,408

TABLE 8.5
Various Types of Pay Range

Job	Pay range	Minimum ($000)	Effective minimum ($000)	Control point ($000)	Effective maximum ($000)	Maximum ($000)
Accountant	A. Market	21.9	27.0	32.5	37.6	45.4
	B. Traditional	–	26.0	32.5	39.0	–
	A. Market	41.1	52.0	54.1	65.0	66.1
Lawyer	B. Traditional	–	43.3	54.1	64.9	–

mining the minimum and maximum values if the control point and percentage spread between the extremes are known. If the spread is 20%, for example:

$$\text{the maximum} = \text{control point value} \times 1.20$$
$$\text{the minimum} = \text{control point value} \times 0.80$$

There are other ways of determining pay range spread. Sauer (1989), for example, proposes using market pay distribution as a basis for determining pay ranges. Thus, an organization wishing to position itself at the market median could use the following reference points to determine its pay ranges:

— *minimum* – 10th percentile of pay distribution: for employees in training or on probation;

— *normal effective minimum* – 25th percentile of pay distribution: for employees who are fully trained or have completed probation;

— *normal effective maximum* – 75th percentile of pay distribution: for employees with many years of work experience and good performance; and

— *maximum* – 90th percentile of pay distribution: for employees whose performance is regularly superior or outstanding.

With this method, for example, the pay range for an accountant who has two to four years of experience and reports to the chief accountant will be Scale A in Table 8.5, whereas Scale B represents what it would be using the traditional approach. The table also compares the ranges for a lawyer with four to seven years of experience.

In a traditional scale, when this mathematical formula is applied, the effective maximum and minimum are usually, respectively, 20% more and 20% less than the control point. In the example, as chance would have it, this roughly corresponds to the market pay distribution for the accountant's job. However, that is far from being true of the lower portion of the lawyer's scale. It would come as no surprise to find organizations that use a traditional scale for their lawyers having to offer pay that is almost at the control point of their scale at hiring. Here the traditional scale fails to reflect market pay distribution. On the other hand, the organization using the traditional scale would hire an accountant at a higher salary than it would if considering market pay distribution.

8.6.5 Intergrade Differentials or Degree of Overlap

The size of the spread between the midpoints of adjacent grades has a direct impact on the degree to which various pay ranges overlap. The larger the pay ranges, the more overlap (or duplication) there will be, because of the small differentials between the midpoints of adjacent grades. The opposite is equally true. The smaller the pay ranges, the less overlap there will be between grades, because of the large differentials between midpoints.

Reasons for Intergrade Differentials

There are essentially two reasons for the overlap or duplication of various pay ranges. First, recognizing individual merit or seniority allows for a more flexible pay structure. In a relatively stable organization, with few opportunities for promotion, a high degree of overlap allows individual employee characteristics to be rewarded monetarily. A high degree of overlap allows for greater monetary recognition of seniority, and pay increases can occur with no change in employee competence. The same argument may be used to justify considering individual performance.

Secondly, the degree of overlap points to the relativity of job evaluation results. The more duplication there is, the slighter the consequences of a classification error on pay. Conversely, the less overlap there is, the more accurate the classification must be, because of the large pay differentials between grades.

Nature of Intergrade Differentials

The differentials between the midpoints of adjacent pay grades may be constant or may increase. Uniform differentials may be easier to justify, but increasing ones are equally acceptable. The reasons for increasing differentials are essentially the same as those for widening ranges: the increasing impact of jobs on organizational results, the progressive income tax rates, the relative scarcity of qualified persons interested in filling the highest jobs in the organizational structure, and actual market pay.

From another perspective, the greater the differentials between midpoints, the more incentive the pay structure provides for promotion.

Size of Intergrade Differentials

In practice, the spread between the midpoints of adjacent grades ranges from 3% to 5% at the bottom of the structure to 25% to 35% at the top. In large organizations, it is not uncommon to find differentials of 40% to 50% between two upper-level job grades. Generally speaking, however, it is relatively common to find a 5% to 7% differential between the midpoints of adjacent grades in pay structures for production or clerical workers. For professionals and support staff, a minimum norm of 10% to 15% is often used for the lower levels.

In this regard, it is interesting to recall Mahoney's findings (1979). He asked students and compensation personnel what pay differentials they believed should exist between jobholders in two adjacent organizational levels, and at the same level. His results indicated that there should be a pay differential of 30% to 40% between jobs in two adjacent upper organizational levels and no more than 2% to 5% for jobs at the same level. His findings agree with salary survey data, and with the standards generally recommended for avoiding problems of pay inequity between two adjacent upper organizational levels.

On the other hand, pay differentials between jobs at the lower organizational levels within the pay structure may be smaller. The standard acceptable differential between the pay of a supervisor and the highest-paid employee reporting to that supervisor is from 20% to 30%. Less than 20% may create a problem of pay compression, making it difficult for the organization to recruit supervisors internally, since employees will lack sufficient financial incentive to accept the job. An organization will also have problems retaining supervisors, who will perceive inequity when they compare their pay with that of their employees (internal inequity).

Before concluding this section, it should be noted that organizational level and job grade are not identical. In fact, there may be more than one grade between the holders of hierarchally adjacent jobs. Consequently, the norms for differentials between two organizational levels do not necessarily apply to intergrade differentials.

Consequences of Intergrade Differentials

Pay overlap between grades is relatively well-accepted in practice. Nevertheless, it seems that the degree to which the duplication is accepted is inversely proportional to the degree of overlap. Here, there appears to have been a change in social standards over the years. Until the late 70s, having two or three grades overlap was generally acceptable, whereas today an overlap of three or four is considered equitable. Beyond the norm of three or four grades, the overlap may well be judged too great and, therefore, inequitable, since employees perceived as having responsibilities that differ greatly in value could be paid the same.

Furthermore, the higher the degree of overlap, the less incentive the pay structure provides for advancing within the structure, and the more promotions create problems with the pay structure. In fact, when there is considerable overlap between job grades that reward merit beyond the midpoint, promoted employees may find themselves collecting pay higher than the midpoint of their new pay grade; the merit maximum becomes their normal maximum. A practical way of solving that problem involves setting the maximums for the lower grades below the midpoints of the higher grades, because promoted employees are generally near their pay grade maximum. For example, when organizational policy calls for a minimum 10% pay increase on promotion, a pay structure with grade maximums approximately 10% below the midpoints of the adjacent higher grades would create no problems of inequity.

Similarly, with organizational decisions about recruiting external candidates, the greater the overlap between grades, the closer to the maximum the pay offer will have to be, and the more problems it creates within the pay structure. This is all the more true when an organization's pay policy is to adhere to the market average. In addition to creating eventual problems of pay progression for new staff, existing employees in the pay grades in question may perceive an inequity in comparing their situation with that of the newcomers.

Intergrade Differentials and Pay Compression

The problem of pay compression, in the form of a high degree of overlap between pay grades, occurs during inflationary periods such as the early 80s. A high inflation rate, a slowing economy, minimum wage legislation, and union pressure result in higher pay for lower level employees, (i.e. result in more pay compression), and reduce the differential between the highest and lowest pay levels within an organization. During periods of relative economic stability, such as the late 80s, the pendulum swings the other way, and the pay differentials between grades increase.

The problem of pay compression and a high degree of overlap between pay grades may be solved by reducing the number of pay grades. Fewer pay grades result in a motivational pay structure with acceptable differentials

EXHIBIT 8.8
Types of Pay Range

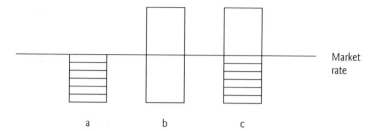

a: Pay range with steps
b: Pay range without steps
c: Mixed pay range

between grades. This solution generally involves reducing the number of organizational levels. The organization may then offset the reduced opportunities for vertical promotion by increasing the possibilities for pay increases within grades.

8.7 Determining Operating Procedure within Pay Ranges

The basic question in operating procedure within pay ranges is whether or not to use steps. In practice, the answer depends on the criteria used to determine individual pay increases. Three solutions are possible: ranges with steps, ranges without steps, and mixed ranges with steps up to the normal maximum. Exhibit 8.8 illustrates these three options.

8.7.1 Pay Ranges without Steps

Most private sector organizations use merit pay ranges without steps. The ranges, however, are graduated, with different performance levels corresponding to different pay levels. Exhibit 8.9 illustrates this type of range.

The control point (normal maximum) corresponds to what the organization wishes to pay compared to the market for satisfactory performance. The minimum represents entry-level pay. The merit maximum is what an employee whose performance is exceptional would be paid. This type of scale tries to match what the market pays for a similar job and equivalent performance. An applicant with no prior experience in the job is hired at

EXHIBIT 8.9
Pay Range Based on Individual Performance

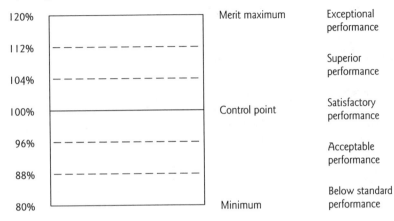

120%	Merit maximum	Exceptional performance
112%		Superior performance
104%		
100%	Control point	Satisfactory performance
96%		Acceptable performance
88%		
80%	Minimum	Below standard performance

the minimum pay. Nonetheless, since organizations consider experience and expected performance when determining a new employee's pay, starting pay is often located somewhere between the minimum and control point. And, since employees accumulate experience more rapidly during the initial months or years of work, pay reviews based on performance are more common at the outset. For example, a new employee's pay may be revised on the basis of performance after three months, six months, one year, two years and, subsequently, every year.

With this type of scale, an employee who does satisfactory work would earn pay in the 96% to 104% range, around the normal maximum. This is rarely the case in practice, however, because pay scales are raised each year, based on market pay increases. For an employee's pay to reach the control point after 4 or 5 years, annual increases of 4% to 5% would be necessary, without considering scale increases. So, if the scale increases by 5% annually, the employee must receive a 9% or 10% annual increase. One way to avoid paying increases of this kind to someone whose performance is satisfactory is to narrow the gap between the minimum and the normal maximum. For example, if an organization decides that an employee whose performance is satisfactory should receive increases of 2% per year and that the normal maximum should be reached in 4 years, the scale minimum equals the control point divided by 1.02^4. For 3% increases over 3 years, the divisor is 1.03^3.

Two comments are in order. First of all, the decision as to the time required to progress from the minimum to the normal maximum may vary from one job cluster to the next. For example, it may be three years for office staff and four for professionals. Secondly, the pay differential between the normal maximum and the merit maximum must correspond to what management considers an appropriate distinction between a satisfactory and an exceptional performance. For example, the scale minimum may be set at 12% less than the normal maximum, the merit maximum, 20% above. In this situation, the term "midpoint" can no longer be used to describe the normal maximum, because it no longer represents the middle of the pay range.

Pay increases above the normal maximum generally take the following form. An employee at the 104% level, whose performance is superior, will rise to 107% or 108% the following year. A second year of superior performance would result in an increase to 110% or 112%. A third year of superior performance would require a smaller percentage increase; otherwise, the employee will move into the exceptional performance range. In practice, however, such a slowdown is difficult for employees to accept. The situation becomes worse if the employee's performance is only satisfactory in the third year; the employee then receives no increase, and the level of pay slips back into the satisfactory performance range. In reality, this logic is never fully adhered to. Pay does not increase as rapidly above the normal maximum as it does below, and an employee's level within the pay scale is generally maintained, if not increased, from one year to the next. Therefore, an employee's salary rarely matches performance level.

8.7.2 Pay Ranges with Scales

Pay scales for unionized employees in general, and clerical staff in particular, generally use seniority as a criterion for individual pay increases. In this case, a number of steps are created within the pay range, hence, the term "pay scale". The number of steps basically depends on the differential between minimum and maximum and on the percentage increase between steps. While a pay range may have anywhere from 3 to 15 steps, most have 6 or 7.

Determining Steps within Pay Ranges

To determine steps, the percentage differential between the minimum and the maximum must first be considered; then, an acceptable percentage for pay increases from one step to the next must be determined. Occasionally, fixed amounts are used instead of percentages. In practice, this means that the value of the steps decreases with time. This may be justified, on the basis that learning primarily occurs early in the job. To create numerous steps, 2% is used as the pay increase rate. Yet, since this rate seems low when one considers the effect of income taxes, some organizations use 3% or 4%. Table 8.6 illustrates this situation. With this type of range, the organ-

TABLE 8.6
Pay Range with Steps

Grade	Minimum	I	2	3	4	5	Maximum
I	405	417	430	443	456	470	484
II	432	445	458	472	486	501	516
III	460	474	488	503	518	533	549
IV	490	505	520	535	550	568	585
V	520	536	552	568	585	603	621
VI	552	569	586	603	621	640	659
VII	585	603	621	639	658	678	699
VIII	620	639	658	677	698	719	740
IX	660	680	700	721	743	765	788
X	700	721	743	765	788	811	836

ization must determine what the various points along the scale will correspond to. For example, will the maximum represent what the organization wishes to pay compared to the market? Or will that be represented by the midpoint between the minimum and the maximum? The value of the steps in this illustration is 3%.

Progressing from One Step to the Next

Once the pay scale and steps have been established, the rule for progressing from one step to the next must be determined. For example, the minimum might represent entry-level pay, and the employee might move up one step each year thereafter. Another option would be to have the employee's pay at the first step after the probation period, at Step 2 after 6 months, Step 3 after 1 year, Step 4 after 3 years, Step 5 after 5 years, and the maximum after 10 years. In brief, the objective (workforce stability, recognition of years of service, etc.) must first be determined, and then the procedural rules established accordingly.

If the objective is workforce stability, seniority might be adopted as the rule. An effective approach in this case is to grant increases more frequently at the beginning (the period when the chances of the employee leaving the organization are higher) and less frequently thereafter.

If the objective is to recognize years of service with the organization, the increases may be annual and, in this case, the number of steps is theoretically infinite. In practice, this gives rise to pay structures with more than 15 steps and, when an individual reaches the maximum, a seniority bonus policy may be applied instead of pay increases. This approach, while somewhat rare in North America, is common in Europe, even for management jobs. Generally speaking, pay increase percentages for seniority are lower. For example, in the chemical industry in France, employees generally receive a 1% annual increase until they reach 15 years of seniority and then 1% every two years to a maximum of 20%. In addition to this, there are special seniority bonuses equivalent to half a month's pay after 20 years of service, 1 month's pay after 30 years, and 2 months' pay after 40 years.

8.7.3 Mixed Pay Ranges

Mixed pay ranges, which are less common, have steps only up to the midpoint. The minimum represents entry-level pay; subsequently, pay increases with length of service to the normal maximum. Beyond that point, individual increases are based on performance that is more than entirely satisfactory. The lack of steps above the normal maximum makes the magnitude of pay increases very flexible.

The speed at which employees progress to the normal maximum may also be based on performance evaluation results. For example, a satisfactory performance may correspond to one step. An individual whose performance is less than satisfactory would receive a pay increase of less than a full step, while another whose performance is exceptional might rise two steps. This approach is suitable for an organization with a policy of granting pay increases based on seniority, which wishes to use another criterion, e.g. performance, without disrupting its existing pay scales too much. Certain employees may then reach the normal maximum for their grade more rapidly.

☐ 8.8 Determining Individual Pay and Adjusting Pay Rates

Once pay ranges have been determined, one must determine the pay employees will receive. Both the type of pay structure an organization adopts and the criteria it uses for pay increases come into play here.

Based on the pay scale illustrated in Table 8.6, and assuming only one incumbent per job, Table 8.7 shows the implications of establishing a new pay scale. The illustration reflects a variety of situations. Present pay may be less than pay under the new scale, or more than the new scale but less than the maximum, or clearly above the new scale.

8.8.1 Solutions for Employees Whose Pay Is Below the New Scale

Employees whose present pay is below the new scale should receive an increase. This applies to Employees C and D in Table 8.7. There may be

TABLE 8.7
Implications of a New Pay Structure

Employee	Seniority (years)	Job grade	Present weekly pay ($)	New weekly pay ($)
A	9	I	516	516
B	14	II	562	562
C	3	II	461	472
D	3	II	461	472
E	0	III	435	460
F	6	III	610	610
G	2	IV	536	536
H	14	IV	620	620
I	0	IV	486	490
J	8	V	650	650
K	6	VI	665	665
L	13	VI	665	665
M	23	VI	706	665
N	1	VI	590	590
O	3	VII	620	639
P	6	IX	800	800
Q	11	IX	800	800
R	35	X	1,166	1,166
S	26	X	923	923

justification, however, for paying less than the new scale. An employee may not be performing all facets of the job as described, performance may fall short of expectations, or the employee may still be learning the job. Various solutions are possible, depending on the situation.

When an employee is only performing part of the job, the job description may be modified to bring it closer to what the employee actually does. This entails re-evaluation and reclassification of the job. When an employee's performance falls short of expectations, an attempt may be made to improve it through training, the employee may be transferred to a more suitable job, or the employee may simply be dismissed. An employee still in the learning phase should be at or slightly above the minimum. In some cases, pay levels below the minimum point (e.g. 10%) are established for employees learning the job.

8.8.2 Solutions for Employees Whose Pay Is Above the New Scale

When an employee's pay is higher than what the new scale calls for, but less than the maximum, the most common solution is a pay freeze until the scale catches up through general pay increases, or through the increase in the employee's years of service with the organization. This applies to Employees G and N in Table 8.7.

When an employee's pay is clearly above the maximum (it then becomes a question of "red circles"), various solutions are possible. The pay may be reduced to the maximum point, but this may affect the employee's motivation.

Another solution is to do nothing, but this does not solve the problem. The injustice persists, whereas the stated objective of establishing a pay structure is precisely to eliminate inequities, especially the most obvious ones.

While the employee's pay may be frozen until the pay scale catches up, the greater the difference between the employee's pay and the maximum, the more this solution penalizes the employee. Employee R in Table 8.7 is a case in point. Another alternative is to slow down the employee's pay increases until the pay scale catches up over time. This solution may take various forms. For example, the employee's pay rate may be maintained, and the employee may receive general increases until a change of job. In this case, it is a matter of correcting a previous management error. Or, the employee may receive only part of the general increases granted by the organization. Yet another option is not to give this employee general increases but to recognize performance by means of bonuses.

One might also consider modifying the job content to make it more demanding. This results in the job being re-evaluated and moved to a higher job grade. This requires a genuine change in the content, and not simply a change in title. Employees are no fools! Note that this solution is only possible when the employee's potential and the nature of the work permit. If these two conditions are met, the possibility of transferring or promoting the employee might be considered.

Allen and Keaveny (1984) conducted one of the rare empirical studies on the effect of partial pay increases on the attitudes and behaviour of employees whose pay was above scale. They found that these employees applied themselves less to their work, took more paid sick leave, and were less satisfied with their pay and their job. Nonetheless, the findings also indicated that these negative effects were less pronounced when the employees concerned saw a possibility of promotion, or of having their job reclassified by changing its content.

TABLE 8.8
Solutions for Adjusting Pay Rates

A. Below the new scale:
    • increase pay to new scale
    • reclassify the job
    • transfer the employee
    • dismiss the employee
    • create a pay level for employees learning their job

B. Above the new scale:
    • status quo
    • maintain the pay until the employee changes job
    • pay freeze
    • partial pay freeze
    • pay freeze and possible performance bonuses
    • modify job content
    • transfer the employee to another job

One final situation is possible when an employee's pay is above what it should be in the new scale, the job has been correctly evaluated, performance is satisfactory, and the pay scale is generally correct. This situation may be caused by market supply and demand for certain jobs. For example, market pay for certain data processing jobs is higher than for different jobs with equivalent requirements. In this case, the salary survey results contradict those of the job evaluation. Under these circumstances, one must above all not change the job classification, for this would have an inflationary effect on the evaluation of other jobs. A common solution is to give these employees more generous pay, but this is only appropriate if their pay is below their grade maximum. Another option is to establish market bonuses for these jobs. For example, some universities award market bonuses to professors of medicine, actuarial science, and accounting, to make it easier to recruit and retain these professionals, who enjoy highly favourable market pay conditions. Market bonuses are a sensitive issue, however, and some organizations reject this approach outright. How can a school of business administration justify market bonuses for accounting professors to professors of other disciplines that lend themselves to business consultation, who could just as well demand similar treatment?

8.9 Relationships between Various Pay Structures

To date, the entire question of developing a pay structure and determining individual pay has been treated as though an organization had a single pay structure. This situation is the exception, rather than the rule. When it does

FIGURE 8.10
Fan-type Pay Structure

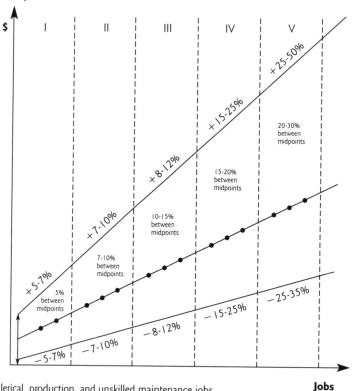

I: Clerical, production, and unskilled maintenance jobs
II: Clerical, production, and skilled maintenance jobs
III: Technical, paraprofessional, and supervisory jobs
IV: Middle management and professionals
V: Senior management and executives

occur, the pay structure generally takes the shape of a fan; Figure 8.10 illustrates such a fan-type structure.

As this indicates, organizations rarely have a single pay structure. There are usually as many structures as there are job clusters, because the jobs in various clusters are often evaluated using a different system. Moreover, since the labour market for different jobs varies, compensation surveys often use different methods.

Nonetheless, one must remember that the ultimate objective of job evaluation is to establish a degree of pay equity within the organization **as a whole**. Establishing pay structures for various job clusters raises the question of equity between pay structures. How can one ascertain that the pay structure for skilled clerical jobs is equitable in relation to the one for supervisory, technical, and paraprofessional jobs?

Henderson (1989) suggests an interesting way of solving the problem of equity between job clusters. The first step is to evaluate the most demanding job in the lowest pay structure with the system used for the highest structure, and to evaluate the least demanding job in the highest structure with the system used for the lowest. The second step is to determine the cash value of these jobs in the pay structure opposite to the one in which they are located. This cross-evaluation makes it possible to identify pay differentials related to structural differences. The final step is to ask the following series of questions about the results.

— Are the incumbents of the jobs in the lowest pay structure favourably evaluated when their job is placed in the highest structure? Conversely, are the incumbents of the jobs in the highest pay structure at a disadvantage when their job is placed in the lowest pay structure?
— Are the pay differentials justifiable?
— Would it be possible to use one pay structure instead of two?
— Are the jobs placed in the appropriate pay structure?

☐ 8.10 Two-tiered Pay Structures

Union pressure to increase pay levels is particularly strong during inflationary periods. During a recession, the parties at the negotiating table require ingenuity to solve the problem of labour costs honourably for both parties. These are the circumstances that gave rise, in the early 80s, to the use of two-tiered (or dual) pay structures in some unionized American organizations.

Basically, a two-tiered pay structure creates a pay differential based on an employee's date of hire. It involves an agreement stipulating that employees hired after a specific date will be subject to a different pay structure from the one governing employees hired before that date. The second pay structure may take various forms; Exhibit 8.11 illustrates this.

Line ADB in Exhibit 8.11 represents the pay structure for existing employees, while CDB represents the most common type of second structure. New employees are hired at a rate below the one for existing employees. Nonetheless, after a certain period (about five years), the second structure converges with the first and, from that point on, all employees are governed by the same structure. The difference between Points A and C usually ranges from 20% to 25%. Line CD represents another type of second structure. In this case, once the pay in the second structure converges with the first, the pay of employees governed by the second structure stops increasing on the basis of years of service. So, pay increases stop more quickly for employees hired after a given date. Finally, the third type consists of two parallel structures (line CE). In this case, new employees are always paid less than those in

EXHIBIT 8.11
Différents Types of Two-Tiered Pay Structures

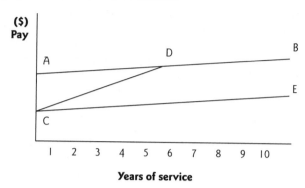

ADB: Pay structure for existing employees.
CDB: First type of pay structure for new employees.
CD : Second type of pay structure for new employees.
CE : Third type of pay structure for new employees.

place before the agreement was signed. The pay differential between the two structures may, in this scenario, be 10% or more.

In the United States, two-tiered pay structures have been implemented primarily in supermarket chains and airlines. For the latter, this system was a means of reducing labour costs and breaking the pattern of management-union relations that had prevailed prior to deregulation in the late 70s (Walsh, 1988). During the subsequent recession, the system allowed existing pay conditions to be maintained, while promising the possibility of lower labour costs in the future.

In Canada, Thériault's survey (1986) found that 5% of organizations had a two-tiered pay structure for their office staff, whereas 11% had one for their production and maintenance personnel. These organizations were mainly in the retail sector and, in virtually every instance, the employees covered by that type of pay structure were unionized.

At first glance, use of a two-tiered structure might seem efficient. Since the people affected by the new approach have not yet been hired, there is no opposition to the new system. Nonetheless, over the intermediate term, it may create numerous work-climate problems. Martin and Peterson (1985) conducted an empirical study of this, involving employees of a major super-market chain. They found that the employees governed by the second struc-ture considered their pay more inequitable, and saw their union as less useful in wage negotiations than did employees subject to the original structure. These negative effects vanished when the employees governed by the second structure did not work at the same location as the others (e.g. if they were in a new store). When they did not work together, employees' perceptions of their pay and of their union were similar. Cappelli and Sherer (1990) also studied two-tiered pay structures. Contrary to expectation, they found that employees in the lower-paid group (subject to the second structure) were more satisfied with their pay, work, and immediate supervisor than the others. These results may be partly due to the fact that this study was conducted only one year after the system had been implemented. When the new employees agreed to work under the new conditions, their reference group was different from that of existing employees, and their expectations were not as high. It would be interesting to see whether the perceptions of these new employees change with time.

Finally, it should be noted that use of two-tiered pay structures has been limited in recent years, and that there are few new agreements along these lines. Bernstein (1987) even found some backpedalling in the aviation industry. In 1986, the contract governing Boeing's approximately 40,000 machinists was amended to narrow the gap between the two pay structures. In 1987, American Airlines also amended its contract with its 5,700 pilots to ensure that the second structure will converge with the first after 10 years, whereas before, the two were parallel.

☐ 8.11 Summary

This chapter has discussed the stages of and possible options for integrating two sets of data: job requirements and market pay. This integration is achieved through the various stages of developing a pay structure. First, job evaluation results must be examined alongside those of the salary survey, and a pay line plotted to reflect the organization's pay policy relative to the market. Next, the organization must decide whether it will establish different pay levels for the various jobs in the structure, or group them in grades with different pay conditions for each. Then, if the organization wishes to consider individual characteristics, such as length of service and employee performance (individual equity), it must create pay ranges and decide how to weigh the factors chosen for determining pay. When all this has been done, the organization has all the rules it needs to determine what to pay each jobholder, and to make any necessary adjustments.

This process of determining what to pay employees within an organization may be rational and logical, but it remains subjective. The resulting pay structure is an image of its designers. Some groups of employees may be favoured or penalized by the application of decisions made throughout the process. This is pay discrimination stemming from conscious as well as unconscious bias. Nonetheless, regardless of the degree of subjectivity inherent in developing a pay structure, this process is how employee pay has been determined in recent years and, there is every reason to believe, will continue to be determined in the years ahead. The solution for penalized groups of employees must therefore be part of the process; this means controlling biases with socially unacceptable consequences. In this vein, the next chapter discusses pay discrimination and how to eliminate it.

REFERENCES

ALLEN, R. and T. KEAVENY, "Some Implications of Having Wages Red-Circled", *IRRA Proceedings*, 1984, pp. 465-472.

BELCHER, D.W. and T.J. ATCHISON, *Compensation Administration*, Englewood Cliffs, New Jersey, Prentice-Hall, 1987.

BERNSTEIN, A., "Why Two-Tier Wage Scales are Starting to Self-Destruct", *Business Week*, March 16, 1987, p. 41.

CAPPELLI, P. and P.D. SHERER, "Assessing Work Attitudes Under a Two-Tier Wage Plan", *Industrial and Labor Relations Review*, 1990, vol. 43, N° 2, pp. 225-244.

GOODE, W.F. and I. FOWLER, "Incentive Factors in a Low Morale Plant", *American Sociological Review*, 1949, vol. 14, pp. 618-624.

HAY, E.N., "The Application of Weber's Law to Job Evaluation Estimates", *Journal of Applied Psychology*, 1950, vol. 34, pp. 102-104.

HENDERSON, R.I., *Compensation Management*, Englewood Cliffs, New Jersey, Prentice-Hall, 1989.

HOLZER, H.J., "Wages, Employer Costs, and Employer Performance in the Firm", *Industrial and Labor Relations Review*, 1990, vol. 43, N° 3, pp. 147-164.

JAQUES, E., "Preliminary Sketch of a General Structure of Executive Strata", in *Glacier Project Papers*, edited by W. Brown and E. Jaques, London, Heinemann, 1965.

MAHONEY, T.A., "Organizational Hierarchy and Position Worth", *Academy of Management Journal*, 1979, vol. 22, N° 4, pp. 726-737.

MARTIN, J.E. and M.M. PETERSON, "Two-Tier Wage Scale Structures and Attitude Differences", *IRRA Proceedings*, 1985, pp. 72-79.

NASH, A.N. and S.J. CARROLL, *The Management of Compensation*, Monterey, California, Brooks/Cole Publishing Co., 1975.

NUNNALLY, J.C., *Psychometric Theory*, New York, McGraw-Hill, 1967.

SAUER, R.L., "A New Approach to Salary Structures", *Compensation and Benefits Review*, September - October, 1989, pp. 57-63.

SLIGHTER, S.H., J.J. HEALEY and E.R. LIVERNASH, *The Impact of Collective Bargaining on Management*, Washington, D.C., The Brookings Institute, 1960.

THÉRIAULT, R., *Politiques et Pratiques en matière de rénumération globale dans les entreprises au Québec*, Montreal, Les Productions INFORT, Inc., 1986.

WALSH, D.J., "Accounting for the Proliferation of Two-Tier Wage Settlements in the U.S. Airline Industry, 1983-1986", *Industrial and Labor Relations Review*, 1988, vol. 42, N° 1, pp. 50-62.

TABLE OF CONTENTS

9

PAY DISCRIMINATION

The opening chapters of this book covered the various factors that must be considered in determining pay, discussing various ways of ensuring internal equity and external competitiveness, while considering the characteristics of individual employees. The preceding chapter looked at how these three forms of equity could be integrated into a structure for determining individual pay. Part IV now ends with a discussion of pay discrimination.

This chapter begins by examining the concept of pay discrimination, then raises the issue, and reviews the main causes, of pay differentials between men and women in the labour market. Finally, the chapter looks at pay legislation in Canada and the United States, and discusses the implication of this legislation for employers.

☐ 9.1 Pay Equity and Employment Equity

Pay discrimination means paying people who do equal work, or work of equal value, differently, because of factors such as their sex, race, or age. In Canada, bias based on sex is the most closely watched form of discrimination. All pay equity programs strive to correct injustices in the compensation paid to women holding jobs that are similar, or of equal value, to those filled by men.

It is important to distinguish between *pay equity* and *employment equity*. Employment equity programs are designed to ensure equitable representation of members of groups protected by law (related to sex, age, race, etc.) in all jobs within an organization, as well as to eliminate discrimination in human resource management activities undertaken to fill positions (recruitment, hiring, promotion, transfers, etc.).

Pay equity is therefore a part of employment equity. The purpose of pay equity is equality in the compensation paid to men and women holding jobs that are similar, or of equal value. Employment equity aims for equality in the representation of protected groups (related to sex, age, race, etc.) in every facet of the job.

9.2 Pay Differentials between Men and Women

One thing is clear. In aggregate women are not as well paid as men in the labour market. Sources indicate differences in men's and women's pay range from 30% to 40%, that is, while men are earning $100, women are being paid only $60 to $70. For example, a 1985 report published by the Province of Ontario (Province of Ontario, 1985) noted a 38% pay differential between men and women holding full-time jobs.

The Government of Manitoba's Pay Equity Bureau (1986) refers to a 34% pay differential. According to Statistics Canada (*La Presse*, 12/22/90), women were paid 65.6% and 65.8% of what men were earning in 1984 and 1989 respectively (34.4% and 34.2% differentials). Sorensen's survey (1990) in the United States found women earning 61% of what men were paid in 1978 (39% differential) and 70% in 1987 (30% differential).

The results of these studies indicate that the pay differential between men and women in the labour market generally ranges between 30% and 40%. Roughly speaking, this means that women are earning $60 to $70, whereas men are being paid $100. Is this discrimination? The answer is not simple. The pay differential between men and women may be the result of sex-based discrimination, but may also have a number of other causes.

9.3 Causes of Pay Differentials between Men and Women

The principal reasons commonly cited to explain pay differentials between men and women are:

- labour supply and demand;
- labour characteristics;
- industrial sector;
- organizational size;
- the nature of jobs;
- unionization rate; and
- job evaluation or pay discrimination.

9.3.1 Labour Supply and Demand

The fact that two jobs are of equal value does not necessarily mean that their incumbents must receive the same pay. Labour market supply and demand may differ from one job to the next (Killingsworth, 1985). For example, a garbage collector's job may be equal in value to that of a payroll clerk, but the garbage collector will be paid more, because more people are interested in working as a payroll clerk. In the same vein, market supply and demand, as well as general job preferences, may justify identical pay for jobs of different value.

9.3.2 Labour Characteristics

Pay levels also depend on various characteristics of the labour pool, such as education, skills, experience, weekly number of hours worked, etc. The market's higher pay for men may reflect the fact that, generally speaking, they possess these characteristics to a greater degree than women. For example, men in Canada work an average of 41.4 hours a week, compared to 36.4 for women.

A study of major corporations (Gerhart, 1990) found female employees paid 88% of what men earned. However once the comparison was narrowed to men and women with similar characteristics (same experience, training, specialization, length of service, performance, job), that figure rose to 95%. Gerhart also found that the persistent pay differential between men and women is largely due to the lower pay received by women at hiring. Once again, there are various reasons for this. Women may have more modest expectations at hiring and be less inclined to negotiate pay, or they may be more prone to accept lower pay because they know about pay discrimination.

9.3.3 Industrial Sector

Some industrial sectors pay less than others because labour constitutes a high percentage of total production costs, and demand for their products is not very elastic. Part of the pay differential between men and women may be explained by this fact, because women work mostly in labour-intensive industries (Hodson and England, 1985). Aldrich and Buchele (1989) found that when the effect of worker characteristics and the nature of their jobs were taken into consideration, the differential between female-dominated (60% or more held by women) and male-dominated jobs is about 19%. This differential drops to 7.9% if industrial sector is also considered.

9.3.4 Organizational Size

As mentioned in Chapter 6, organizational size also influences pay levels. There is a 50% difference between the pay of men working for large corporations and those working for small businesses. Part of the pay differential between men and women may therefore be explained by the fact that women work primarily for small businesses (Oi, 1986).

9.3.5 Nature of Jobs

Market pay also varies with the nature of the jobs in question, their value in the employer's eyes, and the supply of labour to fill them. Doctors in a hospital earn more than social workers, for example, because of the greater value society places on doctors' services, and their relative scarcity.

Labour market pay differentials between men and women may also be explained by the fact that the two sexes tend to hold different jobs. Thus, while women constitute 44% of the United States workforce, they hold 81% of office jobs and 61% of service sector jobs. Eighty-eight percent of women in the United States labour market fall into 25 of the 420 occupations or trades listed in the *Dictionary of Occupational Titles*. Over 50% of women, in fact, hold either an office or service sector job. Furthermore, it would seem that the greater the percentage of women in an occupation or trade, the lower their pay (Treiman and Hartman, 1981). Not only do women hold different jobs from men, but the ones they do hold pay less!

This over-representation of women in certain jobs is the result of various social and historical factors. According to Treiman and Hartmann (1981):

– Women are led, through socialization, to believe that certain jobs are more "suitable" than others.
– Women are trained to fill jobs that fit the image society decrees for them, rather than those that are available.
– Women have less information about the labour market, pay, and working conditions.
– Women tend to invest less in training, because they expect to leave the market because of family obligations.
– Women think certain jobs are out of reach because of discrimination.

However, this situation is changing. In the United States, the number of women holding the jobs of programmer and auditor rose from 28% and 34% in 1979 to 39.7% and 44.7% in 1986 (Milkovich and Newman, 1990). In Canada, from 1981 to 1986, the percentage of female optometrists increased from 17.7% to 32.2%, veterinarians from 17.2% to 35.1%, biologists from 31.9% to 36.9%, and petroleum engineers from 1.1% to 6.5% (Marshall, 1989). Another study showed that the percentage of women in certain faculties or schools of business administration in Canada rose from 33% in 1979 to 50% in 1989 (Vanasse, 1990).

While the nature of jobs held by women and by men does not entirely explain labour market pay differentials between them, it apparently plays a major role. An analysis of the data on 74 jobs held by incumbents of both sexes (Faille, 1989) found that women were paid less than men in 75% of cases. The pay differential, however, amounted to less than 5% in over half these cases, and ranged from 5% to 10% in almost 35% of cases. The remaining 15% of jobs (for which the pay differential between men and women holding the same job was over 10%) were held by a very low percentage of women. Clearly, the labour market pay differential between men and women is not primarily a question of sex-based pay discrimination. Rather, it is the result of the still-significant differences in the nature of jobs held by men and women in the labour market. In effect, pay differentials stem more from sex-based job discrimination than from pay discrimination.

9.3.6 Unionization Rate

Unionization is another argument raised to explain the labour market pay differential between men and women. Studies have found that pay is higher in a unionized than in a non-unionized organization, and women are under-represented in unions in comparison with their share of the labour market.

9.3.7 Job Evaluation and Pay Discrimination

Part of the labour market pay differential between men and women may also be the result of conscious or unconscious systemic discrimination in determining pay, primarily during job evaluation.

Whatever method is used, job evaluation is essentially subjective, because it is based on the existing value system and cultural standards at the time of the evaluation. It is not surprising to find that the results of job evaluation may carry the negative (or positive, depending on one's point of view) effects of the value system on which they are based. By definition, a value system brings out the noble nature of certain jobs and the degrading nature of others, by favouring certain requirements at the expense of others. For example, one need only think about the relative value our society places on intellectual work compared to physical labour. The same applies to so-called male versus so-called female characteristics. Since job evaluation is not immune to this problem, it should come as no surprise that the main, standard, job evaluation methods on the market may have an impact on jobs held by a majority of women (Patten, 1987). Most of these methods were developed between the mid-30s and the mid-60s – a period when there were relatively few women in university, when women were considered a second source of income on the labour market, and when their work was seen as similar to their "natural" maternal role (social work, nursing, light physical labour, teaching).

quote

The neutrality of a job evaluation system rests on judgments as to what is being measured, how it is being measured, who is measuring it, who is participating in the process, and how the factors are weighted. Since there is no associated standard of neutrality, no job evaluation system can be proven to be neutral.* Since job evaluation decisions are basically subjective, research indicates that they may be affected by numerous social and personal biases (McArthur, 1985). For example:

— the availability-of-information error, that is, the tendency of evaluators to favour information they can remember most readily;
— the halo effect, that is, the tendency of evaluators to assign value to an entire job based on the nature of only one of its requirements; and
— the expectations error, that is, the tendency of evaluators to favour information that matches their expectations.

Such biases in job evaluation are related to the way people process information. They are not necessarily conscious, but may have a discriminatory effect. For example, the bias related to the availability of information might favour the jobs held by men, because evaluators will be more inclined to fall back on traditional job evaluation factors, since they come more readily to mind. The halo effect will ensure that certain low value or negative characteristics, which are found more in female-dominated jobs, are recognized, and therefore paid, less (for example, opportunities for promotion, poor job security, and simple, monotonous tasks).

In conclusion, to the extent that job evaluation results in prejudice and discrimination, labour market pay differentials between men and women may be partially explained. This limits job evaluation's value in solving pay inequity problems. However, it in no way diminishes its importance as a means of managing pay.

Prejudice may operate and discrimination may occur at various points in the job evaluation process. Their effects may be seen in the choice of evaluation factors, the weighting of those factors, the sex of the evaluators, and the incumbents' pay levels.

Choice of Evaluation Factors

As the Government of Manitoba's Pay Equity Bureau (1986) notes, the gender stereotypes associated with different jobs influence job evaluation results, so that jobs characterized as female are very likely undervalued compared to those considered male.

---

* Private conversation with Jim Delaney, Principal with William M. Mercer Limited in Toronto on April 25, 1990.

The choice of evaluation factors may lead to pay discrimination between men and women. Certain evaluation factors call for special consideration to keep the evaluation process from being biased in favour of either sex (Remick, 1978). For example, one might think of experience and physical effort. (Paradoxically, these very factors are set forth in different legislation as criteria for assessing the degree of similarity between jobs, to identify whether or not there is any discrimination based on the sex of the incumbent.) Since the experience required to hold jobs dominated by women is generally acquired outside the workplace (at school or at home), these jobs are generally considered to require less job experience than male-dominated ones.

Treiman (1979) illustrates the importance of the experience and working condition factors, by comparing a company's evaluations of the jobs of typist and light truck driver. The job evaluation system contains a factor called "knowledge of the work", which is defined in such a way as to indicate the extent of specialized training, the amount of prior experience considered essential, and the length of on-the-job training required to do the work under normal supervision. The typist's job is rated as requiring one month of training; 12 months is specified for the truck driver. One might think that such ratings are based on stereotypes. In fact, in both cases, the training required to do the work is normally acquired – sometimes formally, at other times informally – prior to hiring. A very strong argument might even be made that the training required to work as a typist should be rated higher than that of the truck driver.

In addition, the typist's job is rated as requiring "very light to light" physical effort, compared to "light to moderate" for the truck driver. Yet, does holding the steering wheel of a truck really require more physical effort than typing on a keyboard? This type of question calls for a re-examination of the common historical definition of "physical effort", which emphasizes the use of physical force, while ignoring the fatigue resulting from performing a task that requires small but frequent physical force. The question then becomes: Is strenuous occasional effort more tiring than light continuous effort?

Weighting the Evaluation Factors

The relative importance assigned to each evaluation factor has a direct influence on job evaluation results. By way of illustration, look at the results of Stieber's study (1959, cited by the ILO, 1960), which evaluated a group of jobs using two methods: CWS and NEMA-NMTA (cf. Table 9.1).

As this table illustrates, the jobs are ranked differently, depending on which method is used. This is hardly surprising, given that evaluation results depend mainly on the choice of factors and the weighting used. In this case,

TABLE 9.1
Ranking of certain jobs evaluated by the CWS and NEMA-NMTA methods

	CWS	NEMA-NMTA
Toolmaker	3	1
Millhand (*blooming*)	1	2
Mechanic	4	3
First assistant (open furnace)	2	4
Unskilled labourer	6	5
Assembler (light benchwork)	5	6

while the factors are similar, the weighting is very different. In the NEMA-NMTA method, the set of factors related to occupational skills represents 50% of the points, while those related to responsibility account for 20%; with the CWS method, these proportions are 31% and 45%. Does this mean that one method is more valid than the other?

As mentioned in Chapter 4, there are essentially four ways of determining the weight of job evaluation factors: judgment, statistical methods based on market pay, statistical methods based on organizational pay, and a combination of judgment and statistical methods. Regardless of how the question of weighting is viewed, the risk of discrimination remains. The use of judgment might contain biases that are socially learned. The adoption of market pay brings the discrimination existing in the market into the organization. Finally, the use of organizational pay replicates existing pay inequities.

Sex of the Evaluators

Another potential source of bias in job evaluation results is the sex of the evaluators (more specifically, the socialization differences between women and men). The guidelines proposed by various agencies responsible for enforcing pay equity legislation strongly recommend the presence of a representative number of men and women on evaluation committees (for example, see the *How To Do Pay Equity Job Comparisons*, published by the Ontario Pay Equity Commission in 1989). Are these guidelines justified in practice?

To date, several researchers have tried to measure the effect of the gender of evaluators on job evaluation results. In 1977, Arvey, Passino, and Loundsbury conducted a study in which they projected a slide illustrating a single job – administrative assistant – accompanied by narration provided by three men and three women, paired by degree of attractiveness and quality of voice. Their findings showed that women tended to assign lower evaluations than did men. On the other hand, the results of a 1985 study by Schwab and Grams revealed that the evaluator's sex had no effect on job evaluation results. In 1988, Caron obtained different results, regardless of what evaluation method was used, or how the factors were weighted. Between 15% and 30% of the jobs were ranked differently, depending on whether they were evaluated by a man or a woman, and in 60% to 100% of cases, the evaluations by women were lower than those by men. Bergeron's study in 1990 found the opposite effect; one third of the jobs evaluated were rated slightly higher by the female evaluators.

These studies indicate that the evaluator's gender appears to influence evaluation results. While this has yet to be confirmed, the effect is apparently not universally present. Until further research is done, it would be prudent to form mixed evaluation committees. If this recommendation seems inappropriate in view of the research finding, it is appropriate from the standpoint of the appearance of justice. A mixed committee gives the evaluations greater credibility, especially when a large number of women hold the evaluated jobs.

Incumbent's Gender

To date, about ten studies have tested the discriminatory effect of a jobholder's gender on evaluation results (cf. Grams and Schwab, 1985; Schwab and Grams, 1985), and found no significant effect. Only two (Mahoney and Blake, 1979; Bergeron, 1990) showed that jobs held by women tended to receive a lower evaluation than those held by men.

Pay Level

Pay levels represent yet another potential source of bias in job evaluation. Jobs held by a majority of women may be evaluated as less demanding because they are less well paid. In other words, if market pay for certain jobs influences the evaluator's judgment, the evaluation results of predominantly female jobs will be affected.

Three of the four studies reviewed on this subject concluded that knowledge of pay levels appeared to have a very strong influence on job evaluation results (Grams and Schwab, 1985; Schwab and Grams, 1985; Mount and Ellis, 1985; and Bergeron, 1990). Schwab and Grams, for example, found that knowledge of pay accounts for up to 40% of the variations in total job evaluation results. Bergeron's is the only study that found that knowledge of pay had no significant effect on job evaluation results. But as the author points out, the credibility of the information conveyed to the evaluators about the pay for the jobs studied is questionable.

Thus, on one hand, job evaluation is one of the factors involved in determining pay. On the other, research indicates that evaluators' knowledge of what the incumbents are presently paid has a strong influence on evaluation results. It is apparently circular. One job is considered relatively less demanding because it is relatively less well paid, and is assigned relatively lower pay because it is considered relatively less demanding. The circle can only be broken by paying particular attention to the evaluation criteria and the evaluation process. This is all the more important when it appears that knowledge of market pay carries more weight in determining pay than job evaluation (Rynes, Weber and Milkovich, 1989).

Conclusion

The preceding discussion has shown that evaluation results are probably influenced by the choice of evaluation factors, their weighting, the sex of the evaluators, and market pay. On the other hand, the sex of the jobholders apparently has no effect on the results. While these conclusions seem clear, further studies on the evaluation process are needed. More must be discovered about how evaluation decisions are made, the consequences of those decisions, and the impact on those decisions of external factors, such as the environment within which the system has been established, as well as the relevant management policies (Schwab, 1985).

9.4 Canadian Legislation

Regardless of how pay differentials between the sexes are analyzed, all indications are that discrimination exists. Against this backdrop, in recent years, job evaluation has been growing in importance. In Canada, there is the force of the Canada Labour Code (1970), the Canadian Human Rights Act (1978), and similar legislation in every province. The United States has the Equal Pay Act of 1963 and Title VII of the Civil Rights Act of 1964. Each of these laws, in its own way, prohibits pay discrimination based on sex when individuals are performing equal, equivalent, or comparable work within the same establishment.

9.4.1 History of the Legislation

Pay equity legislation is a subject of more controversy than any other type of action aimed at redressing discrimination in the labour market. This comes as no surprise, since it bears a direct relationship both to women's compensation, and to the employer's total payroll.

As early as 1919, the International Labour Office, to which most members of the League of Nations (the predecessor of the United Nations) belonged, proposed an international convention against pay discrimination. Countries would agree to ensure equal pay for equal work, regardless of the worker's sex; thus, a man and a woman doing identical work would receive the same pay.

In 1951, the International Labour Organization in turn endorsed the principle of prohibiting pay discrimination in its Convention No. 100. It was no longer a matter of "equal pay for equal work", but rather "equal pay for work of equal value". The convention was ratified by 82 countries, including Canada in 1972. Under this type of legislation, the value of the work, not only the work itself, is compared. Jobs that differ in nature, such as secretary and truck driver, may be compared, and may be expected to command equal pay if they have equivalent value.

Article 119 of the Treaty of Rome, which in 1961 established the European Economic Community, stipulates that members will ensure that men and women doing equal work receive the same pay. Guidelines issued by the Community Council in 1975 make it clear that equal work means the same work or work of equal value.

In the United States, the Equal Pay Act of 1963 uses the phrase "equal work", whereas Title VII of the Civil Rights Act of 1964 refers to "similar work". This principle covers instances in which men and women do similar work, yet have different job titles, such as "janitor" and "cleaning woman". The concept of "work of equal value" has no legal force in the United States.

Canadian legislation against sex-based pay discrimination developed in four stages. The first affirmed the principle of *equal pay for equal work*. The federal law on equal pay for women, adopted in 1956 and subsequently repealed, was based on this principle. Several provinces had similar legislation for a time; however, currently all have laws based on one of the later of the four stages.

The second legislative stage, also common to all the provinces, upheld the principle of *equal pay for similar work*. It was introduced with the Canada Labour Code passed by the federal government in 1970, and was adopted by most provinces during the 70s.

The third stage is based on a principle substantially different from the first two: *equal pay for work that is equivalent or of equal value*. Quebec in 1976, was the first Canadian province to adopt legislation along these lines. It was followed by the federal government in 1978, and by the Yukon (for the public sector) in 1987. Here, the entire problem lies in defining what is meant by "work of equal value". As the Quebec Human Rights Commission

(1980) points out, there are three possible cases. First, the tasks involved are identical. Secondly, the jobs being compared differ only in some of their tasks (in this regard, Canadian arbitration rulings on job classification have set 50% as the minimum amount of tasks that must be identical for jobs to be considered similar). Finally, the jobs involve different tasks that may be considered equal or equivalent in value. Task comparison and evaluation raise problems of evaluation and method.

Before describing the fourth legislative stage, it should be noted that the first three were based on a complaints system, which assumed that discrimination is the exception, rather than the rule. Employers are therefore considered innocent until proven guilty.

The fourth legislative phase – *pay equity* – rests on an altogether different premise. Pay discrimination against women is no longer considered the exception, but the rule. Our economic and social system undervalues the work of women compared with that of men. In other words, there is systemic discrimination. The law now obliges employers to examine their pay practices and change them if they are discriminatory. Unlike the previous stages, based on a complaints system, under pay equity legislation, employers must prove that their pay practices are non-discriminatory. Consequently, the legislation is considered proactive. Manitoba was the first Canadian province to adopt such a law in 1985 for public sector employees; it was followed by Ontario in 1987, Nova Scotia and Prince Edward Island in 1988, and New Brunswick in 1989. Ontario is the only Canadian province – in fact, the only government in the world – that has adopted such legislation for private sector employers.

Table 9.2 presents a synopsis of legislation on pay discrimination across Canada.

Not all action to counter pay discrimination is legislated. In recent years, a number of governments have introduced voluntary pay equity programs for their own employees (e.g. the federal government in 1985, Newfoundland in 1988, and British Columbia in 1990).

9.4.2 Federal Legislation

The first Canadian law on equal pay for both sexes was passed in 1956. The first real legal text on the matter, however, is found in section 38.1(1) of the Canada Labour Code, amended in 1970, which states that

> no employer shall establish or maintain differences in wages between male and female employees, employed in the same industrial establishment, who are performing, under the same or similar working conditions, the same or similar work on jobs requiring the same or similar skill, effort and responsibility.

TABLE 9.2
Canadian pay discrimination legislation

Similar work	Complaints Work of equal value	Proactive Work of equal value
Public and private sectors • Alberta (1980) • British Columbia (1984) • Newfoundland (1971) • Saskatchewan (1978) • Northwest Territories (1966) Private sector • Manitoba (1970) • New Brunswick (1973) • Nova Scotia (1972) • Prince Edward Island (1975) • Yukon (1971)	Public and private sectors • Federal (1978) • Quebec (1976) Public sector • Yukon (1987)	Public and private sectors • Ontario (1987) Public sector • Manitoba (1985) • New Brunswick (1989) • Nova Scotia (1988) • Prince Edward Island (1988)

A similar clause was adopted for section 11 of the Canadian Human Rights Act, on pay discrimination, adopted during the 1976-77 parliamentary session. It replaces the word "similar" with "equivalent", yet retains the same for evaluation criteria: working conditions, qualifications, effort, and responsibility which, along with other terms in the Act, were defined in the 1986 regulations.

The Act is based on a complaints system, and the Canadian Human Rights Commission is responsible for applying the law. From 1978 to early 1990, the Commission received slightly over 200 complaints related to pay discrimination. Most of them have been rejected or withdrawn, or remain under review. Some 12 cases have been resolved by the Commission.

In 1984, the federal government adopted a slightly more coercive approach toward compliance with this law, by establishing a pay equity program that allowed Labour Canada, under the Canada Labour Code, to inspect organizations for compliance with section 11 of the Canadian Human Rights Act. In 1985, the federal government undertook an extensive study of pay discrimination in the public sector. It began acting on its findings in late 1990.

Most labour in Canada comes under provincial jurisdiction. The Canada Labour Code applies only to individuals working for federal agencies or organizations under federal jurisdiction, such as banks and interprovincial carriers. Since federal jurisdiction represents only about 10% of Canada's workforce, provincial legislation is appropriate for review here.

9.4.3 Provincial Legislation

Provincial pay equity legislation in Canada falls into three categories.

Both the public and private sectors in British Columbia, Alberta, Saskatchewan, Newfoundland, and the Northwest Territories, as well as the private sector in Manitoba, Prince Edward Island, New Brunswick, Nova Scotia, and the Yukon, are governed by legislation based on "equal pay for similar work", i.e. most of the governments in Canada.

Quebec and the Yukon public sector have legislation based on "equal pay for work of equal value." These laws are demanding for employers, since they seek to eliminate systemic discrimination. Nonetheless, their application is based on a complaints system.

Finally, Ontario and the public sector in Manitoba, Nova Scotia, Prince Edward Island, and New Brunswick are governed by proactive pay equity legislation.

Legislation does not define the limits of provincial action to counter pay discrimination. In 1988, for example, Newfoundland negotiated an agreement with unions representing public sector employees to implement a pay equity program. Saskatchewan had done the same in 1985 with its executives and professionals, and in 1987 with its support staff. British Columbia embarked on the same course in the fall of 1990.

"Equal pay for work of equal value" legislation is the most complex to enforce. The following sections take a closer look at the two ways in which such laws are applied: on the basis of a complaints system, as in Quebec, or through a proactive approach ("pay equity legislation"), as in Ontario.

Quebec Legislation

The first equal pay legislation in Quebec was passed in 1964. Since June 1976, the issue has been governed by the Quebec Charter of Human Rights and Freedoms.

Section 19 of the Charter states that:

> Every employer must, without discrimination, grant equal salary or wages to the members of his personnel who perform equivalent work at the same place. A difference in salary or wages based on experience, seniority, years of service, merit, productivity or overtime is not considered discriminatory if such criteria are common to all members of the personnel.

Section 81 of the Charter first requires that the Commission tries to bring the parties together to settle their differences. In this spirit, it has produced a document describing the thrust that Quebec lawmakers, in the

TABLE 9.3
Summary of complaints regarding compensation (sect. 19) received by the Quebec Human Rights Commission

	1984	1985	1986	1987	1988	1989	Total
Groundless	20	1	2	–	–	–	23
Withdrawal	11	–	2	–	1	–	14
QCHRF ruling	22	1	–	–	–	–	23
Court judgment	3	–	–	–	–	–	3
Out-of-court settlement	4	–	–	–	–	–	4
Subtotal – closed	60	2	4	–	1	–	67
Pending	19	3	2	16	–	6	46
Total	**79**	**5**	**6**	**16**	**1**	**6**	**113**

Commission's view, wished to give to the principle of equal compensation in the Charter of Rights and Freedoms (Quebec Human Rights Commission, 1980).

While this document has no legal force, it reveals the Commission's perception of the meaning of section 19 of the Charter. It is interesting to note the significance this document assigns to the section. The document notes (p. 58) that the phrase "same place" means a set or group of installations belonging to the same individual or corporation, with all the elements required to function independently and separately. "Salary" and "wages" are defined by the Commission as meaning compensation and employee benefits with a monetary value connected with the job.

Regarding "equivalent work", the Commission document (p. 55) emphasizes the concept of equal value, based on a general estimate of the fundamental dimensions needed for habitually and principally performing such work, namely skills, mental and physical effort, responsibilities, and working conditions.

These criteria are similar to those in the Canadian federal legislation, i.e. qualifications, effort, responsibilities, and working conditions.

Application of the Quebec law is based on a complaints system, which gives it a relatively limited practical application. As long as an employee, group, or the Commission responsible for enforcing the law does not lodge a complaint against an organization, nothing is done to determine whether there is any sex-based discrimination. In fact, there have been very few complaints since the law was introduced. Table 9.3, for example, summarizes the compensation complaints received by the Quebec Human Rights Commission. Except for 1984, the number of complaints filed has not been high. This might be expected, given the tedious procedure for filing a complaint.

In terms of Quebec jurisprudence, one might cite the case of Quebec North Shore Paper Co., whose job evaluation system was used to justify the fact that the jobs were "equivalent". In the case of Industries Valcartier, the CWS system was used to show that the jobs were equivalent. It should be noted that, in every case, the burden of proof falls on the employer, not on the complainant.

Ontario Legislation

Only to Ontario

Ontario pay equity legislation (Bill 154), which took effect January 1, 1988, applies not only to all public sector employers, but also to all private sector employers with 10 or more employees. This is a unique case, because nowhere else in the world are private sector employers subject to this type of legislation. In other words, nowhere else in the world does legislation require private sector employers to assess their pay practices from a pay equity perspective, so as to establish job comparison systems and provide equal pay for predominantly male and female jobs of equal value.

The Ontario legislation does not cover all jobs; employers are not required to evaluate every job in their organization. They must first identify predominantly female jobs (60%), as well as potentially equivalent ones among predominantly male jobs (70%). Next, the employer and the union (if there is one) must agree on the evaluation of these jobs. The subsequent steps outlined below describe the process for implementing a pay equity plan called for by Ontario law. In this respect, the Ontario legislation will not necessarily result in rational compensation structures. An employer may very well pay two jobs of the same value at different rates without doing anything illegal, providing that one is not filled predominantly by women and the other by men. In other words, discrimination, if present, may continue to exist, but must not be a function of the incumbent's sex.

Identifying the Establishment and Number of Pay Equity Plans

The first step in any Ontario pay equity program involves determining the number of pay equity plans the organization must implement. The law stipulates at least one plan for each establishment, and an establishment encompasses all employees in a geographic region. Moreover, one plan is required for each bargaining unit in an establishment, as well as one for non-unionized employees. The law allows the parties, if they so desire, to establish fewer equity plans than the required number. T. Eaton Co. in Toronto, for example, must establish at least one plan for employees of its stores in the Toronto area. It could also, however, establish one or more plans for its employees in the Ottawa region. The law recognizes regional pay differentials.

The situation is not always as clear as our example might lead one to believe. In the fall of 1988, the Ontario Nurses' Association (ONA) filed a complaint in court against the Regional Municipality of Haldimand-Norfolk. The Nurses' Union alleged that the Police Commission was not a separate employer from the Municipality, and since the police and nurses working for the municipality had the same employer, they belonged to the same establishment.

The court ruling in July 1989 is interesting. While the term "employer" is not defined in the Pay Equity Act, in its guidelines on pay equity, the Commission states (series No. 2, March 1988):

> No single criterion governs the determination of who the employer is, but the following concepts have been used in legal decisions:
> - Who exercises direction and control over employees;
> - Who determines compensation;
> - Who hires, disciplines and dismisses employees;
> - Who the employees perceive to be the employer;
> - Whether there was an intention to create an employer-employee relationship.

Further in its guidelines, the Commission adds:

> The definition of employer under the Pay Equity Act will likely be consistent with the decisions of the Ontario Labour Relations Board, Employment Standards adjudicators, the Workers' Compensation Appeals Tribunal, and the courts.

In the case against the Regional Municipality of Haldimand-Norfolk, the Pay Equity Hearings Tribunal ruled in favour of the Nurses. In its decision, however, the Tribunal set four new criteria for determining the definition of the employer. These criteria go well beyond the Commission's guidelines and established jurisprudence on application of the Labour Relations Act.

In rendering its decision, the Tribunal used the following criteria to define the "employer":

1. Who has overall financial responsibility?

2. Who has responsibility for compensation practices?

3. What is the nature of the business, the service or the enterprise?

To those three, the court added a fourth, which it stated as follows:

4. What is more consistent with achieving the purpose of Pay Equity Act?

In brief, to determine the definition of employer in this case, the Tribunal based itself on the objectives and intent of the law, among other things. If application of the first three criteria results in a decision in favour of different employers, and if application of the fourth criterion furthers the objective of the Pay Equity Act, the fourth criterion prevails. In its decision, the Tribunal also noted that additional criteria could be used, if necessary.

This decision was appealed to the Ontario Court of Appeal, the highest provincial tribunal, which in October 1990 upheld the decision of the Pay Equity Hearings Tribunal. According to the Court of Appeal, the tribunal had not overstepped its jurisdiction.

In two other decisions on this matter (CCH Canadian Limited, 180-007 and 180-008, 1990), the Tribunal maintained this orientation, and rejected the standards used in labour relations to identify the employer. The four criteria used in the case of the Regional Municipality of Haldimand-Norfolk were again upheld.

Determining Predominantly Female and Predominantly Male Jobs

The second stage of a pay equity plan in Ontario involves identifying the jobs held predominantly by women and those held predominantly by men, with the norm set at 60% for the former and 70% for the latter. It adds that a predominantly female job category may include any

> job class that a review officer or the Hearings Tribunal decides is a female job class or a job class that the employer, with the agreement of the bargaining agent, if any, for the employees of the employer, decides is a female job class.

Nonetheless, the Commission considered it wise to issue guidelines in this regard. These guidelines are not absolute. Historical data, the number of people filling the jobs, and even stereotypes, must all be considered. For example, an engineering job with one male and two female incumbents would probably be classified as predominantly male, because engineers are usually men.

Specifically, the law states that one must identify not jobs, but rather job classes, on which to base the comparisons. A job class means "those positions... that have similar duties and responsibilities and require similar qualifications, are filled by similar recruiting procedures and have the same compensation schedule, salary grade or range of salary rates." (Pay Equity Commission of Ontario, 1989)

This question of determining female and male predominance raises another: What does one do if one cannot identify predominantly male classes to compare with predominantly female ones? This may happen for two reasons; either no comparison can be drawn within the non-union group of employees or the bargaining unit under consideration, or else there is no comparison within the establishment.

If there is no comparable predominantly male job within the non-union group of employees or bargaining unit under consideration, the law stipulates that one must be found within the organization's other non-union group of employees or bargaining units. This raises the problem of access to information for identifying comparable jobs outside the group under consideration. The Pay Equity Hearings Tribunal has already had to settle several disputes in this area. In the case of Cybermedix Health Services (CCH Canadian Limited, 180-006, 1990), the union claimed that management was refusing to provide information for establishing a pay equity plan. The bargaining unit represented by the union consisted primarily of women. Hence, they had to go outside the unit to find potentially comparable male-dominated jobs, in accordance with the provisions of the law. In this case, the court ordered the employer to provide the union with:

- the titles of all jobs outside the bargaining unit;
- the extent of male or female predominance in each job;
- the pay scale for each job; and
- the description of each job.

This orientation of the Tribunal was upheld by another decision, *Riverdale Hospital v. the Canadian Union of Public Employees* (CCH Canadian Limited, 180-013, 1990). Note that, in both cases, the court did not order the information on actual individual pay to be disclosed, but rather job rate.

A lack of comparable jobs within an establishment is one of the main weaknesses of the existing legislation, according to advocates of pay equity. The Ontario government has promised to amend its legislation to remedy this. There are at least three ways of solving the problem of a lack of male-dominated jobs within an establishment. The first involves proxy comparison, which means identifying a comparable male-dominated job in one of the employer's other establishments. This solution is now being seriously considered by the Ontario government for public sector employees. Secondly, one might use the average adjustment method, by comparing the compensation for a female-dominated job with the average compensation for a set of equivalent male-dominated jobs within a group of establishments or an industry. Thirdly, the method the Ontario government appears to be favouring for predominantly female private sector jobs for which no comparable male-dominated jobs can be found is the proportional value method. This involves a comparison within the same establishment by means of various techniques, including one that entails giving female-dominated jobs for which there are no comparable male-dominated jobs pay adjustments in proportion to those made for predominantly female jobs for which comparable male-dominated jobs could be found. Yet another technique is to pay employees in predominantly female jobs for which there are no comparable male-dominated jobs the equivalent pay indicated by the pay line offered to incumbents of male-dominated jobs.

*[handwritten margin note: whole section * very important]*

Selecting a Gender-neutral Job Evaluation Method

Although the Pay Equity Commission endorses no particular job evaluation method, certain methods appear to be more appropriate than others from the outset. The point method (in its traditional or contemporary form, standard or customized), for example, apparently suits the pay equity objective established by law much better than any other method. Its analytic and quantitative nature allows it to consider the four evaluation factors explicitly, i.e. skills, effort, responsibility, and working conditions. Use of a point method, however, is no guarantee of a gender-neutral evaluation. To determine the gender neutrality of a job evaluation method, one must consider factors such as:

- what is measured, i.e. the criteria used;
- how it is measured, i.e. the definition of those criteria;
- who measured it, i.e. composition of the committee in terms not only of the number of men and women, but also the familiarity with jobs, experience, etc.;
- the weights assigned to evaluation criteria; and
- how the method is applied (evaluation process).

Once adopted, the point method does not guarantee gender neutrality. This method, however, is probably the safest. The others, in fact, create problems. The factor method would seem to be difficult to accept for the purposes of pay equity, because it uses market pay to evaluate benchmark jobs. The same applies to the classification and ranking methods, because of their general, non-analytic nature. This makes it difficult to see how these methods could explicitly consider the four principal dimensions required by law. Yet the Commission (Pay Equity Commission, 1990) agreed to use the ranking method for small businesses with less than 10 employees (who, it should be noted, are not subject to the law). It adds, however, that this method does not enable larger employers to draw relevant distinctions about job requirements.

Unlike legislation in Manitoba, Prince Edward Island, and Nova Scotia, the Ontario law does not oblige employers to evaluate all their jobs with only one system. Each system used, though, must be able to evaluate all the jobs and thereby satisfy the neutrality requirements of the law (MacKinnon, 1990; Weiner and Gunderson, 1990).

Evaluating the Jobs

The law does not attempt to redress all pay inequities, but solely those related to predominantly female jobs. Hence, it does not require all jobs to be evaluated, only the female-dominated ones and the male-dominated ones that would appear to be comparable. *are the ones to be evaluated by law*

In a unionized organization, the union and the employer must agree on the evaluation results. Although the law does not oblige them to use a committee with equal representation of both sides for the evaluation, this approach is generally advantageous.

The results of the comparisons drawn between predominantly male and predominantly female jobs must appear in the pay equity program in accordance with the next two steps.

Determining the Jobs to Be Used for Comparison

The law provides a sequential process of comparison, which makes it possible to determine the predominantly male jobs to be compared to the predominantly female ones. This search for comparable jobs begins within the bargaining unit or the non-union group of employees under consideration within the establishment. If the search fails, another bargaining unit or non-union group of employees must be used. If necessary, it must be reported that there is no comparable male-dominated job. If more than one predominantly male job applies, the employer may select the lower paid.

Comparing Compensation

Another key step in an Ontario pay equity program is to compare forms of compensation: salary, bonuses, employee benefits, etc. In the case of part-time employees, also covered by the law, the cost of employee benefits must be prorated to those of their full-time colleagues.

The law allows some discrepancies in the various types of compensation, if based on the following factors: length of service, temporary training or development assignments, performance evaluation (formal system), red-circling pay, or skills-shortage.

In addition to these five criteria, section 8(2) of the Act indicates that once an establishment achieves pay equity, pay differentials between men and women may still ultimately be created, provided the employer is able to prove that they result from differences in union bargaining power. In other words, the law accepts the fact that union bargaining power influences *future* compensation, but it does not allow its use to justify *existing* or *historical* pay differentials.

Determining the Necessary Adjustments

The next step is to determine, for each predominantly female job, the necessary compensation adjustments, their magnitude, and their effective date.

The law stipulates that for the private sector, the total required adjustments under an employer's various pay equity plans must equal at least 1%

of the preceding year's payroll (excluding employee benefits), or the amount required to achieve pay equity, if less than 1%. This amount must be distributed among the various plans, if there is more than one. In making the adjustments, priority within a bargaining unit or non-union group must be assigned to the lowest paying jobs, rather than to those requiring the most adjustment.

Experience shows the cost of implementing pay equity varies between 2% and 6% of payroll, with an average of 2.5%. The cost is often lower for large, non-unionized organizations, because of the larger selection of comparable jobs. Conversely, the cost is often higher for small employers with a mixture of union and non-union groups, because the scarcity of comparable jobs within a non-unionized group means comparisons must be made with jobs in one of the unionized groups (Delaney and Sullivan, 1990).

Preparing the Pay Equity Plan

The objective of a pay equity plan is to provide relatively detailed information about how pay equity will be achieved in the bargaining unit or the non-union group of employees under consideration. Chapter 13 of the Act specifies the content of a pay equity plan: definition of the establishment, lists of the predominantly male and predominantly female jobs, description of the job evaluation system, evaluation results, pay differentials, explanation of visible differences, any required adjustments, and the dates of the first adjustments.

Announcing the Pay Equity Plan

This step, quite simply, involves posting the pay equity plan in a prominent location, where employees can read it.

The law also stipulates a deadline for posting and making the first pay equity plan adjustments. As indicated in Table 9.4, the implementation dates depend on the number of full- and part-time employees within the organization. While employers with 10 to 99 employees are not obliged to post their pay equity plan, they are required to achieve pay equity.

Resolving Opposition and Official Complaints

Non-unionized employees have 90 days to examine the content of a pay equity plan and respond. In a unionized organization, the program is considered approved when the bargaining agents accept its provisions. Throughout the process, employees or their union representatives may file notices of opposition or complaints with the Commission if they feel their rights are being violated. A review officer then attempts to effect a settlement and,

TABLE 9.4
Deadlines for implementing pay equity programs in Ontario

Size of the employer (number of employees)	Date
All public sector employees	01-01-90
500 or more employees in the private sector	01-01-90
100-499 employees in the private sector	01-01-91
50-99 employees in the private sector (optional)	01-01-92
10-49 employees in the private sector (optional)	01-01-93

in the end, may issue an order. Following the parties' review of the order or decision made by a review officer, a request for a hearing may be made to the Pay Equity Hearings Tribunal regarding the issue(s) in dispute.

By the end of November 1990, 1,866 complaints had been lodged with the Commission's Pay Equity Office. The parties reached an agreement in 431 cases, 104 required review officer orders, 3 were referred directly to the Tribunal, and 1,328 remain under consideration.

The most common complaints involve refusal to disclose information, definition of employer, determining the gender neutrality of the evaluation system, and delays in posting the program. By November 1990, about 100 cases had been brought before the Tribunal; the vast majority of them came from public sector unions (the Ontario Nurses' Association alone filed almost 60).

9.5 American Legislation   Don't worry about this

The principal American legislation against sex-based pay discrimination emerged in the 60s. In 1963, the federal government passed the Equal Pay Act, which was intended to prevent pay discrimination between men and women filling jobs that required the same degree of skills, effort, and responsibility, and involved the same working conditions. The law also stated that pay differentials were legal if justified by length of service with the organization, employee performance as evaluated by a formal system, or any individual characteristics other than sex.

In 1964, Congress passed a major piece of anti-discrimination legislation: the Civil Rights Act and, more specifically, the section known as Title VII. The Civil Rights Act is much more sweeping than the Equal Pay Act, because it affects all employment practices, and not simply compensation. It also opens the way to replacing the concept of "equal work" with that of "work of comparable worth", for it basically prohibits discrimination based on sex and certain other characteristics. The concept of "work of comparable worth", however, has no legal force, because it still has no acceptable working definition (Barrett and Sansonetti, 1988).

As with the Equal Pay Act, application of the law is essentially based on a complaints system. An employer is considered innocent until minimum evidence of discrimination is established.

To date, there has been no real test of the principle of "comparable worth" as a possible interpretation of Title VII of the Act. For example, court decisions have recognized the relevance of both job evaluation and market pay in justifying pay differentials within an organization. When job evaluations and pay surveys have produced conflicting results, the courts have tended to favour the findings of the pay survey, as in the cases of *American Nurses Association v. State of Illinois* in 1985, *Christensen v. State of Iowa* in 1977, *Lemons v. City and County of Denver* in 1980, *Spalding v. University of Washington* in 1984, and *AFSCME v. State of Washington* in 1985 (Rynes, Weber and Milkovich, 1989).

Furthermore, the Commission responsible for applying the law considers complaints valid only insofar as an intention to discriminate can be established. Simply showing that a pay differential exists between two "equal" jobs is insufficient evidence to conclude that discrimination exists.

At the state level, the situation differs somewhat. By early 1991, some 20 states had initiated or completed a pay adjustment program after completing preliminary studies, and just over 20 others are in the process of carrying out their preliminary studies. Some states, such as Minnesota, New Jersey, and Washington, have enacted legislation based on the principle of work of comparable worth; others rest on the principle of similar work. In practice, laws based on the principle of work of comparable worth apply only to state employees.

While the issue of sex-based pay discrimination remains a topic of debate in the United States, the controversy has abated in recent years. There is little likelihood, as Hill and Killingsworth (1989) point out, that the concept of "work of comparable worth" will be applied on a broad scale in the United States during the coming years. While studies and efforts continue at the state and local (municipal) levels, and occasional adjustments may be expected, there is little prospect of real change at the federal level. In fact, several Congressional Bills since 1984 have called for studies of federal government employees, but these have all died on the Senate floor.

Even today, various courts are grappling with such highly complex issues as: When are two jobs equal for the purposes of compensation? Who should determine the worth of a job? What criteria should be used to determine the value of a job? Should the market be the ultimate criterion of equitable pay? Under what circumstances could an employer be found guilty of unintentional discrimination? If the cost of redressing inequities is too high, should the employer be given a reprieve?

This does not mean that nothing is changing. On the contrary, according to an American Compensation Association survey, over half of the existing job evaluation systems have been instituted since the early 80s. Moreover, various states, including New York, California, and Massachusetts, without resorting to legislation, have formed commissions to investigate pay equity among their own employees. Obviously, however, this is a long way from the great social preoccupations of the 60s and 70s. It will definitely be some time before proactive pay equity legislation applicable to private sector employers makes its appearance in the United States.

☐ 9.6 Implications for Employers

Regardless of whether the legislation governing them is proactive or based on a complaint system, Canadian organizations stand to gain from implementing a number of pay equity measures. These measures are not all mandatory but, rather, reflect current practices in organizations interested in providing equitable compensation for their employees, regardless of sex. The measures involve both job evaluation systems and pay determination.

Pay discrimination legislation attaches great importance to job evaluation. Employers must therefore take pains to ensure that no discriminatory bias occurs at the various critical stages of implementing an evaluation system (i.e. job analysis, selecting the evaluation method, choosing factors, weighting them, and the evaluation process) or in determining individual pay.

9.6.1 Job Analysis

It is especially important for employers to have documentation on jobs so that, if necessary, they can prove the absence of prejudice based on the sex of employees.

Regardless of what job analysis method is adopted, the organization must be in a position to demonstrate that the risk of bias in applying it is minimized. It is important that employers keep records on each job. The writing of job descriptions, however, is not mandatory.

9.6.2 Job Evaluation Method

Organizations have a choice of the four principal evaluation methods: ranking, classification, factors, and points. In a pay equity environment, the first three, however, should be adopted with caution. Ranking and classification make it too difficult for an employer to justify evaluation results, because the criteria used to evaluate each job are neither stable nor precise. The factor method, on the other hand, bases job evaluation on market pay data for the benchmark jobs, whereas the intent of the law is precisely to prevent organizations from justifying pay differentials between men and women on the basis of the market, where discrimination exists.

For all practical purposes, legislators favour the point system. It may be predetermined, meaning that the selection of evaluation factors and their weighting may be standardized or customized specifically for an organization. Generally speaking, organizations must exercise caution in using standard point systems (Weiner and Gunderson, 1990). Since the choice of factors and their weighting reflect value systems, close attention must be paid to whether or not the standard method has negative effects on the evaluation of certain jobs.

9.6.3 Selecting Job Evaluation Factors

Organizations must select non-discriminatory job evaluation factors. The four required by law are skills, effort, responsibility, and working conditions. Simply choosing those four factors, however, does not necessarily mean that an organization is obeying the law. Each factor may be more or less discriminatory, depending essentially on how it is defined. This calls for prudence. There are numerous examples of how factor definitions favour predominantly male jobs; take, for instance, the following:

— Human relations
   The skills required for working with people other than subordinates are often excluded from the definition of this factor. In other words, for a nurse's job, the interpersonal skills required to work with patients are not explicitly included.

— Physical effort
   The definition of this factor often emphasizes the weight of the objects that must be lifted whereas, in certain predominantly female jobs, the objects are not very heavy, but the activity is frequently repeated. Ignoring this fact is therefore discriminatory.

Certain evaluation factors more characteristic of predominantly female jobs are often taken for granted or given little consideration:

— Skills
   • Speed and fine motor skills: someone who types 50 words a minute for 5 minutes executes 1,250 finger movements; in addition, no more than 5 mistakes are allowed. For an experienced typist, the requirement may be 90 words a minute, which would involve

7.5 finger movements per second. Based on generally accepted standards, a 9/2,250 errors rate would be tolerable, or 0.4% every 5 minutes. A factor such as this is very rarely found in job evaluation methods. Nonetheless, this skill merits recognition and pay;
  • Operating and maintaining office and production equipment;
  • Writing letters for other people, rereading and revising their work;

— Effort
  • Adapting to rapid changes in office systems or industrial technology;
  • Executing complex task sequences requiring good eye/hand coordination;
  • Coping with frequent interruptions to work requiring concentration;

— Responsibility
  • Training and orienting newly hired employees;
  • Coordinating schedules for large number of people;

— Working conditions
  • Dealing with people who are angry, upset, or irrational;
  • Tension from handling complaints; and
  • Stress caused by noise in an open work area, or by an overcrowded office.

In brief, an organization must not only consider skills, effort, responsibility, and working conditions, but must also ensure that none of these factors is defined in a discriminatory way.

9.6.4 Weighting Evaluation Factors

What has been said about selecting evaluation factors applies equally to their weighting, which must not favour factors associated primarily with male-dominated job categories.

Manitoba's Pay Equity Bureau (1986) provides an example of gender-neutral weighting. In comparing the job of assembler to company nurse, the total number of points before weighting was not based on the same factors, but was similar for both jobs. The assembler's job received more points for physical activity and working conditions, and fewer for task complexity and training. The nurse's job, on the other hand, earned more points for task complexity and training, and fewer for physical activity and working conditions. In this case, gender-neutral weighting means not attaching great weight to the factors for which the assembler obtains relatively more points, and at the same time, less to those for which the job scores lower. In other words, one must not assign a high or a low percentage to factors whose relative importance is exclusive to one job category.

In the above example, assigning 15% to working conditions, 15% to physical activity, and 7% to task complexity would probably be discriminatory toward women, because the assembler's job would be favoured at the expense of the nurse's. A more equitable weighting would be 5% to working conditions, 10% to physical activity, and 15% to task complexity.

Factor weights are often determined statistically, by means of a multiple regression analysis based on the current pay for jobs. This approach simply perpetuates existing discrimination. Treiman and Hartman (1981) have suggested two ways of correcting this discriminatory effect. The first is to include the percentage of women holding the job in the multiple regression equation. Since the effect of the incumbents' sex thereby becomes a constant, the coefficients of the various evaluation factors, i.e. their weighting, are not skewed by that variable. Similarly, other variables, such as length of service or level of training, may be added to the multiple regression equation so as to take into consideration their effect on pay determination.

The second solution is to determine the weighting by performing multiple regression analyses on predominantly male jobs, then applying the results to all jobs. This method is valid only insofar as the characteristics of the male-dominated jobs are the same as those of the female-dominated ones.

9.6.5 Job Evaluation Process

Regardless of what evaluation method is used, there will always be an element of subjectivity in the choice of factors and their weighting. There is also a great deal of subjectivity in job evaluation itself. To avoid any gender bias in the process, an evaluation committee consisting of men and women of different ages and holding different jobs should be formed. The committee members should also receive training in job evaluation. This means, for example, reinforcing the fact that they are evaluating job content, and not the incumbent, that they are evaluating the jobs as they are, not as they should be.

9.6.6 Determining Individual Pay

Once the job evaluation process is complete, an organization must determine each employee's pay. Once again, an incumbent's gender must not influence the determination of that person's pay. While all laws recognize that two employees may receive different pay even though they do work of equal value, the pay scale or various pay rates for their job must be the same. The individual characteristics allowing different pay to be assigned to employees doing work of equal value vary, depending on the legislation. Nonetheless, the following factors are generally accepted and recognized:

- experience relevant to the job;
- length of service with the organization;
- performance evaluation based on a formal system, with predetermined criteria known to employees;
- participation in a training or development program open to both men and women; and
- a labour shortage for the job, resulting in temporarily higher pay for the employee filling it.

☐ 9.7 Summary

After describing the nature of gender-based pay discrimination, this chapter discussed its relative impact on pay differentials between men and women. A review of Canadian legislation on pay discrimination revealed a number of implications for employers. In effect, the best way to prevent legal proceedings for pay discrimination is to establish a gender-neutral job evaluation system. In the United States, proactive pay equity legislation applicable to private sector employers is not likely to be enacted in the near future.

This chapter concludes Part IV, which integrates the concepts of internal equity, external equity, and individual equity. Assembling these three elements makes it possible to develop a pay structure, and to determine each employee's pay. In Part V, we examine various means of rewarding individual and group performance.

REFERENCES

ALDRICH, M. and R. BUCHELE, "Where to Look for Comparable Worth: The Implications of Efficiency Wages", in *Comparable Worth: Analyses and Evidence*, edited by M.A. Hill and M.R. Killingsworth, Ithaca, New York, I.L.R. Press, 1989, pp. 11-28.

ARVEY, R.D., E.M. PASSINO and J.W. LOUNDSBURY, "Job Analysis Results as Influenced by Sex of Incumbents and Sex of Analyst", *Journal of Applied Psychology*, 1977, vol. 62, N° 4, pp. 411-416.

BARRETT, G.V. and D.M. SANSONETTI, "Issues Concerning the Use of Regression Analysis in Salary Discrimination Cases", *Personnel Psychology*, 1988, vol. 41, N° 3, pp. 503-516.

BERGERON, J., *Effet du sexe de l'évaluateur, du sexe du titulaire et du niveau de salaire sur les résultats d'évaluation d'emplois*, directed research for Master's Degree, Montreal, École des hautes études commerciales, Université de Montréal, 1990.

CARON, I., *Étude sur la convergence des résultats d'évaluation de deux méthodes de points d'évaluation des emplois*, Master's Thesis, Montreal, École des hautes études commerciales, Université de Montréal, 1988.

CCH CANADIAN LIMITED, *Canadian Pay Equity Compliance Guide*, Don Mills, Ontario, CCH Canadian Limited, 1990.

COMMISSION DES DROITS DE LA PERSONNE DU QUÉBEC, *À travail équivalent, salaire égal, sans discrimination*, cahier N° 3, Québec, Commission des droits et libertés de la personne du Québec, 1980.

DELANEY, J. and L. SULLIVAN, *Pay Equity: A Survivor's Guide*, Toronto, William M. Mercer Limited, May 24, 1990.

FAILLE, M., "Taux de féminité et taux de salaires moyens selon le sexe dans l'enquête sur la rémunération globale des emplois repères au Québec en 1988", *Le Marché du travail*, August 1989, pp. 62-71.

GERHART, B., "Gender Differences in Current and Starting Salaries: The Role of Performance, College Major and Job Title", *Industrial and Labor Relations Review*, 1990, vol. 43, N° 4, pp. 418-433.

GRAMS, R. and D.P. SCHWAB, "An Investigation of Systems Gender Related Error in Job Evaluation", *Academy of Management Journal*, 1985, vol. 28, N° 2, pp. 279-290.

HILL, M.A. and M.R. KILLINGSWORTH (Editors), *Comparable Worth: Analysis and Evidence*, Ithaca, New York, I.L.R. Press, 1989.

HODSON, R. and P. ENGLAND, "Industrial Structure and Sex Differences in Earnings", *Industrial Relations*, 1985, vol. 25, N° 1, pp. 16-32.

INTERNATIONAL LABOR OFFICE, *La Qualification du travail*, Geneva, International Labor Office, 1960.

KILLINGSWORTH, M.R., "The Economics of Comparable Worth: Analytical, Empirical, and Policy Questions", in *Comparable Worth: New Directions for Research*, edited by H.I. Hartman, Washington, D.C., National Academy Press, 1985, pp. 86-115.

MacKINNON, C., "The Implication of Pay Equity on Job Evaluation Systems", in *Pay Equity in Ontario: A Manager's Guide*, edited by D.W. Conklin and P. Bergman, London, Ontario, The National Centre for Management Research and Development, University of Western Ontario, 1990, pp. 31-44.

MAHONEY, T., S. RYNES and R. BENSON, "Where Do Compensation Specialists Stand on Comparable Worth", *Compensation Review*, 1984, vol. 16, N° 4, pp. 27-40.

MAHONEY, T.A. and R.H. BLAKE, "Occupational Pays as a Function of Sex Stereotypes and Job Context", *Academy of Management Proceedings*, Atlanta, Georgia, 1979.

MARSHALL, K., "Women in Professional Occupations: Progress in the 1980s", *Canadian Social Trends*, Spring, 1989, pp. 13-16.

McARTHUR, L.Z., "Social Judgement Biases in Comparable Worth Analysis", in *Comparable Worth: New Directions for Research*, edited by H.I. Hartmann, Washington, D.C., National Academy Press, 1985.

MILKOVICH, G.T. and J.M. NEWMAN, *Compensation*, Homewood, Illinois, Richard D. Irwin, 1990.

MOUNT, M.K. and R. ELLIS, *Impacts of Pay Level, Job Gender and Job Type on Job Evaluation Ratings*, Des Moines, Department of Industrial Relations and Human Resources, College of Business Administration, University of Iowa, 1985.

ONTARIO PAY EQUITY COMMISSION, "Definition of Employer", *Pay Equity Implementation Series #2*, Toronto, The Pay Equity Commission, March, 1988.

ONTARIO PAY EQUITY COMMISSION, *How to Do Pay Equity Job Comparisons*, Toronto, The Pay Equity Commission, 1989.

OI, W.F., "Neglected Women and Other Implications of Comparable Worth", *Contemporary Policy Issues*, April 1986, pp. 21-32.

PATTEN, T.H., "How Do You Know If Your Job Evaluation System Is Working", in *New Perspectives on Compensation*, edited by D.B. Balkin and L.R. Gomez-Mejia, Englewood Cliffs, New Jersey, Prentice-Hall Inc., 1987, pp. 10-19.

PAY EQUITY BUREAU *Pay Equity: Equality at Work*, Winnipeg, Manitoba, Ministry of Labour, 1986.

PAY EQUITY COMMISSION, *Pay Equity in the Workplace*, Toronto, Ontario Pay Equity Commission, 1990.

PRESSE (LA), Écart de salaires entre les femmes et les hommes", December 22, 1990.

PROVINCE OF ONTARIO, *The Green Paper on Pay Equity*, Toronto, Attorney General and Minister Responsible for Women's Issues, November, 1985.

REMICK, H., "Strategies for Creating Sound, Bias-Free Job Evaluation Plans", *Industrial Relations Counselors Inc. Meeting*, Atlanta, Georgia, September 14 and 15, 1978.

RYNES, S., C. WEBER and G. MILKOVICH, "The Effects of Market Survey Rates, Job Evaluation, and Job Gender on Job Pay", *Journal of Applied Psychology*, 1989, vol. 74, N° 1, pp. 114-123.

SCHWAB, D.P., "Job Evaluation Research and Research Needs", in *Comparable Worth: New Directions for Research*, Washington, D.C., National Academy Press, 1985, pp. 37-52.

SCHWAB, D.P. and R. GRAMS, "Sex Related Errors in Job Evaluation: A "Real-World" Test", *Journal of Applied Psychology*, 1985, vol. 70, N° 3, pp. 533-539.

SORENSEN, E. "The Crowding Hypothesis and Comparable Worth", *Journal of Human Resources*, 1990, vol. 25, N° 1, pp. 55-89.

STIEBER, J., *The Steel Industry Wage Structure*, Cambridge, Massachusetts, Harvard University Press, 1959.

TREIMAN, D.J., *Job Evaluation: An Analytical Review*, Washington, D.C., National Academy Press, 1979.

TREIMAN, D.J. and H.I. HARTMAN (editors), *Women, Work and Wages: Equal Pay for Jobs of Equal Value*, Washington, D.C., National Academy Press, 1981.

VANASSE, D., *La clientèle féminine aux H.E.C. 1979-1989*, Montreal, Recherche institutionnelle, École des hautes études commerciales, March 7, 1990.

WEINER, N. and M. GUNDERSON, *Pay Equity: Issues, Options and Experiences*, Toronto, Butterworths, 1990.

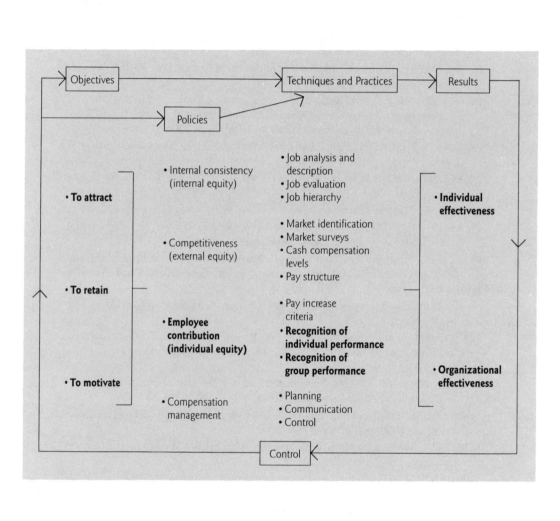

V

REWARDING INDIVIDUAL
AND GROUP PERFORMANCE

The preceding sections have focused on determining what to pay employees within an organization. As mentioned, this is essentially a twofold decision: how much to pay based on the job, and how much, based on employee characteristics. The concepts of job class, midpoint, or normal maximum are important for job-based pay. In some cases, the decision on how much to pay stops there, and everyone holding the same job receives the same pay. In most cases, however, pay also varies depending on specific employee characteristics. In this regard, one of the most universally accepted concepts in compensation management is merit compensation.

Chapter 10 examines work motivation and merit compensation, while Chapter 11 considers individual performance evaluation – the Achilles' heel of merit compensation.

In addition to merit compensation plans, many organizations have recognized the benefits of having incentive plans (variable compensation). These plans, which may apply to different employee categories, are an effective way for an organization to reward both individual and group performance. Chapter 12 describes a range of plans based, first, on short-term performance (normally one year), then on long-term performance (normally three or five years). Long-term plans are generally either real or notional ownership-incentive plans.

TABLE OF CONTENTS

10

MOTIVATION AND MERIT COMPENSATION

Merit compensation is a controversial issue. Some people consider it a myth; others see it as an effective means of increasing organizational productivity. Some support it in principle, yet oppose it in practice. Still others have one reason or another for opposing it altogether. Nonetheless, the concept of individual merit compensation is certainly one of the most widely accepted concepts in pay administration. Failure to give monetary recognition for employees' performance may lead to serious inequities. However, views on merit compensation differ, and not all organizations attach the same importance to it.

This chapter contains a review of merit compensation, beginning with an explanation of the concept of motivation, the various underlying theories, and the role of human needs and how compensation can be used to meet these needs. Presentation of an explanatory model of job performance is followed by a definition of the elements of a merit compensation program. The next section discusses the pros and cons of merit compensation, and the prerequisites for a successful program. The chapter concludes by examining the choice between two means of rewarding individual performance – pay increases and bonuses.

☐ 10.1 Motivation

A decision on the relevance of a merit compensation policy may be aided by an examination of the literature on motivational theory and determinants of job performance. After describing selected theories of motivation, this section discusses the role of human needs and of compensation in motivating employees on the job. Finally, it presents a model of the determinants of job performance that incorporates the role of motivation.

It is generally acknowledged that pay has an impact on employee performance through its effect on motivation. Although there are many different theories of motivation, this chapter focuses on the expectancy theory, for three reasons. First, it has been primarily used to explain work motivation. Secondly, it has received more empirical support in the workplace than the other theories. Finally, the other theories of motivation may usually be incorporated into it (Heneman and Schwab, 1975).

10.1.1. Expectancy Theory

History

Expectancy theory is based on the work of Tolman (1932) and Lewin (1935), which revealed the importance of the concept of instrumentality for, respectively, animals and humans. This theory suggests that individuals have more or less marked preferences for the various objectives or results they pursue. In this regard, it is not a purely psychological theory; it borrows certain concepts from decision-making theory (Edwards, 1954) and economics. Expectancy theory further assumes that employees attach a greater or lesser value to the various rewards they can obtain from their work.

In 1957, Georgopoulos, Mahoney and Jones pointed out that motivation influences performance, and that it depends both on the strength of different personal needs and on an individual's perception of the value of different behaviours in achieving different ends. In 1958, Atkinson began to crystallize the principles of expectancy theory, proposing that motivation is a function of employees' expectations and the nature of the incentives. In 1964, Vroom became the first to place expectancy theory within a genuine cognitive model. His version of expectancy theory, as subsequently modified by various authors, is the one that has begun to be systematically applied in the workplace. According to Vroom, money acquires a valence (value, importance) when an employee perceives its value for achieving certain ends or satisfying certain needs.

Theory

Figure 10.1 illustrates the content of expectancy theory.

According to this model, the effort an individual makes at work (motivation) depends essentially on how that person perceives three factors.

Expectancy   The extent to which an individual perceives a relationship between the amount of effort made and the different levels of performance that result. In other words, it is the probability assigned by individuals to their ability to attain different levels of performance. This perception of

FIGURE 10.1
Outline of expectancy theory

$$\Sigma \{(E \rightarrow P)\ [\Sigma\ (P \rightarrow R)\ V]\} \rightarrow \text{Effort (motivation)}$$

Legend

$E \rightarrow P$:   The relationship an individual perceives between the effort made and the resulting level of performance (the probability that a given amount of effort is linked to a certain level of performance.)

$P \rightarrow R$:   The relationship an individual perceives between different levels of performance and the benefits to be gained by reaching them.

V: The value of the benefits for the individual.

SOURCE: Adapted from Lawler (1971).

probability is influenced by the individual's level of self-esteem and the experience gained in similar work situations. The higher a person's self-esteem, or the more positive experiences that person has had in similar situations, the greater the expectations of achieving a given level of performance. For example, if aspiring managers appreciate a compensation management course, the professor will have more confidence that other students will appreciate the course the next time it is taught.

Instrumentality   The extent to which an individual perceives a relationship between different levels of performance and their potential rewards. In other words, it is the probability that a person assigns to obtaining various rewards for different levels of performance. For example, what probability does the compensation management professor attach to obtaining various rewards for giving a good course to aspiring managers? The more the professor enjoys teaching, the greater the likelihood of experiencing a sense of accomplishment. At the same time, if the professor is paid a fixed salary, the probability of earning a performance bonus will be perceived as nonexistent.

Valence   The amount of importance or value a person assigns to the various possible rewards of work. The more the benefits satisfy different personal needs, the higher the valence. Valence may be positive (something desirable) or negative (something undesirable). To return to our example, giving a compensation management course entails marking exams, which may have a negative valence for the professor. However, giving future managers an understanding of compensation management theory and methods may have a very positive valence.

In short, the more someone thinks they are able to do what is expected of them, and the greater their expectation of more positive than negative results, the greater the effort they will make (the more motivated they will be) to do what is expected of them. This does not mean the person will succeed. Performance (the results achieved at work) depends not only on an individual's motivation, but also on various other factors, which will be discussed below.

The Role of Money According to Expectancy Theory

Expectancy theory does not assume that money itself motivates and serves as an incentive to make a greater effort. Rather, it states that money, or any other reward individuals may gain from their work, has a motivating effect on the amount of effort made, insofar as that reward is linked to job performance and is valued by the employee. Thus, while a merit compensation policy may appear to be an incentive, because it links compensation and performance, the incentive may be low if the resulting pay increases leave very little after taxes. Furthermore, while employee benefits may be perceived as important, they will have no effect on a person's motivation at work, because there is no link between the benefits offered and individual performance.

Criticisms of the Expectancy Theory

Numerous authors have demonstrated the value of expectancy theory as an explanation for employees' behaviour at work (Georgopoulos, Mahoney and Jones, 1957; Lawler, 1966; Graen, 1969; Shuster, Clark and Rogers, 1971; Schwab and Dyer, 1973; Parker and Dyer, 1976; Arnold, 1981). However the theory is also open to criticism. Bergeron et al. (1979, p. 129) point out, for example, that "it is difficult to believe that human beings go through all the mental gymnastics described by the theory to select among the various options open to them." Be that as it may, theories are valued not only for their simplicity, but also for their ability to explain and predict behaviour. Also, one must not conclude that human beings go through such "mental gymnastics" consciously every time they are confronted with a choice. As with computers, people develop routines.

The theory may also be criticized for assuming that employees act logically and rationally. As Simon (1976) indicated, however, while employee behaviour may not be entirely rational, it is at least intended to be so.

Finally, it must be admitted that expectancy theory is not capable of unerringly predicting behaviour. To date, no motivational theory has been sufficiently developed to justify its widespread commercial application in organizations (Pinder, 1977). The risk of malfunction with different theories is high. As Bobko (1978) points out, however, organizations must make decisions, and people have to live with the consequences! The value of a theory must be judged in relation to existing knowledge and ways of doing things and not against some absolute, utopian criteria. As Bobko also notes, the correlation between measurements of the components of expectancy theory (expectancy, instrumentality, valence) and measurements of amount of effort or performance is about 0.40, whereas the correlation between smoking and dying of cancer is 0.08. Various governments, however, consider the latter index high enough to take measures to reduce the consumption of tobacco!

10.1.2 Maslow's Theory

Certain authors focus all their attention on one of the three factors in expectancy theory, namely valence, i.e. the importance or value of the various rewards an individual may gain from work. In this regard, numerous authors have tried to identify the principal human needs. Murray (1938) listed over 40 categories, Tolman (1951), 8.

Maslow's hierarchy of needs (1943, 1954) is probably the one that has gained the most attention in management training courses. According to Maslow, there are essentially five types of needs: physiological, safety, social, self-esteem, and self-actualization. Once one of these needs is met, it no longer motivates the individual. They are met in the order depicted in the following pyramid:

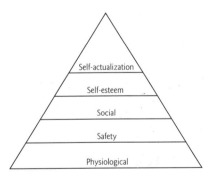

An individual's physiological needs must be satisfied before safety needs influence behaviour, and so on, up the line. By progressing from one level to the next, a person achieves self-actualization, the ultimate goal of human existence.

Criticisms of Maslow's Theory

Maslow's theory has been enthusiastically endorsed (Bergeron et al., 1979, p. 111) because of its apparent logic and its ability to organize and simplify a subject as complex as human needs. Research findings, however, rarely support the theory (Hall and Nougaim, 1968; Miner and Dachler, 1973; Wahba and Bridwell, 1976). According to Alderfer (1972), human needs may equally well fit into three categories, those related to existence, relatedness, and growth. Alderfer's research (1969) also leads one to believe that the more higher needs are met, the more important they become, contradicting Maslow's argument that a satisfied need no longer motivates.

The scarcity of findings in support of Maslow, however, is not enough to discredit his theory. As Locke (1976) mentioned, there is practically no way of verifying the theory for a number of reasons: the imprecise nature of self- actualization needs ("to become more and more what one is"), and confusion between the concepts of need and value, as well as between action and desire.

The Role of Money According to Maslow's Theory

Maslow's theory sheds little light on money's role as an incentive. Pay (money) can satisfy different levels of needs (Lawler, 1971; Maslow 1965; Opshal and Dunnette, 1966), since it is a means of attaining various ends (Vroom, 1964).

10.1.3 Herzberg's Theory

According to expectancy theory, under certain conditions, money may motivate individuals to make a greater effort toward better performance. Herzberg's theory, however, strongly challenges this view.

In the late 50s, Herzberg and his colleagues tried to identify sources of satisfaction and dissatisfaction among 200 American engineers and accountants in the Pittsburgh region (Herzberg, Mausner and Snyderman, 1959). In interviews, the employees were asked to recall a time in their work experience when they felt especially satisfied or dissatisfied, and to indicate the source of that feeling. Compiling their answers enabled Herzberg and his colleagues to identify two sets of factors: those directly related to job content (intrinsic factors) and those related to the environment surrounding the job (extrinsic factors).

The authors discovered that intrinsic factors were primarily cited for moments of satisfaction, whereas extrinsic ones were used to explain, or justify, feelings of dissatisfaction. This led them to conclude that satisfaction and dissatisfaction do not form a continuum. The opposite of satisfaction is lack of satisfaction, and the opposite of dissatisfaction is lack of dissatisfaction. The two states are independent, because they have different causes. Whereas intrinsic factors may cause a person to move from a lack of satisfaction to a state of satisfaction, the theory claims that extrinsic factors cannot make a person feel satisfied. They can only create an absence of dissatisfaction. The next step was to affirm that human beings are motivated only by intrinsic factors (Herzberg, 1966 and 1968). Extrinsic factors cannot motivate a person; at best, they can only lead a person to feel "not dissatisfied".

Pay is among the factors these authors consider extrinsic; it cannot, therefore, serve as an incentive *a priori*. This conclusion contradicts the expectancy theory. Herzberg's theory, however, warrants the closer scrutiny it is receiving from various authors.

Criticisms of Herzberg's Theory

An examination of the findings of Herzberg, Mausner and Snyderman (1959) reveals that pay is far from being associated solely with feelings of dissatisfaction. Opshal and Dunnette (1966) point out that pay is cited in 15% of the cases for feelings of satisfaction, and 17%, for feelings of dissatisfaction. The difference is far less clear than Herzberg (1966, 1968) would have one believe. Generally speaking, Herzberg's results can only be duplicated if the same methodology is used, namely interviews in which the subjects are asked to recall past events (Schwab, Janusaitis and Stark, 1963; Myers, 1964). With other methods, the results differ (Dunnette, 1965; Porter, 1964).

In addition to the fact that Herzberg's results depend on his methodology (House and Wigdor, 1967; King, 1970), the method itself is open to the idiosyncrasies of subjects (Vroom, 1966; Wall, Stephenson and Skidmore, 1971), and there are errors in coding the answers (Schneider and Locke, 1971).

Furthermore, Locke (1976) points out that this type of theory implies a clear dichotomy between mind and body, and completely ignores individual differences. Even Ford (1969), who accepts Herzberg's theory, admits that not everyone necessarily responds positively to work enhancement (intrinsic factors). Locke, Sirota and Wolfson (1976) confirmed this. Some people favour work enhancement only if accompanied by a pay increase.

Finally, what do the terms intrinsic and extrinsic factor really mean? When is a factor related to job content or to work environment? Dyer and Parker's study of members of the Industrial Psychology Division of the American Psychological Association (1975) found that the answer to these questions is far from clear. In fact, classifying the items listed by the authors into intrinsic or extrinsic factors resulted in a veritable hodgepodge in some cases.

Under the circumstances, they simply suggest abandoning the distinction until the conceptual problems it creates are resolved. Brief and Aldag (1977) made an attempt along these lines. According to them, what an employee gets out of a job may be considered intrinsic insofar as the individual gains an advantage from doing the work. It is extrinsic insofar as it may be attributed to an external cause. At least, this is a beginning!

The Role of Money According to Herzberg's Theory

Even without subscribing completely to Herzberg's theory of the different effects of intrinsic or extrinsic factors, the underlying concepts of the theory may be integrated into the expectancy theory. Thus, a job's intrinsic factors stand a greater chance of motivating an employee than do extrinsic ones, such as pay, because the individual gains the former by doing the work. An interesting job gives the employee a sense of doing something interesting. There is no intermediary between the individual and the work. The same is not true for extrinsic factors such as money, since an employee cannot receive a pay increase or performance bonus unless someone within the organization decides to link compensation to performance. The employee does not receive a bonus simply by doing the work. An intermediary between the individual and the work must tell the employee that doing the work in a certain way will result in a bonus.

This more refined conclusion about the role of intrinsic and extrinsic factors allows Herzberg's results to be incorporated into expectancy theory.

10.1.4 Equity Theory

Equity theory also sheds some light on money's role as an incentive for employees. As Lawler (1971), and Campbell and Pritchard (1976) point out, equity theory is virtually integral to expectancy theory.

Distributive justice (equity) has been conceived of and applied in different ways. Pettigrew's review (1967) of the literature on what he calls "social evaluation theory" identifies the following orientations. In psychology, we have the theory of social comparisons (Festinger, 1954), the concept of level of comparison (Thibault and Kelley, 1959), and the concept of subjective identification class (Centers, 1949). In sociology we have the theory of reference groups (Merton and Kitt, 1950; Hyman, 1960), the principle of relative privation (Stouffer et al., 1949), the concept of equitable exchange (Homans, 1961; Blau, 1964), the standard of reciprocity (Gouldner, 1954), and the concept of status balancing (Benoit-Smullyan, 1944; Lenski, 1954). The list is far from exhaustive.

These various ideas are all based on two fundamental propositions.

1. People learn to know themselves by making comparisons of one kind or another.
2. The process of comparison results in a positive, neutral, or negative evaluation in relation to the standards used.

Nonetheless, these concepts or theories of distributive justice (equity) are more or less structured and have inspired little research. Because of this, and because of equity theory's affinity with the workplace, Adams' version of the theory (1963, 1965) is adopted in this chapter.

Adams' Theory

In an article entitled "Toward an Understanding of Inequity", Adams (1963) uses a set of earlier works to present what is now known as the equity theory. This theory contends that individuals compare their contributions and rewards to those of another person they consider significant (*referent other*). According to Adams (1965), a state of inequity exists when people perceive that their contribution-reward ratio is not equal to that of their referent other. The inequity creates tension which people then try to reduce by different means, including:

1. modifying their contribution or reward;
2. withdrawing from the situation that is causing the tension;
3. psychologically modifying their contribution or reward;
4. psychologically modifying the contribution or reward of the referent other;
5. forcing the referent other to withdraw from the situation; or
6. changing referent other.

The degree of difficulty inherent in each option determines the choice. For example, it is much "easier" to modify one's own contribution psychologically than to modify the referent other's. Similarly, it is much "easier" to modify the referent other's contribution psychologically than to modify one's own contribution physically.

In brief, this theory appears to be as much a theory of satisfaction as of motivation. Insofar as the feeling of equity or inequity resulting from the comparison is closely related to the individual's sense of satisfaction, it is a theory of satisfaction. In stating that a situation of inequity (or "subequity") creates tension in the individual, causing that person to seek a means of reducing it, it is a theory of motivation.

In any case, the research done on the different propositions that may be derived from this theory – whether focusing on satisfaction or motivation – tend to bear out its superiority as a theory of satisfaction. Excellent reviews of the literature on this subject are found in Lawler (1968), Pritchard (1969), Goodman and Freedman (1971), and Thériault (1977).

10.1.5 The Effect of Money on Intrinsic Motivation

The role of money remains an unresolved question. A series of studies by Deci (1975, 1987), carrying on the work of DeCharms (1968), develop the thesis that the introduction of compensation as a contingent factor in improving job performance may have the effect of reducing a person's level of intrinsic motivation, and may affect the intensity of the behaviour resulting from that incentive. His findings are confirmed by Lepper, Greene and Nisbett (1973), Lepper and Greene (1975), Calder and Straw (1975), and Pinder (1976).

To date, however, no laboratory research has supported this argument. Moreover, these authors advance a slightly confusing explanation of the role of money. Whereas recognition from someone in authority has a positive impact on employee performance, in these studies, money appears to have a negative effect. Yet a bonus or pay increase for good performance is also a concrete token of recognition. Therein lies both the advantage and disadvantage of money. It may mean several things to the same person, and different things to different people.

☐ 10.2 Job Performance

As mentioned earlier, motivation is but one determinant of job performance. Figure 10.2 illustrates the others. According to this diagram, an employee's job performance (the results achieved) depends not only on behaviour (what the person does), but also on work organization (impact of the work of others), environment (the extent to which it is conducive to achieving the results) and available resources (what is needed to achieve the results). Employee behaviour itself depends not only on motivation (effort), but also on a person's knowledge and skills, understanding of their role (what is expected) and personality (unique way of doing things).

In short, job performance is not simply a question of effort; there is much more involved. An employee's motivation is neither exclusively nor directly related to the pay received. In order for pay to act as an incentive, the individual must feel capable of doing what is expected, must perceive a relationship between a potential level of performance and the money to be gained from it and, finally, must consider the amount of money significant. The real question, then, is to determine whether one can develop such a system of compensation, and whether merit compensation satisfies these conditions.

FIGURE 10.2
Principal determinants of job performance

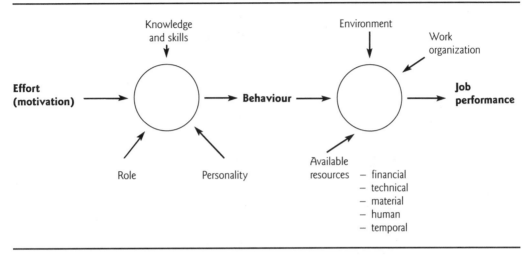

SOURCE: Adapted from Lawler (1971).

☐ 10.3 What Is Merit Compensation?

There is considerable confusion about what is meant by "merit compensation" (Heneman, 1990). For the purposes of this book, merit compensation means pay increases based on the results of an employee's performance evaluation. More specifically, a merit compensation plan has the following characteristics.

1. Employees receive pay increases within their pay scale at regular intervals (usually once each year), with the increases based at least partly on performance.

2. Increases are built into an employee's pay for the purposes of calculating future increases.

3. Employee performance is measured by an evaluation system.

One might add to these characteristics the fact that, generally speaking, merit compensation is intended for non-unionized personnel. In addition, the amount of money to be distributed within each department or division of an organization is based on a standard percentage of the departmental or divisional payroll. This percentage depends on both economic conditions and the position the organization wishes to take relative to the market.

10.3.1 Compa-Ratios

In general, pay increases rarely depend solely on performance evaluation results. Usually the compa-ratio, or relative level of pay within a range, is

FIGURE 10.3
Pay range in relation to employee performance

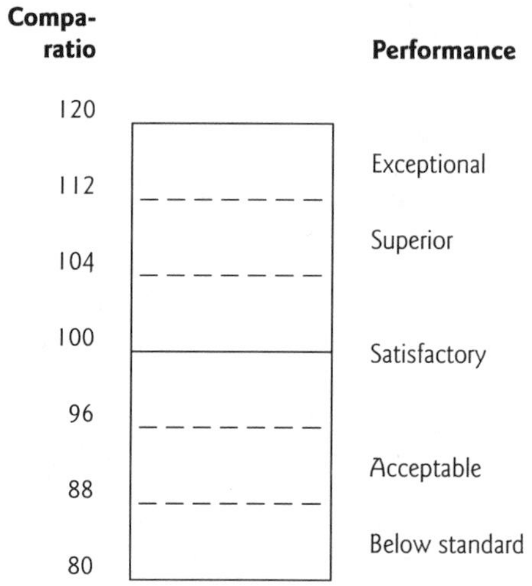

Compa-ratio		Performance
120		
112		Exceptional
104		Superior
100		Satisfactory
96		
88		Acceptable
80		Below standard

also considered. The ratio is calculated by dividing an employee's actual pay by the pay at the control point or normal maximum in that range. So, if an employee's pay is $34,000, and the control point in that range is $30,000, the compa-ratio is:

$$\frac{\$34,000}{\$30,000} \times 100 = 113$$

In a pay structure whose minimums and maximums are located ±20% from the control point, the compa-ratios of employees within that pay range vary from 80 to 120. As mentioned in Chapter 8 on pay structures, the different compa-ratios correspond to various levels of performance, as illustrated in Figure 10.3.

An employee with no previous experience in the job is hired at the range minimum, or a compa-ratio of 80. Entry-level pay may be higher, depending on the incumbent's experience. Subsequent pay increases reflect performance. Given that people gain experience more quickly at the beginning of a job than later on, performance-based pay increases (merit increases) are usually larger at the beginning.

10.3.2 Merit Pay Increase Matrix

Most organizations develop what is known as a merit pay increase matrix to manage merit pay increases more equitably on the basis of compa-ratios.

TABLE 10.1
Pay increase matrix based on pay level and individual performance

Performance	Compa-ratio	Individual pay increases based on compa-ratio (%)				
		80-88	88-96	96-104	104-112	112-120
Exceptional		8-9	7-8	6-7	5-6	4-5
Superior		7-8	6-7	5-6	4-5	2-3
Satisfactory		6-7	5-6	4-5	2-3	0-2
Acceptable		5-6	4-5	2-3	0-2	0
Unsatisfactory		0	0	0	0	0

The matrix considers not only individual performance, but also each employee's compa-ratio. Table 10.1 is an example of such a matrix for an organization having a 4% increase in its salary structure. Thus, an employee whose performance is satisfactory and whose pay is in the control point zone (96-104) would receive a 4% to 5% increase and stay at the same level in the scale. On the other hand, an employee whose performance is better than satisfactory and whose pay is below the control point would receive an increase of more than 4% or 5% and move closer to the control point zone.

Another approach is to vary the length of time between pay increases, in addition to using different percentages. According to the Table 10.1, for example, an employee whose performance is satisfactory and whose pay is in the control point zone would receive an annual pay increase of 4% to 5%. One whose performance is exceptional and whose pay is in the 80-88 zone could receive an 8% or 9% increase, but every 9 months instead of every 12. Doyel and Johnson (1985) show how to construct such matrices, based both on the ideal time for progressing from scale minimum to the control point and on the planned percentage increase in the pay scale.

Using such matrices ensures that the principles adopted for managing merit compensation are correctly applied by managers.

☐ 10.4 Appropriate Merit Pay Increases

Once the portion of a pay increase to be based on merit has been determined, administrators face another question: How much should that increase be? What percentage of a pay increase should be tied to merit? And should this percentage be identical for different pay ranges? The answer given by theorists such as Lawler (1989) is that the potential increase should be significant.

In practice, these questions are usually resolved by pay surveys and the organization's financial position, barring any applicable legislation or decrees. However, the issue of how employees respond to increases of various sizes is rarely raised, aside from saying that they should be happy with what they get.

Some authors have focused on this point. The theory that appears to be most widely accepted is Bernoulli's (1964), which derives from the work of Edwards (1961) and Stevens (1959). The theory advanced by these authors on the value of different pay increases is that the value of the financial gain depends on the individual's income level. In other words, it is a matter of diminishing marginal value.

Thus, the higher a person's income, the lower the marginal value of a fixed amount of pay increase. A constant, or rising, percentage increase must be used to keep the added value constant. In practice, this approach also makes allowance for the progressive nature of tax brackets. It does not, however, consider the effect of the perception of pay equity on the perception of tax brackets. In fact, it seems entirely probable that the more employees consider their pay inequitable, the greater the increase must be for it to be perceived as satisfying. These studies also seem to ignore the fact that money may have not only economic, but also psychological or sociological, significance (cf. Chapter 1). Experience shows that, when pay increases are analyzed as a sociological transaction, the differentials between employees need not be large to be perceptible. In this light, Bernoulli's theory (1964) no longer seems relevant.

☐ 10.5 The Importance of Merit Compensation

In North America, merit compensation plans have enjoyed several waves of popularity since the turn of the century. Tables 10.2 and 10.3 reveal that the most recent wave in both Canada and the United States occurred in the latter half of the 80s.

The percentage of Canadian organizations reporting that they consider only merit (performance) in pay increases for middle management rose from 31% in 1985 to over 40% in 1990. Add to this the organizations indicating that they consider merit in addition to a general increase (based on an increase in pay scales and applied to all employees whose performance is at least satisfactory), and the percentage rises from 60% in 1985 to over 70% in 1990. Table 10.2 further reveals that the percentage of organizations with a merit compensation plan for all non-unionized employees rose from about 55% in 1985 to over 65% in 1990.

TABLE 10.2
Percentage of Canadian organizations considering individual merit
(compensation) in granting pay increases

a)   Middle management

Criteria for pay increases	Year					
	1985	1986	1987	1988	1989	1990
Merit only	31	31	37	40	42	41
Merit and general	30	28	29	29	26	30
General	39	41	34	31	31	29

b)   Non-unionized employees

Criteria for pay increases	Year					
	1985	1986	1987	1988	1989	1990
Merit only	28	28	33	35	38	37
Merit and general	28	29	29	31	27	30
General	44	43	38	34	35	33

SOURCE: Mercer Ltd. (1985, 1986, 1987, 1988, 1989, 1990).

A Conference Board of Canada study of over 150 medium-sized and large organizations considered to be at the leading edge of compensation management found that almost 95% of them used merit alone to determine pay increases (Booth, 1987).

Conference Board of Canada studies (Kapel, 1990) indicate that, not only are merit compensation plans gaining in popularity, but the pay increase differential between employees whose performance is satisfactory and those whose performance is exceptional has also grown in recent years. In 1991, employees of organizations with merit compensation plans will receive an average pay increase of 5.4% for a satisfactory performance, and 8.2% for exceptional. The differential is slightly over 50% (2.8% ÷ 5.4%).

Merit compensation plans are even more popular in the United States, where over 80% of organizations apply them to at least some of their employ-

TABLE 10.3
Percentage of American organizations considering individual merit (compensation) in granting pay increases

a)   Middle management

Criteria for pay increases	Year					
	1985	**1986**	**1987**	**1988**	**1989**	**1990**
Merit only	82	82	87	86	87	87
Merit and general	14	14	10	10	8	9
General	4	4	3	4	5	4

b)   Non-unionized employees

Criteria for pay increases	Year					
	1985	**1986**	**1987**	**1988**	**1989**	**1990**
Merit only	74	74	81	80	81	80
Merit and general	18	18	14	13	11	13
General	8	8	5	7	8	7

SOURCE: Mercer Inc. (1985-86, 1986-87, 1987-88, 1988-89, 1989-90, 1990-91).

ees (Peck, 1984). As Table 10.3 indicates, this resurgence in popularity during the late 80s is greater for increases based exclusively on merit. From 1985 to 1990, the percentage of organizations that based pay increases for middle management and non-unionized employees on merit alone rose, respectively, from 82% to 87% and 74% to 80%.

10.6 Merit Compensation: Pros and Cons

The value of merit compensation has long been debated, and the controversy is far from over. The application of merit compensation to teachers (Scherer, 1983) and federal public sector employees (Silverman, 1983) in the United States during the 80s rekindled the debate there. Meyer (1975, 1976) and

Lawler (1975) are probably the most frequently cited authors in arguing the pros and cons of merit compensation.

10.6.1 Arguments against Merit Compensation

Meyer's research (1975, 1976) at General Electric in the United States led him to observe that merit compensation did not have the anticipated effects on employee attitudes and behaviour. Instead, it was likely to have a negative impact on self-esteem for most employees, since it was shown that a majority of them had a positive self-image and perceived their performance as above-average. In addition, it was likely to have few positive effects, and possibly even negative effects, on employee attitudes and performance on the job. In fact, he reported the following with a merit compensation plan.

1. It was exceptional to find employees working harder to earn a larger pay increase.
2. Some employees pushed for a reduction in performance standards, to maximize their pay increases.
3. Other employees tended to deny the importance of good performance by being absent more often, or arriving late for work.
4. Still others questioned the quality of their immediate supervisor's managerial skills and evaluation of their performance.

Meyer's findings led him to recommend instead the use of intrinsic incentives, such as promotions and feedback, as a means of increasing employee motivation and performance on the job.

While Meyer's argument (1975, 1976) against merit compensation is very well known, it is incomplete. In fact, the cons of merit compensation may be grouped under the following headings.

1. Merit Evaluation

Since there is no objective criterion for evaluating employee performance under a merit compensation plan, personality traits are most frequently relied on. And even if relatively objective performance standards are set, defining good performance always creates problems.

Individual differences in performance are difficult to measure, and most managers are incapable of producing a valid assessment of an employee's performance. Even when managers notice differences in performance, they often look the other way to avoid having to justify their evaluation. Few of them are prepared to assume the role of God that a performance evaluation system assigns to them (McGregor, 1957). Even a manager who sees that one employee's performance is better than another's will consider the fact that giving one a pay increase will create dissension on the team and, therefore, the negative effects will outweigh the positive. The manager will, in all likelihood, give everyone the same increase, an outcome reinforced by society's egalitarian tendencies (Franck, 1979).

In rewarding individual performance, merit compensation also goes against the tendency to promote team spirit (Rollins, 1988) and emphasize the performance of work teams and the entire organization (Pearce, 1987).

Finally, merit compensation budgets assume that merit is distributed along a normal curve, which it is not. In fact, the performance of 80% of employees is rated above-average by their managers.

2. Plan Management

Merit compensation plans are costly and difficult to manage. Pay increases depend not only on individual performance, but also on an organization's capacity to pay, increases in the Consumer Price Index, and an employee's position in the pay scale (compa-ratio).

In addition, the objectives of such plans, namely, to reward individual performance with pay increases perceived as significant and control labour costs (Mount, 1987) are essentially conflictual. Finally, merit pay increases generally remain secret (Lawler, 1989), which tends to lessen their impact on employee motivation.

3. Size of the Pay Increase

The difference in pay increases between employees whose performance is satisfactory and those whose performance is exceptional is not great enough to provide an incentive for increased effort. In fact, it may simply be a disincentive; most increases fall within a ± 2% differential (Teel, 1986). A high inflation rate may consume the budget for increases, leaving nothing for merit pay (Franck, 1979). This problem is aggravated when organizations are forced to recruit employees at pay rates equivalent to what existing employees with superior performance ratings receive. In an inflationary economy with a progressive tax structure, the merit portion becomes ludicrous compared to the general increase (Franck, 1979). Budgetary constraints may also prevent organizations from giving an appropriate increase to all those who deserve one (Miller, 1979; Winstanley, 1982).

4. Employees' Characteristics

Most employees are not motivated by money, but by some other factor, such as the nature of their work, responsibilities, etc. Moreover, the vast majority of employees perceive their merit as being above-average. As a result, an average pay increase undermines self-esteem and destroys motivation (Meyer, 1975, 1976). With a merit compensation plan, the performance and morale of employees rated below-average deteriorates, and they do not voluntarily leave the organization as one might expect (Thompson and Dalton, 1970).

10.6.2 Arguments in Favour of Merit Compensation

In 1975, Lawler replied to Meyer's negative arguments. After reviewing the findings of all the studies on the subject, Lawler concluded that merit compensation had very positive effects on employee attitudes and performance, for the following reasons.

1. When compensation was linked to performance, employees were more motivated to improve their performance and more satisfied with their pay.
2. The employees who tended to leave the organization were those whose performance was inferior, which, in itself, was rather beneficial to the organization.
3. Generally speaking, employees preferred having their compensation tied to performance.
4. Despite the importance of maintaining their self-esteem, employees' self-image must be realistic.

As for Meyer's conclusion that intrinsic incentives are superior, Lawler counters that research has established the importance of informing employees about the results of their work, and giving them feedback in such a way as to improve their motivation and performance. According to Lawler, merit compensation has the advantage not only of enabling such feedback, but also of translating that feedback into concrete, i.e. monetary terms.

Other arguments in favour of merit compensation must not be overlooked. They may be grouped under the following headings:

I. Organizational Productivity and Employee Performance

When an organization or an economy has serious problems with productivity, spending on labour (or investing, depending on one's perspective) must be as cost-effective as possible. This is all the more important during inflationary periods, when there is strong pressure for pay increases. This makes it even more critical to manage payrolls efficiently and equitably, in order to achieve the best individual and team results.

The efficiency of an organization's employees depends on the technology they use, work organization, their skills, their understanding of what their supervisors expect of them, and their motivation. All the research and the lessons to be drawn from current practice indicate that money is an important source of motivation for the vast majority of people.

Furthermore, pay increases based on the Consumer Price Index or length of service never motivate employees to make a greater effort to improve their performance. In fact, such increases have the opposite effect; the standard becomes "not doing a bad job". By emphasizing performance evaluation, merit compensation also allows the organization to make clear what it expects of employees.

2. Employees' Expectations

Employees naturally have a strong need for concrete feedback on how they do their job. Merit evaluation has all the characteristics essential for such feedback. In addition, most employees want at least part of their compensation to be based on merit.

3. Retaining the Most Deserving Employees

Failure to reward relative merit with compensation simply creates serious problems of inequity, resulting in less effort by the most deserving, more absenteeism, less personal involvement in work, etc.

Some authors (for example, Thompson and Dalton, 1970) argue that, with merit compensation, the performance of employees evaluated as being below average deteriorates and, contrary to expectations, they do not leave the organization. This is understandable, given their slim, even nonexistent, chances of finding work elsewhere because of their poor performance. Someone whose performance is superior stands a much greater chance of obtaining another job. Unless an organization offers a monetary reward for superior performance, it risks losing its best employees to competitors that do recognize individual performance.

Finally, merit compensation reinforces the behaviour of top performers and shows other employees that good performance is essential for obtaining a pay increase (Dyer, Schwab and Thériault, 1976; Kopelman and Mihal, 1983).

In short, there are many arguments for and against merit compensation. When added up, however, the two sides certainly do not cancel each other out. In this debate, one must avoid confusing the principle with its application. The more one agrees with the principle of performance-based pay, the more likely that its application will succeed. The fact that most employees perceive no connection between their performance and pay increases (Schieman, 1983) neither negates the advantage of implementing merit compensation, nor explains why one is not in use.

☐ 10.7 Implications for Merit Compensation

While the scales may tilt in favour of merit compensation, this does not mean that any such plan will produce positive effects.

The various motivational theories described at the beginning of this chapter specify a set of conditions that must be fulfilled for money to serve as an incentive for individual performance. Consequently, to be effective, a merit compensation plan must meet certain conditions.

1. Employees must believe that better performance will result in higher income. This implies that:
   a) employees know what good performance means in practice;
   b) they consider the performance evaluation system valid, complete, and reliable;
   c) they see those whose performance is superior earning more.
2. Employees must want a higher income.
3. The benefits of good performance must outweigh those of poor performance. This implies that:
   a) the negative consequences of good performance must be minimized;
   b) employees must perceive performing well as the most profitable form of behaviour;
   c) the amount of money paid for good performance must be perceived as significant and equitable.
4. Non-monetary incentives must also be linked to good performance.
5. The quality of employee performance must be related to the quality of the effort made.

To this, one might add that a merit compensation plan will only be effective insofar as pay is relatively equitable (Hills et al., 1987), the organizational culture supports the principle of merit compensation, and managers are willing to administer it, i.e. make and justify performance distinctions between employees (Sullivan, 1988).

Given the scope of these conditions and the fact that certain theories dispute the motivational effect of money, authors such as Winstanley (1982) question whether compensation has an impact on individual and organizational efficiency. Others, such as Pearce (1987), maintain that it is just as well that merit compensation does not work since its drawbacks would be too great if it did. According to him, organizations that do not base pay on merit should not feel guilty – quite the contrary!

Merit compensation plans must not be abandoned simply because they are difficult to manage. The two biggest problems with merit compensation appear to be inadequate pay differentials between employees and performance evaluation. The following section offers a solution to the problem of differentials, whereas the next chapter deals with the question of performance evaluation.

☐ 10.8 Merit Pay Increase or Performance Bonus?

An organization may use either pay increases or bonuses to monetarily reward the relative merit of its employees. In practice, organizations tend to imitate their competitors in choosing either formula, and their information is drawn primarily from pay surveys. In some cases, pay increases are preferred over bonuses, because of the importance of base salary in calculating numerous employee benefits. As will be seen in Chapter 14, the amount of life insurance to which employees are entitled is generally related to their base salary, e.g. as a multiple of it. The same applies to retirement benefits.

Pay increases are more reassuring to employees than bonuses. Pay increases mean that an employee's income remains stable, or increases from year to year, but cannot decrease. Bonuses, however, are not built into an employee's pay, so the total (salary plus bonus) may increase or decrease. On the other hand, pay increases are less of an incentive to improve performance than bonuses and are also more costly for the organization.

As mentioned in Chapter 8, a commonly used pay structure involves differentials around a midpoint or market pay. This differential is often about ± 20%. An employee is hired at some level between the pay scale minimum and midpoint, depending on experience, and pay increases reflect improvements in performance. Since pay decreases are rare, this type of scale encourages employees to perform excellently at the beginning of their careers, and then to slow down as their pay rises into the upper portion of their scale. This is the result of lower percentage pay increases for employees whose pay is above the control point (cf. Table 10.1, page 293).

Given the pressure on labour costs and the highly motivating effect of performance bonuses, in recent years a growing number of organizations have been modifying their pay structures by replacing the upper portion of their scales with a performance bonus formula.

Thus, pay will increase in line with employee performance until it reaches the level the organization wishes to pay relative to the market. Subsequently, employees whose performance is at least satisfactory will benefit from the new structure. Those whose performance is more than satisfactory are rewarded with a bonus. As Hathaway (1986) noted, bonuses may be much larger than the pay increases they replace, because they are not built into pay. To earn them, an employee's performance must be more than satisfactory. This formula is therefore more advantageous than traditional pay increases for employees whose performance is above average, and less so for those whose performance is satisfactory or average.

The bonus formula supports the charge that merit compensation emphasizes individual as opposed to group performance. Lawler (1989) suggests alleviating this by basing bonuses for employees whose pay is at the top of their scale on organizational performance. This kills two birds with one stone. It encourages cooperation to improve organizational performance, yet recognizes differences by basing the amount of the bonus on individual performance.

☐ 10.9 Summary

Despite all the controversy surrounding merit compensation plans, and the criticism these plans have faced since the 50s, their popularity with organizations is still growing. They remain a favoured means of improving productivity. Nonetheless, certain conditions must be satisfied for merit compensation to affect employee motivation and performance. Organizations wishing to make their merit compensation plan more effective clearly stand to gain from using a bonus formula for employees in the upper portion of their pay scale.

REFERENCES

ADAMS, J.S., "Inequity In Social Exchange", in *Advances in Experimental Social Psychology*, edited by L. Berkovitz, New York, Academic Press, 1965, vol. 2.

ADAMS, J.S., "Toward an Understanding of Inequity", *Journal of Abnormal and Social Psychology*, 1963, vol. 67, pp. 422-436.

ALDERFER, C.P., "An Empirical Test of a New Theory of Human Needs", *Organizational Behavior and Human Performance*, 1969, vol. 4, pp. 142-175.

ALDERFER, C.P., *Existence, Relatedness, and Growth*, New York, The Free Press, 1972.

ARNOLD, H.J., "A Test of the Validity of the Multiplicative Hypothesis of Expectancy – Valence Theories of Work Motivation", *Academy of Management Journal*, 1981, vol. 24, N° 1, pp. 128-141.

ATKINSON, J.W., *Motives in Fantasy, Action and in Society*, Princeton, New Jersey, Van Nostrand, 1958.

BENOIT-SMULLYAN, E., "Status, Status Types, and Status Inter-Relations", *American Sociological Review*, 1944, vol. 9, pp. 151-161.

BERGERON, J.-L. et al., *Les Aspects humains de l'organisation*, Chicoutimi, Gaëtan Morin Éditeur, 1979.

BERNOULLI, D., "Exposition of a New Theory on the Measurement of Risk", in *Mathematics and Psychology*, edited by G.A. Miller, New York, Wiley, 1964.

BLAU, P.M., *Exchange and Power in Social Life*, New York, Wiley, 1964.

BOBKO, P., "Concerning the Non-Application of Human Motivation Theories in Organizational Setting", *Academy of Management Review*, 1978, vol. 3, pp. 906-910.

BOOTH, P.L., *Paying For Performance: The Growing Use of Incentives and Bonus Plans*, Ottawa, Conference Board of Canada, 1987.

BRIEF, A.P. and R.J. ALDAG, "The Intrinsic-Extrinsic Dichotomy: Toward Conceptual Clarity", *Academy of Management Review*, 1977, vol. 2, pp. 496-500.

CALDER, B.J. and B.M. STRAW, "The Self-Perception of Intrinsic and Extrinsic Motivation", *Journal of Personality and Social Psychology*, 1975, vol. 35, pp. 599-605.

CAMPBELL, J.P. and R. PRITCHARD, "Motivation Theory in Industrial and Organizational Psychology", in *Handbook of Industrial and Organizational Psychology*, edited by M. Dunnette, Chicago, Rand McNally, 1976.

CENTERS, R., *The Psychology of Social Class*, Princeton, New Jersey, Princeton University Press, 1949.

DeCHARMS, R., *Personal Causation: The Internal Affective Determinants of Behaviour*, New York, Academic Press, 1968.

DECI, E.L., *Intrinsic Motivation*, New York, Plenum Press, 1975.

DECI, E.L. and R.M. RYAN, *Intrinsic Motivation and Self-Determination in Human Behavior*, New York, Plenum Press, 1987.

DOYEL, H.W. and J.L. JOHNSON, "Pay Increases Guidelines With Merit", *Personnel Journal*, 1985, vol. 64, N° 6, pp. 46-50.

DUNNETTE, M.D., *Factors Structures of Usually Satisfying and Unusually Dissatisfying Job Situations for Six Occupational Groups*, text presented to the Midwestern Psychological Association Congress, Chicago, 1965.

DYER, L., D.P. SCHWAB and R. THÉRIAULT, "Managerial Perceptions Regarding Salary Increase Criteria", *Personnel Psychology*, 1976, vol. 29, N° 2, pp. 233-242.

DYER, L. and D.F. PARKER, "Classifying Outcomes in Work Motivation Research: An Examination of the Intrinsic - Extrinsic Dichotomy", *Journal of Applied Psychology*, 1975, vol. 60, pp. 455-458.

EDWARDS, W., "Behavioral Decision Theory", *Annual Review of Psychology*, 1961, vol. 12, pp. 474-498.

EDWARDS, W., "The Theory of Decision Making", *Psychological Bulletin*, 1954, vol. 51, pp. 380-417.

FESTINGER, L., "A Theory of Social Comparison Processes", *Human Relations*, 1954, vol. 7, pp. 117-140.

FORD, R.N., *Motivation Through the Work Itself*, New York, American Management Association, 1969.

FRANCK, G., *Enquêtes sur les pratiques de gestion du personnel des entreprises dans l'environnement français*, Jouy-en-Josas, France, Centre d'enseignement supérieur des affaires (CESA), 1979.

GEORGOPOULOS, B.S., G.M. MAHONEY and N.W. JONES, A Path-Goal Approach to Productivity", *Journal of Applied Psychology*, 1957, vol. 41, pp. 345-353.

GOLDSTEIN, K., *The Organism: A Holistic Approach to Biology Derived from Pathological Data in Mass*, New York, American Book Co., 1939.

GOODMAN, P.S., "Effect of Perceived Inequity on Salary Allocation Decisions", *Journal of Applied Psychology*, 1975. vol. 60, pp. 372-375.

GOODMAN, P.S. and A. FREEDMAN, "An Examination of Adam's Theory of Inequity", *Administrative Science Quarterly*, 1971, vol. 16, pp. 271-288.

GOULDNER, A., *Patterns of Industrial Democracy*, Glencoe, Illinois, Free Press, 1954.

GRAEN, G., "Instrumentality Theory of Work Motivation: Some Empirical Results and Suggested Modifications", *Journal of Applied Psychology Monograph*, 1969, vol. 53, pp. 1-25.

HALL, D.T. and K.E. NOUGAIM, "An Examination of Maslow's Need Hierarchy in an Organizational Setting", *Organizational Behavior and Human Performance*, 1968, vol. 3, pp. 12-35.

HATHAWAY, J.W., "How Do Merit Bonuses Fare?", *Compensation and Benefits Review*, 1968, vol. 18, N° 5, pp. 50-55.

HENEMAN, R.L., "Merit Pay Research", in *Research in Personnel and Human Resources Management*, edited by K.M. Rowland and G.R. Ferris, 1990, vol. 8, pp. 203-263.

HENEMAN, R.L., D.D. GREENBERGER and S. STRASSER, "The Relationship Between Pay-For-Performance Perceptions and Pay Satisfaction", *Personnel Psychology*, 1988, vol. 41, N° 4, pp. 745-760.

HENEMAN, H.G. and D.P. SCHWAB, "Work and Rewards Theory", in *Motivation and Commitment*, edited by D. Yoder and H.G. Heneman, Washington, D.C., Bureau of National Affairs, 1975.

HERZBERG, F., "One More Time: How Do You Motivate Employees?", *Harvard Business Review*, January-February 1968, pp. 53-62.

HERZBERG, F., *Work and the Nature of Man*, Cleveland, World Publishing, 1966.

HERZBERG, F., B. MAUSNER, and B. SNYDERMAN, *The Motivation to Work*, New York, Wiley, 1959.

HILLS, F.S. et al., "Merit Pay: Just or Unjust Desserts", *Personnel Administrator*, 1987, vol. 32, N° 9, pp. 53-59.

HOMANS, G.C., *Social Behavior: Its Elementary Form*, New York, Harcourt, Brace and World, 1961.

HOUSE, R.A. and L.A. WIGDOR, "Herzberg's Dual Factor Theory of Job Satisfaction and Motivation: A Review of the Evidence and Criticism", *Personnel Psychology*, 1967, vol. 20, pp. 369-384.

HYMAN, H.H., "Reflections on Reference Group", *Public Opinion Quarterly*, 1960, vol. 24, pp. 383-396.

KAPEL, C., "Clear Message; a Must at Salary Review", *Canadian Human Resources Reporter*, December 19, 1990, p. 8.

KING, N., "Clarification and Evaluation of the Two-Factor Theory of Job Satisfaction", *Psychological Bulletin*, 1970, vol. 71, N° 1, pp. 18-31.

KOPELMAN, R.E., Organizational Control Systems Responsiveness, Expectancy, Theory Constructs, and Work Motivation: Some Interrelations and Casual Correction", *Personnel Psychology*, 1976, vol. 29, pp. 205-220.

KOPELMAN, R.E. and W.L. MIHAL, "Merit Pay: Linking Pay to Performance is a Proven Management Tool", *Personnel Administrator*, 1983, vol. 28, pp. 60-68.

LAWLER, E.E., "Ability as a Moderator of the Relationship Between Job Attitudes and Job Performance", *Personnel Psychology*, 1966, vol. 19, pp. 153-164.

LAWLER, E.E., "Comments on Herbert H. Meyer's Pay for Performance Dilemma", *Organizational Dynamics*, winter 1975, pp. 44-49.

LAWLER, E.E., Equity Theory as a Predictor of Productivity and Work Quality", *Psychological Bulletin*, 1968, vol. 70, N° 6, pp. 596-610.

LAWLER, E.E., *Motivation in Work Organization*, Monterey, California, Brooks/Cole Publishing Co., 1973.

LAWLER, E.E., *Pay and Organizational Effectiveness: A Psychological View*, New York, McGraw-Hill, 1971.

LAWLER, E.E., "Pay For Performance: A Strategic Analysis", in *Compensation and Benefits*, edited by L.R. Gomez-Mejia, Washington, D.C., Bureau of National Affairs, 1989, pp. 136-181.

LENSKI, G.E., "Status Crystallization: A Non-Vertical Dimension of Social Status", *American Sociological Review*, 1954, vol. 19, pp. 405-413.

LEPPER, M.R., D. GREENE and R.E. NISBETT, "Undermining Children's Intrinsic Interest With Extrinsic Rewards: A Test of the 'Over-Justification' Hypothesis", *Journal of Personality and Social Psychology*, 1973, vol. 31, pp. 479-486.

LEWIN, K.A., A *Dynamic Theory of Personality*, New York, McGraw-Hill, 1935.

LOCKE, E., "The Nature of Causes of Job Satisfaction", in *Handbook of Industrial and Organizational Psychology*, edited by M.D. Dunnette, Chicago, Rand McNally, 1976.

LOCKE, E., A.D. SIROTA and A.D. WOLFSON, "An Experimental Case Study of the Success and Failures of Job Enrichment in a Government Agency", *Journal of Applied Psychology*, 1976, vol. 61, N° 6, pp. 701-711.

MASLOW, A.H., "A Theory of Human Motivation", *Psychological Review*, 1943, vol. 50, pp. 370-396.

MASLOW, A.H., *Eupsychian Management*, Homewood, Illinois, Irwin-Dorsey, 1965.

MASLOW, A.H., *Motivation and Personality*, New York, Harper and Row, 1954 (2nd ed., 1970).

McGREGOR, D., "An Uneasy Look at Performance Appraisal", *Harvard Business Review*, May-June 1957, pp. 89-94.

MERCER (William M. Mercer Inc.), *Compensation Planning Survey*, New York, New York, 1985-86, 1986-87, 1987-88, 1988-89, 1989-90.

MERCER (William M. Mercer Limited), *Salary Planning Survey for Non-Union Employees in Canada*, Toronto, 1985, 1986, 1987, 1988, 1989, 1990.

MERTON, R.K. and A.S. KITT, "Contributions to the Theory of Reference Group Behavior", in *Continuities in Social Research: Studies in the Scope and Method of 'The American Soldier'"*, edited by R.K. Merton and P.F. Lagerfeld, Glencoe, Illinois, Free Press, 1950.

MEYER, H.H., "The Pay-For-Performance Dilemma", *Organizational Dynamics*, Winter 1975, pp. 44-49.

MEYER, H.H., "Reply to Edward E. Lawler", *Organizational Dynamics*, Winter 1976, pp. 75-77.

MILLER, E.C., "Pay for Performance", *Personnel*, 1979, vol. 56, pp. 4-11.

MINER, J.B. and P.D. DACHLER, "Personnel Attitudes and Motivation", in Annual Review of Psychology, edited by M.R. Rosenzweig, Palo Alto, California, Annual Reviews, 1973, vol. 24, pp. 379-402.

MOUNT, M.K., "Coordinating Salary Action and Performance Appraisal", in *New Perspectives on Compensation*, edited by D.B. Balkin and L.R. Gomez-Mejia, 1987, pp. 187-195.

MURRAY, H., *Explorations in Personality*, New York, Oxford University Press, 1938.

MYERS, M.S. "Who Are Your Motivated Workers?", *Harvard Business Review*, 1964, vol. 42, pp. 73-88.

OSPHAL, R.L. and M. DUNNETTE, "Role of Financial Compensation in Industrial Motivation"", *Psychological Bulletin*, 1966, vol. 66, pp. 94-118.

PARKER, D.F. and L. DYER, "Expectancy Theory as a Within Personal Behaviour Choice Model: An Empirical Test of Some Conceptual and Methodological Refinements", *Organizational Behavior and Human Performance*, 1976, vol. 17, pp. 97-117.

PEARCE, J.L., "Why Merit Pay Doesn't Work: Implications for Organization Theory", in *New Perspectives in Compensation*, edited by D.B. Balkin and L.R. Gomez-Mejia, Englewood Cliffs, New Jersey, 1987, pp. 169-178.

PECK, C., *Pay and Performance: The Interaction of Compensation and Performance Appraisal*, New York, Conference Board, 1984.

PETTIGREW, T.F., "Social Evaluation Theory, Convergences and Applications", in *Nebraska Symposium on Motivation*, edited by M.R. Jones, Lincoln, Nebraska, University of Nebraska Press, 1967, vol. 15, pp. 241-311.

PINDER, C., "Additivity Versus Nonadditivity of Intrinsic and Extrinsic Incentives", *Journal of Applied Psychology*, 1976, vol. 61, pp. 693-700.

PINDER, C., "Concerning the Application of Human Motivation Theories in Organizational Settings", *Academy of Management Review*, 1977, vol. 2, pp. 384-397.

PORTER, L.W., *Organizational Patterns of Managerial Job Attitudes*, New York, American Foundation for Management Research, 1964.

PRITCHARD, R.D., "Equity Theory: A Review and Critique", *Organizational Behaviour and Human Performance*, May 1969, pp. 176-211.

ROLLINS, T., "Pay for Performance: Is It Worth the Trouble?", *Personnel Administrator*, 1988, vol. 33, N° 5, pp. 42-47.

SCHERER, M., Merit Pay: The Greath Debate. What's a Teacher Worth?", *Instructor*, 1983, vol. 93, N° 5, p. 22.

SCHIEMAN, W., *Managing Human Resources, 1983 and Beyond*, Princeton, New Jersey, Opinion Research Corporation, 1983.

SCHNEIDER, J. and E.A. LOCKE, "A Critique of Herzberg's Incident Classification System and a Suggestion of Revision", *Organizational Behavior and Human Performance*, 1971, vol. 6, pp. 441-457.

SCHWAB, D.P. and L. DYER, "The Motivational Impact of a Compensation System on Performance", *Organizational Behavior and Human Performance*, 1973, vol. 9, N° 2, pp. 215-255.

SCHWAB, M.M., E. JANUSAITIS and H. STARK, "Motivational Factors Among Supervisors in the Utility Industry", *Personnel Psychology*, 1963, vol. 16, pp. 45-53.

SHUSTER, J.R., B. CLARK and M. ROGERS, "Testing Portions of the Porter and Lawler Model Regarding the Motivational Role of Pay", *Journal of Applied Psychology*, 1971, vol. 55, pp. 187-195.

SILVERMAN, B.R.S., "Why the Merit Pay System Failed in the Federal Government", *Personnel Journal*, 1983, vol. 62, N° 4, pp. 294-302.

SIMON, M.A., *Administrative Behavior*, 3rd ed., New York, The Free Press, 1976.

STEVENS, S.S., "Measurement Psychophysics and Utility", in *Measurement Definitions and Theories*, edited by C.W. Churchman and P. Ratoosh, New York, Wiley, 1959.

STOUFFER, S. et al., *The American Soldier: Adjustments During Army Life*, Princeton, New Jersey, Princeton University Press, 1949.

SULLIVAN, J.F., "The Future of Merit Pay Program", *Compensation and Benefits Review*, 1988, vol. 20, pp. 22-30.

TEEL, K., "Are Merit Raises Really Based on Merit?", *Personnel Journal*, March 1986, pp. 88-92.

THÉRIAULT, R., *Equity Theory: An Examination of the Inputs and Outcomes in an Organizational Setting*, Doctoral Thesis, Ithaca, New York, Cornell University, 1977.

THIBAULT, J.W. and H.H. KELLEY, *The Social Psychology of Groups*, New York, Wiley, 1959.

THOMPSON, P.A. and G.W. DALTON, "Performance Appraisal: Managers Beware", *Harvard Business Review*, January-February 1970, pp. 149-157.

TOLMAN, E.C., "A Psychological Model", in *Toward a General Theory of Action*, edited by T. Parsons and E.A. Shills, Cambridge, Massachusetts, Harvard University Press, 1951.

TOLMAN, E.C., *Purposive Behavior in Animals and Men*, New York, Century Co., 1932.

VROOM, V.H., *Some Observations Regarding Herzberg's Two-Factor Theory*, text presented to the American Psychological Association Congress, Chicago, 1966.

VROOM, V.H., *Work and Motivation*, New York, Wiley, 1964.

WAHBA, M.A. and L.G. BRIDWELL, "Maslow Reconsidered: A Review of Research on the Need Hierarchy Theory", *Organizational Behavior and Human Performance*, 1976, vol. 15, pp. 221-240.

WALL, T., G. STEPHENSON and G. SKIDMORE, "Ego-Involvement and Herzberg's Two-Factor Theory of Job Satisfaction: An Experimental Field Study", *British Journal of Social and Clinical Psychology*, 1971, vol. 10, pp. 123-131.

WINSTANLEY, N.B., "Are Merit Increases Really Effective?", *Personnel Administrator*, 1982, vol. 27, pp. 37-41.

TABLE OF CONTENTS

11

INDIVIDUAL PERFORMANCE EVALUATION FOR MERIT COMPENSATION

The greatest challenge in merit compensation is evaluating individual performance. After looking at the performance evaluation process, this chapter identifies and describes the nature of the criteria and methods appropriate to merit compensation. It then focuses on managing performance evaluation, i.e. selecting evaluators and reviewers, the frequency and timing of evaluation, communicating the results, and the performance evaluation form. It concludes by considering certain elements that must be considered to ensure that the performance evaluation system for merit compensation functions effectively.

☐ 11.1 The Individual Performance Evaluation Process

11.1.1 Definition of Performance Evaluation

Merit compensation or performance-based pay generally applies to jobs whose content is not standard, e.g. the work of professional, technicians, and most administrative support staff. Since the performance of these employees cannot be measured solely against objective criteria, a more or less subjective judgment must be made about the relative value of each individual's contribution. Performance evaluation may therefore be defined as the act of measuring or judging the relative value of an employee's contribution to the organization.

11.1.2 Performance Evaluation Objectives

A performance evaluation system for determining merit compensation involves an agreement between organization and employee about the rel-

TABLE 11.1
Performance evaluation in a merit compensation context

Subject of the evaluation:	Overall performance
Evaluation standard:	The employee's relative performance
Under evaluation:	Past performance
Evaluator's role:	Judge
Evaluator's required behaviour:	Evaluation
Evaluator's essential qualities:	The capacity to evaluate employee performance properly and motivation to do so
Atmosphere:	Potential conflicts between supervisor and employee over evaluation expectations and results
Evaluation frequency:	Timely

ationship between performance and compensation, based on past rather than future performance. In addition, according to the equity principle, such a system must consider not only how the employees do their work, but also, and above all, their performance compared to that of their colleagues.

A merit compensation system depends largely on the authority of immediate supervisors, who must equitably judge the work of their employees. In this context, supervisors must have the ability to properly fulfil their role as judges representing the organization. They must also be able to weigh a set of relevant factors in evaluating the performance of their employees, such as results achieved or the circumstances surrounding their achievement. Finally, supervisors must be able to link the money paid to employees and the employees' performance evaluation.

Given the financial stakes involved, it is to be expected that performance evaluation gives rise to disagreements in the context of merit compensation. If employees consider the amount of money at stake significant, they will be sure to highlight their own strengths and achievements and blame others for their weaknesses when discussing their performance with their supervisor. Although the dynamics underlying the evaluation interview are generally based on mutual goodwill, this is not always the case. In fact, the evaluation process normally unfolds in an emotionally charged, competitive atmosphere, in which the supervisor has more power, and points of disagreement, rather than agreement, are emphasized. Table 11.1 summarizes this situation.

In view of this reality, over the years, numerous authors have proposed separating performance evaluation for merit compensation from performance evaluation intended to identify training and development needs and other related objectives. This is the recommendation that emerges from the studies conducted by Meyer and his colleagues (Meyer, Kay and French, 1965) at

General Electric in the early 60s. In the early 80s, however, Lawler, Mohrman and Resnick (1984) resumed the studies at General Electric and concluded the opposite, namely that discussing the amount attached to merit compensation had positive effects on the evaluation interview. A recent study focusing specifically on this question (Prince and Lawler, 1986) revealed that discussing pay during the evaluation interview may have a positive impact on the employees' perception of the evaluation process – its contents and results. Various factors account for this positive impact.

1. When the parties have to discuss pay increases, they prepare for the evaluation interview more carefully.
2. A discussion of pay increases generates more interest, resulting in greater participation by the employee being evaluated, and therefore a better understanding of and stronger commitment to work objectives.
3. The discussion also conveys a clearer message about evaluation results: "My boss told me that my performance was satisfactory. But I only got a 4% pay increase, compared to an average 5%, so my performance is not as satisfactory as I thought."

According to Ilgen and Feldman (1983), separating the discussion of merit pay increases from the discussion of training and career planning may only irritate employees. Worse, it may lead to their considering their boss a hypocrite. Distinguishing performance evaluation for pay purposes from performance evaluation intended to identify training and development needs is, therefore, not recommended.

II.I.3 Performance Evaluation Stages

Individual performance evaluation to determine pay increases is not a human resources department program, but rather an integral part of performance management within the organization. The human resource department may develop the system and train managers, but only the latter can make it work (Fay, 1990).

A performance management system implies the six steps illustrated in Figure 11.1.

A performance management system must be built around two basic components: a list of the organization's general objectives and a description of the individual responsibilities of each employee. These two factors (1A and 1B in Figure 11.1) are essential for properly determining performance objectives and expectations. In fact, the objectives set jointly by supervisors and their employees must comply with the organization's strategic objectives and priorities. Failure to consider the organization's strategic objectives may lead employees to set individual priorities that run counter to, or are sec-

FIGURE 11.1
Performance management system

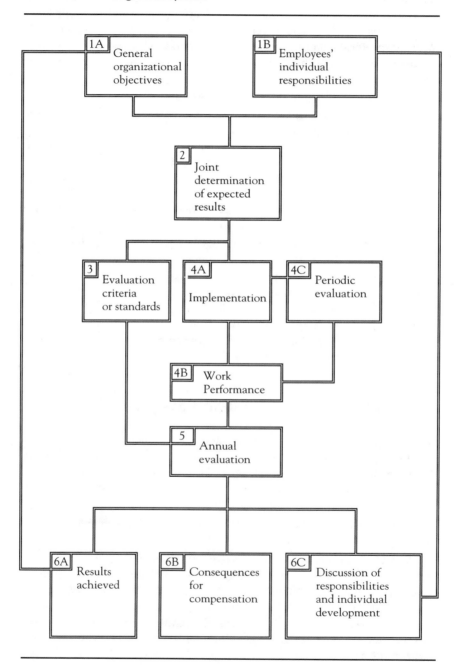

SOURCE: J. Charuest, William M. Mercer Limited, personal communication, October 16, 1990.

ondary to, the organization's priorities. On the other hand, if the employee's individual responsibilities are not considered, the supervisor may set work objectives that should not be assigned to the employee, or that make the employee responsible for achieving objectives with no control over the resources needed to achieve them (such resources being outside the employee's area of responsibility or jurisdiction).

Determining objectives and expected results effectively (Stage 2) leads to establishing evaluation criteria and standards in advance (Stage 3), that is, the precise factors (criteria) on which the evaluation at the end of the annual cycle will be based and the level of expectation (standards) in relation to those criteria. For example, among the criteria used to measure the degree to which the objective of improving union-management relations is achieved might be the number of grievances lodged by the union. In this case, a satisfactory performance might mean improving relationships so that the number of grievances during the year will not exceed the standard of 10.

The fourth stage involves implementation and achievement of results. Here, there are one or two evaluations to ensure that the employee can reasonably achieve personal objectives, and to see what significant changes must be made if circumstances change drastically so that the established crtiteria no longer apply.

The fifth stage is the annual performance evaluation itself. It has two phases: a discussion of achievements compared with expectations and a discussion of the adjustments or action required to develop the employee's abilities.

The annual evaluation has three types of consequences (Stage 6).

1. The achieved results play a role in setting objectives for the following year.
2. The annual evaluation produces a performance rating with consequences in terms of compensation, since the rating is used to determine annual pay increases.
3. The evaluation leads to a discussion of the employee's responsibilities, as well as the measures or action required for personal development to continue. This increases the individual's job satisfaction and commitment to the organization. This discussion occasionally results in changes to the employee's responsibilities, which are reviewed in discussing the objectives for the year ahead.

This enumeration of the stages of a performance evaluation for merit compensation indicates that performance evaluation must not (as is often, unfortunately, the case) be limited to completing an evaluation form every year like a tax return. Upstream, the performance evaluation process springs from work planning and implementation. Downstream, it flows into merit compensation and what is expected of employees in the future.

TABLE 11.2

Examples of performance criteria using an individual's personality traits or personal characteristics

– Conduct and bearing	– Judgment and reason
– Punctuality	– Sense of responsibility
– Teamwork	– Decisiveness
– Interest in work	– Human relations
– Order and method	– Sociability
– Leadership	– Enthusiasm
– Initiative	– Motivation
– Dedication	– Appearance
– Cooperativeness	– Emotional stability

11.2 Individual Performance Evaluation Criteria

Individual performance evaluation means determining to what extent an employee satisfies organizational expectations. While these expectations undoubtedly involve tasks to accomplish and results to achieve, they also imply behaviour that conforms to the organization's philosophy, standards, and preferred way of doing things. Since it is impossible to obtain a complete, instant snapshot of the whole of an employee's contribution to the organization, evaluation criteria must be set. These criteria represent the organization's expectations or the various aspects of an employee's work that indicate contribution. They must reflect what the individual has to do and what is within the employee's control, rather than translate other variables outside the control of the employee.

Evaluation criteria may be divided into three main categories:

– the individual or personality traits;
– the results or standards to achieve; and
– the required process or behaviour.

11.2.1 Personality Traits

An individual's personality traits, or general characteristics, are the most commonly used evaluation criteria, because of the alleged ease with which they may be identified (Lazer and Wickstrom, 1977; Locker and Teel, 1977). Table 11.2 lists examples of these criteria taken from performance evaluation forms. *Examples: Conduct + Bearing, Punctuality*

While these criteria have their defenders in practice, they are the most contested in the literature on the subject. Using such criteria, in fact, raises the question of the relationship among personality traits, attitude, and behaviour. It is one thing to possess certain personality traits, and another to use them appropriately. Even when accompanied by relatively precise definitions, these criteria raise serious problems of interpretation because, generally, they cannot be directly observed. Properly speaking, one does not see someone's leadership. One observes behaviour that is, to a greater or lesser extent, ascribed to leadership. Evaluation then becomes a matter of perspective. And since evaluator and employee have two different perspectives, they will undoubtedly have different interpretations of the evaluation criteria.

11.2.2 Results to Be Achieved

Identifying the results (objectives) to be achieved is based on an analysis of both an employee's expected role, as defined in a job description, and what the organization expects from the employee.

While such criteria may seem appealing at the outset, they nonetheless raise a number of problems.

1. The quantitative nature of certain tasks or responsibilities readily lends itself to setting operational objectives, but this is not as easily achieved with work of an essentially qualitative nature.
2. The need to set operational criteria may result in emphasizing the short term at the expense of the long term.
3. In examining the reasons for the evaluation results, it may be difficult to distinguish employee-related from environmental causes.
4. Since these criteria are tailored to the individual, employee performance cannot be compared for merit compensation purposes.
5. It is one thing to achieve results, it is another to do so by means (behaviour) accepted by, or acceptable to, the organization. The use made of the results stresses the importance of the end, but fails to consider the process, or means, of attaining those results.
6. Such criteria are adequate when an employee manages a large number of projects, but may not be appropriate when applied to routine activities.

Performance evaluation systems based on expected results make it difficult to pass judgment on day-to-day management. One way to avoid this disadvantage is to introduce another type of criterion, such as desired behaviour.

11.2.3 Required Behaviour

As early as 1949, Flanagan proposed using what he termed "critical behaviour" as a performance evaluation criterion. In brief, this involves basing performance evaluation not on an employee's personality traits or characteristics or on the results achieved, but on what the individual does. It focuses the evaluation on the process, i.e. the behaviour that has significant impact, be it positive or negative, on the results. In practice, this involves identifying the type of behaviour desired, and then comparing it to the employee's way of doing things. Smith and Kendall (1963), Dunnette (1966), and Latham and Wexley (1981) are fierce defenders of this type of criterion. Table 11.3 illustrates certain dimensions of management. As with personality traits, one must be cautious when using behaviour as a performance criterion. For example, in reality, usually more than one type of behaviour or way of doing things is acceptable for achieving certain objectives. Identifying appropriate behaviour may become a long and painstaking exercise if one wishes to be very precise. Using behaviour as a criterion also implies that the evaluator has the chance to observe the employee in action, which is not always possible. While such a criterion has its inherent advantages, in practice it is limited.

11.2.4 Selecting Criteria for Merit Compensation

At the beginning of this section, we noted that individual performance evaluation criteria are set because of the impossibility of obtaining a complete, instant snapshot of an employee's contribution to the organization. Performance evaluation criteria must, therefore, be analytic, that is, they must measure employees' effectiveness. But, because of the relationship that must be established between performance evaluation results and pay increase percentages, merit compensation requires an overall evaluation.

From a merit compensation perspective, the type of criteria used matters little, since all of the criteria previously described may serve the purpose. The important thing is for the resulting overall performance rating to be a valid and accurate measurement of employee performance. However, an organization rarely evaluates the performance of its employees solely to determine merit increases. Its objective is generally to identify training and development and other related needs. When performance evaluation takes place in a training and development context, the type of criteria chosen (personality traits, results, or behaviour) becomes important. As mentioned earlier, some of these criteria are not particularly relevant for employee training, i.e. personality traits and results, although the latter have the advantage of reflecting the attainment of objectives, an important dimension for the organization.

In this context, a number of authors suggest using hybrid criteria that combine objectives and behaviour on the job (Beer and Ruh, 1976; Beer et al., 1978). Because objectives appear to be valid, using them has the advantage of pleasing managers. On the other hand, using specific work behaviour as an evaluation criterion gives employees a better idea of what they must do

TABLE 11.3
Illustration of management dimensions

1. Management-related dimensions
   - Achieving results: achieves day-to-day results and carries out the regular responsibilities of the position.
   - Organization and delegation: subdivides projects, distributes and assigns main tasks; delegates authority and the freedom required to achieve objectives; avoids conflicting schedules.
   - Control and follow-up: follows up regularly, establishes performance yardsticks, analyzes the results, and takes corrective action.
2. Conceptual dimensions
   - Initiative and creativity: thinks creatively and suggests new ideas or new ways of doing things.
   - Analytic skills: grasps problems, recognizes and properly weighs the relevant facts.
3. Interpersonal and human resource management dimensions
   - Cooperative relationships: works with colleagues in the organization's best interests.
   - Communication: offers advice, organizes and states facts and solutions in a convincing manner, both orally and in writing.
   - Development of employees: effectively develops employees through coaching, training, advice, and evaluation.
4. Technical or professional dimensions
   - Knowledge of the job: demonstrates competence in handling the technical or professional aspects of the unit being managed.
   - Personal and professional development: enhances technical skills and knowledge of the job; applies the acquired knowledge in different circumstances.

to improve their performance and orient their training and development efforts.

Assigning a performance rating to each hybrid "behaviour-results" criterion is not useful for determining training or development needs. If one decides to weight these criteria, assign them respective values, and add them up to arrive at an overall performance rating that may be used for merit compensation, the final score is useless from a training perspective. It does not identify the behaviour that contributed to, or detracted from, success. Using achievement scores is not only a futile exercise for determining training needs, it also distorts the process of setting realistic objectives, by encouraging employees to pursue goals that they can easily achieve. The higher the monetary stakes of merit compensation, the more this applies.

In brief, the choice of evaluation criteria depends on whether the objective is merit compensation alone, or merit compensation and training and other related objectives. When all of these objectives are pursued, using hybrid criteria (work objectives and specific behaviour) seems preferable. In this case, however, the use of ratings or achievement scores for each objective is not only inappropriate, but also skews the assessment that must be done to determine individual training and development needs. The question of overall evaluation results required for merit compensation cannot be addressed when considering the objective of the evaluation alone. The question must also be addressed in selecting an evaluation method.

☐ 11.3 Individual Performance Evaluation Methods

Finding an appropriate performance evaluation method is undoubtedly the problem that has most concerned and frustrated both academics and practitioners over the years. Apparently, the method used has very little impact on the results (Landy and Farr, 1980), and the choice of method should be based on the purpose of the evaluation (Cummings and Schwab, 1973; Oberg, 1972).

This section does not aim to provide a complete, structured description of each evaluation method with its advantages and disadvantages. Numerous authors have already done that quite competently: Cummings and Schwab (1973), Landy and Farr (1980), Bazinet (1980), Bernardin and Beatty (1984), Bélanger et al. (1988). The purpose, rather, is to identify the most suitable methods for merit compensation.

11.3.1 Performance Evaluation Methods

Performance evaluation methods may be divided into two categories: comprehensive and analytic. Cummings and Schwab (1983), however, propose a subtler distinction. Comprehensive methods consist of those based on comparison, whereas analytic methods may be organized into those that use standards, objectives, or indices; the latter category also includes hybrid methods.

Comparison-based Methods

Comparison-based methods normally have two characteristics. First, performance is evaluated by comparing employees on the basis of appropriate dimensions. Secondly, the comparisons usually include an overall performance dimension that reflects the employee's general effectiveness within the organization. The four best-known methods in this category are straight ranking, alternative ranking, paired comparison, and forced distribution.

Straight ranking involves ranking employees on the basis of their performance. Alternative ranking involves identifying first the employee with the best performance, then the one with the worst performance, and so on, until all employees have been ranked. Paired comparison involves systematically comparing the performance of each employee with that of all the others. Finally, the forced-distribution method requires all the performance evaluations of a group of employees fall into a predetermined distribution; a bell curve is often used for this, e.g. the performance of 10% of employees is considered unsatisfactory, 20% acceptable, 40% satisfactory, 20% remarkable, and 10% exceptional. This method solves the problems that arise from too-lenient or too-harsh evaluators, or those who tend to evaluate every employee's performance as average. Finally, regardless of the distribution chosen, this method is only useful for a relatively large number of employees. While the strict minimum is 10, using forced distribution for less than 20 employees is not recommended.

Standard-based Methods

Standard-based methods differ from comparison-based methods in two ways. First, each employee is evaluated against one or more written standards, rather than against the other members in the group of employees being evaluated. Secondly, this method is analytic rather than comprehensive, i.e. numerous dimensions of an employee's performance are evaluated, rather than a single comprehensive one. Many evaluation methods use performance standards: the critical behaviour or critical incident technique, the weighted checklist, the forced-choice checklist, the standard rating scale, and the Behaviorally Anchored Rating Scales (BARS). Because of the popularity of standard rating scales and the tremendous interest in BARS, only these two methods will be discussed here.

[handwritten: most popular are: Standard Rating BARS]

The Standard Rating Scale Method

The standard rating scale method consists of a list of criteria and an evaluation scale, which may be either numeric (e.g. 1 to 5) or qualitative (e.g. weak to strong).

While this is undoubtedly the most widely used method, its popularity is surprising in view of its limitations. These limitations stem largely from the fact that standard rating scales are often based on criteria that involve the individual, or personality traits, which creates a number of problems for measuring employee performance. Its popularity is, without question, mainly the result of the apparent ease with which a scale may be developed. However, a properly designed rating scale considers a set of psychometric factors that few people seem to be concerned with. This method is also popular simply because it is popular, a human phenomenon best expressed by the advertising slogan for a brand of hot dogs: "More people eat them because they're fresher, and they're fresher because more people eat them."

The BARS Method

The BARS method, an offshoot of standard rating scales, evaluates performance against a set of behavioural aspects or dimensions. The degree of acceptability of each dimension is illustrated by behavioural descriptions typical of the employees whose performance is being evaluated.

There are five steps to developing this method.

1. Persons familiar with the jobs (the incumbents or their supervisors) are asked to provide examples of effective or ineffective behaviour in the jobs in question. These examples represent what are commonly called "critical incidents".

2. A disinterested party (generally an outside consultant) organizes the incidents into a fixed number of dimensions (usually 5 to 10).

3. These dimensions and the list of critical incidents are given separately to a second group of persons familiar with the jobs, who are asked to classify the incidents according to the different dimensions. The critical incidents on which there is a 50% to 80% agreement are then retained.

4. The same group is generally asked to indicate to what extent each retained incident represents effective or ineffective behaviour for the performance dimension in question on a scale (e.g. 1 to 7). The more they agree, the lower the standard deviation of the distribution of answers. With a seven-point scale, incidents with a standard deviation of 1.50 or less are usually retained.

5. The retained incidents for each dimension are placed on each scale at the location that represents the average result for the effective behaviour described by the incidents obtained from the preceding step.

The result of this process is the final evaluation instrument. In view of the specific nature of the behavioural dimensions, the resulting evaluation form may be used to evaluate the performance of persons holding the same or similar jobs.

Taylor (1976), Gartland and Tornow (1977), as well as Beatty, Schneier and Beatty (1977) illustrate applications of this method.

Methods Based on Performance Objectives

The third principal category of evaluation methods consists of those based on performance objectives. Designed as a participatory management and development tool, management by objectives (MBO) was proposed by McGregor (1957, 1960) as a valid option for evaluating performance.

The method involves examining an employee's job description and the objectives of the work team to which the employee is assigned, and establishing a complete set of precise objectives that are subsequently used to evaluate performance. This approach is based on two assumptions. First, the clearer an incumbent's idea of the job, the greater the chances that the incumbent will succeed. Secondly, the level of achievement may be measured solely on the basis of what an employee tries to accomplish.

In practice, MBO varies from one organization to the next in various ways: the nature of the objectives, the extent to which subordinates participate in setting their own performance objectives, and the degree of commitment of the evaluators (McConkie, 1979). As Hodgson (1973) put it, MBO is a little like ice cream — it comes in 29 flavours!

Methods Based on Objective Indicators

The fourth major category of performance evaluation techniques encompasses methods based on concrete, objective indicators, such as productivity or profit levels, absenteeism or employee turnover rates, sales volume, or reject rates.

While this type of measurement instrument is interesting *a priori*, it raises the question of the impact of individual performance on such indicators. Also, these methods may be applicable to production workers and some office personnel, but certainly not to all managers.

Hybrid Methods

In view of the limitations of the different performance evaluation techniques, some authors (Levinson, 1976; Schneier and Beatty, 1979) have proposed the use of hybrid methods, which combine various types of evaluation criteria. As a general rule, the method chosen will consider performance objectives and critical behaviour or incidents. The idea behind this is that a combination of both types of criteria — results and process (behaviour) — may lead to a more satisfactory and complete grasp of the true performance of employees. The use of criteria that refer to the personality traits or the general characteristics of the individual is generally recommended to evaluate employee potential.

Finally, it should be noted that Beer and Ruh (1976) and Beer et al. (1978) provide a good review of the research on this method, in addition to its content and the manner in which it was introduced at Corning Glass to evaluate management performance.

11.3.2 Evaluation Methods for Merit Compensation

As mentioned above, the choice of a method for evaluating performance for merit compensation must be grounded in two fundamental considerations. The method must allow for a comprehensive evaluation of employee performance and must rest on a relative standard, which implies a comparison of performance.

The only two techniques that satisfy both these conditions are comparison-based, namely, the ranking methods and forced distribution. Yet, as noted at the beginning of the preceding section, it is difficult to obtain a comprehensive, instant snapshot of an employee's contribution to an organization; it is preferable to obtain one gradually. Consequently, performance evaluation for merit compensation must first use analytic criteria. The choice of the type of analytic criteria and of the evaluation method may then be selected so as to satisfy performance evaluation objectives other than merit compensation, e.g. training and development needs.

The use of hybrid methods is ideal for identifying training and development needs. As mentioned above, mixed criteria (for example, performance objectives and specific behaviour or performance objectives and specific skills) prove very useful for this. Possible combinations include MBO with the critical incident technique, or with standard rating scales, or with the BARS method.

The hybrid approach first of all allows for an analytic evaluation of performance aimed at employee development. All that remains then is to arrive at a comprehensive, comparative evaluation of employee performance through either a ranking or forced-distribution method.

Ranking methods are more commonly used in practice, because of the disadvantages of forced distribution. In fact, the latter is only valid for a fairly large number of employees (at least 10, but preferably over 20), a situation that applies rarely. Moreover, evaluators do not appreciate being forced to adhere to a predetermined distribution of performance levels.

Of the ranking techniques, the paired comparison method seems preferable, because of its systematic nature. Like all ranking methods, this approach allows the performance of employees reporting to the same manager to be compared, but not the performance of employees under different managers. One advantage of paired comparisons is that the performance of two or three employees may be judged equivalent. This advantage, however, has its drawbacks. Because the performance of more than one employee may receive the same rating, the distribution of all the evaluations in an organizational division or department may appear more concentrated than it is in fact.

This risk of over-concentration is all the greater when employees' pay increases depend on their performance, and few managers have the courage of their convictions. Consider, for example, how people behave when it comes to tipping a restaurant waiter or waitress. Even though the person is a total stranger and the service is poor, it is difficult not to leave at least a substandard tip. Similarly, one may readily appreciate that the pressure felt by managers in a merit compensation situation is not conducive to distinguishing the different levels of employees' performance. Under these circumstances, it is almost essential to use forced distribution, not for each manager's group of employees (the number may not be large enough), but for the employees of a section, department, division, or the entire organization. However, before imposing any form of distribution on evaluation results and stirring up employee resentment, it seems preferable to allow managers to freely evaluate their employees, emphasizing the importance of the distinctive, equitable nature of their evaluations, and then carefully reviewing the evaluation distribution every year.

Even though it is not always appropriate to do a forced distribution of performance evaluations, the need to distinguish the performance of various employees raises two questions: How many performance levels should there be? And what percentage of employees should be at each level?

Number of Performance Levels

Employee performances may be divided into categories or levels: unacceptable, satisfactory, superior, and exceptional. This raises the question of how many such levels there should be. Winstanley (1980) recommends using three levels when evaluating performance for merit compensation. His opinion is based on two points. First, people have problems distinguishing more than three performance levels and, secondly, determining merit compensation depends on factors other than individual performance (individual's compa-ratio, cost of living, etc.).

The argument based on people's limited capacity to draw distinctions has its merits when the evaluators do comprehensive, final evaluations. But this is not the only possible approach. An evaluator may very well be asked to proceed in stages. First, is the employee's performance satisfactory or not? Secondly, if it is satisfactory, is it below average, average, or above average? And so on. In this way, one may define and use more than three performance levels to evaluate a group of employees.

As for the argument that merit compensation depends on factors other than individual performance, this is undoubtedly true. However, using only

TABLE 11.4
Descriptions of Performance Levels

1. Unacceptable: The employee is unable to achieve the minimum performance standards for the job. Even after the employee was told that an improvement was necessary and the required tools and assistance were made available, performance did not improve. Management action (up to and including dismissal) is now necessary.

2. Requires improvement: Even though the employee's performance in different aspects of the job is satisfactory, there are major areas in which it falls short of expectations. Regular work contains too many errors, productivity is too low, or jobs often have to be done over. Particular improvement is necessary to boost the employee's general performance to a fully satisfactory level. Management thinks the employee is capable of making the necessary improvements and deserves its encouragement and support.

3. Fully satisfactory: The employee's performance is fully satisfactory. Work satisfies expectations and the requirements of the job. The employee's judgment and sense of responsibility are reliable, work meets deadlines and standards, and the performance contributes to the success of the unit and the organization.

4. Remarkable: Performance exceeds the requirements of the position and the employee demonstrates a high degree of competence. The employee knows how to take advantage of personal strengths and apply them to achieve outstanding results.

5. Superior: The employee regularly and clearly exceeds standards and requirements in achieving objectives and in relation to the duties of the job. This employee demonstrates a degree of competence and makes a vital contribution to organizational success.

6. Exceptional: The employee's performance is exceptional in every area and enhances the work of other employees. Results significantly surpass expectations, and the employee's behaviour is exemplary. The employee has managed to seize and create opportunities to make a major contribution to organizational success.

three levels tends to weaken the relationship between performance and the merit portion of compensation. This, in turn reduces the motivating effect of compensation.

In practice, management determines the number of performance levels to be used. If management thinks employees' performance may be divided into three or four levels, the distribution should be made accordingly. The same applies if they select five or six. Given human beings' limited powers of discrimination, however, it would not seem advisable to establish more than six or seven levels.

Experience further shows that, even though evaluation forms featuring a choice of six or seven performance levels are not uncommon, only four or five of them are actually used. A greater number of levels complicates interpretation. For example, the description of the "satisfactory" level often leads one to believe that the performance of employees at that level is barely tolerable, whereas the "exceptional" level gives the impression that walking

TABLE 11.5
Percentage of employees at each performance level, based on normal distribution

Performance Level	Percentage of Employees
Exceptional	6
Superior	16
Remarkable	28
Fully satisfactory	28
Requires improvement	16
Unacceptable	6

on water is a requirement! Table 11.4 contains descriptions of performance levels that are less vulnerable to this type of criticism. The meaning of the words used is more positive and, perhaps, more realistic. In addition, unlike many performance evaluation scales, this one has more positive than negative levels.

This evaluation rating system has two advantages. First, it allows nuances in the evaluation. Secondly, exceptional contributions (Levels 5 and 6) may be distinguished from fully satisfactory ones (Levels 3 and 4) without demoralizing the employees concerned (i.e. those with performance levels of 3 or 4).

Percentage of Employees at Each Performance Level

Once the number of performance levels has been determined, the question of the percentage of employees that should be located at each level remains. It is generally recommended that a normal bell curve be used for the distribution. Table 11.5 contains an example of one for six performance levels.

It is questionable whether a normal distribution such as this would reflect the actual performance of employees in an organization. In fact, a normal distribution presumes that employees have been hired at random, and have received no training or advice since. Inasmuch as the employee recruiting and training process is effective, one should find fewer employees in the "fully satisfactory" and lower levels than in the upper ones. The percentage depends on the effectiveness of decisions about selection, training, and promotions. As a result, one may decide to distribute employees among the different performance levels using a different curve. One possibility is illustrated in Table 11.6.

TABLE 11.6
Performance distribution of employees within an organization

Performance Level	Percentage of Employees
Exceptional	0-5
Superior	15-20
Remarkable	25-30
Fully satisfactory	35-40
Requires improvement	5-10
Unacceptable	0-2

☐ 11.4 Managing Performance Evaluation

One important aspect of a performance evaluation system is its management. Managing entails answering questions about the choice of evaluators, appointing reviewers, determining the frequency and timing of evaluations, and communicating the results. The following pages discuss these issues.

11.4.1 Evaluators

In theory, employees should be evaluated by the individual with the best knowledge of how they do their job. This assumes an evaluator in a position to observe the employee at work, one who knows the criteria for evaluating that employee's performance. Generally speaking, this may be done using numerous evaluators: the immediate supervisor, fellow workers, subordinates, and the actual employee. In some circumstances, such as the evaluation of organizational representatives or certain scientists, an external evaluation committee (consisting of outsiders) may be formed, because these persons alone may be in a position (i.e. capable of observing and familiar with the criteria) to correctly appraise performance.

In practice, the immediate supervisor is responsible for evaluating an employee's performance. When someone else does the evaluation, the immediate supervisor remains involved in the process. The immediate supervisor is undoubtedly in the best position to evaluate employees for compensation purposes. Asking employees to evaluate their own performance for pay purposes may be inappropriate, since they would then be both judge and party. The same applies to fellow workers evaluating each other.

This discussion is not applicable, however, when performance evaluation aims to identify training and development needs and other related objectives.

In that case, it is indeed worthwhile to involve the employee (Meyer, 1991) and other people with whom the employee has contact (such as fellow workers). The immediate supervisor's role is then to collect information from all these sources, in order to arrive at an analytic evaluation of the performance of employees, synthesize the data, and discuss it with them. These different sources of information give the immediate supervisor a more accurate appraisal of employee performance. They also provide information useful for arriving at an overall evaluation of each employee's performance, comparing performances, and ranking them to determine merit compensation.

Does this mean that performance should be evaluated by the immediate supervisor alone when its sole purpose is compensation? It seems not. Even when done honestly and with appropriate evaluation criteria and techniques, the results may be skewed by the evaluator's generosity or severity. In addition, if the equity principle applies to employees under the same immediate supervisor, it also applies to employees under different supervisors. First, evaluations by immediate supervisors must be reviewed and, if necessary, adjusted to counterbalance excessive generosity or severity. Secondly, they must be brought into line with the performance of employees under other supervisors. Given that initial evaluations by immediate superiors may be reviewed and amended, the employees concerned should obviously not be informed of the results before they have been reviewed. Until then, the evaluation process is not yet complete, and the information might create false expectations.

II.4.2 Reviewers

Since the evaluator is not God, it is important to consult other people before completing the evaluation or informing the employee of the results. Whether the purpose of evaluation is determining merit compensation, identifying training needs or other related objectives, the results should always be reviewed. This allows consideration of the results in a more global perspective, a curbing of the halo effect, excessive severity or generosity, etc. – in brief, a reassessment of the evaluation. In the case of merit compensation, it is primarily a question of ensuring that the evaluation is equitable, to give employees a clearer perception of the pay-performance relationship. Yet as Schwab and Olson (1990) point out, performance evaluation errors do not seem to be as serious a problem as the pay-performance relationship might lead one to believe. A lack of accuracy in performance evaluation has little effect on perception of the pay-performance relationship.

When evaluating performance for merit compensation, this review must first be assigned to the persons directly above the immediate supervisors, because of the nature of their position and the comparison that must be made among evaluations coming from different immediate supervisors. Their role is to re-examine the performance evaluation results to make sure that they are objective, and to compare the evaluations of various immediate supervisors to establish an acceptable and equitable distribution of employee performance. It is at this stage that human resource department officers (compensation officers) enter the process. Their role is to verify the degree of acceptability of the performance distribution and the consistency of evaluations from different organizational departments or divisions.

On the other hand, in evaluating performance to determine training needs, it may seem less appropriate to have the supervisors of the immediate supervisors participate, because of the "distance" between the former and the employees being evaluated. The same applies to human resource department officers (training and development officers), whose role is to note the training needs of a group of employees, and to determine, together with the immediate supervisors, how those needs may be met.

11.4.3 Evaluation Frequency

Performance evaluations are often conducted annually. Performance evaluations for training and development purposes should be ongoing, with the formal annual evaluation representing an update.

An annual performance evaluation would seem to be more relevant for compensation, since payroll budgets are generally prepared once a year. A shorter evaluation cycle is often recommended for newly hired or newly promoted employees. Employees tend to learn more initially in a job, more frequent pay increases have a greater effect on motivation, and employees have more opportunities to advance toward the control point in their pay scale.

11.4.4 Evaluation Timing

Some organizations schedule individual pay increases for the anniversary of an employee's date of hire or most recent promotion. Performance evaluations for merit compensation are therefore spread throughout the year. This practice has the advantage of de-dramatizing performance evaluation. Nonetheless, it makes performance comparison, of prime importance for compensation, more difficult. Also, spreading performance evaluations across the entire year may have a negative effect on the evaluator's motivation for doing the appraisals and on the quality of the results (Petit and DeCotiis, 1978; Das, 1981). It is therefore preferable to conduct performance evaluations for compensation simultaneously during a relatively brief period. This period should also fit into the organization's management cycle, to ensure its consistency with the employee performance management cycle.

11.4.5 Communicating Evaluation Results

Evaluation results must be communicated twice: to the human resource department and to the employee concerned. These two aspects are discussed below.

Informing the Human Resource Department

One important aspect of a performance evaluation system is determining what information contained on the evaluation form should remain confidential between supervisor and subordinate, or supervisor and reviewer, and what should be passed on to the human resource department.

From a compensation standpoint, performance evaluation results must obviously be passed on to the head of compensation in the human resource department. The head of each department (or division) will convey to the human resource department, after review by organizational supervisors, the results of applying forced distribution (if applicable).

Informing Employees

Informing employees of the results of evaluations intended for merit compensation before they have been reviewed and approved is likely to bias the appraisals. It may also create false expectations. The evaluations by the immediate supervisor may be adjusted, based on the performance of other employees. These evaluations are only one input (however important) in the final, relative performance evaluation for merit compensation.

Once the evaluation process has been completed and the performance distribution accepted, decisions about pay increases must be made and employees notified. Depending on the organization and its operational style, the decisions may be announced by the immediate supervisor or by the human resource department. The decision in some cases is clear and unequivocal; in others, an explanation is necessary. It is therefore important for managers to be prepared to meet with some – or even all – employees to explain and justify the resulting merit increase. In brief, the manager must act as a representative of the organization, and provide a twofold explanation. The first deals with the evaluation of the individual's performance. The parties concerned have already had an opportunity to discuss this point if the overall evaluation is based on a more analytic appraisal used to identify training and development and other related needs. The second aspect of the interview involves the manager's judgment of the employee's performance compared to that of fellow workers. This explanation must be completely frank and direct. When the employee's performance is at least satisfactory, the explanation is all the easier to provide if the rules are precise and known, and other pay increase criteria are used, for example, to protect the employee's standard of living and ensure external equity.

Obviously, most employees will disagree with a less than satisfactory evaluation. Most often, they consider their performance to be at the level their supervisor wants it to be in future (Bernardin and Villanova, 1986). Moreover, employees and their immediate supervisors have different perceptions of the causes of a less than satisfactory performance. Employees attribute the results to factors beyond their control (other employees' absences, lack of administrative support, work overload, lack of adequate equipment, etc.), whereas evaluators attribute them to factors related to the employee (lack of skill, lack of motivation, etc.). The phenomenon is particularly well-documented by the attribution theory (Kelly, 1973; Landy and Farr, 1980; Feldman, 1981; Ilgen and Feldman, 1983). Training programs based on the critical incident technique (Bownas and Bernardin, 1988) have also been suggested to eliminate these disagreements (Bernardin, 1989).

11.4.6 Evaluation Forms

The number and content of evaluation forms depend on the purpose of the evaluation and the method selected. Only two forms may be necessary for performance evaluations exclusively for merit compensation, the first, for the immediate supervisor, to identify each subordinate and assign a relative, overall rating to each, and the second for the department or division head, to synthesize the evaluations of unit members and examine their distribution. If performance appraisals are used for training and development and other related objectives, a separate form must be designed to meet these specific objectives.

☐ 11.5 Prerequisites for Effective Performance Evaluation

Following an in-depth review of the literature on conditions for performance evaluation system effectiveness, DeVries et al. (1980) concluded by emphasizing that implementation of the system is as critical as, if not more critical than, its characteristics. As they described it, performance evaluation is not an event, but rather a process consisting of four stages:

- providing system information and training;
- selecting the target population;
- following up; and
- monitoring the system.

11.5.1 Performance Evaluation System Information and Training

As early as 1950, Mahler's studies found that the accuracy of performance evaluation depended essentially on evaluators – their evaluation skills and motivation. For Mahler, the opportunity to observe employees' work, the need supervisors feel to evaluate employees' performance, as well as the perceived value of the evaluation form in meeting the objective of the process, all affect the ability of supervisors to evaluate the performance of their employees. Supervisors' desire to evaluate performance depends on their understanding of the evaluation system, their acceptance of its objectives, and their attitude towards the management of their organization. More recent studies (Bernardin and Buckley, 1981; Smith, 1986) also consider that evaluators' competence and motivation for doing the evaluations play a critical role in the validity of results.

Evaluation skills are not innate. Moreover, one's motivation for doing something depends on one's perception of the ability required to succeed and the importance attached to succeeding. It seems, therefore, virtually impossible to establish a performance evaluation system without instituting an information and training program for the evaluators. At the very least, the training program may simply contain information about the evaluation system: its purpose, policies and practices, and explanations of the terms used in the forms and related documents. A program such as this may be completely delivered in a minimum of one day.

As mentioned, however, skill in evaluating and, above all, in communicating the results, is not innate. As employee selection and promotion are generally not based on these criteria, it is important to train evaluators (and, to a certain extent, employees as well) to appraise performance and communicate the results effectively. According to Piveteau (1981, p. 45), "the more valuable the supervisor's preparation, the more valuable the interview." Among other things, this preparation means the ability to conduct the interview properly. Establishing a purely informational program is, therefore, clearly inadequate. It is one thing to understand what must be done and quite another to be able to do it.

The content of a genuine training program naturally depends on the evaluation method selected (e.g. an MBO method implies the ability to determine and state objectives). Any training program must try to develop two basic skills: the ability to appraise performance and the ability to communicate the evaluation results (provide feedback). All authors agree on the advantage of having participants play an active role in this type of training program (Warmke and Billings, 1979; Bernardin and Buckley, 1981; Davis and Mount, 1984; Smith, 1986). Since this enables participants to test their skills during training, their expectations as to the types of problems they will face will be all the more realistic. Role-playing and simulations teach them to overcome these difficulties. This type of training program calls for at least two or three days of intensive work.

Finally, regarding the evaluators' motivation to do a good job, it is important to consider how well they perform this task when they themselves are evaluated by their supervisors. If this management responsibility is so important, the effort spent on it must be recognized and acknowledged, not just with fine words, but tangibly.

11.5.2 Selecting the Target Population

There are two ways to introduce a performance evaluation system. The first is to target the entire organization, or an entire category of employees (e.g. managers) for whom the system has been designed. Generally speaking, this strategy calls for considerable resources and would appear risky. In fact, the many and varied problems that may arise when introducing a performance evaluation system cannot be solved speedily enough to satisfy everyone concerned. People get the impression of riding out a storm, but the smart ones wait for it to pass, because they've been through it before.

The second strategy, which is safer and more efficient, involves proceeding in stages. This means selecting a representative pilot group with relatively good chances of success from the outset. The advantage of this approach is that it requires less resources, while providing control over the various components of the system. The system may then be adjusted as problems arise, quickly enough not to compromise the success of the strategy. Ideally, the program should first be implemented among senior management, because of the role it can play in encouraging the lower organizational levels to adopt performance evaluation. Yet, as Beer et al. (1978) point out, senior executives tend to think that performance evaluation is not suitable for them.

11.5.3 Following up on the Performance Evaluation System

Any management system may become routine. To ensure that a performance evaluation system remains relevant, those in charge of it must provide the necessary encouragement and support. Application of the system must be followed up on, and the results of the follow-up must be made known. The evaluators who have been trained to evaluate and communicate the results must apply their knowledge. Those responsible for running the system must be prepared to provide the necessary assistance at the right time and place. As incumbents change, new supervisors must be trained to conduct performance evaluations. Finally, since performance evaluation is not a regular management activity, knowledge may be forgotten and skills lost; therefore, arrangements must be made to organize refresher programs.

11.5.4 Monitoring the Performance Evaluation System

Monitoring is an essential, but often neglected, step in implementing a performance evaluation system. The ongoing effectiveness of the system depends on it. In this regard, DeVries et al. (1980) suggest asking four key questions.

1. Does the performance evaluation system that has been introduced and implemented correspond to what was desired and planned?
2. Are employees using the performance evaluation system in the way in which it was intended?
3. Is the performance evaluation system achieving its objectives?
4. Does the performance evaluation system mesh with the other management systems, especially other human resource management activities?

Finally, it is important to collect the opinions of those being evaluated on the usefulness, accuracy, and equity of the performance evaluation system (Winstanley, 1980). These perceptions influence their satisfaction with pay (Dyer and Thériault, 1976).

In addition to the prerequisites for effectiveness suggested by DeVries et al. (1980), recent studies have revealed the importance of procedural justice (justice of the means or process, as opposed to the results) in developing and implementing performance management in organizations (Folger and Greenberg, 1985; Greenberg, 1986). This perception of justice exists insofar as the employee believes that the immediate supervisor is familiar with the job, that there is two-way communication during the evaluation interview, that the same evaluation criteria are applied to everyone, that the evaluation ratings are genuinely based on employee performance, and that reward systems, such as promotions and pay increases, are based on evaluation ratings. Moreover, Cederblom (1982) stresses the importance of employees being able to make comments during the evaluation interview, and Bernardin and Beatty (1984), as well as Meyer (1991), emphasize the possibility of employees being able to evaluate themselves.

☐ 11.6 Summary

Performance evaluation presents the greatest challenge in successful merit compensation programs. Practically speaking, no performance evaluation system can be fully described, even less so in a book with a broader perspective. The focus has therefore been on the choice and content of various features of a performance evaluation system and on how the different components of such a system interact, with their foreseeable consequences.

Finally, performance evaluation is a challenge in itself, merit compensation another. Above all, it is a matter of principle. Does the organization really want to use compensation to encourage employees to make more effort to improve their performance? This question must be answered before turning to the question of how to implement it. This chapter has tried to offer a few suggestions in this regard. In conclusion, an adequate performance evaluation system for merit compensation must have the following characteristics (Klasson, Thompson and Luben, 1980).

1. The system must be formalized and as objective as possible. It must have specific goals and its use must be mandatory.
2. The system must be based on formal job analysis techniques.
3. The performance criteria (traits, behaviour, or results) must be based on the different dimensions of employees' jobs.
4. The immediate supervisor's subjective evaluation must be only part of the overall performance evaluation.
5. The evaluator must have a real opportunity to observe the employee's performance directly.
6. The overall performance rating of employees must be determined by several evaluators.
7. Performance evaluation training programs must exist, and evaluators must attend them.
8. The administration and recording of evaluation results must be standardized and subject to controls.

REFERENCES

BAZINET, A., *L'Évaluation de rendement*, Québec, Éditeur officiel du Québec, 1980.

BEATTY, R.W., C.E. SCHNEIER and J.R. BEATTY, "An Empirical Investigation of Perceptions of Ratee Behavior Frequency and Ratee Behavior Change Using Behavioral Expectation Scales (BES)", *Personnel Psychology*, 1977, vol. 30, pp. 647-658.

BEER, M. et al., "A Performance Management System: Research, Design, Introduction and Evaluation", *Personnel Psychology*, 1978, vol. 31, pp. 505-535.

BEER, M. and R.A. RUH, "Employees Growth Through Performance Management", *Harvard Business Review*, July-August 1976, pp. 59-66.

BÉLANGER, L. et al., *Gestion stratégique des ressources humaines*, Montréal, Gaëtan Morin Éditeur, 1988.

BERNARDIN, H.J., "Increasing the Accuracy of Performance Management: A Proposed Solution to Erroneous Attribution", *Human Resources Planning*, 1989, vol. 12, N° 3, pp. 239-250.

BERNARDIN, H.J. and R. BEATTY, *Performance Appraisal: Assessing Human Behavior at Work*, Boston, Kent Publishing Co., 1984.

BERNARDIN, H.J. and M.R. BUCKLEY, "Strategies in Rater Training", *Academy of Management Review*, 1981, vol. 6, N° 2, pp. 205-212.

BERNARDIN, H.J. and P. VILLANOVA, "Performance Appraisal", in *Generalizing from Laboratory to Field Settings*, edited by L. Locke, Boston, Massachusetts, Lexington, 1986.

BOWNAS, D.A. and H.J. BERNARDIN, "Critical Incident Technique", in *Job Analysis Handbook for Business, Industry and Government*, edited by S. Gael, New York, John Wiley and Sons, 1988, vol. 2, pp. 1120-1140.

CAMPBELL, J.P. "Contributions Research Can Make in Understanding Organizational Effectiveness", *Organization and Administrative Science*, 1976, vol. 7, N° 1, pp. 29-45.

CEDERBLOM, D., "The Performance Appraisal Interview: A Review, Implications, and Suggestions", *Academy of Management Review*, 1982. vol. 7, pp. 219-227.

CUMMINGS, L.L. and D.P. SCHWAB, *Performance in Organizations: Determinants and Appraisal*, Glenview, Illinois, Scott, Foresman and Co., 1973.

DAS, H., *Performance Appraisal Research: Where Do We Go From Here?* Text presented at the Canadian Association of Science and Administration Congress in Halifax, 1981.

DAVIS, B. and M. MOUNT, "Effectiveness of Performance Appraisal Training Using Computer Assisted Instruction and Behaviour Modeling", *Personnel Psychology*, 1984, pp. 439-452.

DeVRIES, D.L. et al., *Performance Appraisal on the Line, Technical Report N° 16*, Greensboro, North Carolina, Center for Creative Leadership, 1980.

DUNNETTE, M.D., *Personnel Selection and Placement*, Belmont, California, Wadsworth Publishing Co., 1966.

DYER, L. and R. THÉRIAULT, "The Determinants of Pay Satisfaction", *Journal of Applied Psychology*, 1976, vol. 61, N° 15, pp. 596-604.

FAY, C.H., "Performance Management as a Strategy to Increase Productivity", *Compensation and Benefits Management*, 1990, vol. 16, N° 4, pp. 346-353.

FELDMAN, J.M., "Beyond Attribution Theory: Cognitive Processes in Performance Appraisal", *Journal of Applied Psychology*, 1981, vol. 66, N° 2, pp. 127-148.

FLANAGAN, J.C., "A New Approach to Evaluating Personnel", *Personnel*, 1949, vol. 26, pp. 35-42.

FOLGER, R. and J. GREENBERG, "Procedural Justice: An Interpretative Analysis of Personnel Systems", in *Human Resources Management*, edited by K.M. Rowland and G.R. Ferris, Greenwhich, Connecticut, JAI Press, 1985, pp. 141-183.

GARTLAND, T.C. and W.W. TORNOW, *An Integrated R & D Program for Enhancing Managerial Effectiveness at Control Data, Personnel Research Report N° 100-77*, St. Paul, Minnesota, Control Data Corporation, 1977.

GREENBERG, J., "Determinants of Perceived Fairness of Performance Evaluations", *Journal of Applied Psychology*, 1986, vol. 71, N° 2, pp. 340-342.

HODGSON, J.S., "Management by Objectives: The Experience of a Federal Government Department", *Canadian Public Administration*, 1973, vol. 16, N° 4, pp. 422-431.

ILGEN, D.R., and J.M. FELDMAN, "Performance Appraisal: A Process Focus", *Research in Organizational Behavior*, 1983, vol. 5, pp. 141-197.

KELLY, H.H., "The Process of Casual Attribution", *American Psychologist*, February 1973, pp. 107-128.

KLASSON, C.R., D.E. THOMPSON and G.L. LUBEN, "How Defensible Is Your Performance Appraisal System?", *Personnel Administrator*, December 1980, pp. 77-82.

LANDY, F.J. and J.L. FARR, "Performance Rating", *Psychological Bulletin*, 1980, vol. 87, pp. 72-107.

LATHAM, G.P. and K.O. WEXLEY, *Increasing Productivity Through Performance Appraisal*, Reading, Mass, Addison-Wesley, 1981.

LAWLER, E.E., A.M. MOHRMAN and S.M. RESNICK, "Performance Appraisal Revisited", *Organizational Dynamics*, 1984, vol. 13, N° 1, pp. 20-35.

LAZER, R.I. and W.S. WICKSTROM, *Appraisal Managerial Performance: Current Practices and Future Directions*, Ottawa, Conference Board of Canada, 1977.

LEVINSON, H., "Appraisal of What Performance", *Harvard Business Review*, July-August 1976, pp. 30 and ff.

LOCKER, A.H. and K.S. TEEL, "Performance Appraisal: A Survey of Current Practices", *Personnel Journal*, May 1977, pp. 245-254.

MAHLER, W.R., "Let's Get More Scientific in Rating Employees", in *Rating Employee and Supervisory Performance*, edited by M.J. Dooher and V. Marquis, New York, American Management Association, 1950.

McCONKIE, M.L., "A Clarification of the Goal Setting and Appraisal Processes of MBO", *Academy of Management Review*, 1979, vol. 4, N° 1, pp. 29-40.

McGREGOR, D., "An Uneasy Look at Performance Appraisal", *Harvard Business Review*, May-June 1957, pp. 89-94.

McGREGOR, D., *The Human Side of Enterprise*, New York, McGraw-Hill, 1960.

MEYER, H.H., "A Solution to the Performance Appraisal Feedback Enigma", *The Executive*, 1991, vol. 5, N° 1, pp. 68-76.

MEYER, H.H., E. KAY and J.R.P. FRENCH, "Split Roles in Performance Appraisal", *Harvard Business Review*, 1965, vol. 43, N° 1 pp. 123-129.

OBERG, W., "Make Performance Appraisal Relevant", *Harvard Business Review*, 1972, vol. 50, N° 1, pp. 61-67.

PETIT, A., and T.A. DECOTIIS, "La validité des résultats obtenus en évaluation du rendement", *Industrial Relations*, 1978, vol. 33, N° 1, pp. 58-77.

PIVETEAU, J., L'Entretien d'appréciation du personnel, Paris, INSEP, 1981.

PRINCE, J.B. and E.E. LAWLER, "Does Salary Discussion Hurt the Development Performance Appraisal", *Organization Behavior and Human Decision Processes*, 1986, vol. 37, pp. 357-375.

SCHNEIER, C.E. and R.W. BEATTY, "Integrating Behaviorally Based Methods", *Personnel Administrator*, 1979, vol. 24, N° 7, pp. 65-76.

SCHWAB, D. and C.A. OLSON, "Merit Pay Practices: Implications for Pay-for-Performance Relationships", *Industrial and Labor Relations Review*, 1990, vol. 43, N° 3, pp. 237-255.

SMITH, D., "Training Programs for Performance Appraisal: A Review", *Academy of Management Review*, 1986, vol. 11, N° 1, pp. 22-40.

SMITH, P.C. and L.M. KENDALL, "Retranslation of Expectations: An Approach to the Construction of Unambiguous Anchors for Rating Scales", *Journal of Applied Psychology*, 1963, vol. 47, pp. 149-155.

TAYLOR, L.R., *Explorations of the Utility of Behaviorally Based Rating Scales for Performance Evaluation and Counselling*, text presented to the "Managerial Performance Feedback: Appraisal and Alternatives", Greensboro, North Carolina, Centre for Creative Leadership, 1976.

WARMKE, D.L. and R.S. BILLINGS, "Comparison of Training Methods For Improving the Psychometric Quality of Experimental and Administrative Performance Ratings", *Journal of Applied Psychology*, 1979, vol. 64, pp. 124-131.

WINSTANLEY, N.B., "How Accurate are Performance Appraisals", *Personnel Administrator*, August 1980, pp. 55-58.

TABLE OF CONTENTS

12

INCENTIVE PLANS

Incentive plans (production bonuses, profit-sharing, and gain-sharing plans, etc.) are not new to North America or Western Europe. However, they have become more prominent in the discussions of employer and professional associations, because various factors have recently converged: budget cutbacks, low productivity, poor employee motivation, tax pressures, etc. In the United States, for example, more incentive plans, also known as variable compensation plans, were established in the early 80s than in the previous 20 years (O'Dell, 1987). The situation is the same in Canada. A recent Conference Board study (Booth, 1990) confirms a clear trend toward variable compensation. This tendency takes different forms:

- more variable compensation not only for senior executives, but for all employees;
- a greater percentage of total compensation based on the performance of the organization or the employee's unit; and
- an increasingly common blend of short-term and long-term incentive plans that reflect the impact of employees at different levels on organizational performance.

The scientific principles underlying the various types of incentive compensation that recognize individual performance date back at least to the end of the last century (Taylor, 1985). Compensation plans based on group performance appeared as the result of work done at the Hawthorne plant in the United States (Roethlisberger and Dickson, 1939). Compensation plans that consider total organizational performance are said to originate with the Parisian interior decorator Le Claire in 1842 (Jehring, 1969).

The 80s, with their parade of budget cuts, cost controls, pay rollbacks, and productivity problems, saw the emergence of what are often referred to as "alternative reward systems". In most cases, these involved good old technical formulas, updated and renamed. How these plans are used, however, is new. Their implementation and management is now seen as the chosen means of achieving the organization's business strategy.

After classifying and describing the main types of short-term incentive plans, this chapter discusses long-term plans, concluding with a description

TABLE 12.1
Classification of Short-term Profit-sharing Plans

Unit of application	Aspect of performance measured	Type of plan
Individual plan	Cost or productivity standards	Piecework
	Production targets	Individual performance bonus or commission plan
Mixed plan (individual and group)	Production targets, cost or productivity standards, profit levels	Mixed plan performance bonus plan
Group plan	Cost or productivity standards	Gain-sharing
	Profit levels	Profit-sharing

of some organizations' unique approaches, such as suggestion bonuses, special bonuses, recognition bonuses and sales bonuses.

☐ 12.1 Short-term Incentive Plans

The different short-term incentive plans, that is, plans considering performance over a period of one year or less, may be divided on the basis of two criteria:

1. type of performance (individual or group);
2. aspect of performance measured (e.g. production targets, cost standards, profit levels, etc.).

Table 12.1 illustrates this classification.

12.1.1 Individual Piecework Plans

Individual piecework plans are based on employee performance that can be standardized by means of observable, concrete, objective performance evaluations, that is, they involve measuring, rather than evaluating, performance. In practice, these plans are primarily used for blue-collar, not white-collar, workers.

The work of Taylor and his colleagues (1911) at the turn of the century helped spread the popularity of compensation plans in general, and of piecework plans in particular. Their work contributed to the development of better methods for setting standards and measuring employee performance. Since then, various methods have been developed to measure and determine performance standards. No system, however, is truly failsafe, and even the most scientific implies a certain subjectivity. The procedure for determining performance standards is based on a study using a stopwatch, a synthetic study of the time required, or a work sample. Such procedures are generally developed and applied by industrial engineers.

Standard performance is determined by applying the concept of a worker's normal pace. Time-study technicians often refer to the standards of the International Labour Office (ILO), which defines "normal pace" as (1962, p. 250):

> ...the normal rate at which an average worker functions, under the supervision of capable managers, but without the incentive of performance compensation. This pace must be easily sustained day after day, without excessive physical or mental fatigue, and is characterized by making a reasonable, regular effort. Normal pace equals the movement of the limbs of a man of average strength walking, unburdened, along a straight line on even ground at 3 miles per hour...[or to] dealing a set of 52 cards in 0.5 minutes.

The ILO further adds that normal pace "is an appropriate term of comparison for an average worker prepared to make a reasonable extra effort to earn an equitable bonus without having to bear excessive stress." In this regard, according to the ILO, the natural pace of a worker with average experience is definitely above the normal pace. No extra effort is required to work steadily at a pace of 120% to 130%.

Setting performance standards involves certain factors, such as standardization of work methods, supply procedures, the quality of supplies, the type of equipment used and its maintenance, and the development of quality standards for the output. One must also consider personal needs, unforeseen delays, and the representativeness of the employee sample on which the standards are based.

In practice, the various individual piecework plans may be divided into plans with no gain-sharing and those with gain-sharing.

Piecework Plans with No Gain-Sharing

These plans may be subdivided into two categories: those with performance-based bonuses and those with varying bonuses based on different performance levels.

Plans with Performance-based Bonuses

Under these plans, employees are compensated in direct proportion to their performance. A specific percentage increase in performance leads to the same percentage increase in compensation.

These plans generally include guaranteed base pay. On the other hand, certain plans, in which employees' compensation is directly proportional to performance, offer no guaranteed base pay, e.g. in sales.

Plans with Varying Bonuses Based on Different Performance Levels

This type of plan was initially suggested by Taylor (1895), then modified by Gantt (1902) and Merrick (1920).

- The Taylor Plan

The differential bonus plan developed by Taylor (1895) consists of one rate for performance up to a fixed standard, and a higher rate (normally 20% above the first) for all output above the standard.

- The Gantt Plan

Unlike the Taylor plan, the Gantt Plan (1902) offers a guaranteed minimum. Up to a fixed standard, the employee receives base compensation. As the employee's performance improves in relation to the standard, bonuses increase compensation in proportion to the guaranteed base rate.

- The Merrick Plan

The Merrick Plan (1920) discards the notion of a guaranteed minimum in favour of using three different rates, in increments of 10% for a performance from 0% to 85% of the fixed standard, the second, 86% to 100% of the standard, and the third, for all performance above the standard.

Gain-Sharing Piecework Plans

In gain-sharing plans, employees share with the employer the increase that results from performance improvements. These plans were primarily designed for situations involving non-standard work or work subject to variations in materials or procedures. The best-known were developed by Halsey, Bedaux, and Rowan.

- The Halsey Plan

The Halsey Plan (Halsey, 1891), developed by the Canadian engineer of that name, involves a guaranteed minimum pay and is based on hourly standards. Employees who take less time than planned to do their work receive a bonus, which they share equally with the employer. For example, if a job expected to take four hours is done in three by an employee paid $6 an hour, the employee earns:

$$3 \times \$6 = \$18 + (\$6 \times \tfrac{1}{2} \text{ hr.}) = \$21$$

Standard time is based on production sheets or, more frequently, on time studies. Since this system is applied mainly to situations involving non-standardized work, if there is a fluctuation in supply, etc., the norm is set as 62.5% rather than 100% of standard time.

● The Rowan Plan

Developed by Rowan Thomson (Rowan Thomson, 1919) in 1898, this plan involves a guaranteed minimum, with bonuses based on time saved. An employee paid at $6 an hour, who does four hours of work in three, saves 25% of the time, and is paid for time actually worked at the $6 hourly wage, plus 25%, that is

$$\$6.00 \times \$1.25 = \$7.50$$

The hourly minimum wage is guaranteed, if the employee fails to do the work in the prescribed time.

As with the Halsey Plan, time standards are based on production sheets.

Finally, with this type of plan, an employee's compensation increases with productivity, but at a declining percentage and, regardless of productivity, an employee cannot earn more than double the base hourly wage.

● The Bedaux Plan

According to Morrow (1922), the Bedaux Plan was developed by the French engineer of that name around 1910, and is similar to the Halsey Plan. It differs, however, in that the bonuses resulting from time saved are shared 75% by the employee and 25% by other persons directly related to the efficiency, such as supervisors and maintenance workers. Under the Bedaux Plan, standard time is determined by time-motion studies. Scheduled time is set in points or B-units. One B-unit equals the normal amount of work per minute, taking into account a percentage of rest time. Hence, the normal hourly output is 60 Bs. Since a specific number of Bs are assigned to each task, an employee performs different tasks without changing the unit used to calculate bonuses.

For example, the employee paid $6 an hour, who does four hours of work in three, receives a $4.50 bonus, calculated as follows:

240 B (4 × 60) were earned in 3 hours;
240 B − 180 B = 60 B extra;
60 B = $6;
Bonus = 75% of $6 = $4.50.

Subsequent modifications to the Bedaux Plan allow employees to receive 100% of the improvement in their efficiency.

Effectiveness of Piecework Plans

Piecework plans share a number of characteristics.

1. The work is simple, repetitive, and easy to measure.
2. Little, if any, interchange between employees is required.
3. Performance standards are carefully set.
4. They are accepted by the employees for whom they are intended, and by management.
5. There are acceptable procedures for adjusting standards when necessary.
6. The cash incentive is sufficient. In this respect, 25% to 35% more than the standard rate is generally considered adequate and equitable for an above-standard performance.

In addition, effective piecework plans normally include a guaranteed minimum pay, have no ceiling, cover all possible employees, use precise methods for calculating results, create few problems with interruptions in production, and ensure employees of a relatively stable income through work schedules and assignments.

Some might say that it is impossible to satisfy all these conditions in a single situation, and that individual incentive plans are inefficient. In fact, studies by Collins et al. (1946), Dalton (1948), Roy (1952), and Whyte (1955) tend to indicate that employees voluntarily limit their output. There may be cheating involved in setting standards. Employees may refuse to do maintenance work unless paid separately from the standard at a higher rate – the same applies to all non-standardized work. Employees may then use all kinds of excuses to maximize non-standardized work, which results in high compensation for low performance. The cost of maintaining the plan often soars because of the complexity that results over the years. Rates proliferate with the introduction of different products, new rules must be developed to deal with new situations, not to mention the accounting required by all these activities at different rates, depending on the situation. As Brown (1990) points out, piecework definitely has positive effects on productivity, but the measurement and the ensuing plan management problems lead to high costs. As a result, the impact of the plan may be nonexistent or negative. Finally, this situation may also creates an atmosphere of distrust between management and workers, which in turn encourages the establishment of new rules. In this context, it comes as no surprise that most unions are opposed to this form of compensation, because it emphasizes competition between workers, elevates the risk of accidents, and increases the "exploitation" of workers. These plans remain very popular in certain sectors, however, especially the textile and garment, furniture, and rubber industries. On the whole, though, this type of plan has tended to become less common in recent years because of its numerous disadvantages (Lawler, 1989).

12.1.2 Individual Performance Bonus Plans

In individual performance bonus plans, the amount of the bonus depends on the employee's performance, which is evaluated in either an arbitrary or formal manner. The potential amount of the bonus is normally set at a percentage of the employee's pay. Neither group performance nor organizational performance is considered. Since the early 80s, this type of plan, traditionally reserved for senior executives, has become generalized within organizations in both Canada (Thériault, 1986; Booth, 1990) and the United States (Bureau of National Affairs, 1964; Peck, 1986).

As discussed in Chapter 10, given the pressure on labour costs, and the motivating effect of performance bonuses as opposed to pay increases, a growing number of organizations have been modifying their pay structure in recent years, replacing the top portion of their pay scales with a merit bonus formula. Employees' pay progresses, based on performance, until it reaches the level that the organization wishes to pay relative to the market. Subsequently, those whose performance is at least satisfactory receive a bonus. This approach represents a genuine individual performance bonus plan. However, if an organization implements Lawler's recommendation (1989), i.e. the total amount of bonus to be distributed being based on organizational performance, the plan becomes a mixed plan.

In practice, considerable confusion surrounds the popularity of individual performance bonus plans. In fact, close examination of the statistics on the matter reveals that most performance bonus plans are mixed rather than individual. Bonus amounts depend not only on the individual performance, but also on certain performance indicators of the group (cost or productivity), or of the organization (cost, productivity, or profits).

12.1.3 Mixed Performance Bonus Plans

As mentioned, in a mixed performance bonus plan, the amount of the bonuses depends on the performance, not only of individual employees, but also of the group to which they belong, or of the organization as a whole. This is the type of plan normally referred to when discussing performance bonus plans.

Thériault (1986) found that almost 40% of both public and private organizations surveyed offered this type of plan to all their managers, about 15% to non-management employees. For senior executives, the figure rose to 60%. A more recent study (Booth, 1990) of slightly over 100 private progressive organizations in Canada found that 80% have one or more performance bonus plans. In over 90% of these cases, senior executives are eligible for the plan, in 78%, all managers and professionals, in 20%, non-management employees. Most organizations without a performance bonus plan are considering adopting one, and many of those that offer one are studying the possibility of expanding eligibility to lower levels within their organization.

The main advantage of this type of plan is precisely its mixed nature. By considering individual performance, it encourages employees to make the best possible contribution. By considering the performance of the group to which an employee belongs, or the entire organization, it promotes the cooperation vital to organizational success.

Bonus Amounts

There are many ways of determining the amount of a bonus. It may be expressed as a percentage of corporate profits above a certain threshold, distributed among employees based on individual performance. For example, in the case of a plan exclusively for senior executives, 4% of the profits above 15% of net income before taxes might be distributed among those eligible. If the plan applies to all employees, the percentage of profits distributed might, for example, be set at 25% above a certain threshold.

Bonuses may also reflect the performance of the division in which an employee works. In this case, the amounts are first determined by divisional performance, and then distributed within each division on the basis of individual performance. This is a "cascade" plan, the bonuses depending on divisional or organizational performance, which assures the organization of a certain degree of profitability. On the other hand, since the bonuses are not necessarily limited by criteria other than profit level, the organization may find itself forced to pay bonuses it considers very high compared to the market. The bonus plan then falls victim to the organization's success.

Note that this type of plan is essentially based on organizational profits. While this is a suitable criterion of performance, it may prove insufficient or secondary in some situations. If the organizational strategy is to increase market share, for example, or to achieve a financial turnaround, short-term profits are definitely not a preferred criterion of performance.

Bonus amounts may also be expressed as a percentage of employee pay. Plan participants are then entitled to bonuses calculated as a percentage of their pay, based on individual, group, or organizational performance. This formula is more widely used than that based on a percentage of organizational profits.

There are two ways of expressing bonuses as a percentage of pay. In the first, the bonus ranges from 0% to X% of the participant's pay. In the case of a middle manager, for example, the figure might range from 0% to 20%, and for a senior executive, from 0% to 40%. This formula has a major disadvantage, however, in that it provides no indication of what percentage bonus will be paid if objectives are met, i.e. the target bonus percentage.

A second approach, which eliminates this disadvantage, involves setting a target bonus percentage to be paid if objectives are met, along with a maximum percentage. In practice, the maximum often amounts to 150% of the target percentage, although in recent years, a growing number of organizations have adjusted their plan's maximum to 200%. The level of the target bonus varies, depending on the participant's pay. In 1990, it was slightly under 15% for a $50,000 salary, just under 20% for $75,000, and 25% for $100,000 (Mercer Limited, 1990). The figures in the United States are slightly higher.

Finally, there are different formulas for awarding bonuses that are based on both individual and organizational performance:

- the split-award method;
- the multiplier method; and
- the matrix method.

The Split-Award Method

With the split-award method, the bonuses depend equally on individual and organizational performance. Values are assigned to each, and the bonus is based on the average. $(X + Y) \div 2$

For example, assume that the bonus for a target performance is 15% of pay, that an employee's performance is exceptional, rating 150 compared to 100 for a target performance, and that the organization's performance is 100. The performance average, then, is 150 plus 100 divided by 2, or 125. For an employee earning $60,000, the bonus for a target performance would be $9,000 (15% of $60,000). The bonus for the employee in our example would be 125% of $9,000, or $11,250. With this method, the effect of a good individual performance may be cancelled out by a poor organizational performance, and vice versa. Both are equally important.

The Multiplier Method

Another way of determining bonuses based on both employee and organizational performance is the multiplier method, in which the individual

TABLE 12.2
Typical matrix for determining bonuses based on employee category and different performance bases

Employee category	Performance Bases			
	Organization	Division	Employee	Total
Corporate vice-president	75%	0%	25%	100%
Division vice-president	50%	25%	25%	100%
Director	25%	50%	25%	100%
Department head	25%	25%	50%	100%

performance score is multiplied by the organizational performance score. Using the same example, the bonus would be 1.50 times 100, i.e. 150% of $9,000, or $13,500, instead of $11,250. Rather than being averaged by the (x + y)/2 formula, as in the split-award method, individual and organizational performance have a multiplier effect on each other. This results in higher bonuses than the split-award method when individual and employee performance are both over 100, and lower when either or both are under 100.

The Matrix Method

The most widely used method, this involves determining at the outset what percentage of the bonus will be based on individual performance and what percentage on organizational performance. The percentages normally depend on the employee's level in the organization, since the assumption is that, the higher the position, the greater the employee's impact on organizational performance and the greater the proportion of the total bonus that should be based on it. Table 12.2 illustrates a typical matrix for determining individual bonuses in a medium-sized organization, considering individual, divisional, and organizational performance.

Measuring Organizational Performance

The different ways of measuring organizational performance may be classified by whether they represent indicators of operational efficiency (accounting indicators) or the use of financial resources (financial indicators). Profit margin and sales volume increase are accounting indicators, while return on equity, return on net assets, and return on investment are financial indicators.

Generally speaking, performance objectives are based on the organization's budgets, the results measured by its financial statements. Using the budget process to set objectives, however, is contested, because of its subjective nature. A widely suggested alternative is to determine the relative value of the organization's performance indicators and compare them to those of a group of other organizations. For example, the target return on equity (ROE) might be set as the median or the average ROE of a predetermined group of companies.

The comparative approach has numerous advantages. First, it yields more in-depth information. There is a difference between achieving a 15% return on equity and realizing that 15% falls into the bottom quartile of the distribution of that indicator for what management or shareholders consider a comparable group of organizations. Secondly, the comparative approach reflects the impact on organizational performance of economic or other factors over which management has no control, for example, price fluctuations for raw materials or oil prices. Thirdly, a comparison with a group of organizations reinforces the sense of competition, and allows performance to be gauged from the standpoint of a shareholder or potential investor.

Comparison with the market, however, has serious limitations. It does not reflect the organization's unique characteristics, such as business strategy, objectives, etc. An organization with a strategy of increasing sales through massive investments will, in the short term, have a lower return on equity than organizations that are competitors in its industrial sector. Another disadvantage is that the organization has no control over the impact of the comparable organizations' strategic actions on their performance; this is especially important with a small reference group. In the late 80s, for example, many companies used debt financing for their investment, or significantly reduced their working capital to avoid becoming a tempting takeover target. As a result of these strategies, many financial indicators of their performance failed to reflect the true normal situation, and therefore distorted any comparison.

In short, using budgets or comparisons to measure performance is a very complex matter. In the early 90s, the trend is once again toward using budgets, at least for measuring short-term performance. Despite the disadvantages, budgets are basic management tools, and the interactive process by which they are drawn up ensures a certain level of objectivity. Also, in order to limit the impact of external factors beyond management's control, budgets and the indicators derived from them may encompass working assumptions. For example, if oil prices are an important factor in organizational profitability, the performance target might be set at 20%, assuming that consuming crude holds at $14 to $15 a barrel. At year-end, organizational performance may be rated against this objective, taking into account changes in crude oil prices during that period.

Whether an organization's short-term performance is measured against budget or by comparison to a reference group, the main indicators used all have advantages and disadvantages. These indicators are discussed below, in order of diminishing popularity.

Return on Equity

This traditional method is based on the following formula:

$$\frac{\text{Profits*}}{\text{Shareholder's equity}}$$

Return on equity is often used to determine employee performance bonuses. This formula provides protection for shareholders, although in some circumstances may encourage an increase in the organization's debt-equity ratio.

Return on Investment

Return on investment is calculated by the following formula.

$$\frac{\text{Profits}}{\text{Shareholder's equity} + \text{long-term debt}}$$

While used less frequently than return on equity, this method has the advantage of considering both shareholders' equity and long-term debt. Accordingly, it does not encourage an increase in debt and has no effect on the debt-equity ratio.

Return on Net Assets

This method uses the following formula:

$$\frac{\text{Net profits}}{\text{Total assets} - \text{current liabilities}}$$

This method is less commonly used than return on equity or return on investment, but has the effect of discouraging or deferring the investment needed to achieve a better short-term ratio, because it reflects the use an organization makes of its assets, such as equipment, inventory, etc.

Other Methods

Other ratios may also be used, such as:

---

* Readers should consult texts on financial management for a more detailed and complete description of the performance yardsticks discussed in this section.

$$\frac{\text{Sales}}{\text{Total assets}} \quad \text{or} \quad \frac{\text{Profits}}{\text{Sales}}$$

12.1.4 Group Performance Bonus Plans

Individual performance bonus plans are suitable for employees who control their own work pace and whose work does not depend on others. In contrast, because they serve as an incentive for closer cooperation, group performance bonus plans are more appropriate for employees whose work is interdependent. There is nothing, however, to prevent the use of group plans for employees whose work is not interdependent.

Group plans are more effective with small, stable groups of employees, where the pressure that traditionally originates with supervisors and managers comes instead from the group. In this regard, it is interesting to read about the second and third phases of Hawthorne's renowned experiments (Roethlisberger and Dickson, 1939). The pressure exerted by one member of a group on another will be all the greater if the former's performance is superior, and if the latter's inferior performance results in lower compensation. Group plans are less effective with large groups though, because members have difficulty perceiving the relationship between their individual performance and the group bonus (Campbell, 1952).

Although group plans are now less popular than individual ones, they are expected to become increasingly common in the years ahead (Lawler, 1989) because, in North American organizations, job structure is shifting toward more interdependent tasks. With automation and simple jobs moving to countries with lower labour costs, a growing percentage of the workforce is found in the service sector. Individual performance evaluation becomes a problem with interdependent jobs, and a group plan often proves more appropriate.

The different types of group performance bonus plans may be divided into two main categories: gain-sharing and profit-sharing plans. With the former, employees must have a direct impact on productivity or costs to be entitled to a bonus. It might also be noted that productivity increases or cost reductions are not likely to have a significant effect on organizational profits if other factors have a major negative impact on them. Adopting this type of plan, therefore, requires a good deal of courage and faith on the part of management (Schuster and Zingheim, 1989) because the organization may be forced to pay bonuses despite poor financial results.

Gain-Sharing Plans

According to Thériault (1986), about 5% of organizations had gain-sharing plans. However, a more recent Conference Board study of slightly over

100 progressive Canadian organizations found 16% with this type of plan. These plans are generally applied to all employees except managerial personnel.

The best-known formulas are those proposed in the Scanlon, Rucker, and Improshare plans. In practice, however, there are almost as many different plans as there are applications. The instant a standard plan is modified to meet an organization's specific circumstances, one may speak of a different plan.

The Scanlon Plan

● History

In the early 30s, during the Great Depression, Joe Scanlon was President of the local union at a steelmill experiencing grave difficulties. Its equipment was obsolete, there was little market for its products, and profits were virtually nonexistent. At the same time, the workers were trying to improve working conditions, and demanding higher pay. After much discussion with company management and executives of the international union of which the local was a part, Scanlon was encouraged by Clinton Golden, Vice-President of the United Steelworkers of America, to take steps toward saving the steelmill from bankruptcy and securing the workers' pay. The union agreed to drop its demand for an immediate pay increase, and management agreed to increase pay as soon as higher productivity allowed.

A special committee, of which Scanlon was a member, was charged with canvassing employees for suggestions on improving productivity. The approach worked, costs were reduced, and the quality of production improved. A few months later, when the steelmill's survival was assured, employees received better working conditions and pay increases.

This success led to the appointment of Scanlon as Director of Research and Engineering for the Steelworkers, where he went on to apply the technique to other ailing businesses.

The Scanlon Plan only gained real recognition, however, following its implementation at the Adamson Company in 1945. Until then, all the organizations that had adopted Scanlon's solution were facing serious problems. Adamson was flourishing, and its President simply wanted to make a good situation better. Douglas McGregor, who was then at the Massachussetts Institute of Technology (MIT), learned of the matter and invited Scanlon to join him. For McGregor, the Scanlon Plan was a perfect illustration of the results to be achieved by practising his Y-theory.

Not long after, Jack Ali, President of the union at Lapointe Machine Tool Co., and Ed Dowd, Executive Vice-President of the company, read about the Adamson experiment in Life magazine (Chamberlain, 1946). They tracked

Scanlon down at MIT and, in 1947, his plan was implemented at Lapointe. It was so successful that White (1979) called its description by Davenport (1950) in Fortune magazine one of the best-known articles about the Scanlon Plan written for the business world.

● Basic Philosophy

The Scanlon Plan differs from compensation based on results, in that it aims for productivity increases through improved work methods rather than greater effort. In short, the motto of Scanlon Plan defenders is, "Work smarter, not harder." Employees are not necessarily asked to make a greater effort at work, but rather to think about more efficient ways of doing their jobs, and to make recommendations to the appropriate supervisor. A Scanlon Plan consists of two essential elements: worker participation, and bonuses based on the organization's productivity increases.

According to this management philosophy, worker participation, reinforced by payment of bonuses, results in productivity increases. While the Scanlon Plan has been used primarily by unionized organizations, it has also been applied to non-unionized employees.

● How the Scanlon Plan Works

The three essential elements of a Scanlon Plan are the creation of production committees, the establishment of a historical base for production costs (pay), and the adoption of a bonus formula.

Production Committees

As illustrated in Figure 12.1, the production (work, bonus, or productivity) committee system involves a group of such committees reporting to a screening (or central) committee.

A production committee is formed in each major work unit or shop. It may consist of only two members: the supervisor and an elected employee representative (who may be the shop steward). The committee normally meets twice a month. Its role is to canvass employees for ideas on improving productivity, and to follow up on the suggestions. Proposals that involve major changes are referred to the central committee.

The central or screening committee consists of a senior executive and representatives of key personnel (manufacturing, engineering, marketing, control, and human resources), as well as a number of employee representatives from the different production committees. Its role is to review the suggestions made by the production committees and management for improving efficiency and reducing costs. It also ensures that approved suggestions are implemented, reviews the organization's monthly statistics, and draws appropriate conclusions. This committee normally meets once a month,

FIGURE 12.1
Scanlon Plan: How Production Committees Work

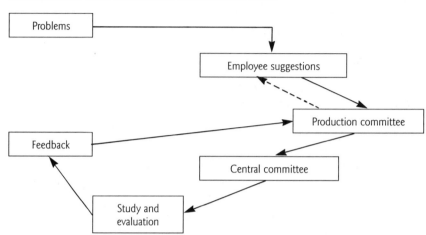

at which time it determines bonus amounts. The minutes of these meetings are distributed to employees. Finally, as Lesieur and Puckett (1969) as well as Moore and Ross (1978) point out, a central committee is an advisory, not a decision-making, body. The decisions are made at the appropriate organizational level.

These essential characteristics of encouraging employee participation and considering all suggestions make the Scanlon Plan more effective than a simple suggestion program (Geare, 1976). In the latter case, an average of one suggestion a year for every three employees is considered satisfactory. A Scanlon Plan receives twice as many suggestions (Schultz and Crisera, 1952). In some cases, the average is as high as one suggestion per employee per year (Lesieur and Puckett, 1969). Also, the suggestions submitted under a Scanlon Plan are usually of a higher quality and more precise. Generally speaking, about 80% (Schultz and Crisera, 1952) to 90% (Lesieur, 1969) are accepted, compared to 25% under a simple suggestion program. The quality of the suggestions stems from how the committees function, because their members must meet with employees to explain why their suggestion was rejected, without discouraging them. Finally, simple suggestion programs usually pay employees relatively small amounts ($25 to $50, according to Thériault, 1986), whereas a Scanlon Plan accurately estimates the value of suggestions, and the increases are distributed to all employees, rather than simply to the author of the suggestion.

Establishing a Historical Base for Production Costs

A historical base must be established for production costs, to determine the amount of the bonus that employees receive. Selecting the base is a critical step. The year must be recent and represent average performance, i.e. it must not be a record year, which would make it impossible to award bonuses, or a poor year, because that would artificially increase the opportunities for bonuses.

The standard base for a manufacturing unit is determined using the following formula:

$$\frac{\text{Total payroll (cost of labour)}}{\text{Product sales (sold and in stock)}}$$

The variation in this index is calculated every month to determine the bonus to be paid to all employees.

The ultimate purpose of a Scanlon Plan is to improve organizational efficiency through a proportional reduction in labour costs, which is shared. Such reductions, however, are not solely the product of greater employee efficiency. Henderson (1989, p. 346) identifies 11 variables that may influence the determination of standard production costs:

— new equipment or a technological change;
— a change in methods or procedures;
— a product modification;
— the availability and cost of raw materials;
— the cost of labour;
— after-sale service requirements;
— delivery procedures;
— inventory policy;
— the selling price of the service or product;
— the method of selling the service or product; and
— the method and cost of financing.

The effect of most of these variables on standard production costs does not necessarily depend on employees. This gives rise to the problem of adjusting the standard production base. As Geare notes (1976), neither management nor employees are likely to demand that the standard be adjusted if the change is to their disadvantage. Under a Scanlon Plan, however, ratios are revised when changes occur.

Bonus Formula

The value of the bonuses depends on the variation in the ratio of labour costs to production value, which is calculated every month and submitted to the production committee. The bonuses are shared between the organization and production workers, office staff, and management. One common formula is 75% for employees and 25% for the organization. Table 12.3 demonstrates how the bonuses are calculated.

TABLE 12.3
Scanlon Plan: Bonus Calculation

1. Sales for the month	$1,100,000
2. Less: returns, discounts, etc.	25,000
3. Net sales (1 − 2)	1,075,000
4. Increase in inventory	125,000
5. Value of production (3 + 4)	1,200,000
6. Standard cost of labour (20% of production)	240,000
7. Actual cost of labour	210,000
8. Funds available for bonuses (6 − 7)	30,000
9. Organisation share (25% of 8)	7,500
Subtotal	$ 22,500
10. Reserve for deficit months (25% of subtotal)	5,625
11. Employee share (75% of subtotal)	16,875
12. Total payroll	168,750
13. Value of bonus (%)	10 %

This table indicates that, for the month in question, the organization could pay plan participants $22,500 in bonuses. If it actually distributed that amount, there would be no reserve for months with negative results. It is, therefore, common practice to provide for a 25% reserve, and make an adjustment at year-end. Hence, in the example in the table, there is a bonus pool of $16,875 or 10% of payroll at the end of the month. Employees will receive a bonus of 10% of their pay.

● Effectiveness

As Frost (1977) points out, a Scanlon Plan is not a panacea. Its approach is not suitable for every organization, and it is no substitute for an adequate pay structure. The plan will not eliminate antagonism between management and a union or employees, nor is it an easy substitute for compensation based on piecework or hourly standards or an excuse for incompetence on the part of senior management. Quite the contrary! As Frost (1977) notes, a Scanlon Plan is not a result, but a process, by means of which all members of an organization are able to manage their resources more efficiently and more effectively. A basic prerequisite for the success of this approach is diagnosis and evaluation of the situation. Nonetheless, published case studies of Scanlon Plans report success more often than failure. One suspects that no one likes to admit failure. The studies by Gilson and Lefcowitz (1957) and Gray (1971) are an exception, however, and Scanlon Plans appear to have been abandoned as often as they were maintained (White, 1979).

In addition, there is very little documented research on the effectiveness of Scanlon Plans. The literature contains more anecdotes than scientific studies. In this regard, Lesieur and Puckett (1969) report the cases of three companies (Atwood Machine Co., Parker Pen Co. and Pfaulder Co.) that had been using a Scanlon Plan for over 14 years. During that period, the average bonuses at the three companies ranged from 4.5% to 19%. There is no indication, however, of how successful each company was and even less as to whether this success was particularly attributable to the Scanlon Plan.

● Conditions for Success

Even the Scanlon Plan's most zealous defenders agree that its success is not guaranteed. Geare (1976) sets forth the following conditions for success.

1. Managers must accept employee and worker participation in decision-making.
2. Senior management must promote the idea that managers are performing well when they encourage suggestions. If managers perceive that their supervisors feel that the managers are doing a poor job when teams make suggestions for improving work methods, the managers may scorn suggestions.
3. Employees must think in terms of the team. The team is more important than the individual.
4. The union must accept employees making a personal commitment (not simply through the organization representing them) and cooperating with management. Where a Scanlon Plan exists, of course, the unions have much more detailed financial information about the organization during wage negotiations.

These conditions imply a sometimes radical change in attitude, if not in actual operating procedures. All indications are that this type of dramatic turnaround can only be achieved through an agent of change (consultant) from outside the organization and union. Geare (1976), for example, cites the case of Kaiser Steel, which had an outstanding, dynamic leader in Edgar Kaiser, but still felt it worthwhile to hire three outside consultants.

Finally, the work by Moore and Goodman (1973), published by the National Commission on Productivity and Quality Working Life (NCPQWL) (1975), stands out because of the scarcity of studies on the effectiveness and conditions for success of Scanlon Plans. Their study spanned three years, with measurements taken before and after the Scanlon Plan was established in three plants of the Chemical Coating Division of De Soto Inc. in Garland, Texas. One of the authors' main conclusions is that employees cooperate to the extent that bonuses are paid.

TABLE 12.4
Rucker Plan: Bonus Calculation

1. Value of production (sales and adjustments)		$1,000,000
2. Less: value of purchases		
— raw materials and supplies	$500,000	
— other purchases (energy, etc.)	160,000	660,000
3. Value added (1 − 2)		340,000
4. Projected cost of labour based on a study over time (3) × 41.18%		140,000
5. Actual cost of labour		120,000
6. Bonuses: funds available (4 − 5)		20,000
7. Organization's share (25% of 6)		5,000
8. Employee's share (6 − 7)		15,000
9. Reserve for deficit months (25% of 8)		3,750
10. Bonus amount (8 − 9)		11,250
11. Total payroll		120,000
12. Value of bonuses (%)		9.4%

The Rucker Plan

The Rucker Plan is based on a management philosophy similar to the one underlying the Scanlon Plan. Its process for determining the standard production base, however, is much more complex. Developed by Allan Rucker of the Eddy-Rucker Nickels Co., the plan calculates bonuses, based on detailed analyses of an organization's financial statements. Adoption of a Rucker Plan presupposes that the financial statements are available and that management will agree to making them available to unions and employees. Like the Scanlon Plan, the Rucker Plan also uses labour costs in measuring productivity. The value of product sales, however, is replaced by the value added in production, to reflect changes in the costs of raw materials, supplies, and any other component that might affect the ratio without a change in productivity. Table 12.4 illustrates the method of calculating bonuses. Savings are shared in the same way as in the Scanlon Plan, i.e. a 75-25 split, with a 25% reserve for deficit months.

According to Belcher and Atchison (1987), there are as many Rucker Plans as Scanlon Plans in the United States. The results of the plans would also appear to be similar. Because of the analyses required to determine the original ratio, however, the bonus formulas for a Rucker Plan are changed less often than those in a Scanlon Plan.

The Improshare Plan

Both of the plans described above are based on a philosophy of genuine participation. Other incentive plans, based on an entire organization, may

TABLE 12.5
Improshare Plan: Productivity Factor and Bonus Calculation

Calculation of the productivity factor during the reference period

$$\text{Standard work hours} = \frac{\text{Total direct hours of work}}{\text{Quantity of production}}$$

Product A: $\dfrac{20 \text{ employees} \times 40 \text{ hours}}{1,000 \text{ units}} = 0.8 \text{ hour/unit or } 0.8 \times 1,000 = 800$

Product B: $\dfrac{20 \text{ employees} \times 40 \text{ hours}}{500 \text{ units}} = 1.6 \text{ hour/unit or } 1.6 \times 500 = 800$

Standard value of total hours = 1,600

$$\text{Productivity factor (PF)} = \frac{\text{Total hours (direct and indirect)}}{\text{Standard value of total hours}}$$

$$PF = \frac{[40 \text{ production employees (direct)} + 20 \text{ (indirect)}] \times 40 \text{ hours}}{1,600}$$

$$PF = \frac{2,400}{1,600} = 1.5$$

Bonus calculation

Product A: 0.8 hour x 600 units x 1.5 = 720
Product B: 1.6 hour x 900 units x 1.5 = 2,160

Standardized hours	2,880
Less: actual hours	2,280
Hours gained	600

Employee share: $\dfrac{50\% \text{ of hours gained}}{\text{Actual hours}} = \dfrac{300}{2,280} = 13.2\%$

be designed without formally involving participation. The qualifier "formally" is used here because, in practice, there is always some participation. What varies is the importance of participation in the plan's design and structure. The Improshare Plan is one example of a plan not based on a philosophy of participation. Unlike the Scanlon and Rucker Plans, in which productivity is measured financially (value of production or value added), the Improshare Plan measures it physically, i.e.:

$$\frac{\text{Total weekly hours of work}}{\text{Quantity of production}}$$

With an Improshare Plan, increases are normally split 50-50 between employer and employees. Table 12.5 illustrates the method of calculating the productivity factor for the reference period, as well as the amount of bonuses.

Organizations using an Improshare Plan generally expect a 60% maximum increase in productivity. If productivity increases by more than 60% and holds at that level for a time, the organization can "buy" the productivity increase, awarding employees a bonus of 30% of their pay — or 50% of the 60% increase. Thereafter, the productivity factor's base rate is increased. As Kendrick (1987) points out, the 60% ceiling protects the organization to a certain extent. In fact, since the standard does not consider the value of sales and the productivity of the industry in which the organization operates, the organization may be required to pay bonuses even if its productivity is inferior to the industry. If productivity increases by 60% at the very most, it would be reasonable to assume that the organization's base productivity factor was lower that might normally have been expected.

According to Fein (1982), who developed this type of plan, a study of 72 Improshare plans established in organizations from 1974 to 1982 indicated that 57 were still being used in 1982 (cf. Kendrick, 1987). Productivity at the organizations that maintained the plan increased by 10.3% during the first three months after the plan was introduced. The average productivity increase for the first year was 24.4%. However, as with case studies of other plans, it is not possible to determine whether this success, or any portion of it, was the result of the Improshare Plan or of other concurrent events.

Conditions for the Success of Gain-Sharing Plans

Based on a study of some 20 gain-sharing plans, Wallace (1990) reached the following conclusions about the characteristics of the organizations where the plans were established:

- the organizations generally had less than 500 employees;
- none of the organizations could be considered at the mature phase, making it impossible to establish historical standards;
- no organization had a simple, precise measure of productivity that was not influenced by factors apart from the employees concerned;
- no organization had a stable product line; most of them were planning to launch new products;
- no organization was operating in a strong market that could absorb productivity increase and was not subject to seasonal fluctuations;
- no organization used a stable technology that was not expected to change;
- no organization projected stable capital investment; and
- most organizations had an open, participatory culture with a high level of trust.

Virtually none of the organizations that had set up such a plan satisfied the prerequisites for success. Nonetheless, they all established a plan. As the author of the study notes, the organizations were all eager to experiment. If cost-based plans (i.e. Scanlon and Rucker) are considered first-generation gain-sharing plans, and those based on standard hours (i.e. Improshare), second-generation, many of the existing plans studied by Wallace (1990) are third-generation plans, based on objectives to be achieved in time rather than production costs or standard hours, and cover several employee groups.

Finally, as Lawler (1989) indicates, these plans have several advantages:

- they encourage cooperation and teamwork;
- they promote the introduction of changes aimed at increasing productivity;
- they bring about a change in employee attitude that calls for greater efficiency and better planning by management; and
- they stimulate employees to work smarter, by encouraging them not only to make an effort, but also to come up with ideas.

On the other hand, a gain-sharing plan is not an incentive for employees whose individual performance could be improved to join and remain with such an organization. This type of plan recognizes group, rather than individual, performance. Moreover, this type of plan is not entirely effective as a cost-control instrument, because the organization might have to pay bonuses even if it earns no profit. In fact, these plans emphasize production costs alone; all other organizational expenses are ignored.

Profit-Sharing Plans

Unlike gain-sharing plans, profit-sharing plans involve a less well-defined relationship between individual or group effort and bonus amounts. Bonuses are based on the organization's overall performance, which is affected by a variety of factors, such as general economic conditions, the costs of financing and supplies, etc. Generally, employees receive an automatic fixed percentage of total profits or of profits above a certain threshold. Strictly speaking, it is not a question of individual or group performance, but purely of the performance of the entire organization.

Definition

The Council of Profit-Sharing Industries (1962) defines profit-sharing as:

> Any system by which an employer pays, or makes available to employees, under certain reasonable conditions, in addition to the pay rates in effect, special sums based on organizational profits, paid immediately or in time.

Le Claire, a Parisian interior decorator, is often considered to be the father of profit-sharing plans. In February 1842, he told his 41 employees that, for one year, he would share with them part of the profits resulting from operations during that fiscal year. The experiment was so successful that it was repeated the following year. In 1972, after 130 years, Maison Le Claire, by then operating under the name of Faucher, Nestier et Cie, was still offering its employees a profit-sharing plan, and the results remained convincing (Metzger, 1973).

Le Claire is considered the father of profit-sharing plans, not because he was necessarily the first to establish one, but rather because his was the first to succeed. According to Metzger (1973), the first profit-sharing plan was established in 1794 by Albert Gallatin in his glass factory in New Geneva, Pennsylvania. One of the oldest plans still in existence in the United States is the one that Procter & Gamble established in 1887.

According to Nalbantian (1987), the popularity of profit-sharing plans increased during the 40s in the United States, after a government finance subcommittee found that profit-sharing was a vital concept – one that could not only improve management-labour relations and productivity, but was also essential for maintaining the capitalist system. As a result of the subcommittee's report, the U.S. government enacted legislation that gave tax breaks to organizations with a registered profit-sharing plan.

Profit-sharing plans enjoyed a resurgence of popularity in the late 70s and early 80s, because of the pressing need to improve productivity to compete internationally, and because of management's desire to bring an element of flexibility to employees' compensation. In 1982, after a sharp drop in American car sales while sales of imports rose, the United Auto Workers in both the United States and Canada finally agreed to major concessions on pay and employee benefits in return for the establishment of a profit-sharing plan. The automotive industry was not alone in adopting this type of arrangement. In the early 80s, similar agreements were negotiated in the steel, aviation, and construction industries. Canadian companies that now have profit-sharing plans include Ipsco, Dofasco, Lake Ontario Steel Co., and Sidbec-Dosco.

Types of Plans

Profit-sharing plans may be classified by the employee groups they cover. Plans that cover all or virtually all employees are referred to as non-selective plans; those that cover distinct categories, such as management personnel or all executives, are referred to as selective.

They may also be divided into three categories, based on how the bonuses are paid:

- *immediate payment:* found primarily in small organizations;
- *deferred payment:* offered primarily by large organizations, and often used to finance the employee pension fund; and
- *mixed plan:* some of the profits are paid immediately, the balance, deferred.

Characteristics of Profit-Sharing Plans

The characteristics of profit-sharing plans differ from one country to the next. In the United States, more so than in Canada, they appear to be used to accumulate retirement savings.

The characteristics of these plans also vary with organizational size. According to a Profit-Sharing Council of America survey (1989) of 400 organizations, employers contributed the equivalent of slightly less than 9% of employees' annual pay to profit-sharing plans from 1983 to 1989. This amount represents about 25% of the organizations' net income in 1984 and 1985, and 20% from 1986 to 1988. Contributions were higher in small organizations (10.5% of pay) than in large ones (6.6%); small organizations were more likely not to have a pension plan. Most small organizations (80%) had a plan with deferred payments, and less than 30% offered employees a pension plan in addition to a profit-sharing plan.

Finally, the characteristics of profit-sharing plans may vary from one organization to the next. In Canada, surveys by both Thériault (1986) and Booth (1987) found that the vast majority (over 70%) of non-selective profit-sharing plans featured immediate payment. In addition, in almost 70% of the organizations, the bonuses were based on net income before taxes, amounted to 10% or less of pay, and were paid annually. Over 20% of the organizations surveyed paid the bonuses more than once a year.

Deferred profit-sharing plans (DPSP), in Canada, are governed by the Income Tax Act.

The Act stipulates that the employer may select the participants and is not bound to continue the plan indefinitely. Employer contributions to a DPSP must be made in the current year or within 120 days of year-end, and the plan must be administered by a trust company. In 1991, the maximum tax-deductible employer contribution was the lowest of:

- the amount actually paid into the employee's account;
- $6,250; and
- 18% of the employee's income.

The $6,250 ceiling for 1991 will increase by $500 a year until 1994, after which it will be indexed to the National Average Wage increase. As of 1991, employees may no longer contribute to a DPSP. Employer contributions to a DPSP must be included in calculating the amount an employee may contribute to a Registered Retirement Savings Plan (cf. Chapter 14). The Act further stipulates that the contributions become vested after, at the most, two years of plan membership. Employers, therefore, are not allowed to stipulate that contributions made to a DPSP on an employee's behalf will vest cumulatively at the rate of only 20% for each year of service. The benefits must be fully vested after two years of membership.

Popularity of Profit-Sharing Plans

The Profit-Sharing Research Foundation (1985) estimates that, in 1945, there were over 2,000 legally registered profit-sharing plans in the United States. By 1974, that number had risen to almost 200,000, and in 1988 was approaching 400,000. In many cases, however, the plans apply to only a very limited number of employees.

Thériault's survey (1986) found that almost 10% of organizations had a non-selective profit-sharing plan, while 15% had a selective plan that excluded administrative support staff and production personnel. A more recent survey by Booth (1990) of about 100 Canadian organizations with progressive compensation management practices found that about 25% of them offer a non-selective profit-sharing plan.

Effectiveness of Profit-Sharing Plans

The purpose of profit-sharing plans is to encourage employees to contribute to organizational success and become more concerned with organizational results.

Profit-sharing plans emphasize improvements in total productivity. They encourage employees to reduce not only labour costs, but also the costs of raw materials, energy, capital, etc. On the other hand, because individual performance has little impact on profits, these plans have little effect on an employee's effort at work.

A Personnel Journal study (1972) compares the performance from 1952 to 1969 of several large American retail chains that had profit-sharing plans with others that did not. The chains with a profit-sharing plan increased sales by 37% more than those without a plan, their increase in net worth was 47% greater, and their earnings per share, 88% higher. Nonetheless, these results fail to prove the effectiveness of profit-sharing plans, because the results may be attributable to many other factors.

Finally, it is interesting to note that employees that belong to a profit-sharing plan are less likely to be laid off during a slump in demand than those paid a fixed amount. Employees with a profit-sharing plan also tend to be more loyal to employers than employees without such a plan (Chelius and Smith, 1990).

☐ 12.2 Long-term Incentive Plans

Long-term incentive plans, i.e. those that consider performance over a period of more than one year (generally three to five years) are usually reserved for senior management, but may be open to all employees. Most are stock ownership plans. While no Canadian statistics are available, it is estimated that, in the United States, 11 million employees working for 8,000 organizations own at least 15% of their employer (Quarrey, Blass and Rosen, 1986).

The eagerness to establish long-term compensation plans for senior executives based on organizational performance is one of the most important changes of the past 20 years in both Canada and the United States. During the same period, the proportion of total compensation dependent on long-term organizational performance also increased significantly. In 1990, long-term compensation accounted for about 20% of total compensation for senior executives in Canada. In the most progressive organization, it is said that this figure should be as high as 50% (Booth, 1990). In the United States, the figure ranges from 35% to 40%.

Organizations generally adopt a long-term incentive plan to:

- create more harmony between employee and shareholder objectives;
- increase employee participation in the organization;
- ensure that long-term organizational objectives are met; and
- enjoy tax breaks (in some cases, lower income taxes).

Long-term incentive plans may be divided into ownership plans and long-term performance bonus plans. The former may be further subdivided into real and notional ownership plans.

12.2.1 Real Ownership Plans

Real ownership plans include stock purchase plans, stock bonus plans, and stock option plans.

Stock Purchase Plans

Stock purchase plans give participants an opportunity to buy a specific number of company shares at favourable terms for a predetermined maximum price. The shares may be new ones, issued from the corporate treasury, or market shares purchased through a trust company.

Stock purchase plans take different forms. For example, an organization may give employees with one year of service an opportunity to buy shares for a total value of up to 6% of their pay. The organization provides 25% to 85% of the purchase price of each share, depending on projected profits. In other cases, the percentage bears no relation to profit and the arrangement constitutes a savings plan for employees.

Stock purchase plans are generally reserved for senior executives. In a typical case, from April 1st to May 1st, executives have an opportunity to acquire company shares at 10% less than the Toronto Stock Exchange closing price on the day before the purchase, for up to 25% of their pay. The executives can borrow 75% of the share price from the company at 10% interest to make the purchase, with the loan repayable over five years through payroll deductions. The shares are kept in trust by the company for at least one year before being turned over to the executives.

According to Booth (1987), almost 40% of progressive Canadian organizations offered employees a stock purchase plan. More (61%) contributed to the employee purchase than discounted the market price (24%) or provided an interest-free loan (15%). In contrast to earlier years, most stock purchase plans were open to a majority of employees. One third of the plans had been introduced since 1985.

Besides encouraging ownership, the plans allow employees to benefit from dividends as well as possible capital gains and therefore tax breaks. As of 1991 in Canada, capital gains are taxed at the individual's marginal rate applied to 75% of the value of the gain. Stock price discounts, governed by securities commission regulations, for example 10% for shares under $5, are treated as a capital gain at the time of the stock purchase, which allows a tax deferral. When the interest rate on a loan to an employee is less than prescribed by law, the difference, expressed in interest, is added to income. However, the employee still never pays full tax on the difference, with the result that a loan at a lower rate remains an advantage for the individual.

On the other hand, stock ownership plans require employees to make a disbursement, and there is always a chance that they may lose money.

Restricted Stock Award Plans

Under a stock bonus plan, an organization gives employees, usually senior executives, a number of its shares. While the participants are then entitled to receive dividends and to vote at shareholder meetings (if granted voting shares), they are not normally allowed to sell the stock for a fixed period, e.g. three to five years, or unless the organization achieves certain results.

This type of plan not only aligns employees' interests with shareholders' interests, but also encourages participants to remain with the organization, which is why they are sometimes referred to as handcuffs for the individuals concerned. They may also serve as an incentive for an individual to join the organization, compensating for the loss of certain benefits, such as retirement benefits. They motivate participants to adopt a long-term outlook in their decisions and approach to work.

According to Booth (1990), restricted stock award plans are offered in almost 20% of about 100 progressive Canadian organizations. Overall, however, less than 10% of organizations have this type of plan, which is almost never open to all employees.

Stock Option Plans

Under a stock option plan, an organization agrees to sell to its employee, at a predetermined price, its own shares or those of a related company. For example, it might allow participants to purchase a fixed number of company shares at the market price on the date the option is awarded. The option may then be exercised over a maximum of ten years, at an annual rate of 20% of the total number of shares, beginning one year after the option award date.

Most companies stipulate a waiting period of one year before an employee may begin exercising an option. In some cases (12% according to Booth, 1990), participants must hold the shares for a fixed period, such as one year, *as a rule* before they are allowed to sell. The options may be valid for periods of up to 10 years, but usually only a fixed percentage (e.g. 20%) may be exercised each year.

Over 50% of publicly traded Canadian companies offer their senior executives a stock option plan. In addition, over 50% of the plans call for options to be awarded regularly. Most companies award options annually, to avoid having to grant them when the share price is high. The options normally depend on the employee's level within the organization. Thus, the annual allowance for Presidents and Chief Executive Officers might be 100% to 150% of their salary. At the next level down, the allowance might be 50% to 60%. Occasionally, organizations extend the plan to a third management layer; in this case, the allowances range from 30% to 35% of salary. Companies generally want their President and Chief Executive Officer to own shares equal to 7 to 10 times their annual salary; at the next level down, the multiple is 3 to 6 times salary.

As Bickford and Lucania (1990) point out, awarding stock options as a multiple of salary is a highly controversial practice in a bull market. For example, if the executive's salary is $150,000, the multiple is 50%, and the shares are priced at $5, the number of options awarded in the first year would be $75,000 divided by $5, or 15,000. If, one year later, the shares are at $7 and the executive's salary is $160,000, the number of options awarded will be $80,000 divided by $7, or 11,428. In the second year, the first year's options have increased in value by $30,000 [15,000 × ($7 − $5)]. The value of the shares will therefore have to rise to $9.63 ($30,000/$11,428 + $7) for the second year's options to have the same value at the end of the second year as the first year's options had at the end of the first. At the end of the second year, the first year's options are worth $69,450, or the amount by which the share price has increased over the two years ($2 in the first year which the share price has increased over the two years ($2 in the first year and $2.63 in the second year) multiplied by 15,000. The opposite effect occurs in a bear market. One solution to this situation is to use a fixed number of options rather than a multiple of salary. In a bull market, however, this approach might seem generous.

These plans are generally intended only for senior executives. However, there are two well-known instances of their application to all employees. In 1989, Pepsico in the United States began offering all of its 100,000 employees an option plan equivalent to 10% of their pay, including bonuses and overtime. The amount is paid each year. Employees may exercise their options at an annual rate of 20%, at the share price on July 1st of the year in which the option was issued. They have 10 years to take advantage of the option. Since a program such as this increases the number of outstanding shares and reduces earnings per share, the company regularly redeems its outstanding shares to reduce the effect of the dilution. According to Pepsico management (Levine 1990), the purpose of the program is to get the message across to employees that, no matter what Pepsico Group subsidiary they work for, they are part of the Pepsi family. Employees of Pepsi-Cola Canada Limited are also covered by this plan.

The second case involves Du Pont. In early 1991, the 4,300 employees of Du Pont Canada Inc. received options to purchase 100 shares of their parent company, E.I. du Pont de Nemours & Cie. The plan was also offered to all of the multinational's 136,000 employees in 50 countries around the world.

Participants in these plans in a publicly owned company are subject to tax when the option is exercised. If those options were issued at a fair market value, the difference between the price when the options were issued and the value of the shares at the time of exercise is treated for tax purposes as employment income, but taxed at 75% rather than 100%. That certainly encourages participants to sell some shares the same year they are acquired, in order to raise the cash needed to pay the income tax on the gain realized by exercising the option. In conclusion, this type of plan involves less risk than a stock purchase plan, because the employee remains free to exercise or not to exercise the option. However, one disadvantage remains; the employee must make a disbursement to exercise the stock option.

12.2.2 Notional Ownership Plans

Notional ownership plans are intended to alleviate two disadvantages of real ownership plans: the requirement that employees make a disbursement and the risk of dilution facing shareholders. The two most common forms of this type of plan are phantom stocks, performance shares or units, stock appreciation rights, and long-term performance bonus plans.

Phantom Stock Plans

Under this plan, an employer gives employees a number of units whose value is generally equivalent to that of the same number of the company's common shares. During the period covered by the agreement, employees receive (or have credited to their account) an amount equal to any dividend paid on common shares. On specific dates or at year-end, employees are entitled to any increase in the value of their units since the plan took effect. The amounts paid are taxable as employment income.

Unlike stock options, there is no mandatory minimum period for holding the units, and no disbursement is involved. For shareholders, there is no dilution of their investment, and the amounts paid under the plan are tax-deductible.

Performance Unit Plans

In a performance unit plan, the employer promises to pay the employee an amount equal to the value of performance units awarded if certain objectives are achieved by the end of a given period, normally three or five years. For example, an employee might receive 1,000 performance units worth $60 each in three years if the company manages to maintain a 15% growth rate in its earnings per share. If the growth rate is 14%, 90% of the bonus is awarded, if it is 13%, 80% of the bonus, etc. If the growth rate is 10% or less, no bonus is paid. Sometimes, instead of paying a sum of money, the employer promises to give the employee a number of company shares; it then becomes a performance share plan rather than a performance unit plan.

This type of plan makes it possible to establish a direct link between the bonuses paid and the achievement of certain objectives that depend primarily on the work of managers. This is an advantage over stock options or phantom stock plans, in which the value of the shares is influenced by numerous factors in no way related to the performance of the managers. Also, a performance unit plan allows the organization to establish predictable levels of merit compensation, rather than being subject to the vagaries of the stock market.

Stock Appreciation Rights

Stock Appreciation Rights (SARs) resemble stock option plans, except that the employee does not have to spend money to obtain the shares. The employee benefits from the increase in the value of shares over a given period. At the end of that time, the employee receives an amount equal to the increase in the market price of the stock for the number of shares allocated by the company.

12.2.3 Long-term Performance Bonus Plans

Except for performance unit plans, all plans mentioned so far depend directly or indirectly on the market value of shares, and are intended mainly for companies whose stock is listed. While the book value of a company's shares may be used, this approach involves a number of practical problems. For companies whose shares are not publicly traded and for public organizations, the only means of rewarding long-term performance is a long-term performance bonus plan. This type of plan is also suitable for any organization interested in keeping bonuses separate from the market value of its shares.

Except for the period covered, the plan operates just like the short-term performance bonus plan described above. The question of measuring organizational performance, however, requires special attention. In addition to verifying the cohesion between long-term financial projections (normally three years) and the expected performance objectives, achieving those objectives must generate an acceptable return for shareholders, (if there are any). If the performance measurement does not consider the performance of other organizations, at a minimum, the performance objectives must consider those of comparable competitors in the market. Performance objectives must also be reviewed regularly to adapt to changing economic conditions. Numerous changes might require adjustment of performance objectives:

- a change in the organization's cost of capital because of a fluctuation in interest rates;
- a major change affecting the entire industry in which the organization operates, such as a substantial variation in the price of oil or raw materials;
- a change in dividend policy, in capital structure, in accounting practices, in tax calculation, etc.

Changes such as these may push objectives up or down. It is important then to ensure that the plan remains effective, protecting its incentive effect and avoiding situations where participants benefit or are penalized as the result of factors beyond their control.

According to Rich and Larson (1987), in the early 80s, most publicly traded companies used earnings per share as a performance criterion. The underlying assumption is that the higher earnings per share are, the higher the value of the shares. This assumption is not completely valid, however, because share price depends on the present value of anticipated income.

Share price increases when a company increases its financial value, not its earnings per share. Earnings per share increase when the company's investments earn more than they cost (return on equity is greater than cost of equity). To offset this limitation, Rich and Larson propose using a long-term performance indicator that considers return on equity, cost of equity, and growth in equity.

Rock (1984) and Ubelhart (1991) suggest using a long-term performance indicator that considers cash flow (e.g. the ratio of cash flow to investments). According to these authors, using criteria that emphasize organizational income, such as earnings per share or return on equity, may be dangerous, because such criteria simply reflect the organization's ability to generate funds. Thus, an organization might increase its revenue while its managers are in the process of liquidating it. Also, organizational revenue is directly affected by inflation. On the other hand, cash flow demonstrates the real value of the funds generated for shareholders, the ultimate purpose of a company. This yardstick, which considers the impact of investments on cash flow, reflects the organization's ability to generate funds better than any other indicator. This performance criterion is, however, more difficult to measure and explain to employees.

In short, as Ubelhart notes (1991), an organization's long-term performance yardstick evolves with the instruments of financial analysis. During the 60s, the performance yardstick was primarily based on the value of shares. In the 70s, organizations began using earnings per share in their business plans, and so this criterion became a performance yardstick. In the 80s, after a relationship between return on investment (ROI) and share values had been established, organizations began using ROI as a yardstick. In the late 80s, when ROI became the target of criticism, using a measurement that considered cash flow was suggested. In the near future, other performance yardsticks will probably come to the fore. In this as in other areas, no single criterion can reflect an organization's overall performance; each has its limitations. The organization must ask itself why it wishes to compensate its executives over the long term, and then use the corresponding criteria as a measure of its performance.

☐ 12.3 Other Incentive Plans

Organizations use many other types of incentive plans.

A prime example is that of the suggestion programs found in certain organizations. In the United States, for instance, General Motors paid approximately $64 million for slightly over 300,000 suggestions in 1985. That same year, Eastman Kodak paid $4.6 million for just over 85,000 suggestions (National Association of Suggestion Systems, 1986). In Canada, Thériault's survey (1986) found that about 10% of organizations had suggestion pro-grams, intended primarily for office, production, and maintenance workers, as well as technical staff. Most of these plans appeared to have been in existence for many years, and were most common in large organizations (over 1,000 employees) in the finance, insurance, and manufacturing sectors. In almost 70% of cases, the minimum bonus was $50 or less, while the max-imum was over $3,000 in large organizations (over 1,000 employees) and $500 in smaller organizations (fewer than 500 employees). A more recent survey by Booth (1990) of about 100 progressive Canadian organizations indicates that 42% have a suggestion program, and that two thirds of the programs were established before 1985.

In-depth studies have not proved the effectiveness of suggestion pro-grams. Approximately 25% of the suggestions submitted by employees are accepted by management. The number of suggestions tends to be high during the first year of the program, and then drops off noticeably. The first year is therefore critical in terms of how employees will later react. In this regard, it is important to make sure that the time required to consider suggestions is relatively short. At the very least, employees must be informed quickly that their suggestion is being considered, so that they perceive the plan as credible, particularly so during the first year, when the number of suggestions is high.

A second type of incentive plan is the special award program. At IBM, for example, the program is based on three levels of recognition of individual performance; the levels correspond to the extent of its impact. At the local level, there is the Informal Award Plan, in which the decision to award bonuses is made by immediate supervisors. The second level, the Outstanding Con-tribution Award, rewards performance that has an impact on an entire divi-sion. Finally, the Corporate Award is reserved for employees whose exceptional performance has an impact on the entire organization. According to Booth (1990), over one third of the approximately 100 progressive Canadian organ-izations have this type of plan, and half of them have introduced it since 1985.

A third approach found in some organizations is a spot bonus plan. With this plan, immediate superiors have a fund from which to pay rec-ognition bonuses "on the spot". The bonuses might be in cash ($25 or $100) or goods (tickets for a sports or cultural event, restaurant gift certificate, etc.).

A fourth type of incentive plan consists of gifts handed out at Christmas or vacation time in the form of bonuses, time off, or a thirteenth month's pay.

Finally, organizations have various incentive bonus plans, primarily intended for sales personnel and their spouses. These bonuses might consist of all kinds of consumer goods, trips, services, etc. Out-of-the-ordinary unusual trips awarded as bonuses include nights on the Nile, a safari on a Kenyan game reserve, or a prisoners' carnival in the streets of Sydney, Australia – not to mention trips to Hawaii, Mexico, and the Caribbean. It is important to remember that such bonuses are generally taxable, unless the trip bears a direct relationship to the organization's business. The market for these incentive bonuses is well-organized. The Toronto-based Canadian Premiums and Incentives Association regularly publishes information about its activities and members.

☐ 12.4 Summary

A growing number of organizations offer their employees various incentive plans in addition to their pay. In some cases, the plans are based on the employee's or the organization's short-term performance (normally one year). In others, they are based exclusively on the organization's long-term performance (normally three years).

Short-term plans consist of individual plans (those based on individual performance) and group plans (those based on the performance of a work unit or of the entire organization). Individual performance bonuses and piecework plans are examples of the former, while gain-sharing plans and profit-sharing plans are examples of the latter.

Long-term plans may be divided into those that result in actual ownership, such as stock purchase and stock option plans, those that simulate ownership, such as phantom stock plans, performance unit plans and stock appreciation rights, and, finally, long-term performance bonus plans.

REFERENCES

BELCHER, D. and T.J. ATCHISON, *Compensation Administration*, Englewood Cliffs, New Jersey, Prentice-Hall Inc., 1987.

BICKFORD, L. and L.A. LUCANIA, "Long Term Incentives for Management, Part 6: Plan Administration", *Compensation and Benefits Review*, May-June 1990, pp. 56-67.

BOOTH, P.L., *Paying for Performance: The Growing Use of Incentives and Bonus Plans*, Ottawa, Conference Board of Canada, 1987.

BOOTH, P., *Strategic Rewards Management: The Variable Approach to Pay*, Ottawa, Conference Board of Canada, 1990.

BROWN, C., "Firms' Choice of Method of Pay", *Industrial and Labor Relations Review*, 1990, vol. 43, N° 3, pp. 165-182.

BUREAU OF NATIONAL AFFAIRS, *Productivity Improvements Programs, PPF Survey 138,* Washington, D.C., Bureau of National Affairs, 1984.

CAMPBELL, H., "Group Incentives", *Occupational Psychology,* January 1952, p. 1521.

CHAMBERLAIN, J., "Everyman A Capitalist", *Life Magazine,* December 23, 1946.

CHELIUS, J. and R.S. SMITH, "Profit-sharing and Employment Stability", *Industrial and Labor Relations Review,* 1990, vol. 43, N° 3, pp. 256-273.

COLLINS, O., M. DALTON and D. ROY, "Restriction of Output and Social Cleavage in Industry", *Applied Anthropology,* Summer 1946, pp. 1-14.

COUNCIL OF PROFIT-SHARING INDUSTRIES, *The Constitution and Bylaws of Profit-Sharing Industries,* Evanston, Illinois, Council of Profit-Sharing Industries, 1962.

DALTON, M., "The Industrial "Rate-Buster": A Characterization", *Applied Anthropology,* Winter 1948, pp. 5-18.

DAVENPORT, R., "Enterprise for Everyman", *Fortune,* January 1950, pp. 55-59.

FEIN, M., *Improved Productivity Through Worker Involvement,* unedited text, Hillsdale, New Jersey, Mitchell Fein Inc., 1982.

FROST, C., *A Conference on Sharing the Gains of Productivity,* text presented at a symposium organized by the Work in America Institute, Plaza Hotel, New York, September 20, 1977.

FROST, C., "The Scanlon Plan: Anyone for Free Enterprise?", *MSU Business Topics,* 1978, vol. 26, N° 1, pp. 25-33.

GANTT, H.L., "A Bonus System of Rewarding Labor", *Transactions of the American Society of Mechanical Engineers,* 1902, vol. 23, pp. 341-372.

GEARE, A.J., "Productivity from Scanlon-Type Plans", *Academy of Management Review,* July 1976, pp. 99-108.

GILSON, T.O. and M.J. LEFCOWITZ, "A Plant-Wide Productivity Bonus in a Small Factory: Study of an Unsuccessful Case", *Industrial and Labor Relations Review,* 1957, vol. 10, pp. 284-296.

GRAY, R.B., "The Scanlon Plan – A Case Study", *British Journal of Industrial Relations,* 1971, vol. 9, pp. 291-313.

HALSEY, F.A., "The Premium Plan of Paying For Labor", *Transactions of the American Society of Mechanical Engineers,* 1981, vol. 12, pp. 755-780.

HENDERSON, R.I., *Compensation Management: Rewarding Performance,* Reston, Virginia, Reston Publishing Co., 1989.

HILDERBRANDT, F.D., "Individual Performance in Incentive Compensation", *Compensation Review,* 3rd Quarter 1978, vol. 10, N° 3, pp. 28-33.

INTERNATIONAL LABOR OFFICE (I.L.O.), *Introduction to Work Study,* Geneva, International Labor Office, 1962.

JEHRING, J.J., "Profit-Sharing: Origine, Situation et Perspective", *Synopsis,* January-February 1969, pp. 37-43.

KENDRICK, J.W., "Group Financial Incentives", in *Incentives, Cooperation and Risk Sharing,* edited by H.R. Nalbantian, Totowa, New Jersey, Rowman & Littlefield, 1987.

LAWLER, E.E., "Pay for Performance: A Strategic Analysis", in *Compensation and Benefits*, edited by L.R. Gomez-Mejia, Washington, D.C., Bureau of National Affairs Inc., 1989, pp. 136-181.

LESIEUR, F., "What the Plan Isn't and What It Is", in *The Scanlon Plan – A Frontier in Labor Management Cooperation*, edited by F. Lesieur, Boston, M.I.T., 1968.

LESIEUR, F.G. and E.S. PUCKETT, The Scanlon Plan Has Proved Itself", *Harvard Business Review*, September-October 1969, pp. 109-118.

LEVINE, H.Z., "The Board Speaks Out", *Compensation and Benefits Review*, May-June 1990, pp. 18-32.

MERCER (William M. Mercer Limited), *1990 Executive Benchmark Compensation Report*, Toronto, 1990.

MERRICK, D.V., *Time Studies as a Basis for Rate Setting*, New York, The Engineering Magazine Co., 1920.

METZGER, B.L., *Profit-sharing in Perspective*, Evanston, Illinois, Profit-sharing Research Foundation, 1973.

MOORE, B.E. and P.S. GOODMAN, *Factors Effecting the Impact of a Company-wide Incentive Program on Productivity*, final report submitted to the National Commission of Productivity, Washington, D.C., 1973.

MOORE, B.E. and T.L. ROSS, *The Scanlon Plan Way to Improved Productivity: A Practical Guide*, New York, John Wiley and Sons, 1978.

MORROW, L.C., "The Bedaux Principle of Human Power Measurement", *American Machinist*, 1922, vol. 16, pp. 241-245.

NALBANTIAN, H.R., "Incentive Compensation in Perspective", in *Incentive, Cooperation and Risk Sharing*, edited by H.R. Nalbantian, Totowa, New Jersey, Rowman and Littlefield, 1987.

NATIONAL ASSOCIATION OF SUGGESTION SYSTEMS, *Annual Statistical Report/1985*, Chicago, May 1986, pp. 15-16.

NATIONAL COMMISSION ON PRODUCTIVITY AND QUALITY OF WORKING LIFE (N.C.P.Q.W.L.), *A Plan-Wide Productivity Plan in Action: Three Years of Experience with the Scanlon Plan*, Washington, D.C., 1975.

O'DELL, C., *People, Performance, and Pay*, Houston, Texas, American Productivity Center, 1987.

PECK, C., "Top Executive Compensation: 1987 Edition", *Conference Board Report*, N° 889, New York, Conference Board, 1986.

PERSONNEL JOURNAL, "As You Were Saying – Share Profits – Don't Freeze Them", *Personnel Journal*, 1972, vol. 54, p. 51.

PROFIT-SHARING COUNCIL OF AMERICA, *Profit-sharing Experience of 400 Companies*, Chicago, Profit-sharing Council of America, 1989.

PROFIT-SHARING RESEARCH FOUNDATION, *Cumulative Growth in Number of Qualified Deferred Profit-Sharing and Pensions in the United States, 1939 through 1984*, unedited text, Chicago, Profit-Sharing Research Foundation, 1985.

QUARREY, M., J. BLASS and C. ROSEN, *Taking Stock: Employee Ownership at Work*, Cambridge, Massachusetts, Ballinger, 1986.

RICH, J.T., and J.R. LARSON, "Why Some Long Term Incentives Fail", in *Incentives, Cooperation and Risk Taking*, edited by H.R. Nalbantian, Totowa, New Jersey, Rowman & Littlefield, 1987, pp. 151-162.

ROCK, R.H., "Pay-For-Performance: Accent on Standards and Measures", *Compensation Review*, 1984, vol. 16, N° 3, pp. 15-23.

ROESTHLISBERGER, F. and W.J. DICKSON, *Management and the Worker*, Boston, Harvard University, 1939.

ROWAN THOMSON, W., *The Rowan Premium Bonus System of Payment by Results*, 2nd ed., Glasgow, McCorquedale Co., 1919.

ROY, D., "Quota Restriction and Gold Bricking in a Machine Shop", *American Journal of Sociology*, March 1952, pp. 427-442.

SCHULTZ, G.P. and R.Pp. CRISERA, *The Lapointe Machine Tool Company and the United Steel Workers of America, case study N° 10*, Washington, D.C., National Planning Association, 1952.

SCHUSTER, J.R. and P.K. ZINGHEIM, "Improving Productivity Through Gainsharing: Can the Means Be Justified in the End", *Compensation and Benefits Management*, Spring 1989, pp. 207-210.

TAYLOR, F.W., "A Piece Rate System", *Transactions of the American Society of Mechanical Engineers*, 1895, vol. 16, pp. 856-905.

TAYLOR, F.W., *The Principles of Scientific Management*, New York, Harper, 1911.

THÉRIAULT, R., *Politiques et pratiques en matière de rémunération globale dans les entreprises au Québec*, Montreal, Les Productions INFORT Inc., 1986.

UBELHART, M.C., "New Direction in Executive Compensation on Shareholder Value", *Perspectives in Total Compensation*, American Compensation Association, 1991, vol. 2, N° 1.

WALLACE, M.J., *Rewards and Renewal: America's Search for Competitive Advantage through Alternate Pay Strategies*, Scottsdale, Arizona, American Compensation Association, 1990.

WHITE, J.K., "The Scanlon Plan: Causes and Correlates of Success", *Academy of Management Journal*, 1979, vol. 22, N° 2, pp. 292-312.

WHYTE, W.F., *Money and Motivation*, New York, Harper, 1955.

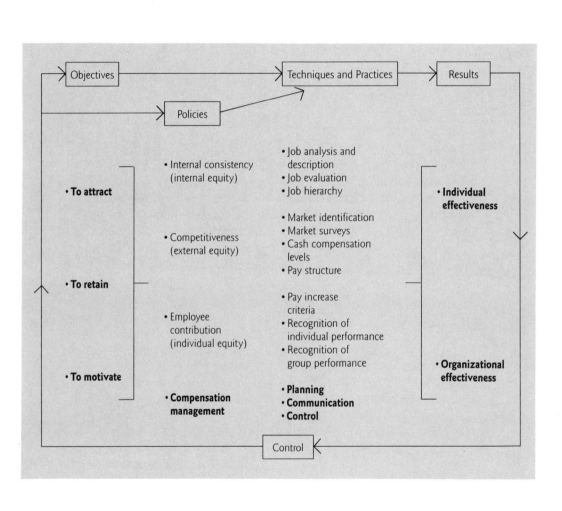

VI

MANAGING PAY

The preceding sections described how an organization develops equitable and competitive pay policies and practices. Once in place, however, their continued effectiveness and consistent application must be ensured.

This section, consisting of a single chapter, first discusses the importance of planning pay increases, then examines various possible criteria for these increases. Organizational objectives, and the compensation policies and practices that support them, are not necessarily communicated to employees. So, the remainder of this chapter demonstrates the need for communication and discusses the impact of a policy of pay secrecy. It concludes by emphasizing the importance of control mechanisms and describing several possible techniques.

TABLE OF CONTENTS

13

PAY MANAGEMENT

It is one thing for an organization to adopt equitable and competitive pay policies and practices; it is another to ensure that they are applied (managed) consistently and efficiently, and that they remain equitable and competitive. After a discussion of the value of planning pay increases, this chapter looks at awarding pay increases. It then focuses on the importance of communication, and concludes with an examination of the problems of selecting methods and techniques of pay control.

☐ 13.1 Planning Pay Increases

The planning of pay increases generally begins three to five months before year-end. The process involves two major decisions: percentage increase in pay scales and increase in total payroll. The latter figure breaks down into overall percentages for each employee category and, further, into individual pay increase percentages.

The percentage increase in pay scales is determined by two factors: the organization's pay policy in relation to the market and the projected market increase in pay scales. The decision on individual pay increases depends on the same two factors, as well as on the organization's capacity to pay. In some years, for example, at a time when market projections indicate 5% to 6% pay increases, an organization with a policy of market parity may, for financial reasons, decide on an average 3% pay increase.

Information about both pay scale and pay increase forecasts derives from annual surveys conducted by various public agencies, such as the Conference Board of Canada and by most compensation consulting firms, who publish their pay increase projections for the year ahead every fall. These forecasts, which generally distinguish pay scale from pay increases, are based on surveys conducted earlier in the year. Some firms publish the information, while others distribute it only to the organizations participating in their surveys, to avoid problems of misinterpretation. Table 13.1 is an excerpt from one such publication. Similar projections are made for the international level,

TABLE 13.1
Pay Increase Forecasts for Canadian Regions

A. Projected average percentage pay structure increases - 1991

	Executives	Middle managers	Technical, professional, supervisory	Administrative support	All
Canada	5.0	5.1	5.1	4.9	5.0
Maritimes	5.0	5.3	5.3	4.6	5.0
Quebec	5.0	5.0	4.9	4.8	4.9
Ontario	5.1	5.2	5.3	5.0	5.0
Prairies	4.7	5.0	5.0	4.9	4.9
British Columbia	5.0	5.1	5.1	4.8	5.0

B. Projected average percentage pay increases - 1991

	Executives	Middle managers	Technical, professional, supervisory	Administrative support	All
Canada	6.1	6.2	6.0	5.9	6.0
Maritimes	6.0	6.0	5.6	6.0	5.8
Quebec	6.1	6.1	5.7	5.7	5.8
Ontario	6.2	6.2	6.2	6.0	6.1
Prairies	6.3	6.5	6.4	5.8	6.2
British Columbia	6.1	5.8	5.8	5.9	5.8

SOURCE: Mercer Limited (1990a).

and firms publish this information for multinational organizations. Table 13.2 contains an example of forecasts for various countries.

☐ 13.2 Awarding Pay Increases

13.2.1 Criteria for Pay Increases

Should an employee who has held a position for six months receive the same pay as another who has held the position for three or for ten years?

TABLE 13.2
International Pay Increase Forecasts

| Country | Projections for 1991 Average Percentage Pay Increase | | |
	Management (%)	Non-management (%)	CPI (%)
Australia	5.0-6.0	5.0-6.0	5.0
Belgium	7.5	5.8	3.5-3.7
Canada	6.1	6.0	6.0-6.2
France	5.0	4.3	3.6-3.8
Hong Kong	12.8-15.0	12.8-15.0	10.5
Italy	11.2	10.2	5.7-5.9
Japan	5.0-6.5	5.7-6.0	2.8-3.1
Mexico	23.0-25.0	18.0-22.0	18.0-20.0
Philippines	16.0-18.0	16.0-18.0	18.0
South Korea	11.0-16.0	11.0-16.0	10.0-11.0
Spain	12.0	8.5	6.4-6.5
Sweden	8.0-8.5	7.0-7.5	9.0
Switzerland	7.0-7.5	6.5-7.0	5.0
United Kingdom	10.1	9.8	5.1-6.0
United States	5.3	5.0	6.7
West Germany	7.0	4.3	3.4-3.6

SOURCE: Mercer Limited (1990b).

Should an employee whose performance is clearly superior receive the same pay increase as one whose performance is barely satisfactory?

Should an employee whose performance, after one year in a position, promises to be very high, making that employee a candidate for promotion, receive the same pay increase as one who does good work but seems to have found a job that fits perfectly and is unlikely to rise higher in the organization?

These three questions raise the issue of pay for performance in its temporal dimensions: past, present, and future. To what extent should past performance be rewarded, compared with present or future performance? The answer to this question invariably raises another: What criteria should be used to measure that performance? Do the criteria selected and the means of applying them refer to anything other than the type of performance desired? For example, is length of service only a measure of past performance? Moreover, what role or part do increases linked to changes in the Consumer Price Index (CPI) and fluctuations in the organization's capacity to pay play in the total pay increases awarded to individuals?

TABLE 13.3
Pay Structure Designed To Promote Workforce Stability

Class	Hiring (min.)	3 mos.	6 mos.	I yr.	2 yrs.	3 yrs.	5 yrs.	10 yrs.	15 yrs. (max.)
					Time				
I	425	438	451	464	478	493	507	523	538
II	459	473	487	502	517	532	548	564	581
III	496	511	526	542	558	575	592	610	628
IV	545	561	578	596	613	632	651	670	690
V	600	618	637	656	675	696	716	738	760
VI	660	680	700	721	743	765	788	812	836

Years of Service

In some cases, a pay increase policy based on years of service (rise in grade or percentage increase determined annually) serves as a means of rewarding an employee's past performance with the organization.

Occasionally, the monetary recognition of years of service also serves as a financial incentive aimed at maintaining workforce stability. Since the chances of involuntary employee turnover are greater during the early years on the job and diminish with time, seniority-based increases occur more frequently at first, then are more widely spaced. Table 13.3 illustrates this situation.

Thus, someone hired at the minimum pay for Grade II would receive a 3% increase after three months, six months and one year. At the end of the first year, that employee's salary would be about 10% more than at the time of hiring. Subsequently, the intervals between increases based on seniority become greater and greater.

The practical effects on the pay scale of using the seniority criterion as a reward for years of service differ from the effects of using this criterion as an incentive for workforce stability (cf. Chapter 8 on pay structures).

From the standpoint of rewarding years of service, the increases or bonuses may last as long as the individuals continue working for the organization. Employees may continue receiving pay increases or seniority bonuses after 30 years of service, if the organization is intent on rewarding length of service.

It would not make sense, however, to award pay increases or seniority bonuses over such a long period if the purpose is to promote workforce stability. Seniority-based pay increases may have an impact on labour stability early in the job, but certainly not after 10 years.

The duration of seniority-based increases, therefore, depends on which of these two objectives the organization is pursuing.

Individual Performance

The use of effectiveness (achievement of objectives) and efficiency (best use of available resources) as performance criteria remains controversial. As mentioned in Chapter 10, some people are for it, others against. Some favour it in principle but not in practice, while others are absolutely opposed to it for one reason or another. Nonetheless, virtually all organizations use this criterion for certain employee categories. Its use implies establishing an individual performance evaluation system (cf. Chapter 11). Whatever evaluation system is used, however, it depends on judgment exercised by the employee's immediate supervisors. Their judgments may be more or less harsh, resulting in higher or lower percentages of employees in the different performance categories. The percentage pay increase to be awarded for different levels of performance must also be determined. In practice, as we have seen in Chapter 10, these percentages depend on the individual's pay level. It is therefore common to develop pay percentage increase grids or matrices, based on the different performance levels and on the pay within pay ranges. These matrices, together with a pay increase budget, then serve as a means of controlling merit pay increases (cf. Section 13.4).

As we have seen in Chapter 10, dealing with pay for performance, organizations rarely have a compensation policy based solely on merit. In practice, other variables are always involved in determining merit pay increase percentages.

The labour market, the increase in the CPI, the merit compensation budget, working conditions, length of service with the organization, the employee's level in the organization, the percentage increase received by the immediate supervisor, and the latter's level of experience are all factors that influence the percentage of merit increases awarded to employees (Heneman, 1990).

Cost of Living

Using the cost of living as a criterion translates, in practice, into more or less automatic indexation of pay to changes in one or more consumer price indexes.

Pay Indexation

According to Cousineau and Lacroix (1980), the first clear instance of an automatic pay adjustment tied to a CPI dates back to 1916. This does not mean, however, as the authors point out, that before that date there were no pay adjustments to match changes in the cost of living; however, it was only in 1910 that a particular CPI was used to adjust pay.

As the same authors point out (p. 9), the relative stability of prices during the 20s, the Great Depression of the 30s, and the policy of price stabilization applied during World War II virtually wiped out any trace of pay indexation in the United States and Canada until the late 40s. The high inflation of the early 50s triggered the return of indexation clauses in labour agreements. The same thing happened throughout the 70s until the mid-80s, when indexation again began to fade.

While allowing organizations to sign longer-term contracts with unions, indexation clauses may also fuel inflation. During the 1976-81 inflationary period, for example, unionized employees received higher pay increases than non-unionized personnel, basically because of indexation clauses. Nonetheless, organizations with such clauses quickly found themselves in trouble in the early 80s, e.g. the automotive, airline, and trucking industries. At that point, job security became an important issue for unionized employees, in dealing with the pressures of global competition and non-unionized organizations.

The Consumer Price Index (CPI)

Cost of living, with or without an indexation formula, generally seems to be accepted as a criterion, partly because of its simplicity, but primarily because of its apparent equity. This simplicity stems more from the fact that an index is published rather than from how the index is determined.

At present, the CPI is based on the value of a basket of products consumed by a target population consisting of families and single persons living in urban centers with a population of 30,000 or more. The cost of the basket of products is compared to the purchases made by the target population during a reference period in the year. The contents and proportions of the basket's components are regularly updated to reflect changes in spending habits. The most recent update occurred in 1986, when the total value of the basket was reset at the base index of 100. The basket contains seven groups of products, each with its relative total weight. Table 13.4 lists those components with their relative weight.

The index is relatively straightforward but reflects an average situation and, therefore, raises numerous questions. For example, the situation of someone who neither smokes nor drinks alcoholic beverages does not cor-

TABLE 13.4
Consumer Price Index Components and Their Relative Weights (base: 1986)

Component	Weight (%)
Food	18.1
Housing	36.3
Clothing	8.7
Transportation	18.3
Health and personal care	4.2
Recreation, reading and education	8.8
Tobacco and alcohol	5.6

SOURCE: Statistics Canada (1989).

respond to the target population's product basket. The same applies to someone who does not use a personal vehicle (which represents 16.4% out of the 18.3% in Table 13.4) or someone who does not eat out (which represents 5% out of the 18.1% allocated for food). Moreover, the index does not consider the possibility of using substitute products or the effect of income taxes.

In fact, very few individuals are in a situation that exactly matches the general average. Furthermore, changes in the cost of living do not have the same impact on a person earning $85,000 a year as they do on one earning $30,000. Some people, therefore, suggest applying a diminishing percentage to each higher pay range for increases based on the CPI, or applying the change in the index only to a fixed amount of pay.

The tendency in Canada is to rely on the national CPI and only rarely on regional variations. Table 13.5 lists the CPI increases for selected Canadian cities from January 1990 to January 1991. A few observations on this table are in order. First, during this period, the average CPI increase in the selected cities is higher than the national average. The size of the city where one is located therefore has an impact on the CPI increase. Secondly, the highest inflation rate (CPI increase) during the period in question is not found in the largest Canadian cities. The rate in Toronto was 5.3%, Montreal 8.2%, and Vancouver 6.9%, compared to 9.3% in Charlottetown and 8.4% in Halifax. Thirdly, the inflation rate may vary greatly from one location to another. Thus, the maximum differential for the reference period and cities specified in Table 13.5 is 4%, or the spread between Charlottetown at 9.3% and Toronto at 5.3%. Finally, all of these comments are based on the reference period from January 1990 to January 1991. They would have been different had another period been selected (the variances in the inflation rate from

TABLE 13.5
Percentage CPI Increase for Canada and Selected Canadian Cities from January 1990 to January 1991

Location	CPI Increase (%)
Canada	6.8
Charlottetown	9.3
Halifax	8.4
Montreal	8.2
Ottawa	6.6
Toronto	5.3
Winnipeg	6.5
Edmonton	7.9
Vancouver	6.9

SOURCE: Statistics Canada (1989).

city to city might differ), but the conclusions would have been the same (inflation rates vary greatly from one city to the next).

In practice, organizations rarely use CPI increases directly as a criterion for pay increases, except with unionized personnel. Instead, they grant general or economic pay increases, which primarily consider the inflation rate, market increases, and the organization's financial position. CPI increases are most often used to adjust pay scales as opposed to individual pay.

Actual Frequency of Criteria Usage

Table 13.6 provides an indication of the criteria used to determine individual pay increases.

On the whole, the table indicates that formal performance evaluation and the inflation rate are, in that order, the two most important criteria for individual pay increases. Also, how frequently these criteria are used varies by employee category. For executives and professionals, pay increases depend on performance evaluation, pay level, and the inflation rate, in that order. In contrast, the criteria used for production and maintenance workers are the inflation rate, performance evaluation, and years of service with the organization, in that order.

In the United States, the Freedman and Montanari (1980) survey of compensation managers at over 200 major organizations produced interesting information about the criteria used to determine pay increases. While the study failed to clearly indicate the employee categories concerned, it appeared

TABLE 13.6
Frequency (%) of Criteria Usage for Individual Pay Increases

Criteria	Executive	Managerial & professional	Technical	Administrative support	Production & maintenance	All categories
		Employee Categories				
Formal performance evaluation	46	51	42	36	27	41
Informal performance evaluation	31	31	32	25	21	28
CPI increase	31	31	38	37	59	38
Length of service	17	20	21	22	24	21
Pay level (compa-ratio)	29	35	32	29	18	29

SOURCE: Thériault (1986, p. 109). Reprinted by permission of the publisher.

to focus primarily on managerial and office staff. Each compensation manager was asked to rate, in the order of importance, 28 possible pay increase criteria. Employee performance emerged as the top criterion, with contribution to organizational success in second place. Increases received by others within and outside the organization ranked 11th and 12th, respectively. CPI increases took 14th place, and seniority, 17th.

In brief, both in Canada and the United States, numerous criteria are used to determine individual pay increases, with performance being the most commonly used.

13.2.2 Timing Pay Increases

During the 70s, most North American organizations reviewed the pay of their non-unionized employees on their anniversary date of hire (Ellig, 1977). Bonuses, on the other hand, were typically awarded once a year, on the same date. This practice has since changed (Thériault, 1986). In most cases, increases now typically occur on the same date.

Anniversary Date of Hire

The main reason cited for using the anniversary date of hire for awarding pay increases is the idea of personalizing pay increases, which makes the process more meaningful for employees. On the other hand, this approach may mask pay increases, complicating comparison between employees whose increases occur earlier or later. Financially, using anniversary dates also allows pay increases to be spread over the entire year.

This approach, however, has some serious disadvantages. For example, it makes it virtually impossible to obtain a realistic distribution of employee performance. It also makes it difficult to get supervisors to carry out pay reviews efficiently, because of other demands of the moment. Inequities may also be created or maintained, since supervisors see no point in examining the impact of each pay decision they make in relation to the general trend within their administrative unit.

Same Date for All

This situation has led authors such as Ellig (1977) to argue in favour of conducting all pay reviews within an organization at the same time. The review should occur after the end of an organization's fiscal year, to enable a better comparison between individual performance and organizational results. This makes it much easier to control pay policies effectively. It also results in more efficient and better use of supervisors' time, and facilitates comparisons between individuals, increasing the chances of achieving equity. On the other hand, in this context, a policy of forced distribution for individual performance is possible and realistic.

Coordinating the Pay Increase Dates of Different Employee Categories

The timing of pay reviews for non-unionized employees in relation to that for unionized personnel must also be considered. More generally, the timing of pay increases for different employee categories must be considered. The following is an example of the problems caused by a failure to coordinate the timing of pay increases for management and unionized employees.

In this organization, unionized employees received their pay increases in September and management, in March. The latter pay increases reflected those received by unionized employees. As a result, supervisors' satisfaction with pay was high in April, May, and June. But after September, when unionized employees had received their pay increases, the pay differential between supervisors and their unionized employees was virtually eliminated and, in some cases, unionized employees earned more. This made supervisors dissatisfied with their pay in November and December, and created a real problem by January and February. The situation would have been avoided if pay increases for the supervisors had been scheduled some time after those for unionized employees, so as to maintain acceptable differentials.

☐ 13.3 **Communicating Pay**

While a compensation policy has the effect of reinforcing its objectives, those objectives are not necessarily communicated to the employees concerned.

A distinction may be drawn between the question of communicating an organization's compensation policies and communicating pay structures and individual pay.

The Freedman and Montanari (1980) survey indicates that, in practice, nearly 70% of responding organizations informed employees of the compensation policies relevant to them, or made the information available. However, sixty percent of the respondents had an official pay secrecy policy for individual pay. A minority of the organizations published information about the minimum-maximum differentials in various pay grades, but did not disclose individual salaries.

In brief, employees concerned are generally informed about formal compensation policies, but not about pay structures and individual pay.

Yet individuals act on the basis of their perceptions. If a compensation element is to have an effect on employee behaviour, employees must first perceive its existence and then attach some value to it. Leaving aside the question of the value of the different elements (cf. Chapter 15), their perceived value depends on communication. It may be shaped by the messages conveyed through a formal, official communication process, or by how employees interpret what they see or conclude from messages received through informal channels. In any case, compensation policies and practices are rarely secret. The content is, in some cases, conveyed officially, in others, informally. Either way, one may not assume that employees know and understand the true situation as management is trying to convey it. This point will be elaborated by considering first the question of formal communication and then the repercussions of secret pay practices.

13.3.1 **Formal Communication Process**

"I know you think you understand what you thought I said, but I'm not sure you realize that what you heard is not what I meant to say." This familiar statement illustrates quite clearly the problem of the meaning and interpretation of communicated messages.

As Figure 13.1 illustrates, communication requires a sender and a receiver.

FIGURE 13.1
The Communication Process

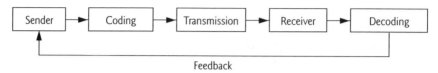

Feedback

Elements of the Process

La Palice coined the saying that the message a sender intends to transmit is rarely the one received. Actually, it could scarcely be otherwise, given the problems that can occur at, and between, each step of the process. In the compensation field in particular, one need only think of the impact of the status differences between sender and receiver, of their different value systems, of the expectations and aspirations of receivers, of the prior perceptions of both sides, and of the motives and intentions each attributes to the other. Then there are the problems of coding (clear and precise statement of the message to be conveyed), transmission (relative effectiveness of the various media), and decoding.

In addition, while messages are transmitted verbally, nonverbal communication is equally important. If verbal messages are difficult to understand, what about nonverbal messages? The most obvious forms of nonverbal communication in an organization are delays, absenteeism, employee turnover, quality and quantity of work, accidents, grievances, and wilful damage. What do these messages mean? And how are they related to compensation policies and practices?

The Dynamic Nature of the Process

The communication process is dynamic, not static. The instant a message is sent, it spreads in different directions. Its reach is not limited to the individual or group for whom it was intended. At the same time, messages come from various sources within an organization, and may reinforce or contradict each other. For example, Nash and Carroll (1975) recount the story of the university department head who, after telling his teaching staff that compensation increases would be based on individual merit, informed them that they were all entitled to a 10% pay increase that year! How are managers to interpret a statement that, henceforth, all management compensation will be based solely on merit, when their actual increases range from 4% to 6%, and the CPI stands at 5%? And what are employees to think of the message that a compensation policy aims "to establish pay structures that promote career planning within the organization", when the pay differential between two adjoining hierarchical levels are less than 10%, or are unknown?

These examples raise the problem of consistency in compensation policy and practice, as well as in the messages an organization wishes to convey to its employees about their compensation and existing practices.

Relative Effectiveness of Communication Media

Another issue is the relative effectiveness of the various media employed to communicate current policies and practices to all organizational levels.

Using an official notice to all employees is definitely the swiftest means of conveying information. However, the sender, i.e. management, has no guarantee of the quality of the reception or the interpretation of the message. This approach is useful for conveying simple information, when employees are already familiar with the subject. Under other circumstances, however, beware! Correcting such a message requires a much more time-consuming set of operations than if the communication had been directed to small groups from the outset.

Unlike notices to all employees, small discussion groups allow for two-way communication – downward and upward. This makes it a greater challenge for the sender, whose message may be called directly into question. Yet by facilitating interaction, this approach increases the chance that the message will be understood. While this method is more dynamic than a notice to all employees, the message received may vary from one group to the next. In addition, the size of the group limits the possibility of interaction.

Finally, individual, face-to-face communication is the easiest way to ensure that messages are understood. However, this form of communication also involves the greatest risk that the message will vary from person to person.

Practical Implications

Three important points emerge from these brief observations on communicating compensation policies and practices, to the extent that an organization wishes to set them forth clearly.

1. One or more official documents signed by an executive must specifically state the organization's objectives and the principal characteristics of the ensuing practices.
2. Information sessions with supervisors must be arranged to allow them to understand, so that they may, in turn, explain the organization's

objectives and how the related procedures apply to their employees. Employee communication flows through organizational supervisors.
3. One or more competent individuals must be responsible at all times for providing supervisors and employees with any clarification they may require.

13.3.2 Pay Secrecy Policies

As mentioned, a minority of organizations publish information about pay structures without disclosing individual pay. In general, employees have access to information about pay policies. They do not know, however, about pay structures (minimum-maximum differentials in the various grades) or, above all, individual pay.

The principal argument in favour of pay secrecy is that it prevents comparisons between employees and limits dissatisfaction. This affirmation is not supported by the theory of social comparisons (Festinger, 1954), or by certain studies dealing with the concept of equity (Homans, 1961; Adams, 1965). Lacking objective points of comparison, employees tend to compare themselves to other employees who constitute their reference group, whose relevant characteristics are then evaluated or estimated based on the perceptions of the person making the comparison. Hence, instead of preventing comparison, a policy of pay secrecy to some extent encourages it (Lawler, 1967).

By assigning higher pay to the most demanding jobs, a pay structure enhances the incentive value of promotions and thereby the motivation to perform better (insofar as promotions are based on performance). For this to occur, however, employees must perceive significant pay differences between jobs. In fact, however, research on the subject indicates that individuals generally underestimate the pay of their organizational supervisors.

Results of Pay Secrecy

Studies by Lawler (1965, 1965a, 1966, 1967 and 1971), as well as by Milkovich and Anderson (1972), indicate that when managers lack information about other managers' pay, they are also incapable of accurately estimating it. These studies reveal a tendency to overestimate the pay of subordinates and of colleagues at the same organizational level, and to underestimate the pay of superiors. In the study by Milkovich and Anderson, the managers had information about pay grade minimums and maximums, and knew their colleagues' grades. Even so, 54% of them overestimated their colleagues' pay – the same percentage as in the case of managers with no information. Does this mean that they lacked confidence in the value of the information they had received, or was the information inadequate? The question is debatable.

Consequences of Pay Secrecy Information

Based on these results, various authors, Lawler (1971) in particular, note that a policy of pay secrecy distorts employee perceptions, causing them to overestimate what their subordinates and colleagues are paid, which, in turn, increases their dissatisfaction (equity theory). Such a policy results in managers not knowing that larger pay increases are awarded to employees whose performance is superior, and vice versa, which, of course, reduces motivation (expectancy theory).

In addition to these effects on satisfaction and motivation for better performance, some studies reveal that a policy of pay secrecy influences pay increase decisions (Leventhal, Michaels and Sanford, 1972). The study by Kidder, Belletirie and Cohn (1977), in particular, revealed an interesting finding. Male participants in the study distributed rewards on a basis of equity when they knew that their decisions would be made public, and on a basis of equality when they knew that their decisions would remain anonymous. Female participants did the opposite; they applied a standard of equality when they knew that their decisions would be published, and a standard of equity when they knew that their decisions would remain anonymous. Analyzing the results of this study, Freedman and Montanari (1980) formulated an interesting hypothesis. Individuals are inclined to follow organizational standards when they know that decisions will be disclosed, and to violate them when they know that their decisions will remain secret.

Remember as well that organizational standards do not necessarily correspond to the official guidelines; in some cases, the opposite is true.

Finally, a study by Reis and Gruzen (1976) found that employees tended to use a standard of equity when they knew that their supervisor would learn the results of their decisions, and a standard of equality when they consider that the colleagues of the person whom the decision concerned were very likely to know the results.

Applied to an organizational situation, these findings illustrate that employees responsible for pay increases may find themselves between a rock and a hard place when official policy calls for performance-based pay increases (equity) and their disclosure (or when subordinates are likely to learn about the increases). Undoubtedly, this accounts, to a large extent, for the small variations actually found in the merit-based pay increases awarded to employees reporting to the same supervisor. It constitutes yet another argument for using forced distribution in awarding merit pay increases.

Reactions to Pay Disclosure

In practice, a minority of individuals seem to agree with disclosing information about pay (Bureau of National Affairs, 1972; Schuster and Coletti,
1973; Burroughs, 1982). As we can see, however, these studies were conducted
some years ago, and the situation may since have changed.

As for the characteristics of these individuals, the study by Schuster and
Coletti found that the higher the performance of employees, the less they
favoured disclosure of pay information. The higher their level of education,
the more they favoured disclosure. However, since this is virtually the only
study on the subject, the issue remains unresolved.

Effect of Disclosing Information about Pay

Studies focusing on pay disclosure are few in number, and are all quite dated.
After examining the results of these studies at the time, Dyer, Schwab and
Fossum (1978) concluded that, given the limited number of studies and
their contradictory results, it was premature to draw conclusions about a
policy of pay disclosure.

In this context, the arguments about the effects of an open pay policy
on employee satisfaction and motivation retain their value. Certain precautions, however, are necessary.

The disclosure of information about pay should probably vary from one
organization to the next, based on existing and prior practices. Informing
employees about the minimums and maximums of the various pay grades,
as well as the median of actual pay is very different from posting a list of
individual salaries on the cafeteria wall.

Nor is there any doubt that, once an organization embarks on the process
of disclosing information about pay, the demand for more openness grows.
It then becomes a question of how pay is determined, who makes the
decisions, the relationship between what the organization pays and what the
market pays, the relationship between what the holders of different jobs are
paid, employee benefits, how benefits are selected, etc. Disclosure may also
reveal the inadequacy of a compensation program, flagrant inequities, and
an inability to explain the rationale for these situations.

An organization should therefore first analyze any information about
compensation and work that it wishes to disclose to employees. The same
applies to what employees want to know about their present and future
opportunities. In addition to such analyses, the adequacy and acceptability
of the compensation program must be ensured. One good way of doing this

is to ensure that job evaluations are current and reflect the organization's requirements.

Finally, an effective policy of pay disclosure will entail the establishment of a training program, to ensure that organizational supervisors understand the compensation program. Since much of the communication within an organization flows through them, they must be in a position to give their employees satisfactory answers, rather than refer them to specialists. The success of a compensation communication program depends on the ability of organizational supervisors to convey information about pay and employee benefits to their employees.

☐ 13.4 Controlling Pay

The control process may be divided into four stages:

- setting objectives and the ensuing standards of effectiveness;
- measuring effectiveness;
- comparing actual results to the standards; and
- determining and implementing corrective action.

The first two steps are fundamental. The value of the remaining two depends both on the quality of the established standards and on the degree of effectiveness achieved.

13.4.1 Standards of Effectiveness

As Belcher and Atchison (1987) point out, standards of effectiveness for compensation policies and practices are not well-developed. While this shortcoming definitely depends on problems of measurement, it is also true that often, organizations have not clearly determined what they want for themselves and what they expect from their employees. Nonetheless, in some cases, specific standards have been developed and used. They apply to the following aspects of compensation:

- indices and ratios: total compensation or payroll as a percentage of sales or production value (cf. Chapter 12 on profit-sharing plans for examples of the content and application of various ratios or indices of this kind);
- direct, indirect, or total labour costs, or labour expense (investment) budget;
- standards for pay rates and differentials;
- pay increase budget: total budget, budget for merit increases, based on merit, promotions, seniority, cost of living, etc.;

- overtime budget for the entire organization and for units (divisions, departments, etc.); and
- pay and compensation distribution standards.

13.4.2 Responsibility for Control

One of the major weaknesses in the compensation control process is undoubtedly the practical division of responsibilities for the various aspects of compensation. While a section of the human resource department is responsible for pay surveys, managers alone, or together with the compensation department, may be in charge of controlling individual pay. The financial manager may be responsible for controlling the payroll, whereas the industrial engineering department may play a role in controlling incentive compensation for production or clerical workers.

In addition, one must also mention the role of the training department in controlling individual performance evaluation systems, of the recruiting and selection department in the starting pay offered, of managers in preparing or approving job descriptions, of the accounting and computer department in pay administration. And of course, the list is far from complete. This division of responsibilities creates serious problems for controlling compensation within an organization. The situation, however, seems to be changing. It is no longer rare to find senior managers concern themselves with compensation issues and demanding an accounting from compensation managers.

13.4.3 Types of Control

Senior management exercises its control in a variety of ways. Sibson's classification (1967) of the types of control remains relevant: by approval, budget, statistics, or influence.

Control by Approval

Control by senior management's approval ensures compliance with compensation policies. However, this approach creates problems at the individual level because senior management has a very incomplete picture of what goes on at that level.

Control by Budget

Control by budget allows decisions to be delegated. In brief, it involves control before decision-making at the level of the total pay budget or the pay increase budget. In practice, however, there is no guarantee of the quality of the decisions that will be made. As discussed in Chapter 10, it is one thing to establish a merit pay increase budget and another to ensure that the budget is really allocated on the basis of employee performance.

Control by Statistics

Statistical control makes it possible to develop standards of effectiveness and to detect potential problems and the required remedial action. This approach, however, provides very little indication of the real source of the problems, and is generally combined with budgetary control.

The advent and development of computers have made it much easier for organizations to exercise statistical control. Already in the early 70s, Meyer (1973) argued in favour of using computers to assist in making compensation decisions. In this regard, Fossum et al. (1974) provide an interesting example of designing and implementing a computerized compensation system for an organization. The number of possible statistical indices is then virtually unlimited. However, two comments must be made.

First, it is important to recognize the critical nature of the programming. Here, as in other fields, many experts suffer from technical nearsightedness. The program must, above all, allow for swift access to the desired information in the simplest and most efficient way possible. The information obtained must be usable, i.e. understandable by managers. It must also be used.

Secondly, in any field, though perhaps especially in compensation, the use of computers raises the problem of the confidential nature of the information. The question of access to data has certainly been studied for many years (cf., for example, Scaletta, 1971), but remains unresolved. Its importance has grown with public awareness about the need to protect individual privacy in our society.

Control by Influence

Finally, control by influence involves helping managers, on an individual basis, to make satisfactory, consistent decisions about the compensation of their staff. To achieve this, there must be specific policies and procedures, and managers must have the information they need to make decisions, be able to rely on support from specialists, have the training needed to make this type of decision, and be responsible for their decisions. Obviously, gaps in any one of these areas will jeopardize the effectiveness of this type of control.

13.4.4 Control Mechanisms

Compensation control mechanisms may focus on employee contributions or rewards.

Control of Contribution

Control of contribution may focus on the work, performance, or individual contribution of employees.

Control of Employees' Work

This involves establishing and applying mechanisms for ensuring that job descriptions and classifications (job evaluation) are updated, and that new jobs are analyzed, described, and evaluated.

This control may be exercised at fixed intervals. As mentioned in the discussion in Chapter 3 on job descriptions and in Chapter 5 on managing job evaluation, annual review of the content of jobs and their position in the pay structure (classification) has its value. The same applies to the general rule of reviewing job evaluation criteria, their value and weighting, or the job evaluation methods used to classify jobs (cf. Chapter 4). Ideally, this should be carried out every five years or so.

Control of Employees' Performance

Generally speaking, these methods have been little developed. The one note-worthy exception involves controlling profit-sharing plans (cf. Chapter 12) as opposed to merit compensation (cf. Chapter 10).

Few standards of effectiveness have been established for merit compensation, even in organizations that use management by objectives. Nonetheless, it is important to repeat the axiom from Chapter 10. A performance evaluation system should be reviewed every two or three years, to ensure the value of the methods by which it is applied and the system's validity with respect to the required behaviour of employees.

Control of Personal Contribution

Control of personal contribution is not practised much in North America, except in determining starting salaries that recognize an employee's previous experience and assign a monetary value to it. The myth of the irrelevance of personal contribution to compensation is also a frequent source of conflict between management and compensation officials with respect to the adequacy of the compensation structure.

On the other hand, monetary recognition of personal contribution as practised in certain European organizations (compensating individuals on the basis of their potential) engenders other conflicts and leads to serious problems of control (cf. Chapter 10 on pay increase criteria).

Control of Rewards

The mechanisms for controlling employee rewards may focus on total payroll, pay levels, pay structure, individual pay, or pay increases.

Control of Total Payroll

Budgets, (payroll budgets for sales personnel, production workers, etc.) or general or specific ratios (pay over sales, payroll over production value, etc.) are normally used to control total payroll.

These budgets or ratios are determined annually. Most organizations, however, use them much more frequently, i.e. on a monthly or even weekly basis.

Control of Pay Levels

This is exercised by conducting compensation surveys. Generally, as indicated in Chapter 7, an annual review of pay changes in the market is necessary. However, as noted, for certain types of jobs and at certain times, the situation is changing so rapidly that semi-annual surveys may prove necessary.

In addition to compensation surveys, other methods may be used to control pay levels, for example, relating pay levels and employee turnover or pay levels and job offer rejection rates. In these two cases, however, a distinction must be drawn between the effect of pay levels and the impact of other variables.

Control of Pay Structure

The best and certainly the ultimate indication of the relevance of a pay structure is the extent to which it is accepted by employees. This obviously assumes that employees are familiar with the pay structure. Employee interviews or surveys then constitute suitable control mechanisms.

However, there are other means of determining the degree to which employees accept the pay structure, for example, keeping track of job re-evaluation requests, and above all, their increase or decrease over time.

Another method would be to examine promotion refusals or difficulties raised at the time of promotions. If employees consider the pay differentials between jobs inadequate based on job requirements (cf. Chapter 8), promotions will be less attractive.

Control of Individual Pay

The mechanisms for controlling individual pay may focus both on the appropriateness of pay rates and on individual pay within grades.

• Control of Pay Rates

With respect to the appropriateness of pay rates, one need only think of the means adopted to verify the pay offered on hiring, transfer, promotion, or individual pay increases. Most organizations, for instance, have a minimum and maximum percentage, with minimal and maximal actual levels for promotions. An organization might decide to have a minimum pay increase of 10% accompany a promotion, with the proviso that the employee's new pay not exceed the maximum of the pay grade for the new job. This rule is generally accompanied by another to the effect that, on promotion, an employee's new pay must be no less than the minimum of the pay grade for the new job.

Applying rules such as these may create certain problems, already discussed in Chapter 8. In fact, if the structure has no differentials between grades that comply with the rules for promotion, for example, the 10% rule may be very difficult to apply, because the differentials between grades are too small or result in promoted employees finding themselves virtually at the maximum of their new pay grade from the outset. In that case, there is no occasion for individual pay increases without surpassing the established grades.

It is equally important to coordinate the use of the individual pay control mechanism at such events by using management mechanisms suitable to the event. For instance, control of starting-pay offers must be closely coordinated with the application of hiring methods, or some, to say the least, embarrassing situations may occur. Take, for example, the case of the student entering the job market a few years ago. Like his classmates, he applied for jobs at a number of companies. One of the jobs was particularly attractive, and the company in question appeared to take his application quite seriously. After several interviews and a visit to the company, the student received an official job offer, specifying his starting pay. The student chose to wait before replying, in order to compare the offer with any others he might receive. Much to his surprise, several days later, he received a note from the company apologizing because an error had been made in the pay stipulated in the offer; the real figure was 15% lower! While this may have been just another way of telling the student that the company had changed its mind about hiring him, it was certainly not a good way to start a working relationship.

• Control of Individual Pay Levels

An organization may control individual pay levels by establishing control points within each pay grade. Compa-ratios are the most commonly used technique for this. As mentioned in Chapter 10, this ratio is calculated by dividing the actual pay of an employee (or group of employees) by the pay for the point corresponding to the normal maximum or the control point of the pay range (or the average of the normal maximums for different employees).

For example, the compa-ratio of an employee earning $34,000 in a pay range with a normal maximum of $30,000 is:

$$\frac{\$34,000}{\$30,000} \times 100 = 113$$

In a pay structure with minimums and maximums located ± 20% from the control point, the compa-ratio of employees within the limits of their pay range will vary from 80 to 120. The significance of the resulting index is then examined in relation to the individual's real situation. If it was determined that an index of 110 corresponds to the pay of an employee whose performance is well above satisfactory in most areas of responsibility, and the performance of the employee in question is only satisfactory, some adjustments are called for.

This index may be used to compare performance of employees in different groups, as well as the relative effectiveness of applying the pay increase policy. On a collective basis, this makes it possible to determine actual pay level in relation to the organization's pay policy. For example, there is a difference between having a pay policy that, overall, calls for control points at the 60th percentile of the reference market and finding that the average compa-ratio is 92 or 105.

In addition to the compa-ratio method, other systems may be used to control pay levels. One method is to set standards for the percentages of employees that should be located at different levels within pay grades.

• Control of Pay Increases

Organizations usually have two ways of controlling pay increases: budgets and a percentage matrix.

As mentioned, a pay increase budget is a basic management tool, like any other organizational budget. It provides the organization with an action guide, and ensures definite control of its activities over the year. Pay increase budgets normally have at least two components: increases related to promotions and increases related to performance.

Most organizations use a matrix for performance-based pay increases, in order to ensure equitable treatment for all. As noted in Chapter 10, this matrix considers both individual performance levels and employee pay levels. According to Table 13.7, employees whose performance is satisfactory and whose pay is in the control point zone (96-104) will receive a 4% to 5% increase, and remain at the same level within their grade. On the other hand, employees whose performance is satisfactory or better and whose pay is below the control point will receive an increase of more than 4% or 5%, which will bring their pay closer to the control-point zone. Note that the matrix contains rather conservative percentages. In fact, according to it, an employee hired at the minimum, whose performance is always satisfactory, would have to wait 10 or 11 years before reaching the control point (100). With a constantly superior performance, that time would be reduced to 6 or 7 years. An organization interested in shortening this period would have to establish a larger differential between the percentages assigned to an employee with satisfactory performance whose pay is in the control point zone (i.e. 4% to 5% in Table 13.7), and those assigned to an employee whose performance is exceptional and whose pay is in the first quintile (80-88 zone) of the scale (i.e. 8% to 9%). Whereas the differential in Table 13.7 is 4%, it could be 6% to 7%.

Nonetheless, this matrix is inadequate as a control instrument, because it provides no indication of the number or percentage of employees that should be found in each performance category. An organization might remedy this shortcoming by adopting a forced distribution method for its evaluations.

TABLE 13.7
Pay increase matrix based on pay level compa-ratio and individual performance*

Individual Performance	Individual pay increases based on compa-ratio (%)				
	80-88	88-96	96-104	104-112	112-120
Exceptional	8-9	7-8	6-7	5-6	4-5
Superior	7-8	6-7	5-6	4-5	2-3
Satisfactory	6-7	5-6	4-5	2-3	0-2
Acceptable	5-6	4-5	2-3	0-2	0
Unsatisfactory	0	0	0	0	0

* Projected pay increases for a 4% scale increase.

This practice, is however, strongly contested (cf. Chapter 10). Another approach would be to give managers a pay increase budget along with the matrix. The manager would no longer be required to use a forced distribution of evaluations which, in any case, might not be appropriate with a small number of employees. Nonetheless, the application of the pay increase matrix must adhere to the budget.

Conclusion

There is no single means of establishing effective control mechanisms for compensation policies and practices. A number of rules and techniques have been proposed in the preceding pages. These rules and techniques, however, deal with specific aspects of the compensation program. Since no organization operates in a vacuum, a compensation policy or practice will only remain adequate and satisfactory through constant observation of the economic, social, and legal changes that occur and affect both employees and operations.

Given the importance, as well as the complexity, of compensation for organizations and employees, it is essential to undertake a formal, systematic evaluation of employee reactions to various aspects of compensation. This is the only way to adequately appraise the return on investment in total compensation.

Such surveys provide an excellent means of identifying groups of employees that are experiencing problems and the nature of the main difficulties. Since any organization has limited resources, it is important that they be used intelligently.

☐ 13.5 Summary

After ensuring that its pay policies and practices are equitable and competitive, an organization must make certain that they are applied (managed) consistently and efficiently, and that they remain equitable and competitive.

One principal instrument of pay management is an organization's operating budget. By means of the budget's payroll item, the organization gives a concrete expression to its pay policies, as well as the strategy it will emphasize in the year ahead. An important part of the budget deals with pay increases, which may be based on various criteria, such as employee performance, the inflation rate, or length of service with the organization.

A second important factor in pay management is communication: who communicates what and how? In keeping with the will of the majority, individual pay and pay increases are often kept secret (except in the case of unionized employees). This, however, reduces the relative effectiveness of compensation policies and practices.

Finally, control is the third factor to consider in pay management. This control must focus on different aspects of pay, and be exercised in different ways. Compa-ratios are an important control instrument for pay trends within the organization, whereas matrices and budgets are excellent tools for controlling pay increases.

REFERENCES

ADAMS, J.S., "Injustice In Social Exchange", in *Advances in Social Psychology*, edited by L. Berkovitz, New York, Academic Press, 1965.

BELCHER, D. and T.J. ATCHISON, *Compensation Administration*, Englewood Cliffs, New Jersey, Prentice-Hall Inc., 1987.

BERNOULLI, D., "Exposition of a New Theory on the Measurement of Risk", in *Mathematics and Psychology*, edited by G.A. Miller, New York, Wiley, 1964.

BUREAU OF NATIONAL AFFAIRS, *Personnel Policies Forum: Wage and Salary Administration*, Survey N° 697, Washington, D.C., Bureau of National Affairs, 1972.

BURROUGHS, J.D., "Pay Secrecy and Performance: The Psychological Research", *Compensation Review*, vol. 14, N° 3, 1982, pp. 44-54.

COUSINEAU, J.M. and R. LACROIX, *L'indexation des salaires*, Montreal, École des relations industrielles, Université de Montréal, 1980.

DYER, L., D.P. SCHWAB and J.A. FOSSUM, "Impacts of Pay on Employee Behaviors and Attitudes: An Update", in *Perspectives on Personnel/Human Resource Management*, edited by H.G. Heneman and D.P. Schwab, Homewood, Illinois, Richard D., Irwin, 1978, pp. 234-241.

ELLIG, B.R., "Administering Salaries and Short-Term Incentives", *Compensation Review*, vol. 9, N° 2, 1977, pp. 15-30.

FESTINGER, L., "A Theory of Social Comparison Processes", *Human Relations*, vol. 7, N° 2, 1954, pp. 117-140.

FOSSUM, J.A. et al., "An EDP Monitoring System for Compensation Plan", *Compensation Review*, 2nd quarter 1974, pp. 28-39.

FREEDMAN, S.M. and J.R. MONTANARI, "An Integrative Model of Managerial Reward Allocation", *Academy of Management Review*, vol. 5, N° 3, 1980, pp. 381-390.

HENDERSON, R., *Compensation Management*, Englewood Cliffs, New Jersey, Prentice-Hall, 1989.

HENEMAN, R.L., "Merit Pay Research", *Research in Personnel and Human Resources Management*, vol. 8, 1990, pp. 203-263.

HOMANS, G., *Social Behavior: Its Elementary Forms*, New York, Harcourt, Brace and World, 1961.

KIDDER, L.H., G. BELLETIRIE and E.S. COHN, "Secret Ambitions and Public Performances: The Effects of Anonymity on Reward Allocations Made by Men and Women", *Journal of Experimental Social Psychology*, vol. 13, 1977, pp. 70-80.

LAWLER, E.E., "Managers Perceptions of Their Subordinates Pay and of Their Superiors' Pays", *Personnel Psychology*, vol. 18, 1965, pp. 413-422.

LAWLER, E.E., *Pay and Organizational Effectiveness: A Psychological View*, New York, McGraw-Hill, 1971.

LAWLER, E.E., "Pay for Performance: A Strategic Analysis", in *Compensation and Benefits*, edited by L.R. Gomez-Mejia, Washington, D.C., Bureau of National Affairs, 1989, pp. 136-181.

LAWLER, E.E., "Secrecy About Management Compensation: Are There Hidden Costs?", *California Management Review*, vol. 9, 1966, pp. 11-22.

LAWLER, E.E., "Should Managers' Compensation Be Kept Under Wraps?" *Personnel*, vol. 2, 1965a, pp. 17-20.

LAWLER, E.E., "The Mythology of Management Compensation", *California Management Review*, vol. 9, 1966, pp. 11-22.

LEVENTHAL, G.S., J.W. MICHAELS and C. STANFORD, "Inequity and Interpersonal Conflict: Reward Allocation and Secrecy About Reward as Methods of Preventing Conflict", *Journal of Personality and Social Psychology*, vol. 23, 1972, pp. 88-102.

MERCER (William M. Mercer Limited), *1990-1991 Salary Planning Survey for Non-Union Employees in Canada*, Toronto, 1990a.

MERCER (William M. Mercer Limited), *Mercer's 1991 Global Compensation Planning Report*, Toronto, 1990b.

MEYER, H.E., "A Computer May Be Deciding What You Get Paid", *Fortune*, November, 1973, pp. 168-176.

MILKOVICH, G.T. and P.H. ANDERSON, "Management Compensation and Secrecy Policies", *Personnel Psychology*, vol. 25, 1972, pp. 293-302.

MITCHELL, D.J.B., "Should the Consumer Price Index Determine Wages?", *California Management Review*, Fall, 1982, pp. 5-19.

NASH, A.N. and S.J. CARROLL, *The Management of Compensation*, Monterey, California, Brooks-Cole Publishing Co., 1975.

REIS, H.L. and J. GRUZEN, "On Mediating Equity, Equality and Self-Interest: The Role of Self Perception in Social Exchange", *Journal of Experimental and Social Psychology*, vol. 12, 1976, pp. 497-503.

SCALETTA, P.J., "The Computer as a Threat to Individual Privacy", *Data Management*, January, 1971, pp. 18-23.

SCHUSTER, J.R. and J.A. COLETTI, "Pay Secrecy: Who is For and Against It?" *Academy of Management Journal*, vol. 16, 1973, pp. 35-40.

SIBSON, E.R., *Wages and Salaries: A Handbook for Line Managers*, New York, American Management Association, 1967.

STATISTICS CANADA, *Consumer Price Index Reference Document*, Ottawa, Supply and Services Canada, 1989.

STATISTICS CANADA, *Consumer Price Index*, Ottawa, Supply and Services Canada, February, 1991.

STEVENS, S.S., "Measurement Psychophysics, and Utility, in *Measurement: Definitions and Theories*, edited by C.W. Churchman and P. Ratoosh, New York, Wiley, 1959.

THÉRIAULT, R., *Politiques et pratiques en matière de rémunération globale dans les entreprises au Québec*, Montreal, Les Publications INFORT Inc., 1986.

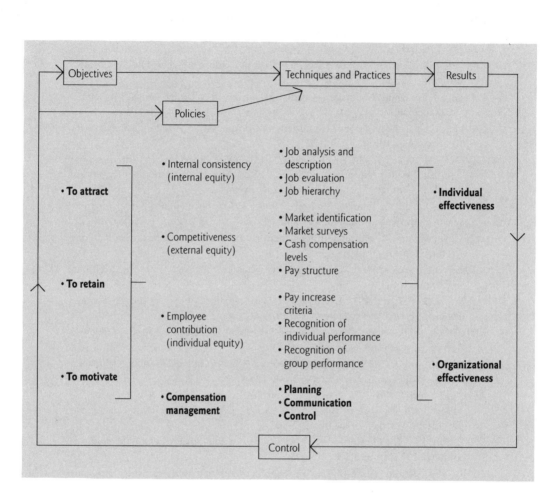

VII

EMPLOYEE BENEFIT PLANS

Regardless of how the employer-employee transaction is viewed, direct or cash compensation (i.e. pay, bonuses, and incentive plans) is an important component of it. Yet indirect compensation, including employee benefits and perquisites, paid time off, and working conditions, is equally important.

Given the contention around what constitutes an employee benefit and what does not, the purpose of employee benefits, the cost and value of their various components, etc., decisions about employeee benefits (indirect compensation) are generally more complex than those about pay.

The importance of indirect compensation within overall compensation is a relatively recent phenomenon. Until the end of the 19th century, cash was the only compensation workers received for their services. Industrialization intensified the old risks surrounding income security, and created new ones. Organizations' increasing productivity led to the adoption of job-security programs as part of benefit plans.

The industrialization process was accompanied by significant social changes, including urbanization and, consequently, greater family dependance on pay. The politicians of the day (like all politicians) did not remain indifferent to this shift in public attitude.

The unionization of large industrial organizations (among others) also played a role in the introduction of various employee benefit plans.

Finally, the role of certain employers in instituting and generalizing particular benefit plans must be mentioned. Concerned with protecting their employees, distinguishing themselves from other employers by offering attractive plans, and retaining a competent efficient workforce, some employers adopted a proactive rather than reactive approach to the various components of indirect compensation.

All this has definitely made managing indirect compensation increasingly complex and costly. What can be said, then, about how such plans are managed, and about their effect on organizational productivity and on how employees respond to their work and to the organization?

Separated form the question of pay until very recently, indirect compensation plans are coming more and more to be considered an integral part of employees' pay. One speaks, therefore, of total compensation rather than, on the one hand, pay and incentives and, on the other, benefits and working conditions.

Chapter 14 identifies and describes the main benefit plans offered, while Chapter 15 describes various factors involved in managing benefit plans, as well as managing total compensation.

TABLE OF CONTENTS

14

EMPLOYEE BENEFIT PLANS: A DESCRIPTION

This chapter begins with a short historical review, followed by a definition and classification of employee benefits, then briefly describes the different plans offered by organizations.

☐ 14.1 Historical Review

The importance of employee (often called "fringe") benefit plans in total compensation is relatively recent. Until late in the 19th century, cash was the only compensation workers received for their services.

The spread of industrialization meant less income security, and was accompanied by major social changes, including the development of urban life and the ensuing greater dependence of families on pay. The politicians of the day, like their contemporary counterparts, sensed the shift in public attitudes. Canada's Old Age Security Act, for example, dates back to 1927; it provided government assistance for senior citizens who were unemployed and in need. The first income protection plan, the Direct Assistance Program, appeared in the 30s.

The Canadian government made its first significant impact on employee benefits almost unwittingly in 1941, when it instituted wage controls and imposed very high taxes on corporate profits to control inflation. As a result, companies introduced "fringe benefits", as they were called at the time, to attract and retain the labour they needed. The presence of unions in large industrial corporations, which could generally afford to pay more, also contributed to the establishment of such plans. As for public income security plans, the Unemployment Insurance Act was passed in 1940, the first benefits paid two years later. Canada's original family allowance plan was enacted in 1944.

Government played an essentially supplementary role in this area until the early 50s. Since then, it has gradually become an incentive role. In 1952, the Old Age Security Plan was transformed into the Old Age Security Act (OAS). Financial need was no longer a criterion; the pensions became payable to all who reached age 70. The minimum age was later reduced to 65 and, in 1967, the Guaranteed Income Supplement (GIS) was introduced. In 1965, Ontario passed the first Canadian legislation on pension benefits, followed by Quebec in 1966, Alberta and the federal government in 1967, and most other provinces since. Around the same time, in 1968, the federal government passed its Medicare Act to replace the 1958 Hospital Insurance and Diagnostic Services Act, and all the provinces followed suit. In 1971, the Unemployment Insurance Act was thoroughly revamped to provide greater accessibility and more generous benefits. For the first time, women became eligible for unemployment insurance benefits while on maternity leave.

This and subsequent legislation had a profound effect on the evolution of income security plans. The role of private enterprise and unions was no longer to initiate in this sphere, but rather to offer and demand complementary employee benefits. Consistency between private and government plans therefore became crucial.

The evolution of employee benefits and particularly income protection plans and governments' role in them, vary considerably from country to country. This is also true of methods of financing: by taxes and by employer and employee contributions. For example, as Belcher and Atchison (1987) point out, Americans have decided to solve the problems of insecurity in an industrial society by relying primarily on private initiative. As a result, unionized employees at large companies in urban centres are relatively well-protected and entitled to considerable paid time off. On the other hand, non-unionized employees working for small businesses have limited protection, some of them, none at all.

14.2 Classification of Employee Benefit Plans

As mentioned in Chapter 1, some elements of total compensation require a cash disbursement by the employer, others do not. The former, in addition to pay and incentive plans, include the principal employee benefit plans (indirect compensation), and other benefits, or perquisites. The elements involving no disbursement consist of payment for time not worked and working conditions, as illustrated in figure 14.1.

Income security benefits generally comprise pension plans and various insurance plans (life, health, disability) provided by most organizations. *Other benefits*, or perquisites, include the automobiles provided for certain employees, employee parking, subsidized meals, tuition fees, financial advice, employee assistance programs, etc.

FIGURE 14.1
Components of Employee Benefit Plans

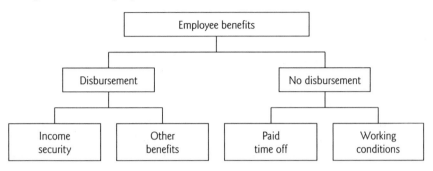

While certain benefits, such as *payment for time not worked* and *working conditions*, involve no additional disbursement, (because, in practice, the cost of these benefits is already included in calculating pay), they remain a significant expense for employers. Payment for time not worked, of which many organizations offer more than the legally required minimum, takes a variety of forms: annual vacations, holidays, special leave, sick leave, maternity and paternity leave, leave for civic duty, bereavement, marriage, etc. The amount of time off has a direct impact on the cost of total compensation for time worked. The same applies to benefits related to working conditions. Some, such as working hours, have a direct effect on compensation for time worked, while others, such as unpaid leave and work schedules, have an indirect effect. Granting unpaid leave, for example, is likely to mean training and developing new employees to replace those on leave, more overtime and, possibly, work of inferior quality.

In brief, while the different employee benefit plans may be divided into public and private schemes, the plans may also be arranged by category, based on the objectives pursued. This chapter adopts the following, generally accepted classification:

1. Income security:
   a) health and accident insurance,
   b) disability benefits,
   c) pension plans,
   d) life insurance,
   e) severance pay;
2. Payment for time not worked:
   a) vacations,
   b) holidays and paid leave;
3. Other benefits (perquisites); and

4. Working conditions.

These benefits are discussed in the order given.

□ 14.3 Income Security

The different forms of income security aim to protect individuals against five major hazards of life. As Magnan (1979) notes, everyone faces the risk of incurring *medical expenses* (illness), of having their income interrupted because of a *disability,* of growing (too!) old and outlasting their savings, of reaching *retirement* age, and of *dying* ("a premature death", as insurers put it). Furthermore, some people are more likely than others to have their *income interrupted by unemployment.* As La Fontaine put it in *The Animals Stricken by the Plague,* "Not all died, but all were afflicted."

The different types of public and private protection against these events are described below.

14.3.1 Health and Accident Insurance

In Canada, medical expenses are covered by two major public plans in each province and territory: hospital and health insurance. (There are also public automobile insurance plans in certain provinces, including Quebec, Ontario, and British Columbia).

Public Hospital Insurance*

Since the 60s, each province and territory has provided hospital insurance. The plans, adopted by provincial governments, are funded with federal assistance. Under the Canada Health Act, which took effect April 1, 1984, the federal government may impose financial sanctions on provinces that fail to provide reasonable access to health services, or set up any sort of obstacles. These plans cover hospital expenses in a public ward, as well as a variety of related services, including ordinary nursing, use of the operating room, laboratory services, or emergency treatment in out-patient clinics. Patients must pay for a semi-private or private room if they wish one; the rate varies by hospital and by province. (This expense is often covered by private hospital insurance provided by employers.) All provinces cover, in varying degrees, expenses incurred outside their territory.

---

*   The description of the various public plans is based primarily on Coward (1988) and Mercer Limited (1991).

Public Health Insurance Plans

Every province and territory also has a health insurance plan, covering all doctors' fees incurred at home, at the doctor's office, or at the hospital. The plans also encompass a variety of other forms of care, although the specifics vary from one province to the next, including vision care, dental care, prostheses, and orthopedic devices. Coverage also applies outside the insured's province or territory.

Financing Public Insurance

Hospital and health insurance premiums are mandatory in some provinces. In Quebec and Ontario, they are paid entirely by employers, who contribute 3.75% and 1.95% of gross pay (1991), respectively. In Ontario, a lower percentage applies to payrolls of less than $400,000. Contributions for self-employed workers and public servants in these two provinces are taken from personal income tax revenues. Other provinces, such as Alberta and British Columbia, require residents to contribute directly.

Private Medical Assistance Plans

In addition, virtually all Canadian employers (Pay Research Bureau, 1990) offer their employees medical assistance plans, whose coverage goes beyond that offered by public plans. These plans generally reimburse expenses incurred by employees and their dependents for prescription drugs, semi-private or private hospital rooms, paramedical services, nursing or private-duty nursing care, prostheses and other medical equipment, vision care required as the result of an accident, and sometimes dental care following an accident.

Employees usually become eligible for these plans after reaching a certain level of seniority. Most plans are mandatory (Pay Research Bureau, 1990), and their costs are borne entirely by the employer in slightly more than 50% of cases.

Dental Care Plans

The vast majority of organizations offer dental care plans separate from extended medical coverage (Pay Research Bureau, 1990). These plans have become increasingly popular in recent years, particularly as a result of collective bargaining. Whereas only 40% of Canadian employers offered dental care plans in 1978, that figure rose to 67% in 1980, 83% in 1982, and 90% in 1989 (Pay Research Bureau, 1983 and 1990).

Dental care plan coverage falls into three main categories:

1. basic preventive and minor restorative care: check-ups, cleaning and scaling, x-rays, extractions, fillings, space maintainers, endodontal and periodontal work;
2. major restorative care: crowns, inlays, fixed bridges, and dentures; and
3. orthodontic care.

Almost 90% of plans cover major restorative care in addition to basic preventive care, and about 60% cover orthodontic expenses.

These plans are generally compulsory although, in some cases, coverage may be waived when employees are covered under their spouse's plan. With mandatory plans, the cost of basic preventive care is fully paid by the employer in about 50% of cases; that figure drops to 40% for major restorative and 30% for orthodontic care. In most cases, there is no deductible for basic preventive and major restorative care. However, a deductible applies in most cases for orthodontic care (Pay Research Bureau, 1990).

Vision Care Plans

At present, very few employers offer employees a vision care plan; however, the percentage of those who do has been increasing over the years.

Like dental care, vision care plans are affected by the phenomenon of antiselection. This means that, when these plans are optional, they are more likely to be selected by employees who need them than by those who do not, with the result being higher unit costs for those who do enrol. Membership in these plans is, therefore, generally mandatory.

Vision care plans normally cover a limited range of services: eye examinations (if not covered by provincial health insurance), eyeglass frames, and lenses. The cost of frames and lenses and of contact lenses, is subject to a ceiling of $100 or $200 every 12 or 24 months.

14.3.2 Disability Benefits

A disability may be short-term (temporary) or long-term (permanent); it may also be partial (the employee can handle certain jobs or duties) or total (the individual cannot work at any job). The type of disability is a factor in both public and private income protection plans. Some cover certain types of disability but not others, and vice versa.

Public Disability Plans

At least five public plans have provisions covering disability: the Canada or Quebec Pension Plan (C/QPP), the Unemployment Insurance Act, administered by Employment and Immigration Canada, the automobile insurance act in certain provinces, workers' compensation legislation and, in some provinces, the social assistance act. Most of these plans will be dealt with in the context of their primary objectives (retirement, death, or unemployment), so they are only briefly described in this section.

To qualify as disabled under the C/QPP, a contributor must be wholly incapable of performing the duties of any gainful employment; the disability must be presumed to be terminal or indefinite in length. Those who meet this and other eligibility criteria (i.e. who have contributed for at least five of the last ten years, etc.) are entitled to monthly benefits beginning in the fourth month following the onset of the disability. The plans provide benefits for both contributors and their children.

Under certain conditions, the Unemployment Insurance Act also provides employees, disabled because of illness or non-occupational injury, with benefits for up to 15 full weeks.

In some provinces, particularly Quebec, the automobile insurance act provides all drivers, passengers, cyclists, or pedestrians, disabled as a result of bodily injury suffered in a traffic accident, with non-taxable income replacement benefits of up to 90% of net income, up to an annually indexed gross income ceiling. The Régie de l'assurance automobile, which administers the act in Quebec, may also take any necessary measures and incur any expenses it considers appropriate to further rehabilitation, and to facilitate the victim's return to normal life and re-entry into the job market.

Every Canadian province has workers' compensation legislation, which provides non-taxable disability benefits (based on a percentage of insurable earnings) that vary with the nature and expected duration of the disability. In British Columbia, Prince Edward Island, and Manitoba, these benefits are indexed to the cost of living and set at 75% of eligible gross income. Elsewhere, they amount to 90% of eligible net income. The disability must be caused by a work-related accident or illness.

Finally, in certain provinces, including Quebec, social assistance legislation provides welfare benefits based on the difference between what a family or single person needs and their income, provided they are not excluded because of the value of their assets. In other words, if the total benefits received by the disabled person from various public and, if applicable, private plans are below a specified ceiling, social assistance payments make up the difference.

Table 14.1 summarizes the different arrangements.

TABLE 14.1
Disability Coverage* of Public Income Protection Plans

Type of Disability	Cause	Plan
Temporary	Traffic accident	Automobile insurance act**
	Work-related accident or illness	Workers' compensation legislation
	Other	Unemployment Insurance Act
Permanent	Traffic accident	Automobile insurance act
	Work-related accident or illness	Workers' compensation legislation
	Other	C/QPP

* If disability benefits fall short of a specified ceiling, in some provinces the individual may apply for social assistance.

** Some provinces, including Alberta and the Maritime provinces, have no automobile insurance act; their residents must obtain private coverage.

Financing Public Plans

Public plans that protect income in the event of a disability are financed in different ways. The tax treatment of benefits also varies. The C/QPP is financed equally by employer and employee. Contributions are tax-deductible and benefits are taxable. In the case of Unemployment Insurance, employers contribute 1.4 times the employee's premium. In 1991, contributions amounted to $3.92 and $2.80, respectively, for each $100 of insurable weekly earnings. Benefits are taxable and contributions are tax-deductible. Automobile insurance is generally financed by contributions included in vehicle registration fees and fees for obtaining and renewing a driver's license. These contributions are not tax-deductible and benefits are not taxable. Benefits under workers' compensation legislation are financed solely by employer contributions. Benefits are not taxable, and contributions are tax-deductible for the employer. Finally, social assistance payments are financed by tax revenue.

Private Disability Plans

Private plans to protect income in the event of disability may be classified according to their duration: short-term (ordinarily less than one year), referred to as "salary insurance" or long-term (one year or more).

Short-term Disability

Short-term disability plans guarantee a defined amount in the event of a disability caused by a non-occupational accident or illness. Many of the plans are self-funded, in the sense that the benefits are paid as though they were salary. In some cases, employers pay premiums to an insurance company, which pays the benefits. Employees normally receive benefits at the same frequency as their pay, usually for a period of 26 weeks.

The benefits vary, depending on the types of employees covered. For office personnel, they often amount to full pay. For production and maintenance workers, they generally range from 66⅔% to 80% of pay. Benefits from these plans are usually coordinated with benefits from public plans.

Sick-leave Plan

Many organizations have an official sick-leave plan to cover short-term disability payments. The number of days allowed normally depends on the illness. In some cases, sick leave accumulates at the rate of one-half day to two days for each month of service. Employees are rarely allowed to accumulate sick leave for more than one year.

At the end of each year, employees may be paid for their unused sick leave. This practice, however, has been criticized. Doyel and McMillan (1980) make an interesting suggestion. They recommend pooling sick leave, so that if an employee is entitled to 10 days a year, that number is reduced to seven and the three remaining days are placed in a common pool. This pooling, which is managed by an employee committee, helps employees with greater needs.

Long-term Disability

Disability insurance plans are generally used to protect income in the event of a long-term disability. The cost is generally paid by employers. Over 90% of organizations offered this type of plan in 1990, compared to about 75% in 1980 (Pay Research Bureau, 1990).

Normally, benefits amount to 60% or 70% of the employee's gross pay, and there is almost always a fixed ceiling. The waiting period before plan benefits may be received is coordinated with short-term disability coverage, and often covers 26 weeks. Ordinarily, for a total disability, benefits are paid until normal retirement age. For a temporary or partial disability, they are paid for up to two years. Most organizations insure all employees, regardless of category.

14.3.3 Pension Plans

Pension plans are undoubtedly the most complex of all employee benefits.

In this discussion, a distinction is drawn between true pension plans, retirement allowances, and Old Age Security. These three types of plan are described below.

Pension Plans

Here again, there are both public (statutory) and private plans.

Public Pension Plans

The Canada Pension Plan (CPP) (applicable to all provinces except Quebec) and the Quebec Pension Plan (QPP) took effect January 1, 1966. Both are mandatory public plans, which pay benefits in the event of retirement, death or, as mentioned above, disability.

At present, benefits are limited to an income replacement rate of about 25% of the average industrial wage.

The plans are financed equally by employer and employee contributions, at the rate of 2.3% of that portion of earnings between the basic annual exemption and the Year's Maximum Pensionable Earnings (YMPE). The basic annual exemption is 10% of the YMPE, which stands, in 1991, at $30,500. The YMPE is indexed annually to increases in the Average Industrial Wage.

In practice, at this rate of contribution, paid by employers and employees, the plans are only partially capitalized. Since the ultimate objective is to ensure sufficient funds to cover two years of pension benefits, a schedule for increasing contributions has been drawn up. The schedule, which extends to 2011, must be reviewed every five years. The existing law provides for employer and employee contributions to increase at the rate of 0.075% of pensionable earnings from 1992 to 1996 inclusive.

Pension benefits, which amount to 25% of average pensionable earnings, as mentioned above, are paid starting at age 65, regardless of the pensioner's subsequent earnings from employment. They are indexed every year, according to increases in the cost of living. The plan allows for benefits, reduced by 6% per year of anticipation, to be drawn as of age 60, or increased by 6% per year of postponment if retirement is postponed until age 70. The benefits are taxable, while employer contributions are tax-deductible and employee contributions give rise to a tax credit.

Private Pension Plans

Private pension plans may be divided into registered pension plans and Registered Retirement Savings Plans (RRSP).

● Registered Pension Plans

Private group pension plans (also called sometimes "supplemental pension plans") offered by employers are governed by a body of relatively strict and complex laws. Under the Canadian constitution, most pension plans come under provincial jurisdiction. Accordingly, all provinces, except for British Columbia, Prince Edward Island, and New Brunswick, have passed similar pension plan legislation. The terms and conditions, financing, and administration of private pension plans are regulated and must comply with certain standards. Most of the provincial legislation was thoroughly revamped in the 80s. British Columbia has tabled a bill on private pension plans, which is scheduled to take effect January 1, 1993. Prince Edward Island and New Brunswick have both passed pension plan legislation, but no dates have been set for implementation. The federal government has also passed a law governing employees under its jurisdiction.

In addition to complying with provincial legislation, pension plans must also be registered with Revenue Canada for tax purposes. By agreement, such registration also applies for Revenue Quebec. This section of the federal Income Tax Act was also overhauled in the late 80s, and certain new measures adopted in June 1990 took effect on January 1, 1991. Others will come into force later. Quebec adjusted its legislation at the same time as the federal government.

Generally speaking, the plans are governed by an administrative committee, usually formed of representatives chosen by the employer. In Quebec, however, the plans must be administered by a pension committee consisting of at least three members: two elected by members at an annual meeting and a third independent party. There is no limit on employer representatives. The role of the administrative or pension committee is to administer the plan and oversee application of both legislative and plan provisions. More specifically, they must provide members with personal pension statements every year, produce the information required by the provincial agency that regulates pension plans, oversee management of the pension fund, have actuarial reports prepared as required every three years, make sure benefits are paid, etc. In Quebec, the pension committee must also convene an annual meeting of members, draw up the agenda, chair the meeting, etc.

The participation rate in private pension plans offered by employers stood at 37% in Canada in 1988 (Statistics Canada, 1990). Yet if workers who cannot participate in such plans are excluded, i.e. the self-employed, unpaid homemakers, and the unemployed, the participation rate rises to 44.9%, or 37.2% for women and 51% for men. This rate varies little from province to province, with the exception of Prince Edward Island, where the rate is 35.4%.

The situation in the public sector differs greatly from that in the private sector. Not only are practically all public servants covered, but they are also protected by different provisions with regard to funding agencies, benefit levels, employee contribution rates, retirement age, and indexation provisions during retirement.

The rate of participation in pension plans offered by employers also depends on whether or not employees are unionized. In 1986, 75% of active unionized workers belonged to a pension plan, compared to only 46% of all active workers.

Funding Private Pension Plans

Funding a pension plan involves accumulating assets, made up of employer contributions, employee contributions (if any), and investment income, so that the plan can pay the promised benefits. As Coward (1988) notes, most plans are underwritten with a view to:

— ensuring that employees who belong to the plan receive the promised pensions;
— properly controlling the plan's financial position and avoiding excessive increases in plan costs;
— taking advantage of a significant tax shelter; and
— complying with applicable legislation.

Since pension plan membership implies contributing now in order to receive benefits in 20, 30, or 40 years, the cost of the plan depends on the rate of return earned on the fund and the age of members at death.

As an indication of the importance of rate of return, a simple mathematical formula may be used to calculate the approximate time required for an amount to double in value: 72 divided by the rate of return. For example, at a compound rate of 7%, a pension fund's assets will double in 10 years (72/7).

As for age at death, obviously, the longer pensioners live after their retirement, the longer they receive benefits and the more expensive the plan becomes. According to the mortality tables currently in use in Canada, at age 65, the average life expectancy of a man is 15 years, and of a woman, 19 years. For purposes of actuarial valuations, a different mortality table may be used for each sex. However, some provinces prohibit sex-based discrimination in paying benefits and assessing employee contributions.

A plan's cost depends on other variables, in addition to rate of return and the age of members at death. These include retirement age, employee turnover rate, pre-retirement mortality rate, rate of pay increases, inflation, and the percentage of men and women in the plan.

These variables, given their nature, may also be expected to change over the next 20, 30, or 40 years. The actuarial assumptions concerning them are of tremendous importance in funding a plan. Supplemental pension plan legislation requires that each plan be valuated every three years, primarily to ensure that it has sufficient funds to meet its obligations. Any shortfall must be covered by the employer over a period of 5 to 15 years, depending on the type of deficit. A surplus may be used to improve the plan, or to reduce the employer's pension fund contributions. Plan provisions regarding surplus, however, must also be considered.

Financing Pension Plans

Pension plans may be distinguished by the source and method of their financing.

As Table 14.2 illustrates, 54% of plans, covering some 70% of members, are contributory, i.e. their costs are covered by employers and employees. The table also reveals a marked difference between public and private sector.

Whereas virtually all public sector employees contribute to a pension plan together with their employer, half of private plans are non-contributory, meaning the employer alone contributes. This difference between the two sectors holds if the number of members is taken into account. In fact, 55% of private sector employees covered by a pension plan do not contribute to it; the cost is borne entirely by employers.

Contributory plans have certain advantages: they are less costly for employers and make employees more aware of their pensions. On the other hand, non-contributory plans are easier to manage. Under the new laws, employers must contribute for at least 50% of the pension from a contributory plan.

As Coward (1988) points out, contributory plans are more popular in Canada than in the United States, because in Canada employee contributions are tax-deductible. Moreover, social security contributions are much higher in the United States, which means that employees may be more reluctant to accept an additional payroll deduction.

With respect to the financing method, Table 14.2 indicates that pension funds are managed by insurance companies in 73% of cases. However, these plans cover only 14% of all plan members. In other words, insurance companies primarily administer the pension funds of small plans. In terms of number of members, the lion's share in fact goes to trustees, mainly trust companies and individual trustees. Finally, 15% of members are covered by plans funded through a government's consolidated revenue fund.

Eligibility

Employers are not obliged to offer their employees a pension plan. If they do, they must comply with existing legislation. Before the new provincial pension legislation was adopted, most plans specified a minimum length of service and, sometimes, a minimum age before employees could join the plan. The amendments passed in certain provinces, including Ontario, Manitoba, Alberta, and Nova Scotia, as well as by the federal government for employees under its jurisdiction, require employees in the categories covered by the plan to become eligible after no more than two years of service,

TABLE 14.2
Characteristics of Employer Pension Plans

Characteristics	Public Sector		Private Sector		All	
	Plans %	Members %	Plans %	Members %	Plans %	Members %
1. Financing						
a) Source:						
Contributory	94.3	99.6	51.8	45.5	53.7	69.8
Non-Contributory	5.7	0.4	48.2	54.5	46.3	30.2
b) Method:						
Insurance company					73.0	14.0
Trustee					24.9	67.0
Government consolidated revenue fund					0.1	16.0
2. Integration with public plans (Canada and Quebec)						
Integrated plans (all)	40.3	90.7	23.1	46.2	23.9	66.2
Plans with partially defined benefits					54.0	89.0
Defined contribution plans (money purchase)					10.0	25.0
3. Type of plan						
Defined benefit					32.0	71.4
– final average pay					18.6	60.1
– career average pay					13.4	11.3
Flat benefit					7.0	20.0
Defined contribution plans (money purchase)					59.8	7.6
Other (hybrid or defined contribution, etc.)					1.1	0.9
4. Benefit Rate						
Defined-benefit plans 2% or more per year of service	–	98.6	–	47.6	–	78.4
Flat-benefit plans						
– monthly pension of less than $10 per year of service					28.8	12.3
– de 10.00 to $14.99					28.9	18.7
– $15.00 to $19.99					15.7	14.3
– $20.00 to $24.99					6.2	14.8
– $25.00 to $49.99					5.3	10.6
– $50.00 and over					3.4	11.6
5. Contribution rate						
Less than 5.00%	–	0.6	–	24.1	28.4	9.1
5.00% to 5.99%	–	12.8	–	44.5	46.7	24.2
6.00% to 6.99%	–	14.7	–	10.3	4.2	13.1
7.00% and over	–	70.7	–	1.6	3.0	45.8
Other (e.g. fixed amount)	–	1.1	–	19.5	17.7	7.8
6. Normal retirement age						
60 years	7.1	16.5	7.6	2.6	7.6	8.8
65 years	86.6	63.5	90.0	93.3	89.9	80.0
Other (service plus age, etc.)	6.4	20.0	2.3	4.1	2.5	11.2

SOURCE: Compiled from Statistics Canada (1990) data.

regardless of age. Part-time employees are eligible if their compensation reaches a certain percentage (generally 35%) of YMPE, or, in the case of Ontario, if they have worked for 700 hours in each of two consecutive calendar years. In Quebec, employees in the categories covered by the plan must become eligible at the beginning of the calendar year following the one in which their compensation reaches 35% of the YMPE, or in which they worked 700 hours. Membership may be compulsory or optional, depending on a plan's provisions (except for Manitoba, where membership is mandatory).

Integration with Public (Statutory) Plans

The question of integrating or coordinating private with public (statutory) plans first arose with the introduction of the C/QPP. Plan coordination entails a harmonization of benefits or contributions, or both, in relation to all or part of the YMPE. It may also involve deducting all or part of the C/QPP benefits from the pension. Before new legislation was introduced, the coordination could also apply to Old Age Security payments. This however, is no longer permitted for the years following pension reform, except in the case of plans subject to federal law.

While coordination may take many forms, the most popular method (Coward, 1988) consists of applying lower pension and contribution rates to the portion of annual pay below the YMPE, and higher ones to the portion above the YMPE. For example, an employee's pension for each year of service might be 1.3% of pay up to YMPE, and 2% of pay above the YMPE. Contributions might be 3.5% of pay up to the YMPE, and 5% of pay above the YMPE.

As Table 14.2 illustrates, nearly all plans covering public sector employees are integrated with the applicable public (statutory) plan (C/QPP). In the private sector, this is true of only 46% of members and 23% of plans.

Types of Plan

Most pension plans may be divided into three types: defined benefit, defined contribution, and hybrid (Coward, 1988).

With a defined benefit plan, the employer agrees to pay a predetermined pension and assumes final responsibility for funding these pensions. Pension benefits may be completely defined (flat benefit), i.e. the amount is specified in advance (for example, $20 a month for each year of service) or partially fixed (unit benefit), in which case they represent a percentage of pay (for example, 2% of pay multiplied by number of years of service). In the latter case, different formulas are used to determine pay: final average earnings (e.g. the average earnings for the last three years), best years' average (e.g. the highest average for three consecutive years), career average, etc. As table 14.2 indicates, career average is used almost as frequently as final average,

TABLE 14.3
Pension Plan Types

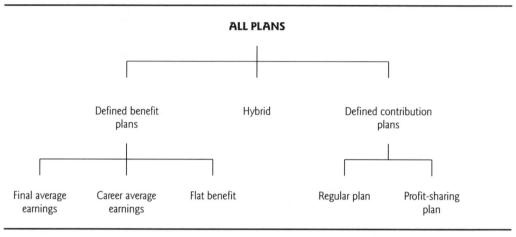

SOURCE: Coward (1988, p. 12).

although the latter applies to the largest number of plan members. This statistic is primarily skewed by public sector plans. Whereas the pensions of 94% of public sector members are based on final average pay, the corresponding figure for the private sector is only 32%.

With a defined contribution (money purchase) plan, the employer and, if applicable, the employee agree to contribute a predetermined amount each year. The money is used to fund pensions that vary in amount, depending on the size of contributions, the pension fund's investment income, and economic conditions at retirement. The amount of the contributions may be predetermined (e.g. 5% of pay (regular)) or based on the organization's net income (profit sharing). While these types of plans are fairly widespread, as Table 14.2 indicates, they apply to very few members and are offered primarily by small organizations.

Finally, there is a third type of pension plan, whose characteristics combine those of defined benefit plans and defined contribution plans. They are appropriately called mixed, or hybrid, plans. One example is the "service plus annuity" plan, in which the employer pays the entire pension based on service, while employee contributions are used to purchase a pension additional to the service pension.

Benefit Rates

Given the nature of defined contribution plans, it is not possible to compile statistics on their benefit rates. Statistics are only available for plans with partially or completely defined benefits.

The rate for partially defined benefit plans is generally 2% of pay for each year of service. Under Canadian tax law, the amount of pension paid by a plan may not exceed 2% per year of service multiplied by average of the highest-paid three consecutive years of earnings, with a ceiling of $1,722 per year of service until 1994, inclusive. Until then, the annual maximum pensionable earnings for a pension plan with a 2% benefit rate is $86,111 ($86,111 x 2% = $1,722). After 1994, the ceiling will be indexed to the Average Industrial Wage.

As for flat benefit plans, Table 14.2 reveals that, for almost 50% of members, monthly benefits are less than $20 per year of service. It should be pointed out that this type of plan is usually negotiated for unionized employees.

Contribution Rates

As mentioned earlier, almost all public sector and close to 50% of private sector plan members make individual contributions to their pensions. These contributions are generally based on a percentage of their pay.

Table 14.2 indicates that, for almost 45% of private sector plan members, this percentage ranges from 5% to 6% of pay (usually 5%) above the YMPE, and is 7% or more for 70% of public sector plan members.

Since 1974, there has been a definite trend toward increased contributions. While only 1% of plan members contributed over 7% of their pay in 1974, by 1988, over 45% did. This increase is primarily the result of contributions to certain large public sector plans.

Retirement Age

Normal Retirement

Normal retirement age means the age specified by the plan when members may retire and begin receiving their full, unreduced pension. It represents the age at which most members retire. For many years in Canada, that age has generally been 65. As Table 14.2 indicates, this is particularly true of the private sector. In the public sector, a relatively large number of plan members are entitled to a full pension at age 60, or according to some other formula, such as the sum of age and years of service.

In the past, the normal retirement age often differed by sex, e.g. 65 for men and 60 for women. Today, the law considers this practice discriminatory.

Setting a normal retirement age does not necessarily mean that an employer is allowed to force employees to retire when they reach it. Mandatory retirement has come under increasing fire, and has been abolished in certain provinces. Some plans, however, start paying pensions at the normal retirement age (or at the deferred retirement age discussed below), even if the employee continues working.

Early Retirement

Nearly all plans have a provision for early retirement, which allows employees to receive a proportionately reduced pension before normal retirement age.

Such benefits represent the actuarial equivalent of the full pension payable at normal retirement age, or the pension may be reduced by a fixed percentage (generally 0.5% or 0.25% a month) for each month or year preceding the normal retirement date.

The recent pension reforms give all employees the right to take early retirement 10 years before their normal retirement age. If the normal retirement age is 65, an employee may take early retirement at 55. The pension in such cases must be no less than the actuarial equivalent of the amount payable at the normal retirement date.

Under new tax legislation, a full pension may be paid in the event of early retirement to members:

– who have reached age 60;
– who have at least 30 years of service;
– whose age and years of service with the employer total 80; or
– who have a total, permanent disability.

More generous rules may apply under certain conditions.

Deferred Retirement

Many plans allow members to continue accumulating credits after their normal retirement date and to receive a higher pension when they actually retire. In other plans, the deferred pension may be the actuarial equivalent of what would be received at normal retirement age. In Canada, in 1988, 98% of plans covering 92% of members allowed retirement to be deferred beyond the normal age. Tax laws, however, stipulate that retirement may not be deferred beyond age 71. Members must begin receiving their pension benefits at that age, although they may continue working.

Death Benefits

Death benefits are paid in two instances: death before, and death after, retirement.

Before the legislative amendments of the 80s and early 90s, no plan was obliged to provide benefits other than reimbursement of employee contributions, with interest, in the event of death before retirement. However, a vast majority of public sector plans and a number of major private sector plans paid the surviving spouse a pension, or reimbursed the employer's, along with the employee's, contributions. Under the new legislation, in most provinces, the total amount of pension accumulated after passage of the applicable law must be paid to the spouse (or to the estate if there is no spouse) in the form of a pension or equivalent lump sum. In certain provinces, including Quebec and Ontario, the present value of the pension paid to the spouse must be 100% of the discounted value that would have been payable to the member on the date of the member's death. Elsewhere, such as Alberta, that figure may be 60%.

In the event of death during retirement, the new legislation provides for a spouse's pension equal to at least 60% of the member's pension while alive. The percentage differs in some provinces, such as Manitoba (66 2/3%) and Saskatchewan (50%).

Termination of Employment

Along with indexation, which is discussed in the following section, one of the most serious problems faced by plan members until the late 80s was termination of employment.

Until that time, most federal and provincial legislations in Canada stipulated than only employees at least 45 years old and with a minimum of 10 years of plan membership were obliged to leave their contributions in a pension fund and receive a deferred pension. Employees who failed to meet the minimal conditions when their employment was terminated were entitled to the return of their own contributions only. They were not entitled to their employer's contributions, unless the plan had more generous provisions. Individuals who changed employers often might contribute to plans throughout their career, yet in some cases be entitled to only a very low, if any, pension (if, for example, the plans were non-contributory).

The new legislative measures generally require pensions accumulated after the reform date to be vested after two years of plan membership. Manitoba stipulates two, and Alberta, five years of service. The provisions for vesting and locking in of pensions accumulated before the reform remain the same, i.e. generally 10 years of plan membership and age 45.

Inflation/Indexation

In Canada, in 1988, few private pension plans contained an automatic indexation of benefits clause. In the few that did, the clause was usually based on the Consumer Price Index (CPI). These few plans covered over 33% of plan members, most of whom (67%) contributed to public sector plans. The corresponding figure for the private sector is less than 8%. In most cases, indexation was only partial (Statistics Canada, 1990).

Since the early 70s, considerable public attention has focused on inflation and the erosion of purchasing power. The need for protection is felt for pensioners, who are more vulnerable.

Different solutions to this problem have been proposed over the years (cf., among others, Cofirentes +, 1977; Calvert, 1977; and Pesando, 1978). By January 1990, only Ontario had announced its intention of indexing pension benefits based on inflation. As of early 1991, however, the formula had not yet been established. In the late 80s, certain large negotiated plans, including those in the pulp and paper, automotive, and aviation industries, though not required to do so, adopted partial pension indexation clauses, based on the CPI, for a limited period.

There are other indexation methods besides the automatic one based on the CPI. For example, monthly pensions may be increased from time to time, with no guarantee of future increases. This type of pension revaluation is popular with employers, because it enables them to control costs. The formula allows them to consider the inflation rate, the organization's financial position, and changes in social security plans.

● Registered Retirement Savings Plans (RRSPs)

A Registered Retirement Savings Plan (RRSP) is a personal retirement savings plan that an employee may contribute to, even while belonging to a group pension plan offered by an employer. However, employees must deduct the value assigned by Revenue Canada to the employer's plan (the "pension adjustment") from the amount of their eligible contributions. There are both individual and group RRSPs. The latter are essentially a set of individual RRSPs with a common administration. Employees may contribute to their group RRSP through regular payroll deductions to benefit from immediate tax breaks. Given the increasing complexity of registered pension plan legislation, group RRSPs are growing in popularity, especially as an alternative to small pension plans.

According to Statistics Canada (1990), these plans have increased significantly since 1957, when the Income Tax Act first allowed individuals to deduct RRSP contributions from their taxable income.

According to the same source, since 1977, the amount of RRSP contributions has exceeded the total amount of contributions paid by employees to all employer-sponsored pension plans. In 1987, about 40% of RRSP contributors also contributed to a pension plan offered by their employer.

For employees, RRSP contributions are an attractive alternative to voluntary contributions to their employer's group pension plan. For the self-employed, an RRSP is an outstanding means of saving for retirement.

An RRSP offers employees more flexibility than a group pension plan in terms of the availability of funds, contributions, investments, or types of income at maturity. Individuals may also deduct contributions to their spouse's RRSP from their own income.

Bill C-52, "An Act to amend the Income Tax Act and related Acts", passed June 27, 1990, made major amendments to the tax treatment of retirement savings. The new rules aimed to eliminate inequities among taxpayers, some of whom had been enjoying more advantageous tax breaks than others because of the type of plan to which they contributed. The law set a ceiling of 18% of income, subject to an absolute dollar limit, on the amount of tax-deductible retirement savings. The 18% figure is the product of a number of studies. Based on trends in pay and return on investment, persons whose active working life spans 35 years must save 18% of their pay each year to receive a pension of 70% of the average of their final years of pay, which will be protected against inflation and will provide benefits for a surviving spouse.

To determine how much they may contribute to an RRSP each year, employees must know the value of pension adjustment (PA). Employers calculate the PA, and every fall Revenue Canada confirms the maximum RRSP contribution. The PA is the estimated value of benefits credited to the employee's account for membership in a pension plan or deferred profit-sharing plan (DPSP), if applicable. The PA considers not only contributions to a pension plan, but also the value of benefits accumulated during the year. Employees who do not belong to a pension plan have a PA of 0. Employees who belong to a money purchase plan have a PA equal to the total of their own and their employer's contributions. In the case of a DPSP, the PA equals the employer's contributions to the plan on behalf of the employee. For a defined benefit pension plan, the following formula is used to calculate the PA:

PA = (9 × value of pension accumulated during the year) − $1,000

The factor 9 is based on the assumption that one dollar of pension income per year of service is equivalent to $9 in annual contributions, if a plan has a number of supplementary benefits such as pension indexation and survivor benefits. To receive a pension of $100 per year of service at retirement, it is assumed that a person will have to contribute $900 a year for their entire working life. Many private pension plans, however, have much less generous supplementary benefits than those assumed by the factor 9. To reduce the discrepancy caused by variations in supplementary benefits, the $1,000 reduction is applied. Employees whose plans have generous benefits are therefore at an advantage.

Table 14.4 provides an example of how to calculate the PA.

A person's maximum annual RRSP contribution equals their income multiplied by 18%, subject to a dollar ceiling, minus their PA. The annual ceiling on contributions of $11,500 in 1991 is scheduled to rise by $1,000

TABLE 14.4
Pension Adjustment (PA) Calculation

Assumptions: – Defined benefit: 1.3% of pay up to YMPE
2% of pay above YMPE
– Annual income: $55,000
Pension accumulated during the year:

1.3% × $28,900*	= $376
2% × ($55,000 − $28,900)	= 522
	$898

PA: ($898 × 9) − $1,000 = $7,082

* YMPE in 1990.

a year until 1995. Increases for 1996 and beyond will be pegged to the Average Industrial Wage. Potential contributions not made during a year may be carried forward indefinitely (subject to a maximum amount). Taking the example in Table 14.4, and assuming that the employee's actual earnings amounted to $55,000, the potential RRSP contribution in 1991 would be:

($55,000 × 18%) − $7,082 = $2,818

If the employee contributes only $1,000 instead of the $2,818 to which he or she is entitled, the following year a contribution of $1,818 more than the ceiling for that year will be allowed. This carry-forward was not permitted before 1991.

● Supplemental Executive Retirement Plans (SERPs)

Since 1976, the Income Tax Act had allowed payment of a maximum annual pension of about $60,000, or $1,715 per year of service for a 35-year career ($1,715 x 35 = $60,025). This ceiling will not increase before 1995, aside from a technical adjustment raising it to $1,722 in 1992. Further increases will be based on the Average Industrial Wage. The maximum pensionable earnings are $85,750 for a plan that provides for annual pension accrual based on 2% (the maximum allowed) of the average of the highest paid three years for each year of service, to a limit of 35. As a result, executives whose annual pay exceeds that level have increasingly less protection as their income rises. Table 14.5 illustrates this situation.

The capacity of pension plans to pay senior executives adequate pensions has decreased considerably since 1976, when this ceiling was set. To deal with this situation, some organizations have established a supplemental executive retirement plan (SERP). A Mercer survey found that 70% of major Canadian organizations have a SERP (Zilli and Connor, 1990).

TABLE 14.5
Effective Percentage of Pension Payable by Pay Level

Assumptions: – Pension: 2% of final average earnings per year of service
– 25 years of service
– Objective: pension equal to 50% of final average earnings

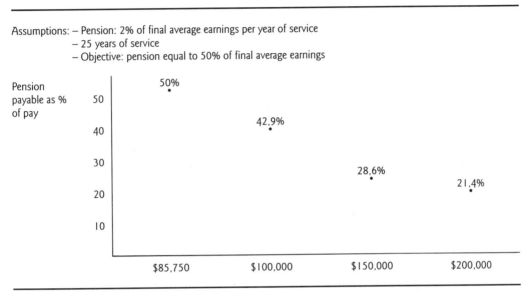

SOURCE: Blais and Magnan (1989).

In general, a SERP is a promise made by the employer to pay an executive, for example, a pension equal to a percentage (e.g. 2%) of average or final pay multiplied by years of service, with amounts payable under the registered pension plan subtracted from the result. A SERP may be funded or unfunded. In the latter case, no funds are set aside for the SERP, and payments are drawn from the organization's current revenue. Most SERPs are of this type, primarily because the tax implications for the employer can increase their cost. Yet executives may be offered a certain level of security, in the form of letters of credit, insurance policies, special appropriations of assets, or guarantees from a parent company (Mercer, 1990).

Retirement Allowance

A retirement allowance program, whether in the form of a severance bonus or severance pay, is in no sense a pension plan. Rather, it represents a payment by an employer in recognition of an employee's record of service or for the loss of a job. This allowance may be paid when an employee retires, or when employment is terminated, even if the employee goes to work for another employer. The payment is generally a gratuity.

Tax legislation allows employers to deduct the amount of a retirement allowance from income, as long as the amount is reasonable under the circumstances.

Employees must include severance pay in their taxable income, unless they elect to defer taxation (subject to certain limits) by transferring the money into a pension plan sponsored by their employer or, more often, into an RRSP.

Old Age Security

Canada's elderly are financially supported by a three-tiered system:

- Old Age Security (OAS) and Guaranteed Income Supplement (GIS) programs;
- the contributory C/QPP based on employment income and covering all workers; and
- private pension plans offered by employers, Registered Retirement Savings Plans, and other forms of personal savings.

In Canada, as in most other countries, in addition to their other pension income, individuals are entitled to a monthly OAS pension at age 65, regardless of their financial resources. To be eligible, they must meet certain minimal residence criteria.

In its present form, the Canadian plan dates back to 1952. Monthly benefits are indexed every quarter according to increases in the CPI. A few years ago, a provision was adopted to recover the pension from individuals whose income exceeds a certain level; the ceiling is $51,765 in 1991.

In addition to the Old Age Security pension, individuals whose financial position so warrants may receive benefits from GIS. This plan, which took effect January 1, 1967, pays benefits to everyone over age 65 who receives an OAS pension and whose financial resources are below a certain limit. Benefits are reduced by $1 for each $2 of income, excluding the OAS. GIS payments are also indexed to the cost of living. In 1987, 46% of 3 million OAS recipients received GIS payments (Statistics Canada, 1990).

Both OAS and GIS plans are financed by tax revenues.

14.3.4 Life Insurance

One of life's hazards is death or, as life insurers put it, "premature death".

Nearly all unionized and non-unionized employees in Canada are protected by a group life insurance plan (Pay Research Bureau, 1990). The

TABLE 14.6
Group Life Insurance Rates for an Average-Sized Group

Age	Premium per $1,000 of coverage	Percentage of the premium charged at age 45
25	1.68 $	35 %
45	4.80 $	100 %
65	27.96 $	583 %
75	75.72 $	1,578 %
85	170.40 $	3,550 %

SOURCE: Coward (1988, p. 153).

insurance is generally term, as compared to permanent or whole-life insurance.

There are two types of plan. Under the first, the deceased's family receives a lump sum. Under the second, the family receives a generally lower lump sum than in the first case, plus a survivor's pension payable to the deceased's spouse for life. This pension is a percentage of the employee's pay at the time of death. This amount is supplemented by family allowance benefits, if applicable, C/QPP benefits (spouse's and orphans' pensions), workers' compensation if the death is caused by a work-related accident or illness (spouse's and orphans' pensions), and, in certain provinces, automobile insurance act benefits if death is the result of a traffic accident (spouse's pension and lump sum for minor children).

Employers generally pay the cost of these life-insurance plans. The extent of coverage is usually based on the employee's pay, frequently 100% or 200% of annual pay. In addition, there are often optional plans allowing employees to obtain more coverage and also to protect their dependents.

Most life insurance plans provide for a waiver of premiums in the event of disability.

Many employers also offer their pensioners a life insurance benefit (usually reduced). Such plans may be costly, since every $1,000 of life insurance requires the insurer to disburse $1,000. Table 14.6 is a schedule of annual life insurance premiums for an average-sized group. As indicated; it costs as much to insure one 85-year-old as it does to insure 35 45-year-olds. Since employees are taxed on their employer's contributions for group life insurance of more than $25,000, the premiums for active employees should be separated from those for pensioners, to avoid imposing a large taxable benefit on active employees.

Aside from these three life insurance plans (basic life insurance, supplementary life insurance and insurance for dependents), most employers also have a travel insurance plan. This employer-paid insurance pays a benefit in the event of an employee's death, or in some cases disability, that occurs while the employee is travelling on business.

Finally, many employers also offer a group accidental death and dismemberment insurance plan. Coverage generally extends to all employees, with, in most cases, the employers paying the cost. The benefits are usually a multiple of pay (e.g. 1, 2, or 3 times). Many of these plans also allow employees to obtain additional coverage if they wish, as well as protection for their dependents.

14.3.5 Unemployment Insurance

Finally, the fifth hazard of life that can jeopardize an individual's financial security is loss of employment. Some people are more vulnerable than others; however, virtually no one is completely immune. One need only think, for example, of the 1981-82 recession, or the one in the early 90s, when many executives and professionals found themselves unemployed.

Canada has had an Unemployment Insurance Act since 1940. In its present form, the law dates back to 1971. The amendments introduced that year extended coverage to public sector employees, and also required them to contribute. Benefits also increased considerably and eligibility rules were thoroughly revamped.

The 1971 Act provides for benefits equal to 60% of insurable earnings (50% in the case of voluntary termination of employment). The ceiling on insurable earnings is indexed annually to the cost of living. The maximum insurable earnings in 1991 are $680 a week, which means maximum benefits of $408 a week. The plan is financed by both employer and employee contributions.

Workers are eligible for unemployment insurance benefits if they lose their job after working a certain minimum time, and after a two-week waiting period. Workers may also receive unemployment insurance benefits for a maximum of 15 weeks in the event of pregnancy, illness, or accident.

In the case of job loss, the duration of benefits depends on the number of weeks the person was employed and the regional unemployment rate. The maximum benefit period is 50 weeks.

☐ 14.4 Payment for Time Not Worked

Time not worked includes holidays, vacations, and other types of leave.

14.4.1 Holidays

Holidays generally include statutory holidays (such as Christmas Day), additional holidays (such as Boxing Day), and floating days off offered to employees.

Aside from floating days off, organizations generally give their employees 10 to 13 holidays a year. These figures vary little from one employee category to the next. In Canada, in 1990, about 30% of organizations offered 11 paid holidays a year, and almost 40% offered 12 or 13 (Pay Research Bureau, 1990).

In addition to paid holidays, almost 50% of organizations gave their employees floating days off. This normally means one, two, or three such days a year.

14.4.2 Paid Leave

In addition to holidays and floating days off, most employers give their employees leave in special circumstances, such as death, marriage, or jury duty. Employers also offer maternity leave (in addition to what is required by the Unemployment Insurance Act), paternity leave (for the birth or adoption of a child), leave in the event of a move, etc. The number of days off depends on predetermined rules and special circumstances.

14.4.3 Annual Vacations

Two interesting trends in vacations have emerged since the mid-60s: vacations have tended to become longer and employees become eligible for longer vacations sooner.

The length of vacations most often depends on seniority, and virtually all employers stipulate a maximum number of weeks. The ceiling may be as high as seven weeks, but is usually five or six.

Public sector employees, in many provinces, are entitled to four weeks of vacation from their first years of employment. In the private sector, it is becoming increasingly common to give three weeks after one, two, or three years of service.

Legally, the labour code in most provinces stipulates a minimum of two weeks of vacation for employees with one to four years of service, and three weeks for those with five or more years of service. There are exceptions, however. Saskatchewan, for example, requires 3 weeks after 1 year and 4 weeks after 10 years; Quebec requires 3 weeks after 10 years (which will gradually be reduced to 5 years at the rate of one year annually from January 1, 1992 to January 1, 1995).

14.4.4 Sabbaticals *Education Leave*

Following the lead of major North American universities, certain employers are giving employees (usually executives or senior executives) paid sabbaticals. The maximum length is normally 12 months and the period is primarily used for graduate studies leading to a degree or for revitalization. Some employers, including the Federal government, the Quebec government, the City of Toronto, and York University, offer to set aside part of their employees' pay each year (e.g. 20% of regular pay) so that they can take a paid sabbatical of six months to one year (Cornell, 1991).

14.5 Other Benefits (Perquisites)

The third category of employee benefits is composed of different personal services. The nature of these benefits, which in some cases are called "perquisites", varies greatly. The list may include more than 50 items, ranging from subsidized meals to housing assistance to theatre tickets. Some benefits, however, are more commonly available than others. The following are intended for general information.

14.5.1 Automobile

In addition to having a policy of reimbursing expenses incurred when using a personal vehicle for business purposes, many organizations provide their employees (at least senior executives) with a vehicle.

If the vehicle is also available for personal use, it is considered a taxable benefit. The amount added to an individual's taxable income depends on the percentage of personal use, although there is a minimum amount called a standby charge. A few years ago, a maximum was also set on the price of the vehicle. This maximum, however, only affects employers, i.e. there is a limit on the amount of lease payments, or, in the case of a purchased vehicle, capital cost allowance deductible by the employer. Employees are taxed according to the same system, regardless of the automobile's price.

14.5.2 Parking

Many employers provide their employees with parking space, or pay the costs of parking. This benefit is primarily available to executives and senior executives, although a number of organizations offer this benefit to all their employees. It is a taxable benefit for employees.

14.5.3 Discounts on Products and Services

Many organizations (about 50% according to Thériault, 1986) offer their employees discounts on the products and services they supply. In some cases, the discounts apply only to senior executives, but, more often than not, all employees are eligible for them. These discounts commonly range from 10% to 25%. In other cases, the product or service is billed at cost, or at the wholesale price.

14.5.4 Employee Loans

Extending loans to employees for work-related moves is a relatively common practice in Canada. Some organizations offer their employees, particularly executives and senior executives, loans at reduced interest rates. The purpose of such loans is generally specified. It may be to purchase company shares, pursue further education, cope with unexpected financial problems, buy a home or consumer goods, etc. Most programs set a ceiling on loans, often based on pay, i.e. the employee's capacity to repay the loan. Maximum terms for loans are also stipulated.

The practice of offering loans at reduced rates has been subject to the Income Tax Act since January 1, 1978. Before that time, the resulting benefit was non-taxable. Since then, a minimum interest rate (restated quarterly) is prescribed. Employers who extend loans at a rate below the prescribed rate must add the difference between the interest actually paid and the required minimum to the employee's taxable income.

14.5.5 Housing

Most employers offer housing to employees required to work in isolated areas. As a general rule, a token rent is charged. In addition, a few employers provide housing to certain employees (particularly senior executives).

In principle, the value of housing is a taxable benefit. An exception, however, is made for employees working at a special construction site or in a remote region.

14.5.6 Subsidized Meals

Some organizations have an employee cafeteria, with the employer providing the necessary space and equipment. Meal prices are sometimes subsidized.

Certain organizations also have dining rooms, which are often only for executives.

Partly subsidized meals are not a taxable benefit for employees unless the prices are "unreasonably low".

14.5.7 Tuition Fees for Employees

Most organizations (at least medium-sized and large ones) have a policy of reimbursing tuition fees, generally for courses related to the employee's work and in which the employee receives a passing grade. If a course benefits the employer more than the employee, the reimbursed tuition fees are not a taxable benefit. Otherwise, the reimbursement must be included in taxable income, and the employee may claim a corresponding deduction.

14.5.8 Tuition Fees for Dependents

Some organizations have a scholarship program for their employees' dependents. The number of scholarships varies considerably from one employer to the next. Some employers may offer more than 100 scholarships. The awarding of the scholarships is based on various conditions, including merit, academic record, etc.

14.5.9 Conference and Convention Expenses

Most organizations allow executives, as well as scientific and professional staff, to attend conferences and conventions on a theme related to their work. The opportunity is generally made available on a selective basis. The same applies to reimbursing dues for membership in professional associations.

Convention expenses reimbursed to an employee are not a taxable benefit; neither are professional dues.

14.5.10 Club Memberships

Quite a large number of organizations (over one quarter, according to Thériault, 1986) pay dues and fees for employees' memberships in social, athletic, or health clubs. This benefit generally applies only to executives and senior executives.

These expenditures are not tax-deductible for the employer, and are generally not a taxable benefit for employees.

14.5.11 Financial and Legal Advice

While the practice of offering financial and legal advice as an employee benefit is not yet widespread in Canada, it is growing in popularity. Financial advice might cover such areas as retirement and estate planning, insurance, financial planning, etc.

The advice, provided primarily for senior executives, may be given on an individual or group basis. Fees paid by an organization for individual financial or legal advice are a taxable benefit for the employee. This rule does not apply if the advice is given to a number of employees simultaneously.

14.6 Working Conditions

The fourth and final category of employee benefits consists of various working conditions. While some, such as working hours, have a direct impact on compensation for time worked, the impact of others, such as unpaid leave and work schedules, is indirect.

14.6.1 Working Hours

Most office, managerial, and professional staff have an official 35 or 37.5 hour work week (about 30% and 35% respectively). For production and maintenance workers, the normal work week is 40 hours (60%). Since 1980, the number of organizations with a 37.5 hour work week for office staff and 40 hour for production and maintenance workers has been declining steadily (Pay Research Bureau, 1983 and 1990).

Generally speaking, production and maintenance workers are paid 150% and sometimes 200% of their base pay for overtime. Managers are usually not paid for overtime.

14.6.2 Unpaid Leave

Some organizations allow employees to take unpaid leave. In many cases, this applies to unionized employees. Such leaves are attractive for employees, because they are assured of a job when they return. For employers, however, allowing such leaves may create staff-planning problems, not to mention the cost of training replacements for employees on leave.

14.6.3 Work Schedules

The issue of work schedules consumed a great deal of union as well as management energy during the 70s. Since then, things have stabilized. Some organizations have accordingly developed new work schedules including, in most cases, significant core time.

☐ 14.7 Summary

After defining and classifying employee benefits, this chapter provided a brief description of the different benefit plans offered by organizations.

The content of these plans is evidently very complex. One need only think of pension plans as an example. Moreover, most of these plans are relatively new. This makes it understandable why, in many organizations, employee benefits and pay are treated as separate issues. There is all the more reason for doing so if plan management and costs are considered.

However, as the next chapter will show, the question of costs, and the more general question of managing employee benefits are closely related to pay. In this respect, it becomes less and less a question of pay and employee benefits as separate entities, and increasingly one of these items as components of the compensation package offered by organizations.

The next chapter discusses the administration of employee benefits, not as a process distinct from pay administration, but as a major component of total compensation.

REFERENCES

BELCHER, D. and T.J. ATCHISON, *Compensation Administration*, Englewood Cliffs, New Jersey, Prentice-Hall Inc., 1987.

BLAIS, R. and A.C. MAGNAN, *Loi du Québec sur les régimes complémentaires de retraite*, text presented at the symposium organized by the Conseil du patronat du Québec, Montreal, September 14, 1989.

CALVERT, G.N., *Pensions and Survival: The Coming Crisis of Money and Retirement*, Toronto, MacLean-Hunter, 1977.

COFIRENTES +, *La Sécurité financière des personnes âgées au Québec, Rapport du comité d'étude sur le financement du Régime de rentes du Québec et sur les régimes supplémentaires de rentes*, Quebec, 1977.

CORNELL, C., "Sabbatical Leave is Good Business for Human Resources Professional", *Info Ressources Humaines*, April, 1991, pp. 30-31.

COWARD, L.E., *Mercer Handbook of Canadian Pension and Welfare Plans*, Don Mills, Ontario, CCH Canadian Limited.

DOYEL, H.W., and J.D. McMILLAN, "Low Cost Benefit Suggestions", *Personnel Administration*, vol. 25, N° 5, 1980, pp. 54-57.

MAGNAN, A.C., *Ré-affectation du budget des avantages sociaux*, text presented as part of the work group organized by the Conference Board of Canada, September 13, 1979.

MERCER (William M. Mercer Limited), "Impact on Executives", *Tax Reform and Retirement Savings: The New Era*, N° 4, October 31, 1990.

MERCER (William M. Mercer Limited), *Benefits Legislation in Canada – 1991*, Toronto, William M. Mercer Ltd., 1991.

PAY RESEARCH BUREAU, *Benefits and Working Conditions – 1982*, Public Service Staff Relations Board, 1983.

PAY RESEARCH BUREAU, *Benefits and Working Conditions – 1990*, Public Service Staff Relations Board, 1990.

PESANDO, J.E., *Private Pensions in an Inflationary Climate: Limitations and Policy Alternatives*, Economic Council of Canada, 1978.

STATISTICS CANADA, *Pension Plans in Canada – 1988*, Ottawa, Supply and Services, 1990.

THÉRIAULT, R., *Politiques et Pratiques en matière de rémunération globale dans les entreprises au Québec*, Montreal, Les Productions Infort Inc., 1986.

ZILLI, K. and D. CONNOR, "The Top-Up Two-Step", *Benefits Canada*, June 1990, pp. 15-18.

TABLE OF CONTENTS

15

MANAGING BENEFIT PLANS AND TOTAL COMPENSATION

The previous chapter described different employee benefit plans. This chapter focuses on managing these plans and on managing total compensation. After indicating the importance of a policy on employee benefit management, this chapter describes the value of such plans. This is followed by a section on the evaluation of employees' needs in terms of benefits, and on flexible benefit plans. A discussion of benefit communication follows, and the chapter concludes with an examination of the principal factors to be considered in total compensation management.

☐ 15.1 Employee Benefits Management Policy

In view of the magnitude and steady growth of the costs of employee benefit plans as a component of total compensation, it is surprising to find that employers pay relatively little attention to them. Most organizations have a detailed compensation policy, as we saw in Chapter 2. In reality, however, such policies almost always apply to the cash portion of total compensation alone, if not exclusively to salary. For example, a policy might state, "The company's compensation policy is based on the principles of internal and external equity, merit increases, and advancement within the pay range." Occasionally, this is followed by a sentence about employee benefit plans, such as "Benefits will be adapted to employees' needs and location." Terse as it may be, this policy statement is quite significant.

While it is true that few organizations have policy statements or a management philosophy on employee benefits, this does not necessarily mean that only a few pay close attention to benefit plan administration. In contrast to pay, however, few organizations appear to have given serious thought to determining the guiding principles on which their employee benefit plans should be based. In this respect, Magnan* suggests a list of questions that

---

* A.C. Magnan, Principal, William M. Mercer Limited, personal communication, April 4, 1991.

management might consider in determining the guiding principles of an organization's employee benefit plan. For example, the list covers the following items.

1. How interested is the organization in obtaining employees' views of their needs and perceptions?
   – How will employees' needs be defined?
   – What role will the union play?

2. To what extent is the organization interested in satisfying employees' needs?
   – Will its attitude be paternalistic, rigid, flexible, or progressive?
   – Will the organization give special consideration to the needs of employees who are not the sole provider for their family or their survivors?
   – What attitude will the organization adopt toward dependents' benefits?

3. To what extent is the organization willing to consider sociological changes?
   – Will employee benefits cover common-law and same-sex spouses?
   – Will the organization consider the growing demand for sabbaticals, leisure time, day-care facilities, and job security?

4. To what extent does the organization wish to acknowledge or favour certain groups?
   – Will the organization offer all employees a universal plan, or adopt different plans based on hierarchical level or employee category, e.g. a separate plan for part-time employees?

5. To what extent does the organization wish to take into consideration benefits payable from government plans?
   – Will employees know that the organization contributes to the public plans?
   – Will the organization take full advantage of all government assistance available?

6. To what extent does the organization wish to consider its ability to pay?
   – What percentage of compensation will be allocated to employee benefits?
   – Will the long-term repercussions be compatible with the organization's financial strategy?

7. To what extent does the organization wish to react to inflation?
   – Will economic adjustments be ad hoc or guaranteed?
   – Will the provisions governing increases in the economic adjustments apply to every level of plan benefits or only up to a certain ceiling?

This framework for reflection may be used to identify guiding principles used to develop or review the appropriateness of various benefits and pension plans. But as McCaffery (1989a) points out, a number of other factors must be considered to ensure that plans are properly formulated:

- the organization's objectives in terms of personnel increases or reductions, geographical dispersion or centralization, acquisitions, etc.;
- workforce characteristics;
- legal requirements;
- the relative cost of employee benefits; and
- total compensation strategy.

The management of employee benefit plans in most organizations may be described as traditional (McCaffery, 1989b).

1. The various plans are managed by different people and total costs are not consolidated.
2. The emphasis is on the pay structure.
3. Benefits are based on a one-dimensional vision, i.e. stemming from the employer's social responsibility.
4. Plans are based on a narrow view of employees, namely that they are all married men whose wives are homemakers, who have two children, and have a large mortgage to pay.
5. The benefits represent vested interests and plan features are ironclad, e.g. the $25 deductible for medical expenses set in 1975 has not changed since.

However, things are beginning to change as McCaffery (1989b) also notes.

1. Some organizations are beginning to manage their benefit plans in a strategic fashion, and the responsibility for communicating them lies with one person.
2. The management of benefit plans has been integrated with pay management.
3. A philosophy and specific policies underlie the different plans.
4. Employees' perceptions are considered and employees are offered various options.

15.2 Value of Employee Benefit Plans

15.2.1 Plan Costs in Canada and the United States

Determining the costs of employee benefit plans is a highly complex matter, even more so attempting to compare the costs at different organizations. It is worthwhile, however, to establish the relative and total costs to organizations of their employee benefit plans by means of surveys.

First of all, it is important to note that plan costs vary with the benefits offered, the composition of the organization's workforce, and certain organizational and industrial as well as cultural characteristics.

1. The higher the percentage of women within an organization, the lower the cost of a life insurance plan, because women have longer average life expectancies.
2. The higher the average age of employees, the higher the cost of certain pension plans (employees have fewer years of contributions before reaching retirement age) and insurance coverage (higher risk of death).
3. An increase in organizational pay levels raises the cost of most income protection plans, since contributions and benefits are usually based on pay.

Having said that, exactly how much do employee benefits cost?

Benefit Costs in Canada

From 1939 to 1945, the relative cost of employee benefits in Canada rose from 5% to 13% of total payroll, largely as a result of the 1941 Wage Control Act. Benefit costs were 15% in 1953, 21% in 1960, and 31% in 1976 (Thorne Riddell Associates Ltd., 1977). As these figures indicate, costs have more than doubled from 1953 to 1976. While costs have continued climbing since the late 70s, they have remained at relatively the same percentage of pay. In 1989, benefits cost about 30% to 35% of pay (Institut de recherche et d'information sur la rémunération, 1989). Table 15.1 contains a breakdown of these figures for various benefits available to Quebec employees. Figures in other Canadian provinces are similar to those of Quebec.

Benefit Costs in the United States

According to a survey by the United States Chamber of Commerce (1979), the cost of employee benefits as a percentage of pay at a group of identical American organizations rose from 16% in 1947 to 24% in 1957, and from 30% in 1967 to 37% in 1978. Since then, the percentage has remained essentially the same (United States Chamber of Commerce, 1990).

As these statistics indicate, the cost of employee benefits in the United States is slightly higher than in Canada. The difference is due primarily to the cost of health insurance and income protection plans, particularly to cover illness. There are fewer government plans in the United States than in Canada (and no basic general medicare coverage). In addition, certain American income protection plans, such as old age security, are financed by employer and employee contributions, whereas in Canada they are financed through tax revenues.

TABLE 15.1
Different Employee Benefit Plans Available to Certain Categories of Quebec Public Sector Employees and Other Quebec Employees as a Percentage of Pay

	Professional		Office Personnel		Maintenance and Service Employees		All categories	
	Public	Other	Public	Other	Public	Other	Public	Other
Other direct compensation								
– Paid sick leave	0.5	0.1	0.8	0.2	1.4	0.4	0.9	0.2
Income security plans								
– Pension plan	5.3	7.8	5.1	7.2	5.0	4.2	5.1	6.6
– Salary insurance	0.6	0.3	2.1	0.6	5.1	1.1	2.6	0.7
– Other insurance	0.1	1.6	0.3	1.8	0.2	1.7	0.2	1.7
– Paid personal leave	0.2	0.2	0.5	0.3	0.1	0.0	0.4	0.2
– Government plans	7.4	7.4	8.9	8.8	9.4	10.6	8.8	9.0
– Total income security plans	13.6	17.3	16.9	18.7	19.8	17.6	17.1	18.2
– Total other direct and income security	14.1	17.4	17.7	18.9	21.2	18.0	18.0	18.4
Payment for time not worked								
– Holidays	5.0	4.6	5.0	4.7	5.0	4.6	5.0	4.7
– Annual vacations	7.7	7.5	7.8	7.2	7.8	7.5	7.8	7.4
– Other time off	1.9	2.9	2.5	3.3	2.3	1.8	2.3	2.8
– Total paid time off	14.6	15.0	15.3	15.2	15.1	13.9	15.1	14.9
Total employee benefits	28.7	32.4	33.0	34.1	36.3	31.9	33.1	33.3

SOURCE: Institut de recherche et d'information sur la rémunération (1989, p. 21). Reproduced by permission of the publisher.

15.2.2 Impact of Benefit Plans on Employees' Attitudes and Behaviour

While pay ensures employees of a certain standard of living, benefits allow them to maintain it. However, employee benefits are not tied to performance. Rather, they are based on the employee continuing to be a part of the organization, and sometimes depend on the position held within the organization. At least in their present form, employee benefit plans provide employees with no incentive to make a greater effort and improve performance. As indicated in earlier chapters, for a reward to serve as an incentive to improve performance, the employee must consider the reward significant and it must be linked to performance.

However, is it true that employee benefits provide incentive to employees to continue working for an organization? It is logical, and certain studies reveal that employee benefits do help bind employees to the organization (Mitchell, 1983; Schiller and Weiss, 1979). Private pension plans may be the benefit most likely to create this type of linkage. However, this effect is still far from having been proved. The person in charge of organizing a 1990 Cornell University conference on the effects of compensation policy found that none of the 14 papers presented dealt with the impact of benefit plans on attracting, retaining, and motivating employees (Ehrenberg, 1990, p. 9). The amount of research in this area remains very limited. However, we may expect to see more studies in the future, because of the aging of the population and the rising costs of benefit plans.

Employees are notoriously ignorant of the benefits they receive (Wilson, Northcraft and Neals, 1986). While most know that certain plans exist, they often know neither the value of the benefits nor the costs incurred by their employer to provide them. Many employees think that plan costs are based on the extent to which a plan is used, so they believe, for example, that a group health care plan (medication) or dental insurance is more expensive than a pension plan. This ignorance does nothing to increase the impact of benefits on employees.

This does not mean, however, that employees do not consider benefits important. For example, one need only think of the demands for pension plan indexation during negotiations of collective agreements with organizations such as the leading automakers, Air Canada, and Bell Canada.

15.2.3 Importance and Evolution of Employees' Needs

The management of employee benefits must not be a question of costs alone, but also of employees' needs. Undoubtedly, costs generally carry more weight than needs. A good example of this is the relative popularity of life insurance plans compared to long-term disability coverage, when the situations covered by both plans are potentially equally problematic.

Some say that things cannot be otherwise, that costs must outweigh needs because the organization's financial health depends on it. However costs being equal, the criterion of relative need should predominate. In practice, this is not always the case. For example, why offer a dental care plan that includes orthodontic expenses when employees, particularly those with the largest financial needs, lack adequate life or disability insurance? In this case as well, it is far from certain that the proposed dental care plan costs the same as additional life or disability coverage.

Relative Importance of Needs

It is important to have a clear understanding of "relative needs", and, above all, to analyze them properly. For example, the amount of income protection required varies according to a number of factors, such as age, marital status, and family responsibilities. The need for income protection depends on three variables: the needs of the employee, the needs of the employee's spouse in terms of ability to enter the workforce, and the needs of their children: age and marital status. For example, the need for income protection is not as great in the event of the employee's death as it is in the case of a permanent disability. The "employees' needs" variable is irrelevant in the first instance, but not in the second.

Changing Needs over Time

Needs change over time, depending not only on individuals and their dependents, but also on inflation, as well as increases in pay and the cost of living. Updates are therefore essential, and must be based primarily on changes in employees' needs rather than on results of market surveys. Updates must also consider changes in social legislation. In this regard, an analytical grid by event, as Bessette (1978) suggests, is definitely useful. It involves determining the availability and level of protection of public and private plans for each possible event, such as death before retirement or long-term disability. This type of analysis reveals shortcomings as well as any duplication in existing plans.

15.2.4 Relative Value of Benefit Plans

The full range of employee benefits requires sound management based on costs and relative needs. For instance, what is the relative value of a plan that provides mortgage assistance in the event of a move, but no help for the spouse in finding a satisfactory new job?

One might also ask questions of a more general nature, such as the value of giving employees four or five weeks of annual vacations when their pay is relatively low. One certainly cannot offer everything; choices must be made. This raises the issue of the relevance of those choices to the individuals concerned. In a broader perspective, organizations should consider the possibility of slightly increasing pay rather than improving employee benefits, given the relative impact of these two compensation elements.

☐ 15.3 Evaluating Benefit Needs

As mentioned earlier, market surveys of benefits must be conducted to arrive at a more satisfactory comparison of total compensation. The measurement of total compensation must also provide some indication of the cost of an effective employee benefit plan. This measurement, however, provides little indication of employee needs, nor does it give any indication about what structural changes should be made to benefits. Finally, it may have a dysfunctional effect by encouraging the introduction of new plans, or changes to existing ones, not because that is what employees need or want, but because that is what other organizations are doing. To this might be added the fact that many plans, in view of their highly complex nature, are managed by specialists likely to be more concerned with technical details than the relative value of benefits to employees. In this context, measuring employees' needs is of prime importance.

As Katcher (1991) notes, decisions on what changes to make to employee benefit plans are often based on management's opinion concerning benefits, management's preferences or wishes, legal and tax considerations, knowledge of market trends and what competitors are doing, or management's perception of employees' needs. This approach is very risky. In fact, the resulting changes are not likely to meet needs, considering costs and the objectives pursued. In some cases, for example, management will solicit the views of a group of executives on the assumption that their answers will be representative of all employees. This assumption may lead to false conclusions, because the executives are in a different financial position from workers – they are paid more. Also, in some organizations, executives are older and their family status differs from that of employees working in subordinate positions. If the organization interviews five male executives whose wives are homemakers and who have three children ranging in age from 12 to 20, their needs are likely to differ completely from those of the vast majority of employees who, for example, may be much younger and have very different perceptions. In such a case, one should survey the needs of a sample of employees, or all of them.

15.3.1 Precautions in Changing Existing Plans

Certain precautions must be taken, however, in conducting such surveys.

1. The surveys will invariably arouse employees' expectations, which makes it important to ensure that all or at least some of them can be satisfied. In addition, expectations must be adequately controlled, by clearly conveying the objectives of the survey and what the organization intends to do with the results. If management does not plan to make changes as a result of the survey, it is preferable not to conduct a survey at all.
2. Employees must be assured of the confidential nature of their responses. The information gathered by such surveys is personal.

There is no need to identify individuals other than as members of certain groups. To gain employees' confidence, absolute confidentiality of responses must be guaranteed.

3. All employees must be allowed to participate in the survey. In view of its objective, namely to identify employees' needs, it is preferable not to use samples. If, ultimately, an organization's size makes it impractical to survey all employees, management must clearly communicate the approach it favours, the reason for it, and, above all, the sampling technique used. In this case, employees who are not part of the sample group should also be given an opportunity to express their views if they wish. While giving all employees the chance to express themselves, it is also important to obtain a maximum response rate. This is an area in which generalization is difficult and risky.

4. Employees must be given feedback about the survey results. This demonstrates the seriousness with which management considers employees' needs in administering benefits, and also helps employees understand subsequent decisions.

15.3.2 Methods of Determining Needs

The numerous methods for determining employees' needs may be divided into two types: focus groups and questionnaires.

Focus groups are small groups of employees with similar characteristics, who are interviewed to obtain their views on the areas under survey. This is a valuable way of developing assumptions and obtaining feedback from employees on existing or proposed benefits. However, it provides no statistical base for establishing projections that may be applied to the entire target population.

The second method involves questionnaires, which may take different forms.

1. Open questions: this type of questionnaire asks employees, for example, what benefits, other than those currently offered, they would like to receive. This approach produces information similar to what is obtained from focus groups, but allows for clearer responses. However, some employees have a better knowledge than others of what the organization offers, and this method provides no indication of employee preferences.

2. Rating scales: Employees might be asked, for example, to rate their degree of satisfaction with each benefit offered, on a scale of 1 to 5. While this method definitely reveals employees' perceptions and feel-

ings, it is not very discriminating, because it does not allow the relative importance of the resulting perceptions or feelings to be determined.

3. Ranking in order of importance: This approach avoids the problems of using rating scales, but ranking provides no indication of the extent to which one benefit is preferred over another. The preference differential between benefits is not constant from rank to rank.

4. Paired comparison: Employees are asked to state their preferences systematically for each pair of benefits. This technique results in a true indication of preferences, but fails to consider variations in the monetary value of benefits.

5. Percentages: Employees are asked to assign a percentage of their compensation to each plan or option, whose monetary value has been determined. This provides indications of employee preferences while considering the monetary value of the different plans.

6. Ranking and paired comparison: These methods may be adjusted to present options of equivalent monetary value. Although the paired comparison method is much more difficult to apply than ranking, it does provide a relatively accurate idea of employees' preferences.

In theory, the problem appears to be solved. But in practice, the solution is not that clear. Studies by Milkovich and Delaney (1975) found that the method chosen may influence preferences. The authors asked three groups of employees in the same organization to indicate their preferences among certain benefit options. The monetary value of each option had been established as equivalent. One group had to using ranking, the second paired comparisons, and the third had to allocate a percentage of their pay among the various options.

Comparing the results of the three groups revealed significant differences, even after the creation of more homogenous subgroups based on age (under 30 and over 40 years old). Are these differences related to the methods used or to other characteristics of the study population, such as variations in seniority or family status from group to group? The study provides no indication. However, once the authors created more homogeneous subgroups based on age (under 30 and over 40 years old), significant differences between subgroups were found when the same method was used.

It makes sense, then, to use several methods of determining employees' preferences, to see how the results compare. The use of a single method risks yielding conclusions that reflect the effects of the method more than employees' real preferences. One might first form focus groups to identify potential changes, and then collect feedback from employees on the proposed changes by means of a questionnaire that uses different measurement techniques. Interpretation of the responses to the various measures would indicate employees' relative preferences.

On the other hand, instead of interpreting, it is possible to use what is known as "joint measurement", a more complex technique used primarily in marketing to identify consumer preferences. It allows the simultaneous effect of two or more variables on the ranking of another variable to be measured (Luce and Tukey, 1964; Green and Rao, 1971; Kienast, Maclachlan and McAlister, 1983).

☐ 15.4 Flexible Benefit Plans

Most conventional employee benefit plans, developed mainly in the 50s and 60s, are based on the needs of a married male employee with a homemaker wife, two children, and a heavy mortgage. This stereotype applies to only 7% of today's working population (Wender and Sladky, 1984).

Even today, many group life insurance plans fail to consider personal situations. They offer all employees the same amount of coverage, regardless of need. The amount is usually two or sometimes three times basic annual pay, regardless of personal circumstances. This approach entirely ignores the fact that individual life insurance needs vary from person to person, as well as over time.

The same applies to employees' needs and preferences in relation to the features of various income protection plans, whose differences are based, not only on personal characteristics, such as age, education, marital status, dependents, etc., but also on the organizational group to which the employees belong (Schuster, 1969; Jain and Janzen, 1974; Jain, 1977; Thériault, 1980).

Current practice indicates that management allocates employee benefits on the basis of either egalitarian justice, i.e. the same benefits for all, or distributive justice (equity), i.e. to each according to their contribution. In the latter case, the contribution of the employee category, rather than of the individual, is used. While distributive justice (equity) appears to provide a generally accepted standard for pay distribution, in practice, employees do not use this type of norm to assess the value of their benefits. They consider a justice based on needs more appropriate. Awarding employee benefits based on egalitarian or distributive justice rather than needs explains the lack of interest most employees have in the benefits they receive, and their ignorance of them.

15.4.1 Definition

In view of this situation, in the late 60s, compensation specialists (Taylor, 1969; Laplante, 1969) proposed using flexible or "cafeteria" (as they were called at the time) benefit plans. Taylor's idea was to establish a number of "fixed menus" of employee benefits (rather than a single one for all personnel), based on what he described as the different stages in a person's life. Each menu would apply for about five years.

Taylor's idea was subsequently pursued, and modified into a full self-serve approach. In a 1970 article published in the *Harvard Business Review*, Gordon and LeBleu predicted the following scenario for 1985:

> Automation allows for a wide variety of employee benefit programs. Employees now select the compensation packages (pay plus benefits and perquisites) that suit their individual needs from the menu provided by the benefits counsellor.

Drucker (1971) took up the idea and, in turn, suggested modelling employee benefits on needs, at least for the main employee categories, to reduce the enormous amount of money wasted (in his view) on employee benefits. With that, the idea became popular.

In practice, there are many types of flexible benefit plans, each of which requires the employee to make a choice.

Core plan plus options, with employer credits: Employees enjoy a basic or core level of protection and a range of optional benefits. Generally, the credits come from the savings realized by reducing the existing program, as well as from new employer contributions. Employees may generally improve their benefits through additional voluntary contributions.

Core plan plus options, without credits: Employees may enhance their plan through voluntary contributions to obtain, for example, optional life insurance or medical benefits, etc.

Modular plan: Different benefit modules are offered, based on the demographic characteristics of certain employee groups. The modules are equal in value and employees may increase their coverage through additional voluntary contributions.

Reimbursement account: Employer deposits contributions in separate accounts for each employee. The employee may then draw on the funds to cover eligible medical or dental expenses excluded from the basic plan.

15.4.2 Advantages

Flexible benefit plans offer both employer and employees numerous advantages. They:

- make employees more aware of the nature and cost of the benefits they receive and, therefore, more satisfied with them (Taplin, 1988);
- meet individual needs without increasing the level of protection for all employees;
- give employees an opportunity to choose, which employees are likely to appreciate, not only because they can adapt their protection to suit their needs, but simply because they have a choice;

- reduce demands for improved benefits at the employer's expense;
- give employers more flexibility at a lower cost in trying to conform with legislation against discrimination based on an employee's sex or age;
- allow new benefits to be offered at a lower cost to employees, and allow the range of benefits to be broadened to more adequately meet the need to maximize employees' net income; and
- provide an extra incentive for employees to remain with the organization, as long as they see no other employer offering equivalent benefits.

15.4.3 Disadvantages

On the other hand, flexible or cafeteria benefit plans have a number of disadvantages or limitations. They:

- represent a departure from current practice, and run counter to many employers' paternalistic attitudes toward employee benefits;
- require a precise monetary value to be attached to the various components of the compensation package; this may prove to be a very complex task, with highly subjective results (Famulari and Manser, 1989);
- raise the problem of identifying employee needs;
- increase plan costs through antiselection, i.e. the tendency of individuals to select the option that has the most value to them;
- entail a considerable amount of work and costs for plan development and administration; and
- assume that it is possible to provide employees with the information they need to make choices.

Introducing a cafeteria plan has virtually no effect on employee motivation to make more effort to improve performance, because the choice of benefits is not related to job performance, but solely to needs. Employees with identical needs receive the same benefits, regardless of differences in performance. In fact, it is even possible that employees with superior performance receive fewer benefits than others, simply because they have fewer needs.

Finally, application of the cafeteria approach in its entirety has certain drawbacks.

1. It enormously complicates compensation accounting (counterargument: computers may be used).
2. It only applies to non-unionized employees, because unions are opposed to it (counterargument: this assumption has not been proved).

3. It calls into question the tenet that employees should have income protection whether or not they want it (counterargument: basic plans may provide minimum protection, although this eliminates the concept of a pure cafeteria plan).

4. The cost of many plans usually depends on the number of participants (counterargument: employee surveys may be used to estimate the potential number of participants and projected costs – the disadvantage (if it is such) in cost must be weighed against the advantage of allowing employees to choose).

5. It may imply giving up some benefits in exchange for others, and a forced choice in face of uncertainty is always difficult.

15.4.4 Frequency of Use

In the United States, cafeteria benefit plans were pioneered by TRW Inc. (1974), the Educational Testing Service (1974), and American Can Co. (1978). Other companies, such as Pepsico Inc., Ingersoll-Rand, Procter & Gamble, Xerox, and American Airlines have since followed suit.

A turning point in the introduction of flexible benefit plans in the United States came with the 1978 tax amendments, which took effect in 1980, and made it possible to offer employees a choice between taxable and non-taxable benefits through what are called "reimbursement accounts". At the beginning of the year, employers credit each employee in the covered categories with an amount that employees may use at their discretion during the year. Any balance at year end simply reverts to the employer (a legal requirement, failing which the employee pays income tax on the surplus). A recent American survey (Hornsby, Kuratko and Wallingford, 1991) found that 40% of flexible plans were of this type.

Canada's Income Tax Act has no specific provisions governing flexible benefits. In practice, this clouds the tax treatment of certain flexible plan benefits, and renders it more complex. For example, an employee who agrees to a $2,000 pay cut to acquire dental care coverage is taxed on the benefit. On the other hand, if the employer offers the employee a 3% instead of a normal 5% pay increase, plus dental care coverage valued at 2% of pay, the benefit is not taxable. Revenue Canada officials provide very few guidelines in this area, and very often their answers differ from existing practices. This lack of clear tax legislation is undoubtedly a deterrent to the development of cafeteria plans in Canada, because of the uncertainty facing employers.

In 1985, Stonebraker reported that about 150 American companies offered a cafeteria plan. The corresponding figure for Canada in 1990 was an estimated 40 (IBIS Review, 1990). On the other hand, a 1989 Mercer survey of 5,000 major American organizations found that 47% either offered, or planned to offer, some of their employees a flexible benefits plan, compared to 23% five years earlier (Wall Street Journal, 1990). The figures seem contradictory, but they are not actually; the answers reflect the question. There are many more flexible than genuine cafeteria plans. Meisenheimer and Wiatrowski (1989) estimated that 13% of full-time American workers were covered by this type of plan in 1988. There are no equivalent statistics for Canada. Since the early 70s, a growing number of employee benefit plans offer a wider choice of options, for example, optional levels of life insurance coverage. In many cases, these plans were drawn up after consulting employees.

While these new formulas make benefit plans more flexible, they differ fundamentally from the cafeteria approach, in that they lack full freedom of choice, and the options available do not include the possibility of re-allocating employer contributions. Finally, the flexibility they offer is based on employees' willingness to make additional contributions to obtain coverage more in line with their needs.

Despite the disadvantages of the cafeteria approach, employers really have no choice but to make employee benefit plans more flexible. The reasons for this are the same as in the past, except that they have become more compelling: the rising cost of benefits, the greater or lesser degree to which employees appreciate their benefit plans, the limited choice of benefits available to employees, employees' ignorance of benefit costs, etc.

15.4.5 Example

In this context, Coward (1988) proposes a prototypical flexible benefits plan. For example, the employer provides identical minimum protection for all employees covered. Employees may not exchange any component of the basic plan for cash or some other component.

In addition to the employee benefits required by law, the minimum program might include:

- a non-contributory basic pension plan;
- life insurance coverage equal to one year's pay;
- travel accident insurance;
- health insurance to cover major expenses, with a substantial deductible;
- minimum dental insurance, with the emphasis on preventive care;
- a salary continuance or short-term disability plan;
- a long-term disability plan that provides 50% to 60% of pay; and
- an annual vacation policy that requires employees to take the first two or three weeks, and allows them to exchange the remainder, or part of it, for other benefits.

In addition, a flexible plan might allow employer credits or employee contributions to be used for additional benefits.

This type of plan is still far from a cafeteria approach, which in its purest form may not be realistic in North America. Nevertheless, any increase in plan flexibility is a step in the right direction.

☐ 15.5 Communicating Benefit Plans

Although communicating employee benefits is an integral part of managing them, communication warrants special attention because of its importance.

15.5.1 Communicating Program Content

Before determining the content of a communication program, the following steps must be taken.

1. Establish the program's objectives.
2. Identify the target public, its needs and expectations.
3. Formulate the message to convey to each audience.
4. Predict employees' reactions in order to prepare responses.
5. Be prepared to make adjustments along the way.
6. Ensure that all key parties concerned feel responsible for the communication program's success.

The communication program must provide employees, on a regular, ongoing basis, with accurate, up-to-date information adapted to the receiver and the medium chosen.

The communication program should regularly remind employees of:

– the value of benefits to all employees;
– the total value of the benefits provided for each employee; and
– the value of benefits compared to their cost if employees had to obtain them privately.

In this context, explanations of the technical details of different plans and organizational policy appear to be less essential and less effective. The effectiveness of an employee benefit communication program increases, not only with employee knowledge of the technical details of various options, but also with the value they attach to them.

15.5.2 Legal Requirements

At present, employers have no legal obligation to provide their employees with information about the benefits they receive, with two exceptions –

contract group insurance and pension plans. With regard to group insurance, the Uniform Life Insurance Act applies to all provinces with the exception of Quebec. According to this Act, insurers must issue, for delivery by the policyholder to each group life insured, a certificate or other document in which are set forth information such as the name of the insurer, the amount, or the method of determining the amount, of insurance on the group life insured, etc. For all practical purposes, an equivalent Act exists for the province of Quebec. As for pension, before the major overhaul of pension plan legislation in the late 80s, only a few Canadian provinces required employers to provide employees with a minimum of information about their pension plan. For example, employees had to be given access to the plan's provisions, to actuarial valuation results, and to a personal statement after each such valuation, i.e. every three years. Since the reform, however, employers in every province except British Columbia, Prince Edward Island, and New Brunswick, whose legislation is not yet in force, must provide pension plan members with a personal statement. Members must be notified of changes to the plan, as well as receive other information, such as termination and death benefits, the plan's financial position, and actuarial valuations. As mentioned, the legislation applies only to pension plans and group insurance. Providing information about other benefit plans is left to the employer's discretion.

15.5.3 Impact of Communication on Employees

A benefit is only valued if it is perceived as a benefit. In addition, one must know that something exists before one appreciates its value.

The purpose of communication is not only to allow employees to appreciate benefits, but also to convey a precise message. Benefits based on employee categories may serve as an additional incentive to aspire to a higher category, if the benefits in the two categories differ significantly. The supplementary pension plans some organizations offer their executives, for example, may have such an impact on employees who are not eligible, or whose plan has fewer benefits.

Based on actual needs, benefits may provide employees with additional incentive to remain with the organization – even more so when employees realize that other employers offer less.

Finally, as Dreher, Ash and Bretz (1988) note there is a positive correlation between the amount of information employees receive about their benefits and their satisfaction with those benefits.

15.5.4 Communication Media

Organizations usually prepare documents explaining their different employee benefit plans. These documents, which employees receive when they are hired or when major changes are made to a plan, have limited value as a source of information, because of their static nature. Many organizations use a full spectrum of media to complement these documents, and to make the communication process more dynamic and effective.

Some use traditional media such as in-house newsletters, news releases, annual employee reviews, bulletin boards, information sessions with audio-visual presentations, and a designated individual or group responsible for providing clear, immediate answers to employees' questions.

Other organizations resort to original high-tech solutions, such as installing interactive computer systems that provide employees with information through such means as personal computers, touch-sensitive monitors, touch-tone telephones, or video-conferences (private satellite links).

These different media all have their advantages, but their impact will be all the greater if they are simply one integral component of an overall strategy for informing employees about their benefit plans.

A properly designed strategy gives both employer and employees the best return on the money and effort invested in a communication program. It makes use of a multi-media approach, with high-quality visuals and text, giving employees information in doses they can absorb.

15.5.5 Personal Statements

One of the most effective means of informing employees about the value of their benefits is a personal statement of total compensation. It consists of a summary and personal statement of the different plans, what the employee is entitled to, the cost of each plan for the employer and the employee, and the amount paid for time not worked. This gives employees a better idea of their compensation and its various components.

By indicating plan costs, the statement helps create awareness of the employer's total expense (or investment) for each employee.

Table 5.2 contains excerpts from the personal statement provided by Alcan Aluminium Limited.

TABLE 15.2
Excerpts from a Personal Statement of Total Compensation
(Alcan Aluminium Limited)

PERSONAL STATEMENT

Prepared for: SAMPLE
Perm. no.:   002158
Date of Birth: August 17, 1943

This statement has been prepared using the personal information on Alcan's files as of *December 31, 1989.* If you notice any discrepancies, please notify your benefits officer.

ABOUT YOUR STATEMENT

Designed to give you personal benefit information, this statement illustrates how the Alcan Benefits Program combines with your salary to form your total compensation.

Pension estimates and life insurance coverage are based on your pensionable earnings and Alcan service as of December 31, 1989. Life insurance premiums are those you were required to pay as of April 1, 1990. Any benefit resulting from 1990 earnings will be reflected in future statements. [...]

IF YOU INCUR HEALTH EXPENSES

PROVINCIAL HEALTH CARE PLANS

Most basic medical expenses, including doctors' services, hospitalization in standard ward, certain procedures undertaken in hospital and other medically necessary services, are paid by your province's health care plans.

The provincial health care plan is paid for through general tax revenues, both federal and provincial, and by the employers' payroll.

ALCAN HEALTH CARE PROGRAM

Some of the additional medical expenses you or your covered eligible dependents may incur are reimbursed to you through the Alcan Health Care Program, for which premiums are paid entirely by Alcan.

Hospital Expenses
If you are hospitalized in Canada, the Program will pay:
- 100% of the charges for semiprivate accommodation;
- 90% of the charges for private accommodation, above the semiprivate rate, after you have paid a $25 annual deductible, to a maximum of $50 a day. [...]

Medical Expenses
The Program pays 90% of eligible medical expenses after you have paid an annual deductible amount of $25 of eligible medical expenses, including charges for private hospital accommodation.

Eligible medical expenses include: [...]

IF YOU INCUR DENTAL EXPENSES

PROVINCIAL DENTAL COVERAGE

Children under 16 years of age are covered for 100% of dental fees for certain treatments.

ALCAN DENTAL CARE PROGRAM

Dental expenses, based on the current fee guide, will be reimbursed as follows: [...]

IF YOU BECOME DISABLED

ALCAN DISABILITY PLANS

Short-term Disability Benefits

If you become disabled because of illness or injury, and are not able to carry out your normal duties, you will receive, based on your December 1989 salary, $3,595 per month for up to 12 months. This benefit includes the amount of any benefits you may be eligible to receive from the Canada or Quebec Pension Plan (C/QPP), Workers' Compensation, or any provincial automobile insurance plan.

Your participation in other Alcan benefit plans continues, provided you make the required contributions.

Long-term Disability Benefits

If you are still unable to work at your regular job once your STD benefit period has expired, you will receive, subject to the insurer's approval, $1,977 a month. This before-tax amount includes the amount of any benefits you are eligible to receive from government plans, such as C/QPP, Workers' Compensation, or a provincial automobile insurance plan. In addition, a monthly benefit might be payable from C/QPP for your eligible children. [...]

IN THE CASE OF DEATH

BEFORE RETIREMENT

In the event of your death before retirement, your designated beneficiary would receive a lump-sum payment:

$ 43,000	of Basic life insurance
n/a	of Contributory life insurance (2 units)

$ 43,000	total life insurance on death from any cause

In addition, your beneficiary would receive:

$215,700	from the Business Travel Accident Plan, if you die as the result of an accident that takes place while you are travelling on company business.

Your beneficiary, or your spouse when required by provincial pension legislation, would also receive from the Alcan Pension Plan a lump-sum amount equal to the present value of your accumulated pension, or $20,949 as of January 1, 1990. [...]

AFTER RETIREMENT

The benefits you build up in the Alcan Pension Plan throughout your career will play an important part in your financial security during retirement.

When you retire, you will be entitled to a lifetime pension from APP, based on:
- your Credited Plan Service, recognized under APP for the purpose of the pension formula;
- your Highest Average Earnings, the annual average of your 36 highest-paid consecutive months of pensionable earnings with Alcan; and
- the average Year's Maximum Pensionable Earnings (YMPE) during the same 36-month period.

To estimate the pension you have earned as of January 1, 1990 in this statement, we have used:
- your Credited Plan Service under the plan at December 31, 1989, of 10 years and 7 months;
- the average of your highest three consecutive calendar years of earnings, or $40,276 (estimated if you have less than three years of Credited Plan Service); and
- the average YMPE for the same period, or $26,700.

In projecting the pension benefits earned after 1989, we have used these same earnings. Please note that this is a change from last year's statement, in which projection of benefits to retirement was, in most cases, based on the latest calendar year's earnings. We have also assumed that you will continue to accumulate Credited Plan Service without interruption, and be eligible for the maximum benefits payable from C/QPP and Old Age Security (OAS) as of January 1, 1990.

NORMAL RETIREMENT

If you continue to participate in APP until September 1, 2008, your normal retirement date, you will be entitled to:

$ 474	from APP, for your Credited Plan Service to December 31, 1989;
$ 836	from APP, estimated for your Credited Plan Service between January 1, 1990 and your normal retirement date;
$ 577	from QPP/CPP;
$ 340	from OAS;
$2,227	total estimated monthly pension.

EARLY RETIREMENT

While your normal retirement date at age 65 is September 1, 2008, our records indicate that you would be eligible to retire as early as September 1, 1998, when you reach the age of 55 years, at which time you would receive 68.00% of the pension you had accumulated at that time. However, if you retire on or after August 1, 2006, when you reach the age of 62 years and 11 months, you would be entitled to receive 100% of the pension earned to that date.

If you retire early [...]

SAVING FOR TOMORROW

AESP, one of our most popular employee benefit plans, offers you a very effective way to save money. Your contributions are made easy through regular payroll deductions. Your savings are further built up by company contributions and income earned from your chosen investment funds.
Depending on your investment and savings objectives, the plan provides for short and long-term investments, as well as tax sheltering opportunities.

In 1989, you contributed $1,682 in regular contributions, including any contributions you may have allocated to your spouse's account. Alcan contributed $1,009 in your name; these contributions vested to you on January 1, 1990. The value of **your** account balance on that date was $5,791.

Using this account balance, and assuming that, each month in the future, you contribute to your own account $144, your December regular contribution, the following table illustrates how much **you** could accumulate in AESP over the next 10 years, including Alcan's contribution based on your credit service. This accumulation will, of course, vary according to the actual rates of return on your chosen investments in AESP. [...]

YOUR TOTAL COMPENSATION

Alcan recognizes that your contribution is important to the company's success and provides valuable income security for you and your family through your benefits program. The cost of the benefits program makes up a significant portion of your total compensation.

Your *total compensation* for 1989 amounts to $47,189. This amount is made up of your 1989 *cash compensation* of $42,040, which includes the following important elements:

$37,027	regular work and short-term disability
$ 3,234	vacation entitlement
$ 1,779	statutory holidays

Note: Your cash compensation is equal to the figure shown in box "C" of your T4 slips less any taxable benefit figures shown.

It also includes your *non-cash compensation* of $5,149, made up of Alcan's contribution towards:
$2,348   the cost of your benefits
$2,801   government benefits

In 1989, you contributed $3,780 towards your benefits, as follows:

Alcan Disability Plans	$ 105
Alcan Life Insurance Plan	n/a
Alcan Pension Plan (Canada)	$ 948
Alcan Employee Savings Plan	$1,682
Canada/Quebec Pension Plan	$ 525
Unemployment Insurance	$ 613

In addition, both you and Alcan contribute to the financing of government plans such as Old Age Security through income, sales and other taxes paid to the federal and provincial governments.

SOURCE: Alcan Aluminium Limited. Reprinted by permission of the Company.

15.6 Managing Total Compensation

15.6.1 Determining Total Compensation Budgets

The disbursements section of an organization's budget indicates how it intends to invest and spend its money in a given year, and stems directly from the business strategy adopted for the coming year. It consists of at least two components: operating expenses and capital expenditures. Compensation managers are most interested in the operating expenses component, because employee compensation comprises a large part of it, in some cases 50% or more. Table 15.3 lists the main items to be considered in preparing a compensation budget. As it indicates, in addition to forecasting pay increases in

TABLE 15.3
Main Factors to be Considered in Preparing the Compensation Budget

- Current employees' pay at year end.
- Cost of employee benefits and perquisites.
- Planned pay increases for reasons other than promotion.
- Planned pay increases because of promotions.
- Planned incentive and other bonuses (if applicable).
- Overtime and temporary help.
- Cost of the impact of pay increases, bonuses (if applicable), and overtime on employee benefits and perquisites.

Less: Effect of employee turnover rate.

Plus: Effect of planned hiring.

FIGURE 15.1
Possible Interactions among the People Who Have an Impact on the Compensation Budget

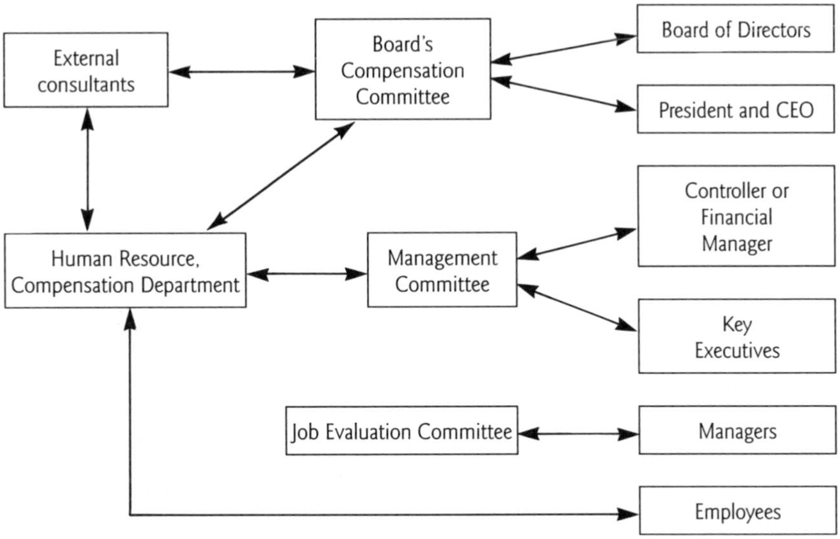

SOURCE: Adapted from Henderson (1989, p. 470).

the coming year, one must also determine the impact of anticipated employee turnover on compensation costs. The budget therefore depends not only on compensation managers, but also on the organization's human resource planners and, above all, on all managers who need employees to carry out their role.

Participants in the Compensation Budget Process

Figure 15.1 illustrates some of the possible interactions among the people who have an impact on the compensation budget.

The President and Chief Executive Officer is the person who makes the final decision on the compensation budget and must ensure consistency between the budget and the organization's business strategy. In this respect, the CEO is involved primarily at the beginning of the process, establishing guidelines and at the end, approving the budgets. In doing so, the CEO is primarily supported by the Compensation (or Human Resource) Committee of the Board of Directors, which approves the compensation received by the organization's President and CEO and leading senior executives. The Human

TABLE 15.4

Frequency (%) of the Sources of Decisions on Individual Pay Increases by Employee Category

		Employee Category				
Source of Decision	Executive	Managerial and Professional	Technical	Administrative Support	Production & Maintenance	All Categories
President and CEO	32	34	23	24	26	20
Immediate supervisors & personnel managers	10	21	26	24	15	19
Immediate supervisors	8	13	16	17	11	13
Personnel managers	0	1	2	3	9	3
Board of Directors	35	17	11	12	16	19
CEO & personnel manager	10	4	3	2	1	4
Others	5	10	19	18	22	14

SOURCE: Thériault (1986, p. 112). Reproduced by permission of the publisher.

Resource Department may provide the Compensation Committee with any information it needs on market compensation policies and practices, or the Committee may turn to outside consultants.

As mentioned, pay increases account for a major portion of compensation budgets. In practice, as Table 15.4 indicates, it is rare to find only one person involved in the pay increase process.

As this table indicates, pay increases are generally approved at the upper echelons of the organizational hierarchy, rather than in the human resource department. It is also surprising to note the relatively high percentage of instances in which the President and CEO has a say in approving pay increases for administrative support as well as production and maintenance staff. This is largely a factor of organizational size. For example, whereas the President and CEO alone approves pay increases at 30% of small organizations (less than 250 employees), that figure drops to 15% for large organizations (over 1,000 employees) (Thériault, 1986, p. 113).

In practice, many factors may come into consideration in determining who is in charge of pay increases. One need simply think of how the organization is structured. To what extent are its operations organized by profit centres or by more or less autonomous divisions? More specifically, the choice of those responsible for determining pay increases depends on the degree of decentralization of the organization's human resource function. The type of financial controls used, and the role assigned to immediate supervisors, as well as their habits and relative efficiency also come into play.

Based on the existing literature, it is difficult to draw precise conclusions. However, two trends may be noted. First, decision-making responsibility for pay increases is assigned to the personnel department official in charge of compensation. This is usually the case at large organizations. Second, organizational managers participate actively in the decision-making. The human resource department serves more as an enforcer of established policies. This is generally true of medium-sized and large decentralized organizations.

15.6.2 Measuring and Comparing Total Compensation

As mentioned, the effectiveness of an employee benefits plan depends on the criteria of cost and need. There is an important difference, however, between the employer's standpoint and that of the employee. A benefits plan may not cost the employee the same as it does the employer. In some cases, in fact:

— benefits are non-taxable, i.e. purchased with before-tax dollars;
— the benefits granted to a large group of employees fail to meet the specific needs of certain individuals; and
— the cost to the employer is less than the market cost to the employee of the same benefit because of volume discounts and the impact of antiselection on those with special problems.

As Thériault (1977) notes, for an element to be part of the exchange process between employee and organization, the employee must perceive its existence as well as consider it relevant. This does not apply to all employee benefits granted by employers. Moreover, the value (cost) of a benefit to an employer and its value to an employee are not necessarily the same.

The value of total compensation must therefore be determined from one or the other of these perspectives. In practice, at present, total compensation cannot take into account the appeal of particular material and psychological benefits for employees. Perceptions of the value or usefulness of compensation elements vary with need, expectations, and certain individual or social characteristics (e.g. the perceived value of a pension plan for a young employee, compared to its value for an older employee). This also applies to the value a life insurance plan equal to two or three times the pay of a 40-year-old married employee with three or four children, compared to that of a single or childless person.

One can do the same thing with each component of total compensation. The adoption of a more flexible approach to employee benefits, such as the personalization of benefits described above, is an effort to respond to the variety of situations that exist.

As Martel (1981) points out, there are numerous advantages to measuring employee benefits and, consequently, total compensation.

1. It enables employers to achieve two compensation objectives:
   a) position themselves within the labour market; and
   b) attain a level of total compensation costs acceptable to the organization.
2. Depending on what method is used, it provides employers with a better estimate of the financial impact of changes on compensation elements, as well as their more prudent development.
3. It may facilitate assessment of the various possible trade-offs during negotiations.
4. It may simplify informing employees about certain compensation elements.
5. It may facilitate and improve the administration and evaluation of total compensation.

There are three types of methods of measuring total compensation: combined, integrated, and others.

Combined Methods of Measurement

Combined or summary comparison methods are the most common means of comparing the total compensation offered by various employers. These methods involve a comparison of pay data as well as of the characteristics of the benefits offered by each employer. The two items are presented separately. Chapter 7 describes the advantages and disadvantages of various methods of presenting pay data. Employee benefits may be presented descriptively (cf. Table 15.5), or in a form indicating each element's relative weight and characteristics (cf. Table 15.6). The first is particularly useful for analyzing employee benefit plans, while the second allows different employee categories to be compared.

The principal advantages of this method are its simplicity and the possibility of observing differences between employers or employee categories for compensation elements.

On the other hand, it does not indicate the relative value of the various elements, or combine pay and incentives with benefits to determine the cost of total compensation.

TABLE 15.5
Comparison of Principal Provisions of Employee Benefit Plans

BENEFIT	REFERENCE MARKET	ORGANIZATION A
Life insurance		
Cost sharing		
— management	Employer — 100%	Employer — 100%
— non-management	Employer — 50%	Employer — 50%
Coverage		
— management	I to 3 times pay	I times pay
— non-management	I to 3 times pay	I times pay
Optional	Yes	Yes
Dependents' coverage	Yes	Yes
Accidental death and dismemberment insurance		
Cost sharing		
— management	Employer — 100% or 50%	Employer — 65%
— non-management	Employee — 100%	Employee — 100%
Coverage		
— management	Variable	I times pay
— non-management	I to 4 times pay	2 times pay
Supplementary health care		
Cost sharing		
— management	Employer — 100%	Employee — 100%
— non-management	Employer — 50% or more	Employer — 100%
Dependents' coverage	Yes	Yes
Dental care insurance	Yes	No
Cost sharing	Employer — 100%	N/A
% of treatment covered		
— basic	80%	
— major	50%	
— orthodontic	50%	
Short-term disability insurance		
Cost sharing	Employer — 100%	Employer — 100%
Waiting period		
— management	None	None
— non-management	None	5 to 10 days
% of pay	75%–85%	75%
Benefit period		
— management	26 weeks	104 weeks
— non-management	26 weeks	15 semaines
Long-term disability insurance		
Cost sharing	Employer — 100%	Employer — 92%
Waiting period		
— management	26 weeks	104 weeks
— non-management	26 weeks	26 weeks
% of pay	66.6–70%	70%
Pension plan		
Type	Defined benefit	Defined contribution
Employer's contribution	5.3–7.5% of pay	5.0–7.5% of pay

TABLE 15.6
Comparison of Dental Care Plan Characteristics for Two Employee Categories

BENEFIT	PROFESSIONALS	TECHNICIANS AND OFFICE STAFF
Dental care coverage:		
– Frequency	40%	11%
– Treatment covered		
• Basic	100%	100%
• Major restorative	100%	100%
• Orthodontics	98%	26%
– Basic:		
Mandatory	58%	95%
Optional	42%	5%
– Major restorative:		
Mandatory	58%	95%
Optional	42%	5%
– Orthodontics:		
Mandatory	57%	26%
Optional	43%	74%
– Treatment coinsurance:		
• Basic	100%	100%
• Major	60%	60%
• Orthodontics	50%	50%
– Deductible	...	...
– Maximum	$1,200	$1,000
– Fee guide	1988	1988
– Retirement coverage	19%	24%
– Employer's contribution:		
• Basic		
Mandatory	76%	85%
Optional	50%	50%
• Major restorative		
Mandatory	76%	85%
Optional	50%	50%
• Orthodontics		
Mandatory	76%	100%
Optional	50%	0%

SOURCE: Institut de recherche et d'information sur la rémunération (1990). Reproduced by permission of the publisher.

Integrated Methods of Measurement

As their name suggests, integrated methods of measuring total compensation allow the costs of pay and incentives to be combined with employee benefits. This integration is based on the cash value of employee benefits.

Integrated methods include the disbursement (employer's expense or cost) method and the simulated cost method.

Disbursement Method

Various government and private statistical agencies and management consulting firms have been using the disbursement method for many years. For example, the statistics in Chapter 14 on the cost of employee benefits, which were derived from Statistics Canada (1990) and United States Chamber of Commerce (1990) sources, are based on the disbursement method.

This method involves quantifying the different benefits, by way of their cost to each employer. One possible variation of this technique involves considering only the net cost to the employer, i.e. deducting, if applicable, employee contributions to various benefit plans (e.g. the pension plan). The cost is expressed in monetary units or as a percentage of base pay. In terms of presentation, the results may apply to all employees in an organization, or be broken down by employee category. The latter approach is all the more valuable, because benefits vary with each category and, in many cases, such as pension plans, their cost also varies by category.

Table 15.7 contains a comparison of total compensation, based on the disbursement method, for three employee categories in both the public and private sector.

There are both advantages and disadvantages to this method.

● Advantages

1. Data collection is relatively simple. The employer determines the cost of each benefit for survey purposes.
2. The results are easy to interpret, because they are expressed in monetary units or as a percentage of pay. This makes it possible to determine the value of total compensation.
3. Various techniques may be used to estimate the cost of certain benefits for which there are no exact figures.

● Disadvantages

1. This method considers the various benefits in terms of their cost to the employer only. It provides no information about the true value

TABLE 15.7

Comparison of Total Compensation Based on the Disbursement Method for Three Employee Categories in the Public and Private Sector

	Professional		Office workers		Maintenance and service personnel	
	Public	**Private**	**Public**	**Private**	**Public**	**Private**
		$		$		$
Direct compensation						
Average pay for category[1]	43,942	43,337	22,508	24,194	23,040	28,449
Paid sick leave	202	74	169	44	332	94
Total direct compensation	44,144	43,411	22,677	24,238	23,372	28,543
Indirect compensation						
Pension plan	2,333	2,774	1,143	1,420	1,145	953
Live insurance	26	247	20	92	16	125
Health insurance	35	142	35	116	38	108
Dental care	0	195	0	137	0	106
Vision care	0	38	0	19	0	12
Salary insurance	277	204	477	184	1,170	370
Long-term disability insurance	0	225	0	104	0	100
Parental leave compensation	97	43	122	48	18	6
Subtotal: insurance, etc.	2,768	3,868	1,797	2,120	2,387	1,780
Quebec Pension Plan	505	516	374	382	385	427
UIC	905	953	650	685	666	794
Quebec health insurance	1,415	1,395	725	779	742	916
Worker's Compensation	417	498	252	298	376	893
Subtotal: government plans	3,242	3,362	2,001	2,144	2,169	3,030
Total indirect compensation	6,010	7,230	3,798	4,264	4,556	4,810
Annual compensation	50,154	50,641	26,475	28,502	27,928	33,353
	(Hours)		**(Hours)**		**(Hours)**	
(Direct and indirect compensation)						
Annual regular hours of work[1]	1,826.3	1,916.2	1,825.9	1,905.5	2,021.5	2,099.4
Weekly hours of work[2]	35.0	36.7	35.0	36.5	38.7	40.2
Paid time off						
Annual vacations	141.2	141.3	142.4	136.2	157.7	158.2
Moveable holidays	91.0	89.0	90.9	90.9	100.7	95.9
Used sick leave	32.1	40.0	41.8	43.8	42.1	24.3
Parental leave	1.1	1.3	0.4	1.1	0.8	0.4
Personal leave	2.2	6.5	3.7	5.1	3.4	4.0
Total paid time off	267.6	278.1	279.2	277.1	304.7	282.8
Reduced schedule	0.0	1.9	0.0	3.1	0.0	0.8
Hours at work	1,558.7	1,636.2	1,546.7	1,625.3	1,716.8	1,815.8

1. Average pay and regular hours of work are obtained by weighting the data for each sector by the number of employees in it.
2. Weekly hours of work are obtained by dividing annual regular hours by 52.18 weeks.
SOURCE: Institut de recherche et d'information sur la rémunération (1990). Reproduced by permission of the publisher.

of the benefits. For example, the pension plans offered by two employers may cost the same, but not necessarily provide the same degree of income protection for employees. The same applies to a life insurance plan.

2. The cost of many benefits is not simply a function of their quantity and quality, but also of certain individual characteristics, such as employee's age, sex, seniority and pay level, organizational characteristics (such as employee turnover rate), and industrial characteristics (such as the risks of accident or industrial disease or the technology used). For example, because of its employees' age and sex, a life insurance plan may cost one employer half as much as a similar plan costs another, yet offer more generous benefits. In absolute values, a benefit as simple as days off may cost one employer more than another that grants the same number of days off, because pay levels differ.

3. Many employers have developed computerized accounting systems that do not record benefits by plan. Costs are usually consolidated by module, or else only total-cost information is available. In this case, appropriate techniques must be used to estimate the costs of individual plans.

Simulated Cost Method

In the simulated cost or compensation level method, the organization determines what it would cost if its employees received the same benefits as those provided by other employers. The organization identifies the principal characteristics of the other employers' plans, then simulates costs, based on the characteristics of its own workforce. + visc versa

For example, if Organization A wishes to compare the cost of the paid time off or the vacations it offers to the cost of offering the same plan as Organization B, it must simply calculate what the plan would cost, using the characteristics if its own workforce.

Table 15.8 illustrates how this method is applied. It indicates the average number of days of vacation that Organization A's employees would be entitled to if it offered the same plan as Organization B. In this case, the analysis reveals that, on average, Organization A's office workers are better off under the plan they have than they would be under Organization B's plan. The cost of both plans could quite simply be calculated by multiplying the number of days of vacation by Organization A's average pay for office workers.

This example is relatively simple, for two reasons. First, in both cases, the length of vacation depends on seniority. A more realistic example might have involved different seniority systems for determining vacation length; then the distribution of Organization A's employees according to Organization B's seniority system would have to be calculated. Secondly, the very nature

TABLE 15.8
Use of the Simulated Cost Method to Compare Two Annual Vacation Plans

Years of service	Number of days of annual vacation offered by:		Number of office wokers at Organization A	Total number of days of annual vacation under the plan of:	
	Organization A (1)	Organization B (2)	(3)	Organization A (3) × (1)	Organization B (3) × (2)
0 to 1	10	15	10	100	150
2 to 14	15	15	40	600	600
15 to 29	20	20	35	700	700
30 and over	25	20	20	500	400
			105	1,900	1,850

Average number of days of annual vacation for the group under the plan offered by Organization A
$$\frac{1,900}{105} = 18.1 \text{ days; Organization B } \frac{1,850}{105} = 17.6 \text{ days.}$$

of the example makes this method seem simple. A comparison involving a life insurance plan or a pension plan would require actuarial expertise to determine costs based on the relevant characteristics of employees at the organization for which the comparison is being made.

The method has a number of undeniable advantages.

1. It allows employee benefits to be combined with pay and incentives and total compensation to be measured.
2. It allows for comparisons based on a common unit of measure, i.e. the cost per hour of work.
3. It allows the relative value of various elements of total compensation to be determined and compared, individually and in aggregate.
4. It is based on more reliable data and produces better survey results than other methods.

Its principal disadvantage is its complexity, which is primarily the result of actuarial valuations of insurance and pension plan costs.

Other Methods

There are several other methods for estimating the value of employee benefits. These include the cost of collective agreements method and the qualitative index method.

TABLE 15.9
Point Grid for Measuring Total Compensation by the Qualitative Index Method

Benefit	Relative importance based on cost		Points	
1. Paid time off	60%		12,000	
• Annual vacation		41%		4,920
• Holidays		26%		3,120
• Rest periods		26%		3,120
• Maternity leave		4%		480
• Personal leave		2%		240
• Family leave		1%		120
2. Pension plan	20%		4,000	
....		..		...
....		..		...
3. Disability insurance	15%		3,000	
....		..		...
....		..		...
4. Insurance	5%		1,000	
• Dental care		60%		600
....		..		...
Total	100%		20 000	

SOURCE: Institut de recherche et d'information sur la rémunération (1987). Reproduced by permission of the publisher.

● Cost of Collective Agreements Method

The main purpose of this method is to determine the cost of a collective agreement for an employer. Developed primarily in Canada by Félix Quinet (cf. in this regard, Quinet, 1974) the method uses standard costing techniques to determine the cost to an employer of innovations or modifications to an existing collective agreement.

Simply put, the method involves projecting the costs of the collective agreement in the year before it expires over the life of the new agreement, on the basis of assumptions about personnel, the Consumer Price Index, etc.

● Qualitative Index Method

This method, illustrated in Table 15.9, involves using a point system to organize the elements of employee benefits according to their value. The first step is to identify employee benefits and their principal characteristics. A given number of points is then distributed among the benefits, based on their relative importance. Next, the points assigned to each benefit are distributed among its principal components, based on their relative value. Finally, a number of points are assigned to characteristics of the different plans under study based on whether or not they are offered and their relative value.

Note that the initial distribution of points represents the maximum value a characteristic may have. The point total indicates the relative value of an employee benefit plan offered by an employer.

This method is reminiscent of the point method of job evaluation.

Like its counterparts, the qualitative index method has its advantages and disadvantages.

Advantages

1. It makes it possible to qualify and compare different employee benefit plans.
2. It allows different employee benefits to be organized by value and certain statistical calculations to be made.
3. It indicates relative importance and reveals the strengths and weaknesses of a plan.
4. It readily allows for employee participation in determining the value of employee benefit plans.

Disadvantages

1. It is difficult to include all possible characteristics of different plans.
2. It does not allow employee benefits to be combined with pay and incentives to determine total compensation.
3. The allocation of points is a subjective process.

This last disadvantage, however, proves relative. As discussed at length in previous chapters, people respond based on what they think, and their judgments are essentially subjective.

Measuring Total Compensation for Each Job

As mentioned, combined methods of measuring total compensation do not allow pay to be integrated with the cost of employee benefits. Combined methods that do allow pay to be integrated with employee benefits are primarily used to measure the total compensation of employee categories or of all employees. In practice, however, there may be some value to measuring total compensation for each job, especially in the case of senior executives. Unlike other employee categories, the various elements of total compensation for senior executives may vary more from one job to the next. Non-pay elements may make up a much greater proportion of total compensation. While the competitiveness of senior executives' compensation definitely depends on pay, there should really be a greater emphasis on total compensation.

In response to these needs, in recent years, consulting firms have developed computer programs for measuring total compensation for each job. While the programs may be used for any job, because of cost considerations, their use until now has been limited to senior executive positions. With this software, an organization can determine the competitiveness of the cash compensation of their senior executives and the total compensation for each job relative to its labour market. Table 15.10 contains an excerpt from a report produced by such a program. The leading consulting firms in the field of total compensation, including Mercer, Hewitt, Sobeco, TPF & C, Wyatt and MLH + A, have developed this type of software. Content may vary from one firm to another, based on the number of total compensation elements the program can handle, the technique for determining the value of the different components, and the nature of the personal information that may be used, i.e. real or hypothetical characteristics, or measures of statistical trends.

15.6.3 Monitoring the Efficiency of Total Compensation Management

The questions raised by McCaffery (1981) in the early 80s are still valuable for assessing the efficiency of employee benefits management.

1. **Responsibility for managing employee benefits**
   Who is responsible for managing employee benefits? In practice, responsibility is often shared, based on the plans or various aspects of them. However, centralizing responsibility for employee benefits may lead to efficient management in achieving program objectives.

2. **Coordinating pay and employee benefits**
   How much coordination is there between direct and indirect compensation programs? Coordinating these programs definitely has a positive impact on budget preparation and forecasts, on collecting information about total compensation and analyzing it, and on the appropriate allocation of financial resources among the various components of total compensation.

TABLE 15.10
Part of a Report on Total Compensation by Job

Job no. : 14
Country : Canada

Job title : Division manager
No. of organizations : 14
No. of incumbents : 45

Compensation element	Organization ABC (Annualized $ value)	Rank	No. of incumbents	No. of organizations	Organizations studied (annualized values)			
					1st quartile	Median	3rd quartile	Average
Total compensation	101,098	2	45	13	89,000	95,000	101,000	95,500
Cash compensation	83,355	2	45	13	72,900	75,100	81,900	74,950
Annual pay	71,700	10	45	13	70,900	72,300	80,100	71,800
Time worked	62,500	11	45	13	62,600	70,400	78,500	70,900
Vacations	6,200	6	45	13	4,500	6,100	7,900	6,000
Holidays	3,000	7	45	13	2,700	3,200	4,000	3,350
Short-term disability	900	7	45	13	750	985	1,300	1,050
Short-term incentive bonus	10,755	4	32	9	7,400	9,500	10,800	9,400
Long-term incentive bonus	0	13	9	7	9,000	11,000	15,000	10,100
Retirement savings	6,453	1	45	13	4,600	5,100	6,000	5,200
Defined benefit	4,302	1	45	13	3,600	3,800	4,200	3,750
Deferred profit sharing	2,151	3	29	7	1,900	2,100	2,400	2,000
Employee benefits Health insurance (public and private)	6,790	2	45	13	4,300	5,900	6,900	5,950
Dental insurance	3,585	4	45	13	3,200	3,500	3,700	3,650
Life insurance	900	3	45	13	700	800	875	850
Long-term disability	750	5	45	13	650	750	800	750
Reimbursement account	1,555	7	40	10	1,400	1,600	1,900	1,700
Perquisites	0	13	4	2	Insig.*	Insig.	Insig.	Insig.
Automobile	4,500							
	4,500							

* Insig.: Insignificant
SOURCE: Adapted from a report produced by William M. Mercer Limited's TREFLEX, a total compensation management software program.

3. Priority of objectives

Are specific objectives arranged in order of priority for the purpose of managing all the employee benefits offered? Doing otherwise would be tantamount to launching a new product without a marketing plan, or building a new factory without considering the conditions for recruiting employees. It is management by improvisation.

4. Satisfying employees' needs

To what extent do the benefit plans offered correspond to employees' needs? Market surveys are definitely useful and necessary. Making changes based on that single source of information, though, may prove hazardous in terms of satisfying the relative needs of the employees concerned, and in terms of finances.

5. Government plan availability and coverage

To what extent has the availability and coverage of government plans been considered by the organization in developing its own plans? The issue here is to avoid duplicating coverage and costs, as well as to arrive at adequate, satisfactory, complementary protection.

6. Information provided in recruiting

How much information do recruiting officials have about the benefits offered, and do they use that information when interviewing candidates? Recruiting officials often act as though there are no significant differences in benefits from one organization to the next. Is that really true?

7. Information conveyed to employees

What information, besides the minimum required by law, is regularly conveyed to employees? If employees are to value the benefits they receive, an effective communication program is essential. Knowledge of a benefit precedes appreciation.

8. Answering requests for information

What mechanisms have been established for quick understandable answers to employees' questions about benefits? Providing information about the various benefits is one thing. Quickly providing clear answers to individual employees is another. Instituting an information program for employees enhances their interest in benefits.

Normal channels generally are not useful for providing clear, satisfying answers to questions about benefit plans. Nor is referral to the appropriate section of the benefits manual much more helpful. It is important to assign responsibility for this task to a clearly identified individual or group within the organization. The effectiveness of their work will depend on their knowledge of the benefits and their ability to convey answers that the ordinary person can understand, but also on their accessibility. An employee who needs information wants it immediately.

If the individual or group in charge is accessible, the information can usually be provided on the spot.

9. **Cost/benefit relationship for employees**

   How effective are the costs and benefits, both collectively and individually, of employee contributions to the different plans? A cost/benefit analysis is important from the employer's point of view. Most organizations use one. But the same is not true of employees. If employees contribute to the plans, a cost/benefit analysis raises all kinds of questions. Employees may wonder about their employer's contributions to different plans. The question of how costs are distributed among employees might also be raised. Are plan costs distributed equitably among employees based on differences in seniority, pay, etc.?

   Comparing what an employee contributes to employer's plans with the costs of participating in similar individual or other group plans also arises. At first glance, the plan offered by the employer appears more attractive. Yet is that really the case? And is it true of every plan and for every employee?

10. **Organizational objectives and employees' needs**

    How effective are benefit plans in terms of achieving organizational objectives? How effective are they at satisfying employees' needs? These are fundamental issues. The answer to the first of these questions is simple, if objectives are arranged in order of priority for the purpose of managing all the employee benefits offered. The answer to the second, however, is not so simple. The traditional approach is to rely on comments made during chance encounters with employees. This approach may be satisfactory and sufficient for small organizations, but is definitely not for medium-sized or large ones. In the latter cases, the best instrument is a questionnaire, surveying employees' attitudes and opinions about the relative importance of various benefits and the effectiveness of the available plans. While some organizations conduct such surveys regularly, they remain the exception rather the rule.

☐ 15.7 Summary

The management of employee benefit plans depends largely on consideration of justice, based on needs, motivation, and external competition. These considerations imply determining the need for benefits and perhaps eventually establishing a flexible benefits program. If an organization wishes its benefit plans to motivate employees, it must evaluate their needs and institute an effective communication program. Finally, considerations of competitiveness, or external equity, raise the problem of comparing total compensation from one organization to the next.

REFERENCES

BELCHER, D. and T.J. ATCHISON, *Compensation Management*, Englewood Cliffs, New Jersey, Prentice-Hall, 1987.

BESSETTE, L., "Rationalisation des régimes de protection du revenu et l'approche par événement", *Industrial Relations*, vol. 33, N° 3, 1978, pp. 524-532.

COWARD, L.E., *Mercer Handbook of Canadian Pensions and Benefit Plans*, Don Mills, Ontario, CCH Canadian Limited, 1988.

DREHER, G.F., R.A. ASH and R.D. BRETZ, "Benefits Coverage and Employee Cost: Critical Factors in Explaining Compensation Satisfaction", *Personnel Psychology*, vol. 41, N° 2, 1988, pp. 237-254.

DRUCKER, P., "What Can We Learn From Japanese Management", *Harvard Business Review*, March-April 1971, pp. 110-122.

EHRENBERG, P., "Introduction: Do Compensation Policies Matter?", *Industrial and Labor Relations Review*, vol. 43, N° 3, 1990, pp. 3-12.

EMPLOYEES COUNCIL ON FLEXIBLE COMPENSATION, *Flexible Compensation Sourcebook*, Washington, D.C., 1991.

FAMULARI, M. and M.E. MANSER, "Employer Provided Benefits: Employer Cost Versus Employee Value", *Monthly Labor Review*, vol. 112, N° 12, 1989, pp. 24-32.

GORDON, T.J. and R.E. LeBLEU, "Employee Benefits, 1970-1985", *Harvard Business Review*, January-February 1970, pp. 93-107.

GREEN, P.E. and V.R. RAO, "Conjoint Measurement for Quantifying Judgemental Data:", *Journal of Marketing Research*, vol. 8, 1971, pp. 355-363.

HENDERSON, R.I., *Compensation Management: Rewarding Performance*, Reston, Virginia, Reston Publishing Co., 1989.

HORNSLEY, J.S., D.F. KURATKO and C.A. WALLINGFORD, "Flexible Benefits in Smaller Firms", *Compensation and Benefits Management*, vol. 7, N° 2, 1991, pp. 14-20.

IBIS REVIEW, "Survey Reveals Few Flexible Benefit Plans", *IBIS Review*, June 1990, p. 30.

INSTITUT DE RECHERCHE ET D'INFORMATION SUR LA RÉMUNÉRATION, *Mise à jour du quatrième rapport sur les constatations de l'IRIR*, Montreal, May 1989.

INSTITUT DE RECHERCHE ET D'INFORMATION SUR LA RÉMUNÉRATION, *Modèles de rémunération globale*, Montreal, IRIR, 1987.

INSTITUT DE RECHERCHE ET D'INFORMATION SUR LA RÉMUNÉRATION, *Sixième Rapport sur les constatations de l'IRIR: État et évolution comparés de la rémunération globale des salariés du secteur public et parapublic et des autres salariés québécois*, Montreal, IRIR, November 1990.

JAIN, H.C., "Employee Pay and Benefit Preferences at Canadian National: New Evidence", *Industrial Relations*, vol. 32, N° 3, 1977, pp. 449-452.

JAIN, H.C. and E.P. JANZEN, "Employee Pay and Benefit Preferences", *Industrial Relations*, vol. 29, N° 1, 1974, pp. 99-110.

KATCHER, B.L., "Using Employee Survey to see if your Benefit Program is meeting the needs of your Employees", *Compensation and Benefits Management*, vol. 7, N° 2, 1991, pp. 8-13.

KIENAST, P., D. MACLACHLAN and L. McALISTER, "Employing Conjoint Analysis in Making Compensation Decisions", *Personnel Psychology*, vol. 36, N° 2, 1983, pp. 301-314.

LAPLANTE, S., "La satisfaction des employés face aux bénéfices marginaux", *Actualité économique*, October-December 1969, pp. 447-473.

LUCE, R.D. and J.W. TUKEY, "Simultaneous Conjoint Measurement: A New Type of Fundamental Measurement", *Journal of Mathematical Psychology*, vol. 1, 1964, pp. 1-27.

MARTEL, P., "La quantification des avantages sociaux", *Annual Conference*, Montreal, Association of Human Resources Professionals of the Province of Quebec, 1981.

McCAFFERY, R.M., "Employee Benefits and Services", in *Compensation and Benefits*, edited by L.R. Gomez-Mejia, Washington, D.C., BNA Inc., 1989a, pp. 101-135.

McCAFFERY, R.M., "Employee Benefits: Beyond the Fringe?", *Personnel Administrator*, vol. 26, N° 5, 1981, p. 26 and ff.

McCAFFERY, R.M., "Organizational Performance and the Strategic Allocation of Indirect Compensation", *Human Resources Planning*, vol. 12, N° 3, 1989b, pp. 229-238.

MEISENHEIMER, J. and W. WIATROWSKI, "Flexible Benefit Plans: Employees Who Have a Choice", *Monthly Labor Review*, vol. 112, N° 12, 1989, pp. 17-23.

MILKOVICH, G.T. and M.J. DELANEY, "A Note on Cafeteria Pay Plans", *Industrial Relations*, vol. 14, N° 1, 1975, pp. 112-116.

MITCHELL, O., "Fringe Benefits and the Cost of Changing Jobs", *Industrial and Labor Relations Review*, vol. 37, N° 1, 1983, pp. 70-78.

QUINET, F., *Collective Bargaining in Canada*, Don Mills, Ontario, CCH Canadian Ltd., 1974.

RANDOLF, D., "More Workers are Getting a Chance to Choose Benefits Cafeteria-Style", *The Wall Street Journal*, July 14 1981, pp. 25.

SCHILLER, B. and R. WEISS, "The Impact of Private Pensions on Firm Attachment", *Review of Economics and Statistics*, Vol. 61, N° 3, 1979, pp. 369-380.

SCHUSTER, J.R., "Another Look at Compensation Preferences", *Industrial Management Review*, vol. 10, Spring 1969, pp. 1-18.

SHEA, J.H., "Caution About Cafeteria-Style Benefits Plans", *Personnel Journal*, vol. 60, N° 1, 1981, pp. 37-38 and 58.

STATISTICS CANADA, Pension Plans in Canada - 1988, Ottawa, Supply and Services Canada, 1990.

STELLUTO, G.L. and D.P. KLEIN, "Compensation Trends into the 21st Century", *Monthly Labor Review*, vol. 113, N° 2, 1990, pp. 38-45.

STONEBRAKER, P.W., "Flexible and Incentive Benefits: A Guide to Program Development", *Compensation Review*, vol. 17, N° 2, 1985, pp. 40-53.

TANE, L.D., "Guidelines to Successful Flex Plans: Four Companies' Experiences", *Compensation and Benefits Review*, vol. 17, N° 3, 1985, pp. 38-45.

TAPLIN, P.T., "Flexible Benefits after Two, Three, and Five Years", *Employee Benefit Plan Review*, June 1988, pp. 30-34.